WEEKS of PURSUIT

Volume 2

Mark G. Trotter

LIVING
FAITH
BOOKS

Dedication

To my beautiful and precious wife, Sherry: my beloved help meet and soul mate, who has "adorned" herself with "the ornament of a meek and quiet spirit, which is in the sight of God (and me!) of great price" (1 Pet. 3:4).

Copyright © 2019 by Mark G. Trotter. All scripture quotations are taken from the King James Authorized Version.

First published in 2019 by Living Faith Books.

All rights reserved. This book or parts thereof may not be reproduced in any form, stored in any retrieval system, or transmitted in any form by any means—electronic, mechanical, photocopy, recording, or otherwise—without prior written permission of the publisher and/or author, except as provided by United States of America copyright law.

Living Faith Books
3953 Walnut St
Kansas City, MO 64111

Cover Design: Brandon Briscoe
Page Design: Joel Springer
Page Editing: Melissa Wharton
Photography: Nick Coury of Coury Photography

ISBN: 978-1-950004-02-0
Printed in the United States of America

TABLE OF CONTENTS

WEEK 27 / Psalm 90-119	17
WEEK 28 / Psalm 120-150, Proverb 1-8	27
WEEK 29 / Proverbs 9-28	38
WEEK 30 / Provers 29-31, Ecclesiastes 1-12, Song of Solomon 1-8, Isaiah 1-6	49
WEEK 31 / Isaiah 7-39	59
WEEK 32 / Isaiah 40-66, Jeremiah 1-4	69
WEEK 33 / Jeremiah 5-26	79
WEEK 34 / Jeremiah 27-49	89
WEEK 35 / Jeremiah 50-52, Lamentations 1-5, Ezekiel 1-16	99
WEEK 36 / Ezekiel 17-36	110
WEEK 37 / Ezekiel 37-48, Daniel 1-6	120
WEEK 38 / Daniel 7-12, Hosea 1-14, Joel 1-3	129
WEEK 39 / Amos 1-9, Obadiah 1, Jonah 1-4, Micah 1-7, Nahum 1-3, Habakkuk 1-3	138
WEEK 40 / Zephaniah 1-3, Haggai 1-2, Zechariah 1-14, Malachi 1-4, Matthew 1-4	148
WEEK 41 / Matthew 5-20	159
WEEK 42 / Matthew 21-28, Mark 1-6	169
WEEK 43 / Mark 7-16, Luke 1-6	178
WEEK 44 / Luke 7-21	187
WEEK 45 / Luke 22-24, John 1-14	197
WEEK 46 / John 15-21, Acts 1-10	206
WEEK 47 / Acts 11-28	217
WEEK 48 / Romans 1-16, 1 Corinthians 1-6	227
WEEK 49 / 1 Corinthians 7-16, 2 Corinthians 1-13, Galatians 1-6 Ephesians 1-6	237
WEEK 50 / Philippians 1-4, Colossians 1-4, 1 Thessalonians 1-5, 2 Thessalonians 1-3, 1 Timothy 1-6, 2 Timothy 1-4, Titus 1-3, Philemon 1	250
WEEK 51 / Hebrews 1-13, James 1-5, 1 Peter 1-5, 2 Peter 1-3	262
WEEK 52 / 1 John 1-5, 2 John 1, 3 John 1, Jude 1, Revelation 1-22	274

FOREWORD

Coming from an unchurched background in Miami, Florida, I was radically saved my sophomore year of high school in 1972. For the next several decades, alongside my formal Bible College education, I became the beneficiary of godly men who took a vested interest in my growth and personally invested their lives and their teaching into me. Other men made significant investments in me without ever knowing my name through the access I had to their teaching resources.

Through the investment of these men—and through the outworkings of their influence over the course of several decades—I fell in love with the word of God and made my life about consuming its truth. In addition to reading and studying the Bible, I read commentaries, listened to sermons, attended conferences and took extensive notes on every sermon I heard. I am mentioning all of this to say that, though I wrote the material in the following pages, it reflects an approach to the Bible that I learned from other men. And the accumulation and conglomeration of their teaching is, no doubt, so woven into my understanding, my vocabulary, and my presentation of the word of God that footnoting the enclosed material to give proper credit was simply an impossible task. Obviously, all direct quotes have been footnoted.

In the name of giving credit where credit is due, however, some of the people who have been major influences in shaping my thinking from a biblical standpoint in the early years were men like Warren Wiersbe, John Phillips, David D. Allen, Clarence Larkin, Harold Wilmington, A.W. Tozer, Andrew Murray, John MacArthur, and Jeff Adams. Though I have probably landed in a different place theologically than each of the men listed, this is my official recognition of their investment, along with my sincerest thanks.

I also give special thanks to my editor, Shannah Hogue; my graphic design artist, Brandon Briscoe; and to my precious wife, Sherry, for the countless hours invested in literally every aspect of this project.

Mark G. Trotter
WordStrong Ministries

INTRODUCTION

One of the most impactful passages of scripture in my life is Colossians 3:1-2. The reason it has proved to be so impactful to me is because of the tremendous depth I have found in its simplicity (2 Cor. 11:3). In Colossians 3:1-2, the Holy Spirit inspires Paul to make clear the wholesale change that is to be evidenced in the life of every person who has experienced God's transforming power in salvation. Paul writes, "If ye then be risen with Christ, seek those things which are above, where Christ sitteth on the right hand of God. Set your affection on things above, not on things on the earth."

The phrase "if ye then be risen with Christ" takes us back to Paul's explanation of salvation in Colossians 2:12. He explained that when we called on the name of Christ for salvation, from a spiritual standpoint we were (1) placed into Christ's death and died with Him, (2) placed into Christ's burial and buried with Him, and (3) we were placed into His resurrection — and the power of God which raised Christ from the dead is the same exact power He put into operation to raise us to new life in Him! Wow! That is some unbelievable power!

So, when Paul says in Colossians 3:1, "if ye then be risen with Christ" again, his point is since we have experienced such glorious transforming power, we are now to live the remainder of our lives in constant pursuit of the spiritual realities that are above our heads in the unseen world — not the things we can see down here on the earth, things that are part of the system of evil Satan used to hold us captive, and almost landed us in an eternity forever separated from God in the lake of fire! He's letting us know that the resurrection power of Christ has not only raised us out of the world's system, but above it, and, therefore, the pursuit of our life, for the rest of our life, should be to seek Christ and the things that are part of His everlasting kingdom. And, of course, both the Old and New Testaments are clear that the way God has chosen to reveal Himself to us is through His holy, inspired, infallible, inerrant and preserved word (Psa. 18:1-2; Heb. 4:12). That is actually what is behind the title of this devotional study: *52 Weeks of Pursuit: Pursuing God Through the Pages of His Word*. And that is why the theme verse for this study is Jeremiah 29:13: "And ye shall seek me, and find me, when ye shall search for me with all your heart."

52 Weeks of Pursuit is designed to provide a structure for reading through the Bible in a year, while also providing enough commentary to keep the reader focused on the big picture, as well as some of the more pertinent events that are key to comprehending God's purposes, plan and will in His unfolding revelation of scripture. Most of the 52 weeks reading assignments are based on a five-day reading schedule, though there are several weeks where it became necessary to include a sixth day. Though this book is laid out according to a 52-week format, the pace may certainly be increased or decreased according to the preference and learning style of each individual.

To receive the maximum benefit from this study, however, it is important to be aware of some of the basic biblical presuppositions that have framed its content.

1. THE BIBLE IS A SUPERNATURAL BOOK.

52 Weeks of Pursuit was written with a firm, overarching belief that the Bible is a supernatural book. By that I mean that the Bible is a book that was not only supernaturally **inspired** as *"holy men of God spake as they were moved by Holy Ghost"* (2 Pet. 1:21), but a book that has also been supernaturally **preserved** by God (Psa. 12:7; Mat. 5:18).

Because of the Bible's supernatural quality, the Apostle Paul let us know in 1 Corinthians 2:9–13 that our natural human *eyes* can't *see* its wisdom… our natural human *ears* can't *hear* it… and our natural human *hearts* can't *comprehend* it (1 Cor. 2:9). Its wisdom must, therefore, be *"revealed"* to us — a work the Holy Ghost is more than willing to do (1 Cor. 2:10) — as we employ the biblical principle of *"comparing spiritual things with spiritual"* (1 Cor. 2:13); or, comparing scripture with scripture. It is both the design and intent of *52 Weeks of Pursuit* to direct the reader into this God-ordained method which the Spirit uses to reveal His supernatural truth. That is why the **HIGHLIGHTS & INSIGHTS** section in each day's commentary is laden with numerous cross references.

2. THE BIBLE HAS THREE TREMENDOUSLY SIGNIFICANT LAYERS OF APPLICATION.

One of the key ways we are able to clearly see the supernatural quality of the Bible is by identifying its three layers of application.

1) The HISTORICAL Application.

This layer of application is simply understanding that the Bible always details for us a record of history that is 100% accurate. The events recorded in scripture really happened to real people, exactly as they have been recorded.

2) The DOCTRINAL (or PROPHETIC) Application.

This is the layer of application of which many believers are unaware, and yet this is the layer of application that actually brings the Bible to life! It is based on the belief that as God was inspiring the human authors of the Old Testament to record the events of history, He did it in a fashion such that they perfectly and graphically picture New Testament principles and truths that are sometimes hard to conceptualize.

3) The INSPIRATIONAL (or DEVOTIONAL) Application.

Because of the timeless quality of the Bible, the historical events we find in Scripture, along with their doctrinal (or prophetic) counterparts, have a very practical and powerful inspirational, or devotional, application to believers throughout history (1 Cor. 10:6,11; Rom. 15:4).

Perhaps an illustration can help to clarify these three layers of application.

In the Old Testament, God's people were in bondage in Egypt. Egypt at that time in history was the world power and was under the domination of a wicked king, who was called Pharaoh. Day in and day out, God's people labored under the taskmasters' whip, longing for a deliverer so they could be released from their bondage. Finally, God delivered them… and He did so through the blood of the Passover Lamb. That biblical account details exactly how the events unfolded, and reflects the HISTORICAL Application.

But what's interesting about that story is that more column inches are given to the record of that histori cal event than any other event in the entire Bible! The story of God's deliverance of Israel encompasses the books of Exodus, Leviticus, Numbers, Deuteronomy — and even on into the book of Joshua! Understanding the amount of biblical space given to this event causes us to have to step back and ask the obvious question: WHY? Why devote *one chapter* to something as monumental as the record of creation (Gen. 1), for example, and almost *five entire books* of the Bible to the account of God delivering the children of Israel out of their bondage in Egypt? The reason is simply this:

> *The "exodus" is not just a **portion** of Israel's history.*
> *It is a **portrait** of the Christian life!*

Because the fact is…

We, too, were in bondage in "Egypt." Egypt in the Bible is always a picture of sin and the world. And the Bible teaches us that this world's system is under the domination of a wicked "king," who is called Satan. And in our bondage, day in and day out, we labored under the taskmasters of sin, self and Satan, longing for a deliverer. And finally, God brought us out (which is what the word *"exodus"* means!) through the blood of the "Passover Lamb" (1 Cor. 5:7 says that Christ is our Passover!). Understanding that New Testament connection to Old Testament history reveals to us the DOCTRINAL or PROPHETIC Application.

Making that biblical connection, we are then able to see that this entire Old Testament section of scripture chronicling Israel's exodus, their wilderness wanderings and their ultimate entrance into the place of abundance in Canaan (Exodus–Joshua) is illustrating our journey as New Testament believers. We ought to allow God, by His Spirit and word, to help us navigate through the "wilderness" that lies between our exodus out of the kingdom of darkness and our entrance into the new type of existence God intended us to experience in this life – what Jesus referred to as the *"abundant"* life (Joh. 10:10b). And this, of course, reveals to us the INSPIRATIONAL or DEVOTIONAL Application.

God even helps us to make this devotional and inspirational application to our lives through Israel's exodus by specifically saying to us in 1 Corinthians 10:6, *"Now these things were our examples, to the intent we should not lust after evil things, as they also lusted"* And lest we still fail to make the connection that Israel's exodus was a picture of ours and that it has tremendous practical application to our individual lives, God repeats Himself five verses later, saying: *"Now all these things happened unto them for ensamples: and they are written for our admonition…"*

Throughout *52 Weeks of Pursuit*, the reader will find many references to these three layers of application.

52 WEEKS OF **PURSUIT**

3. THE BIBLE IS REALLY ALL ABOUT JESUS!

Perhaps the clearest and most beautiful explanation of what the Bible actually is is how the word "Bible" is expressed by our deaf friends through sign language. In this vehicle of communication, the word for "Bible" is conveyed by a combination of signs for two separate words: first, the sign for the word "Jesus" followed by the sign for the word "book." Quite simply, our deaf brothers and sisters refer to the Bible as the Jesus Book! And from a biblical standpoint, there could not be a more *precise* and *concise* explanation of the Bible! The Bible is God's book that is literally all about Jesus! And throughout His ministry, Jesus Himself repeatedly made that abundantly clear. For example...

In John 5:39, Jesus is in the midst of a discourse with the religious leaders of His day, the Pharisees, about the fact that He healed a man on the Sabbath. Recognize, of course, that Jesus is actually the Lord of the Sabbath (Mar. 2:28)! Jesus wants them to face the reality of who He is! So, He says to them, *"Search the Scriptures; for in them ye think ye have eternal life: and they are they which testify of me."* What Jesus is actually saying to them is, "Look: you pride yourself in knowing the Old Testament because you think you'll obtain eternal life because of what you know. But," he says, "you're actually missing the point! Because the entire Old Testament is really all about ME! And eternal life isn't about *what* you know — it's about *who* you know!" Jesus is revealing that the Old Testament is actually about *Him!*

In this same discourse with the Pharisees in John 5, Jesus says in verse 46, *"For had ye believed Moses, ye would have believed me; for he* (that is, Moses) *wrote of ME* (Jesus!)." By *"Moses"*, Jesus is referring to the Old Testament books written by Moses — Genesis, Exodus, Leviticus, Numbers, and Deuteronomy. Wow! Is that actually to say that these first five books are all about Jesus? Really? Where?

In another passage, at the beginning of Jesus' public ministry, John records the account of Jesus calling His twelve disciples. He says in John 1:45, *"Philip findeth Nathanael, and saith unto him, We have found him, of whom Moses in the law, and the prophets, did write, Jesus of Nazareth, the son of Joseph."* And once again, here is a very clear New Testament reference revealing to us that the entire Old Testament (the law and the prophets) is really all about Jesus!

In Luke 24, we read of the 40 day period after Christ's resurrection when He was teaching His disciples about the kingdom of God (Acts 1:3). Luke says of Jesus in Luke 24:27, *"And beginning at Moses and all the prophets, he expounded unto them in all the scriptures the things concerning himself."* And here is that same truth yet again! The New Testament quite clearly and repeatedly reveals that the Old Testament is really all about Jesus!

But again, if it really is all about Him, we would have to ask the obvious and glaring question: *where?* Or maybe the question is: *how?* How is it all about Him?

One of the key purposes of the Old Testament section of *52 Weeks of Pursuit* is to show exactly *where* and *how* Christ is revealed in the Old Testament. It is for this purpose that, in each day's reading assignment, after providing an **OVERVIEW** of the chapters, and **HIGHLIGHTS & INSIGHTS** concerning their content, there is a section entitled **CHRIST IS REVEALED.** In it, you will find *how* and *where* Christ actually is in the chapters in that day's reading with corresponding New Testament cross references.

As you make this incredible journey through the word of God, may *"the God of our Lord Jesus Christ, the Father of glory... give unto you the spirit of wisdom and revelation in the knowledge of him: the eyes of your understanding being enlightened; that ye may know what is the hope of his calling, and what the riches of the glory of his inheritance in the saints, and what is the exceeding greatness of his power to us-ward who believe, according to the working of his mighty power."* (Eph. 1:17–19)

Volume 2

WEEK 27, DAY 1: **TODAY'S READING: PSALM 90-99**

OVERVIEW:
God's eternality and man's transitoriness; the security of the one who trusts in the Lord; praise for God's goodness; the majesty of the Lord; the vengeance of the Lord; a call to sing, worship, and praise the Lord; the Lord's power and dominion; praise for the Lord's righteousness; the exaltation of the Lord as our holy King.

HIGHLIGHTS & INSIGHTS:
Psalm 90 is a highly unique psalm. It was the first psalm ever written (which also makes it the oldest!). And it was written by Moses! Third, the psalm's focus on time is incredibly unique.

Let's start with the prophetic application of Psalm 90:4: "For a thousand years in thy sight are but as yesterday when it is past, and as a watch in the night." In the Old Testament, there were three watches to a night (Judg. 7:19). In the New Testament, there are four watches of the night (Mark 6:48). Christ was born (His first coming) in the "first watch of the night," and He will return (His second coming) in the "fourth watch of the night" (Matt. 14:25) also called the "morning watch" (Mark 13:35). And that morning, the Day of the Lord, is when the "Sun of righteousness" (Mal. 4:1–2) will arise!

In Psalm 90:12, Moses admonishes us to "number our days." Paul calls it "redeeming the time" (Col. 4:5; Eph. 5:16), but either way, we are to make the absolute most of each day! And just how many days is that?

Psalm 90:10 tells us, "The days of our years are threescore years and ten." In other words, the normal lifespan for a typical man before the Second Coming of Christ is seventy years. (For those born during the millennium, men will live to be several hundred years of age [Isa. 65:20], just as Genesis 5 indicates they did in some Old Testament times.) And if we break that down literally, we gain an important perspective on our days.

- At age 20, you have 18,250 days to live.
- At age 25, you have 16,425 days to live.
- At age 30, you have 14,600 days to live.
- At age 35, you have 12,775 days to live.
- At age 40, you have 10,950 days to live.
- At age 45, you have 9,125 days to live.
- At age 50, you have 7,300 days to live.
- At age 55, you have 5,475 days to live.
- At age 60, you have 3,650 days to live.
- At age 65, you have 1,825 days to live.
- At age 70, you are now on "borrowed" time!

Remember, though, that none of us are guaranteed seventy years. That's just the average lifespan! As Proverbs 27:1 says, "Boast not thyself of tomorrow; for thou knowest not what a day may bring forth!" Even more importantly, remember what time it is on God's clock! We are the generation whose days will, no doubt, be shortened by the rapture, so we must live each day as if it were the last (Psalm 90:12)—because it might just be!

Psalm 91, also written by Moses, is another personal favorite. Without understanding the Prophetic application of Scripture, however, people often get tripped up here, claiming promises that aren't intended for them or that aren't intended for them in *this* life.

Verse 12 is clearly a prophetic reference to the Lord Jesus Christ; Satan makes this identification in Matthew 4:6, and the Holy Spirit records it to reveal to us (1 Cor. 2:10, 13) this truth of Psalm 91. In fact, Psalm 91 also applies prophetically to the remnant of Jewish saints in the Great Tribulation (vs. 3, 5–6, 10).

It is not, however, God's people in the church age who are promised protection from "the terror by night; nor for the arrow that flieth by day; Nor for the pestilence that walketh in darkness; nor for the destruction that wasteth at noonday" (91:5–6). An estimated 50 million people in the early church sought with everything within them to "dwell in the secret place of the Most High" but still experienced all that the devil could imagine and convince people to do to God's precious saints. They were shot through with arrows, sewn in the skins of animals and thrown to wild beasts, and placed on the rack to have their bodies ripped to shreds. They were burned at the stake, crucified, boiled in oil, and more. And over the centuries, millions more have been struck down in times of war or by sickness or disease (pestilence).

Clearly, the promises of Psalm 91 are not for the church age. There are, however, incredible Devotional applications for those of us living in the church age:

1. There is a "secret place" (v. 1) of intimacy with Christ that we can experience in our relationship with Him that others don't experience (See Isa. 57:15; 4:6; 32:2; Song of Sol. 2:3, 6.)

2. Our eyes will one day "behold and see the reward of the wicked" (v. 8), when we, as members of the armies that follow the Lord out of heaven at His Second Coming, watch Him return to the earth to unleash His judgment (See Rev. 19:11–16; Isa. 63:1–4)

3. Once we have been raptured and have entered into our physical "secret place" (v. 1; John 14:3), then "shall no evil befall [us], neither shall any plague come nigh [our] dwelling" (v. 10)

4. We will be delivered at the rapture, at which time He will "set [us] on high" (v. 14)

5. In the church age, the Lord has not promised us the *absence* of trouble in this life, but He has promised His *presence* through it (v. 15) (See Heb. 13:5; 2 Cor. 12:9)

6. The Lord has and will "deliver" and "honor" us (v. 15) (See John 5:44; 12:26)

7. We will be satisfied with "long life" (v. 16) beyond our wildest dreams! Jesus called it "eternal life," and I think you'd agree, that's a long, long time! (See John 3:15)

As you read the remainder of the psalms in today's reading (92–99), take time to thank God for the many incredible Prophetic and Devotional truths that you are beginning to identify and apply for yourself.

CHRIST IS REVEALED:

As the *God who Covers with His Feathers* – Psalm 91:4 (Matt. 23:37)

As the *Rock of our Salvation* – Psalm 95:1 (1 Cor. 10:4)

As the *Lord who Judges the Earth in Righteousness and Truth* – Psalm 96:13 (Rev. 16:5–7)

As the *Lord who Returns in Flaming Fire* – Psalm 97:4 (2 Thess. 1:7–9)

52 WEEKS OF **PURSUIT**

WEEK 27, DAY 2: **TODAY'S READING: PSALM 100-105**

OVERVIEW:
Exhortation to praise God; the psalmist's profession of uprightness; the prayer of an afflicted man for mercy upon himself and Zion; praise for the Lord's mercies; praise for the Lord's majesty; the wonderful works of the Lord in behalf of Israel.

HIGHLIGHTS & INSIGHTS:
Psalm 100: 1, calls us to "make a joyful noise unto the Lord, all ye lands." God's passion is, and has always been, the worldwide worship of His Son—among every kindred, tongue, people and nation. In light of the full scope of our commission to make disciples of "all nations" (Matt. 28:19), we would do well to ask some pertinent questions:

- In what ways am I actively allowing the Lord to work out through me His passion to see His Son glorified in all lands?
- Am I presently discipling someone? More precisely, am I reproducing a reproducer of reproducers?
- When was the last time I actually presented the gospel to someone who is lost?
- Am I actively and financially supporting the cause of missions in the world through my local church?

God calls us to join Him, not out of guilt or obligation, but "with gladness" (Ps. 100:2). The Son deserves our praise for all that He does (v. 3) and all that He is (v. 5). Let us, with all people everywhere, "enter into his gates with thanksgiving, and into his courts with praise" (v. 4).

Psalm 101 offers clear warnings about who and what we allow to influence us. Verse 3 says, "I will set no wicked thing before mine eyes." In a world that caters to the "lust of the eyes" (1 John 2:16), this verse is a doozy! In fact, for many believers, it's hard to accept. They call it legalism to suggest this verse applies to many (even most) movies, TV shows, commercials, magazines, advertisements, and websites today. They refuse to take the phrase "no wicked thing" literally. After all, they claim, we have been given liberty in Christ (Gal. 5:1)!

And they aren't wrong. We are gloriously free in the Lord Jesus Christ, but these believers miss the bigger picture. Our liberty is not an excuse to live in sin (Gal. 5:13; 1 Pet. 2:16). We have still been commanded to "cleanse ourselves from all filthiness of the flesh and spirit, perfecting holiness in the fear of God" (2 Cor. 7:1). There are still things the Spirit of God intends that we willfully and aggressively separate ourselves from, and we would be wise to take seriously—even literally—the psalmist's admonition about what we put before our eyes!

If Psalm 101:3 is a warning about *how* we spend our time, verse 4 warns us about *who* we spend it with. We have been called to reach the lost, but who we spend our time with will influence us. As 1 Corinthians 15:33 says: "Be not deceived: evil communications [also translated "company"] corrupt good manners [or morals]." Our most intimate associates must be brothers and sisters in Christ, those who have also surrendered themselves to Christ's lordship instead of everyone "that worketh deceit" or "that telleth lies" (101:7).

Psalm 102 is a great place to find refuge when life gets tough. Notice the title (listed in most Bibles): "A prayer of the afflicted, when he is overwhelmed, and poureth out his complaint before the Lord." On a Devotional level, let this psalm minister to you in whatever your affliction is today. But there is, of course, more going on here. Prophetically, this psalm points, once again, to the nation of Israel at the end of the Tribulation when the Lord Jesus Christ will "arise, and have mercy upon Zion: for the time to favour her, yea, the set time, is come" (v. 13). Note also the definite references to the Second Coming in 102:16 and 102:21–22.

Considering the admonition in Psalm 103:1, I know I've sought to bless the holy name of the Lord from my soul—I'm just not certain I've ever actually done it with "all that is within me." Have you? I'm absolutely certain that's what the worship of heaven will be (Rev. 4), the difficulty is in bringing the worship of heaven to earth—and to our lives now!

Psalm 103 begins and ends the same way: "Bless the Lord, O my soul." This psalm is about God's *mercy*—the nature of mercy (vs. 4), the measure of mercy (vs. 8), the scope of mercy (vs. 11), and the duration of mercy (vs. 17). The more we learn about and grow to appreciate the incredible mercy the Lord has extended to us, the more we will genuinely "bless the Lord" in our souls and with "all that is within" us (103:1).

Interestingly, Psalm 104 also exhorts us to "bless the Lord, O my soul" in its first and last verses. But while Psalm 103 addresses God's *mercy*, Psalm 104 is all about God's *majesty*—displayed in the wonder of creation.

Psalm 105 is the first of five Psalms that feature the phrase, "O give thanks unto the Lord." (See Psalm 106, 107, 118 and 136.) Along with Psalm 106, it highlights Israel's history much like we observed in Psalm 78. The first five verses contain nine (which is the number of fruit-bearing in the Bible) exhortations that should be carried out by every child of God in any dispensation:

1. "Give thanks" (105:1a)
2. "Call upon his name" (105:1b)
3. "Make known his deeds" (105:1c)
4. "Sing unto him" (105:2a)
5. "Talk ye of all his wondrous works" (105:2b)
6. "Glory ye in his holy name" (105:3a)
7. "Rejoice" (105:3b)
8. "Seek his face" (105:4)
9. "Remember his marvelous works" (105:5)

CHRIST IS REVEALED:

As the *Creator* ("It is He that hath made us") – Psalm 100:3 (John 1:3; Eph. 3:9; Col. 1:16; Rev. 4:11)

As the *One who forgives all our iniquities* – Psalm 103:3 (Matt. 9:6)

WEEK 27, DAY 3: **TODAY'S READING: PSALM 106-109**

OVERVIEW:
A recounting of Israel's rebellion and the Lord's faithfulness to deliver them; the deliverance of the Lord in the troubles of life; the psalmist's praise of the Lord and his cry of supplication for victory; the vengeance of God meted out upon His enemies.

HIGHLIGHTS & INSIGHTS:
In Psalm 106, the psalmist continues his praise and thanks to the Lord as he recounts God's mercy through Israel's history. But it also contains a monumental declaration—God's ultimate purpose for Israel's deliverance through the exodus. Verse 8 says, "Nevertheless he saved them for his name's sake, that he might make his mighty power to be known." This is a foundational truth, and it is repeated throughout the Old Testament, just so we don't miss it!

In Exodus 9:16, God declared his ultimate goal for the exodus: "that my name may be declared throughout all the earth." Ezekiel reminded the elders of Israel that God "wrought for my name's sake, that it should not be polluted before the heathen, among whom they were, in whose sight I made myself known unto them, in bringing them forth out of the land of Egypt" (20:9). God repeatedly tells Israel, "What I did and how I worked was not, first and foremost, for *you*. It was for *Me*, for My name! I saved you so the whole world could know Who I really am, so My power could be known."

1 Corinthians 10:1–6 and 11 give us another perspective. The exodus is a historical fact which happened exactly as the Old Testament described. But biblically, Egypt also represents sin and the world, so *Israel's* exodus from bondage in Egypt is a picture of *our* exodus from bondage to sin and the world! (See 2 Tim. 2:26; Eph. 2:2.) This means that God's motivation for *our* exodus was the same as it was for *Israel's* exodus! God's purpose in saving us wasn't, first and foremost, for *us*, it was for *Him*. To display His glory, to make much of His name.

Now clearly God's salvation provides us incredible benefits! But we are not God's ultimate focus. The theme of the Bible, the theme of salvation and every dimension of existence is not us! It's not *about* us or *for* us—it is about our holy, magnificent, omnipotent, omniscient and omnipresent God!

And this is *huge*! Because the truth concerning God's real purpose in our salvation is rarely taught even in our fundamental, Bible-believing churches in the Laodicean Age. But understanding this truth is the difference between a "me-centered" Christianity and a "Christ-centered" Christianity.

The Christianity *of our day*:

1. Says that Christianity is primarily about God benefiting His creatures (God exists for us)
2. Says that the most important thing to God is people
3. Asks, "How should I position my life to gain the most blessing?" (Seeks God's hand)

The Christianity *of the Bible*:

1. Says that Christianity is primarily about God glorifying His Son (We exist for God)
2. Says that the most important thing to God is His glory (His name)
3. Asks, "How should I position my life to bring God the most glory?" (Seeks God's face)

No wonder Paul said, "In the last days perilous times shall come" (2 Tim. 3:1) and that "in the latter times some shall depart from the faith, giving heed to seducing spirits, and doctrines of devils" (1 Tim. 4:1). Not everything we hear is biblically accurate. We must be very careful and discerning!

Psalm 106 records even more of Israel's history for us. Based on 1 Corinthians 10:6 and 11, we can learn from these events so that what happened to them doesn't happen to us. Devotionally, then, the truths the psalmist lays out in this psalm provide limitless application for our lives.

The psalms are ancient poems, and they often used repetition for emphasis. In Psalm 107, repetition reveals the psalm's major theme. Verses 8, 15, 21 and 31 say, "Oh that men would praise the Lord of his goodness, and for his wonderful works, to the children of men!" The rest of the psalm describe these "wonderful works" the Lord has done for his people, providing specific things to praise Him for. Again, the Devotional application of these verses to our lives is virtually limitless.

Psalm 108 is interesting in that the first five verses are a replica of Psalm 57:7–11 and verses 7–10 are a replica of Psalm 60:6–9.

Psalm 109 certainly has a Historical application to David's life, but it is not primarily about David. It is about the Messiah's humiliation, His confrontation with Satan, His exaltation over death, and the ultimate vindication of His life as the Father executes His vengeance. Though it was David who composed this Psalm under the inspiration of the Holy Spirit, the words are actually the prayer of the Lord Jesus Christ—and every aspect of the prayer will be answered to the letter!

CHRIST IS REVEALED:

As the *One who makes the storm a calm* – Psalm 107:29 (Matt. 8:27; John 14:27)

WEEK 27, DAY 4: **TODAY'S READING: PSALM 110-118**

OVERVIEW:

The Lord gives dominion to the King; the psalmist's praise for the works of the Lord; the blessed man; the Lord's exaltation of the humble; God's deliverance of Israel from Egypt; the heathen idols contrasted with Jehovah; thanksgiving for deliverance from death; a psalm of praise; thanksgiving for the Lord's saving goodness.

HIGHLIGHTS & INSIGHTS:

Psalm 110 is a very significant (and magnificent!) psalm. It is a messianic psalm, meaning it contains prophetic references which were (or will be) fulfilled in Jesus. In verse 1, a thousand years before Jesus Christ was born in Bethlehem, David recognized that the Messiah not only existed ("The Lord said unto my Lord"), but that He was his Lord ("The Lord said unto *my* Lord," emphasis added), and that the Messiah would one day come in judgment upon His enemies ("Sit thou at my right hand, until I make thine enemies thy footstool").

Psalm 110 is quoted seven times in the New Testament, more than any other psalm (Matt. 22:43–44; Mark 12:36; Luke 20:42–43; Acts 2:33–34; Heb. 1:13; 5:6; 7:17). In Matthew 22, Jesus himself uses Psalm 110 to prove His deity to the Pharisees: "Jesus asked them saying, What think ye of Christ? Whose son is he? They say unto him, The Son of David. He saith unto them, How then doth David in spirit call him Lord, saying, The Lord said unto my Lord, Sit thou on my right hand, till I make thine enemies thy footstool? If David then call him Lord, how is he is his son? And no man was able to answer him a word, neither durst any man from that day forth ask him any more questions" (Matt. 22:42–46).

Psalm 111 is a psalm of praise for the "works of the Lord" (111:2), which are mentioned in five different verses and described in nine different ways.

1. God's works are ... great (111:2)
2. God's works are ... to be sought out (111:2)
3. God's works are ... honorable (111:3a)
4. God's works are ... glorious (111:3b)
5. God's works are ... wonderful (111:4a)
6. God's works are ... to be remembered (111:4b)
7. God's works are ... powerful (111:6)
8. God's works are ... true (111:7a)
9. God's works are ... judgmental (111:7b)

Psalm 111:10 is a great reminder to those of us living in the last days: "The fear of the Lord is the beginning of wisdom." Notice that it doesn't say reverential trust or holy reverence. It says *fear*. This is not what many churches teach, but it is true as it stands. Rather than fearing what God told us *not to fear* (2 Kings 17:7, 25) and not fearing what God *told us to fear* (Exod. 20:20), we must recognize that we get to choose. We will either fear God—or we will fear men (Prov. 29:25).

This is why Jesus commands us in Matthew 10:28, "And fear not them which kill the body [men], but are not able to kill the soul: but rather fear him [God] which is able to destroy both soul and body in hell!" Clearly Jesus is more concerned that we get this right than that we bow to tact and political correctness.

Psalm 112 describes the "blessed man" that we met in Psalm 1. Psalm 113 describes the millennium.

Psalm 114 is a very brief review of events recorded in Exodus and Joshua, which will be repeated at the Second Coming of Christ.

In Psalm 115:9–13, the psalmist admonishes three groups of people to "trust in the Lord" because "he is their help [aggressive action *against* the enemy] and their shield [protection *from* the enemy]." The three groups are Israel, the "house of Aaron," and those "that fear the Lord." Prophetically, Israel refers specifically to Jews in the Tribulation. The "house of Aaron" is the Levitical priests who will be serving in the millennial temple, and those who "fear the Lord" are the Gentile converts during the Tribulation. The millennial application of verse 18 provides even more beauty and significance: "We will bless the Lord from this time forth and for evermore. Praise the Lord." Won't that be awesome? Hallelujah!

Psalm 116 is another messianic Psalm, and Psalm 117 is short ... and sweet!

Psalm 118 is the exact middle of the Bible—specifically verse 8: "It is better to trust in the Lord than to put confidence in man." Verses 22 and 23 are incredibly significant: "The stone which the builders refused is become the head stone of the corner. This is the Lord's doing; it is marvelous in our eyes." Jesus quoted these verses to the chief priests, scribes, and elders of Israel to show them that they were about to fulfill the prophecy (Matt. 21:42; Mark 12:35–36; Luke 20:42–43). When Peter preached to the high priest, scribes, rulers and elders of Israel, he quoted this verse to show that they had actually fulfilled this prophecy (Acts 4:5–11). And Paul was inspired to use these verses to reveal the mystery of the church, the body of Christ, in Ephesians 2:19–21.

CHRIST IS REVEALED:

As the *One seated at the Father's right hand* – Psalm 110:1 (Eph. 1:20; Col. 3:1)

As the *Stone which the builders refused* – Psalm 118:22 (Matt. 21:42; Mark 12:35–36; Luke 20:42–43)

WEEK 27, DAY 5: **TODAY'S READING: PSALM 119**

OVERVIEW:
The greatness, power, and perfection of God's holy Word.

HIGHLIGHTS & INSIGHTS:

Psalm 119 is nothing short of a masterpiece. It is an alphabet Psalm, meaning that the 22 eight-verse stanzas begin with the 22 consecutive letters of the Hebrew alphabet (Aleph, Beth, Gimel, etc.). But even more, there is no greater treatise concerning the Word of God in the entire Bible (or anywhere else for that matter) than Psalm 119. Of the 176 verses, 173 specifically refer to the Word of God, using at least eight different terms: Law, Testimonies, Way/Ways, Precepts, Statutes, Commandments, Judgments, and Word/Words. All eight of these terms are found in the first nine verses.

It is difficult to simplify this intricate and incredible work of art. There are so many pieces to consider that any overview has the potential to diminish the beauty and significance of this psalm. However, anyone who is serious about God and His Word needs to immerse themselves in this psalm repeatedly and continuously!

Psalm 119 teaches us that it is impossible to separate the God of the Word from the Word of God! We cannot love the God of the Word without also loving His Word. In fact, Psalm 119 reveals the absolute necessity of developing an all-encompassing love for the Bible (John 14:15, 23).

But how do we define a love for God's Word? It can't be measured by what we know about the Bible, how often we read the Bible, or how much of the Bible we've read. At this point in the *52 Weeks of Pursuit*, we have read half of the Bible, but that accomplishment doesn't *prove* that we love God's Word. *Knowing about* His Word is not the same as *knowing God* through His Word (1 Cor. 8:2). We can easily read the Bible just to say we did it or to feel good about ourselves, and thereby display a love, not for the Word, but for *ourselves*. Sadly, love of self (2 Tim. 3:2) often disguises itself in a very spiritual-looking package!

But if faithfully reading God's Word and knowing about God's Word do not prove we love God's Word, how can we determine biblically whether or not we do, in fact, love it?

Thankfully, Psalm 119 also provides God's answer to that question. Interestingly, in all the psalms God inspired David to write, only twice does David declare his love for the Lord Himself (Ps. 18:1; 116:1). But in Psalm 119, David passionately expresses his love for God's Word eleven separate times! And each time, God inspired him to pair that expression of love with a characteristic this love produced in his life. Taken together, then, David's eleven statements provide a practical and observable checklist that we can use to assess our own love for God's Word.

SEVEN WAYS TO KNOW IF YOU LOVE THE WORD OF GOD:

1. You know you love the Word of God *by what you hate* (119:127–128)

    a. You will hate *every false way* (119:127–128)

    b. You will hate *lying* (119:163)

    c. You will hate *vain thoughts* (119:113)

2. You know you love the Word of God *by the holy attitude with which you view it* (119:140, 160, 164, 72, 93, 103, 128, 131, 161)

3. You know you love the Word of God *by what consumes your thoughts* (119:97, 15, 23, 48, 78, 99, 148)

4. You know you love the Word of God *by the joy you receive from getting into it and living it* (119:47)

5. You know you love the Word of God *by your surrender to it* (119:48)
6. You know you love the Word of God *by your inability to be offended* (119:165)
7. You know you love the Word of God *by the desire in your innermost being to obey it* (119:166–167)

David understood the qualities that actually proved his love for God's Word. We must likewise determine whether those characteristics are present and observable in our own lives. Based on those seven divinely inspired characteristics, can you honestly say that you love the Word of God?

CHRIST IS REVEALED:

By the *Psalmist who delighted in fulfilling God's will* – Psalm 119:47 (John 4:34; 6:38; 15:10)

WEEK 28, DAY 1: **TODAY'S READING: PSALM 120-135**

OVERVIEW:

Prayer for deliverance from lying lips; the Lord as the Keeper of Israel; prayer for the peace of Jerusalem; prayer for the Lord's help; praise for the Lord's deliverance of Israel; the blessing of trusting God; thanksgiving for the return from captivity; prosperity comes from the Lord; the blessedness of the fear of the Lord; prayer for the overthrow of Zion's enemies; hope in the Lord's forgiveness; childlike trust in the Lord; prayer for the Lord's blessing upon the sanctuary; the blessedness of unity; the blessing of the night watchers; praise for the Lord's works, and the vanity of idols and idol worship.

HIGHLIGHTS & INSIGHTS:

Devotionally, Psalm 120 is a powerful reminder for times of temptation. Imagine how different the woman's story would have turned out if, when the serpent (Satan) tempted her in the Garden, she had declared the first verse of Psalm 120: "In my distress I cried unto the Lord, and he heard me." Imagine what the outcome might have been had she made verse 2 the cry of her heart: "Deliver my soul, O LORD, form lying lips, and from a deceitful tongue." In the same way, consider how our stories might have gone differently had we applied these verses at key times of temptation. Obviously, we can't change the voice we may have heeded in the past—but we can choose carefully the voice we listen to today … and for the remainder of our days!

Also, keep in mind that, Prophetically, Psalm 120:2–7 points to the Antichrist during the Tribulation Period.

Psalm 121 also has incredible Prophetic implications for Israel. When her "help" comes, it will come from "the hills" (v. 1). God clearly names these hills in His Word:

1. Mount Sinai (Deut. 33:2; Judg. 5:5; Ps. 68:8)
2. Mount Seir (Ezek. 35:2–3, 7)
3. Mount Paran (Deut. 33:2; Hab. 3:3)
4. Mount of Olives (Zech. 14:1–6)

Psalm 121 describes how, during the Tribulation Period, God will establish the nation of Israel (v. 3), He will "preserve [them] from all evil" (v. 7), and from "this time forth" (the Second Coming and throughout the millennium) they will come in and go out of Jerusalem (v. 8).

Psalm 122 describes what will take place in the millennium.

From a Devotional standpoint, if you find yourself in the midst of a trial that's got your back against the wall and you are crying out to God to have mercy upon you, Psalm 123 will bless your heart! To grasp the Prophetic application, read the psalm from the perspective of a Jew in the Tribulation Period awaiting the arrival of the Messiah.

Psalm 124 describes Israel's literal deliverance from a literal flood and from literally being devoured by the enemy. If you have time to read more, some key cross references are Isaiah 6:13; Revelation 6:9–11; 12:15; 20:4; Psalm 35:22; 44:22; Daniel 9:26; Jeremiah 51:34.

The Prophetic context of Psalm 125 is the beginning of the millennium which verse 2 clearly identifies with the phrase "from henceforth even for ever."

Psalm 126 refers to the Second Coming of Christ when He "turn[s] again the captivity of Zion" (v. 1) and establishes His kingdom on the earth. The soul-winners in verses 5 and 6 are also described in Ecclesiastes 11:1–6, though from a Devotional standpoint, the phrase can certainly apply to us. When we travail in prayer for the lost, watering the seed of God's Word (Luke 8:11) that we have sown in the soil of men's hearts with our tears, we will reach people with the gospel. God help us do so while we still have time (John 9:4b).

We must be careful to understand and apply the truth of Psalm 127:1 to our marriages, our families, our churches, and our nation: "Except the Lord build the house, they labour in vain that build it!" Likewise, Psalm 128 is an important and practical psalm that also speaks to our marriages and families.

Psalm 129 describes the scourging endured by our Lord Jesus Christ in His first coming and also points to the execution of His judgment at His second coming. Prophetically, Psalm 130 is a messianic Psalm, but Devotionally, it has tremendous practical implications as well. Psalm 131 is predominantly practical with Prophetic (millennial) overtones in verse 3, and Psalm 132 is literally filled with millennium references, especially verses 11 and 13–18.

The "brethren" of Psalm 133:1 are the "brethren" of Matthew 25:34–42 and Matthew 28:10. Devotionally, however, it is also very "good" and "pleasant" when all of the "brethren" in a local church "dwell together in unity" (1 Cor. 1:10). God help us to experience that good and pleasant unity.

Psalm 134 is the second shortest psalm (only Psalm 117 is shorter) and its context is obviously the millennium. The "house of the Lord" in verse 1 is a literal house that will be built on this earth during the millennium (Ezek. 40–44), and the "servants of the Lord" mentioned in this same verse will stand in that house again.

By now, hopefully you are learning to recognize the Prophetic context of the Psalms—identifying the Tribulation, Second Coming, and millennium references—while still applying these verses to your life Devotionally in a practical sense. Try your hand at it in Psalm 135!

CHRIST IS REVEALED:

As our *Protector, the One who preserves our going out and coming in* – Psalm 121:8 (John 10:9)

As *David's fruit [descendant] who will sit upon David's throne* – Psalm 132:11 (Luke 1:32; Acts 2:29–30)

WEEK 28, DAY 2: **TODAY'S READING: PSALM 136-143**

OVERVIEW:
Thanks for the Lord's goodness to Israel; response to Israel's captivity; thanksgiving for the Lord's blessing; God's omniscience, omnipresence, and omnipotence; prayer for protection against the wicked; prayer for sanctification and protection; prayer for help in trouble; prayer for deliverance and guidance.

HIGHLIGHTS & INSIGHTS:
Psalm 136 masterfully and beautifully declares who the God of the Bible is:

- "*The* Lord" (v. 1)
- "The God of gods" (v. 2)
- "The Lord of lords" (v. 3)
- The God of creation (vs. 5–9)
- "The God of heaven" (v. 26)

He is also tremendously merciful: 26 times in 26 verses we are reminded that "his mercy endureth for ever." In fact, He has been demonstrating His mercy throughout all of history (vs. 5–26). And what is mercy? A quick way to contextualize and deepen our appreciation of His mercy is to remember that …

- Justice is God giving us *what we deserve*
- Grace is God giving us *what we do not deserve*
- Mercy is God *not* giving us *what we do deserve*

Psalm 137 is a tremendously sad song about God's people being taken captive by the godless Babylonian empire (which represents Satan's false kingdom of religious systems in the Bible). Likewise, this song (psalm) can and should be felt and sung by those of us living during this time of Laodicean captivity (Rev. 3:14–22).

Psalm 138:2 is one of the most important statements in the Word of God concerning itself: "Thou hast magnified thy word above all thy name." Given what the Lord's *name* actually is (the sum total of all of His attributes) and what the Lord says regarding His own name ("Blessed be thy glorious name, which is exalted above all blessing and praise," Neh. 9:5), how could anything possibly be exalted *above* His name? God magnified His Word *above* His name because only the Word of God reveals to us all that God is (His name), and only through His Word can we learn how to "magnify"—or exalt, bless, and praise (Neh. 9:5)—His glorious name!

We live in a world that's obsessed with using plastic surgery to "fix" what we don't like about how God created us. But Psalm 139 teaches us that the God who is omniscient (139:1–6), omnipresent (139:7–12) and omnipotent (137:13–17) created us to look the way we do—for His purposes! Rather than being depressed about how He made us, we can accept it, and use what he gave us to fulfill His purposes for our lives! It is a wonderfully freeing day when we can thank God for the physical features that at one time we would have changed if we could!

Psalm 140:1 says, "Deliver me, O Lord, from the evil man: preserve me from the violent man." We will get more detail about the evil man in the book of Proverbs where we'll discover that, Prophetically, he is the Antichrist of the Tribulation. Though the references to the evil man and the violent man in verse 1 are both singular, as if the psalmist were referring to just one individual, the pronoun in verse 2 is plural: "Which imagine mischiefs in their heart." 1 John 2:18 helps clarify the psalmist's terminology: "Little children, it is the last time: and as ye have heard that antichrist [singular] shall come, even now are there many antichrists [plural]; whereby we know that it is the last time."

As in many other psalms, Psalm 140 refers Doctrinally to the end of the Tribulation when the Antichrist will have united the nations for war against Israel. Verse 2 concludes, "continually are they gathered together for war," and at the end of verses 3, 5, and 8, we see our key word—*Selah*. Once again, God reveals that one day, as the nations of the world unite to wipe Israel off the map—when Israel looks utterly helpless and hopeless—our Lord Jesus Christ will return to judge His enemies and establish His rule and rest in His millennial kingdom as the King of Israel! That's the context of the entire Psalm: that day when "the upright shall dwell in thy presence" (140:13) on the earth. It's amazing the doors that open in the Word of God with just a few simple keys of Bible study!

Verse 2 of Psalm 141 ("Let my prayer be set forth before thee as incense") has beautiful scriptural ramifications. In the Old Testament tabernacle, the altar of incense sat just outside the veil where the Lord dwelt in the Holy of Holies. The incense burned there provided a delightful and beautiful aroma that made its way into the Lord's presence. But the Old Testament tabernacle is also a picture of the "true tabernacle" in heaven (Heb. 8:2, 5), and when John was caught up to see that heavenly tabernacle, he wrote in Revelation 5:8: "And when he [the Lord Jesus Christ] had taken the book [the title deed to the earth], the four beasts and four and twenty elders [the church] fell down before the Lamb, having every one of them harps, and golden vials full of odours, which are the prayers of saints." Our prayers are now the beautiful and delightful aroma that arises as incense to become a sweet savor in our Lord's presence! May that incredible reality motivate us to pray ever more fervently!

The Historical context of Psalm 142 is given in the title, "Maschil of David; A Prayer when he was in the cave" — the cave where David hid when Saul was seeking his life. David models in this psalm how we can be completely honest with God about the circumstances of life and how they make us feel. Times when …

- We find ourselves pressed by our "trouble" (142:2)
- Our spirit is "overwhelmed within [us]" (142:3a)
- Our enemies have "laid a snare" for us (142:3b)
- We feel we've been forsaken by everybody and nobody "cared" (142:4)
- We've been "brought very low" (142:6a)
- We've been persecuted (142:6b)
- It feels like our very soul is in prison (142:7)

Pouring our souls out before the Lord in this way is not only necessary, but spiritually healthy. But we must never forget that there are billions of people alive today who have no idea that this Psalm, which is so descriptive of their spiritual condition, even exists! And if no one tells them, even if they were able to articulate their spiritual condition, they would also repeat with David, "I looked on my right hand, and beheld, but there was no man that would know me: refuge failed me; no man cared for my soul" (v. 4). May God use us to be the man or woman today (and every day) who genuinely and passionately *cares for* the souls of the lost, pointing them to the refuge, the mighty cross!

CHRIST IS REVEALED:

As the *One who delivers souls from prison* – Psalm 142:7 (Luke 4:18)

52 WEEKS OF **PURSUIT**

WEEK 28, DAY 3: **TODAY'S READING: PSALM 144-150**

OVERVIEW:
Prayer for rescue and blessing; the Lord extolled for His goodness and greatness; praise for the Lord's help; praise for Jerusalem's restoration and prosperity; the whole universe and all of creation invoked to praise the Lord; Israel invoked to praise the Lord; everything that hath breath invoked to praise the Lord.

HIGHLIGHTS & INSIGHTS:
Psalm 144 is a a song of blessing and praise to God. David personalizes God's great attributes and power in verses 1 and 2. Notice the beautiful repetition of *my* in these verses! May we also bless the Lord today recognizing that…

- He hasn't just strengthened us—He *is* our "strength" (144:1)
- He hasn't just made us good—He *is* our "goodness" (144:2)
- He hasn't just taught us to defend ourselves against the enemy—He *is* our "fortress," He *is* our "high tower," and He *is* our "shield" (144:2)
- He hasn't just made a way of escape for us—He *is* our "deliverer" (144:2)

May those blessed realities preach to our souls today! But David doesn't stop there. In verse 3, He cries out, "Lord, what is man that thou takest knowledge of him! Or the son of man, that thou makest account of him!" David is essentially saying, "O Lord, in light of who You are, who in the world are we?" And I love the exclamation points God placed in His perfectly preserved Word! Because both parts of verse 3 are actually questions, but they're followed by exclamation points. What are we to make of that? Perhaps the psalmist understood that, in light of God's incredible *greatness* and man's incredible *sinfulness*, there could never be suitable answers to the questions. So instead the *questions* become major *statements* of just how incredible, wonderful and awesome God is!

And in light of God's unequalled and incomprehensible awesomeness, Psalm 144 ends with, "Happy is that people, whose God is the LORD" (v. 15). Perhaps we should all ask ourselves: "Am I happy?" And if not, maybe we should ask ourselves some penetrating questions about the reality of Christ's lordship in our lives!

Psalm 145 is a song of praise. The psalmist cries out: "I will extol thee, my God, O king; and I will bless thy name for ever and ever. Every day will I bless thee; and I will praise thy name for ever and ever" (vs. 1–2). And in verses 3–21, he does exactly that, lifting up his praise and worship to the Lord. A.W. Tozer once said that "worship is the missing jewel in modern evangelicalism."[1] May the cry of David's heart be the genuine cry of our hearts today. May his words become our words, as we seek to rediscover that "missing jewel" for ourselves!

Psalm 146 continues the theme of praise. With the psalmist, we can express to the Lord our wholehearted resolve to praise Him for the remainder of earthly lives and for all eternity: "Praise ye the LORD. Praise the LORD, O my soul. While I live will I praise the LORD: I will sing praises unto my God while I have any being" (vs. 1–2). And Psalm 147:1 reminds us of the reason we praise the Lord: "for it is good to sing praises unto our God; for it is pleasant; and praise is comely [beautiful]."

The point of Psalm 148 is that praise is to be jubilantly declared from every place in the entire universe! This psalm teaches us about the three "heavens" (148:1; 2 Cor. 12:2) from which our praise is to burst forth.

- The *first heaven* (vs. 7–14) is from the earth to the clouds. It's where birds and airplanes fly, what we call the earth's atmosphere.
- The *second heaven* (vs. 3–6) is that which is above the clouds to the frozen face of the

deep (Job 38:30), billions and billions of miles above our heads. It's what we call outer space.

- The *third heaven* (vs. 1–2) is the abode of God, above the frozen face of the deep. This is what John saw in Revelation 4:6 when he said, "And before the throne there was a sea of glass like unto crystal."

How incredible is the glorious simplicity of the exhortation in Psalm 149 to those who have been beautified with the precious gift of salvation (v. 4), whom he calls His saints (v. 5a). We must have two vital things in place. From a joyful heart giving Him glory (v. 5a), we are to let "the high praises of God be in [our] mouth" (v. 6a) and "a two-edged sword in [our] hand" (v. 6b; Heb. 4:12; Rev. 19:15; Eph. 6:17). As we pursue God today (and every day), may those two simple admonitions define our objective!

Could there be a more glorious way to end the book of Psalms than with Psalm 150? In verse 1, the psalmist exhorts us to "praise ye the Lord" in the place where He dwells ("in His sanctuary," or in His presence) and in all places that His presence and power are found ("in the firmament of His power"). In other words—everywhere! In verse 2, we are to praise Him for all that He *does* ("His mighty acts"), which proceed out of all that He *is* ("his excellent greatness"). And in verses 3–5, we are to praise Him with any and all musical instruments in existence, but most importantly, with the instrument of our mouth!

The book of Psalms ends with this final admonition: "Praise ye the Lord" (150:6). To adapt a phrase: let us just do it!

CHRIST IS REVEALED:

As the *One who gives sight to the blind* – Psalm 146:8 (Matt. 9:27–30; Mark 10:46–53; John 9:1–41)

---

[1] A. W. Tozer, in *The Best of A. W. Tozer*, as quoted in *Making New Discoveries* (Anaheim, Calif.: Insight for Living, 1996), 29. https://www.insight.org/resources/article-library/individual/discovering-the-missing-jewel-of-the-church

WEEK 28, DAY 4: TODAY'S READING: PROVERBS 1-4

OVERVIEW:
The purpose for the book of Proverbs; the enticement of sinners; the need for wisdom; the prerequisites for obtaining wisdom, knowledge, and understanding; the power of wisdom and knowledge to protect from the evil man and the strange woman; the rewards of wisdom; the instruction of a father.

HIGHLIGHTS & INSIGHTS:
The book of Proverbs is the revelation of wisdom from "the son of David, king of Israel" (1:1). That introduction gives us an amazing opportunity to explore the the three applications of Scripture. (Check out the "Highlights and Insights" in Week 25, Day 5.)

THE HISTORICAL APPLICATION
In the book of Proverbs, Solomon, the king of Israel, imparts his wisdom to his son, Rehoboam. (Twenty-three times, he specifically addresses his advice to "My son.") He is writing to teach a king's son how to rule, to employ the practical principles of life and leadership that flow out of understanding the difference between...

- The *wise* (wisdom) and the *fool* (foolishness)
- What is *right* and what is *wrong*
- The *godly man* and the *evil man*
- The *virtuous woman* and the *strange woman*

THE DOCTRINAL/PROPHETIC APPLICATION
From a Doctrinal or Prophetic standpoint, Proverbs is the revealing of wisdom to the nation of Israel during the Tribulation. (God identifies Israel as "my son" in Exodus 4:22.) It is written by Israel's king to warn them against the Antichrist (the ultimate personification of the evil man) and the seductive draw of false religion (the doctrinal application of the strange woman) during that time.

THE DEVOTIONAL/INSPIRATIONAL APPLICATION
From a Devotional or Inspirational standpoint, the book of Proverbs is the revelation of wisdom from Israel's true King—the King of kings, the Son of David, the Lord Jesus Christ (Matt. 9:27; 15:22; 20:30–31)—to all who have been made his sons (John 1:12; 1 John 3:1). The King's wisdom will teach a young man, first, how to live and to lead in the kingdom of his own *life*! Once he has learned how to rule his heart, mind, emotions, passions and desires, then he can take on the responsibility of marriage and bringing up children. After learning to rule well in the kingdom of his *home* (1 Tim. 3:4), he is ready to apply the King's wisdom in the kingdom, as it were, of the *church* (1 Tim. 5:17).

Even more, as he applies the wisdom revealed in Proverbs, the young man will learn to rule in his spirit over the pitfalls that disqualify men who fall into them from ruling in their homes and in the church:

- The love of self (2 Tim. 3:2)
- The love of pleasure (2 Tim. 3:4 – self-gratification, seduction of the strange woman, etc.)
- The love of money (1 Tim. 6:10)
- The love of this present world (2 Tim. 4:10)

While a young man learns to apply the King's wisdom to his life and subsequent kingdoms, if a young lady will likewise apply His wisdom to her life, God will develop in her the character of a virtuous woman, and the two will inevitably, in God's sovereignty and wisdom, find each other. The godly young man will recognize her character as one to whom he should offer a marriage proposal, and the godly young woman will recognize his character as one whose proposal she should accept. By applying the wisdom of Proverbs, he would be perfectly suited to fulfill his role representing the Lord Jesus Christ (the "godly man") in the home, and she would be perfectly suited to fulfill her role representing the church (the "virtuous woman") in the home (Eph. 5:24–25). As the home's "keeper" (Titus 2:5) or "guardian" (Prov. 31:27, "looketh well" = watchman), she would report to her husband the things that might put the kingdom of the home in jeopardy. As the home's head (Eph. 5:23), he would be poised to make the decisions that would provide spiritual security and safety in the home.

On a practical note, the thirty-one chapters of Proverbs easily connect to the thirty-one days of the month. Because of the importance of the book's subject matter and purposes, many have found it a valuable spiritual discipline to go through the book of Proverbs monthly, reading the chapter that coincides with the day of the month.

As we explore the book itself, we will begin with its purpose. In the first four verses, God reveals that Proverbs was actually designed to accomplish nine specific things:

1. To know wisdom and instruction (1:2a)
2. To perceive the words of understanding (1:2b)
3. To receive the instruction of wisdom (1:3a)
4. To receive the instruction of justice (1:3b)
5. To receive the instruction of judgment (1:3c)
6. To receive the instruction of equity (1:3d)
7. To give subtlety to the simple (1:4a)
8. To give the young man knowledge (1:4b)
9. To give the young man discretion (1:4c)

In the Bible, nine is the number of fruit-bearing, so we could say that Jesus wrote this book to teach us how to have a fruitful life!

Chapter 1 also provides the context of our need for wisdom. Like me, you probably look at the world and wonder how society could have degenerated so far. Gangs threaten safety in every major city (and many smaller ones) around the world, and everywhere we see extreme and senseless violence. According to Solomon, this is nothing new! Proverbs 1:10–19 reveals that something in our depravity finds such behavior appealing. Sinners will always "entice" us (v. 10). Depravity will be a part of any culture where there is no "fear of the Lord" (1:7) and where children do not "hear the instruction" of their fathers and "forsake" the law of their mothers (1:8).

When you become frustrated because you can't always make heads or tails of what you read in the Bible, take heart! Trust God's promise to "pour our my spirit unto you, and ... make known my words unto you" (1:23; 1 Cor. 2:9–13). Proverbs 2:6 contains a related promise: "For the Lord giveth wisdom: out of his mouth cometh knowledge and understanding." But the chapter actually begins, "My son, *if thou wilt*," followed by seven prerequisites to receiving God's wisdom, understanding, and knowledge (vs. 1–4, emphasis added).

1. We must *receive* His *words* (2:1a)
2. We must *hide* His *commandments* with us (2:1b)
3. We must *incline our ear* unto *wisdom* (2:2a)
4. We must *apply our heart* to *understanding* (2:2b)
5. We must *cry out* for *knowledge* (2:3a)
6. We must *lift up our voice* for *understanding* (2:3b)
7. We must *seek* and *search* for God's *wisdom* as we would for silver and hid treasure (2:4)

"Then," verse 5 says, "shalt thou … find the knowledge of God." After those seven prerequisites are fulfilled, *then* verse 6 will be a reality! Why does God give us prerequisites? He is basically making it clear that "you gotta want it!" When people don't know God's Word and, as a result, do not receive His wisdom, understanding, and knowledge, it's because, simply put, they don't really want it.

And when you really do want it, and by God's grace "wisdom entereth into thine heart, and knowledge is pleasant unto thy soul" (2:10), it provides an internal defense mechanism against sin. God's wisdom, understanding, and knowledge protect us from the "ways of darkness" (2:13) and "the frowardness of the wicked" (2:14). Solomon says, "Discretion shall preserve thee, understanding shall keep thee: to deliver thee from the way of the evil man … to deliver thee from the strange woman" (2:11–12, 16). Those are some incredible benefits!

But who exactly are the evil man and the strange woman that God's wisdom protects us from? These two are key characters in the book of Proverbs—and in life! Again, in a Historical and Devotional sense, every culture has evil men, those who speak perversely ("froward things" 2:12), who love to do evil and to pull others into their wicked ways (2:14). Similarly, every culture has strange women—women who are seductive, loose, or whorish—who seek to lure and allure men sexually.

From a Prophetic standpoint, though, the evil man refers to those in whom dwells the "spirit of antichrist" (1 John 4:3)—the personification of the very devil himself. They are found in every culture and will ultimately be represented in the Antichrist (Satan in a human body, 1 John 2:18). He is *the* evil man! The strange woman in a Doctrinal sense, refers to the "harlot," the false religious systems of the world that seduce mankind into bed and hold them there (Prov. 2:19).

The evil man and the strange woman are to be avoided in a Devotional sense because they make people's lives a "living hell"! The evil man and the strange woman are to be avoided in a Doctrinal sense because they send people to a literal "eternal hell"!

Finally, chapter 4 ends with the command to "keep [your] heart with all diligence" (v. 23). This is a choice we must make to protect and guard our hearts, so as not to be lured away from our surrender to Christ's Lordship. Understanding the benefits of wisdom is a major part of that process. We must attentively hear the father's instruction (v. 1), so we can understand his doctrine (or teaching, v. 2), so we can ultimately keep our hearts by not forsaking the instruction we have been given.

CHRIST IS REVEALED:

As the *Son of David, Israel's wise king* – Proverbs 1:1 (Matt. 9:27; 15:22; 20:30–31)

As the *Creator who founded the earth* – Proverbs 3:19 (Col. 1:16; Eph. 3:9; Heb. 1:2–3)

As the *Teacher of wisdom* – Proverbs 4:7, 11 (Col. 2:3)

52 WEEKS OF PURSUIT

WEEK 28, DAY 5: **TODAY'S READING: PROVERBS 5-8**

OVERVIEW:
The dangers and pitfalls of sexual immorality; the father's counsel to his son; the wiles of the strange woman; the blessing of wisdom, understanding, and truth.

HIGHLIGHTS & INSIGHTS:
In today's reading, we discover the powerful truth that God's wisdom and understanding can help us preserve the purity of our God-given sexual desires. These desires are actually holy, though they are to be reserved for the chamber of a covenant marriage bed (Heb. 13:4), but they are also an area of major temptation. In every phase of life, the enemy of righteousness is committed to destroying our personal purity. In any way he can, he will tempt us to satisfy our sexual desires in the heat of passionate compromise. But doing so will defile the body of Christ, contaminate communities, and ultimately condemn entire countries by invoking God's judgment.

In 5:1–2, the father passionately admonishes his son to "attend" (pay close attention to) his wisdom, understanding and knowledge. They provide the spiritual fortitude to avoid falling for the sexual allurements and enticements of the strange woman (5:3). Instead of focusing on momentary pleasure, he tells his son to look to "her end" (v. 4). Ultimately, he'd be left bitter and shredded to pieces by her two-edged sword. With corruption and death in every part of life that really matters, his entire life would be turned into a living hell (5:4–5).

Proverbs 5:8 advises us to get as far away from her as we possibly can, or she will cause irreparable damage:

1. Our honor will be given to others (5:9a)
2. Our years will be given to the cruel (5:9b)
3. Strangers will control our money (5:10a)
4. The things we've worked for will be given to strangers (5:10b)
5. Our health will be destroyed (5:11)
6. Cycles of regret and depression will haunt us (5:12–14)
7. We'll miss God's plan for us to experience the pure, fulfilling love of our life-mate (5:15–19)
8. We may develop sexual addictions (5:22)
9. We'll forfeit the potential we once held in life forever (5:23)

These losses lead progressively in chapter 6 to the warning against idleness (often called by same "the devil's workshop") and deceit, which will themselves lead to sudden calamity and total brokenness (6:15). The "wicked man" (v. 12) is characterized in 6:17–19 by six things that the Lord "hates," with the seventh being an "abomination" to Him:

1. A proud look (6:17a)
2. A lying tongue (6:17b)
3. Hands that shed innocent blood (6:17c)
4. A heart that deviseth wicked imaginations (6:18a)
5. Feet that are swift to run into mischief (6:18b)
6. A false witness that speaketh lies (6:19a)
7. Sowing discord among the brethren (6:19b)

Devotionally, this can describe any "wicked man," but Doctrinally, Solomon is describing "*the* man of sin," the very Antichrist himself (2 Thes. 2:3).

Solomon concludes his advice about avoiding the pitfalls associated with the strange woman with a simple and clear admonition in 6:20–24: Obey your father and mother! (See Eph. 6:1–2)

In 6:25, Solomon, the son of David, makes clear that the allure of the strange woman isn't primarily a *body* issue—it's a *heart* issue! Adultery begins in the *heart* through lust, which then finds its expression in the *body*. Similarly, our Lord Jesus Christ, the son of David, said in Matthew 5:28: "But I say unto you, That whosoever looketh on a woman to lust after her hath committed adultery with her already in his heart"!

Chapter 7 continues the admonition to keep the father's words and commandments as a guard against the lure of the sensual and sexual involvement so prevalent in every generation. Solomon warns that the young man who is "simple" and "void of understanding" (v. 7) is easy prey for the strange woman, especially when his curiosity lures him into her neighborhood (7:8). Curiosity won't just kill the cat; it'll also kill this "cool cat" because being cool is often just being stupid. (And, if I may interject a loose paraphrase here, "There is none cool, no, not one!" Every young man would do well to recognize that.)

In chapter 7, it is clear that the strange woman only catches in her snare those who want to be caught. Sure, there's seduction involved, but any man should be able to see her coming a mile away just by the way she's dressed, or (in this case) undressed (7:10). In addition, Solomon lists three other characteristics that indicate who she is: She is *loud*, *stubborn*, and doesn't like to *stay home* (7:11). Young men, use caution if you see these traits in a young lady you find attractive. Young women, consider whether any of these qualities have begun to surface in your life. Culture often encourages Teenage girls to act this way, but it is an absolutely disastrous path to be on! Finally, parents, recognize that we are not just bringing up sons; we are bringing up future *husbands* and *fathers*! And we aren't just bringing up daughters; we are bringing up future *wives* and *mothers*! The stakes are incredibly high, and sexual sin is extremely costly! (See 1 Cor. 6:18–19)

In 7:15–18, the strange woman tempts the simple young man by describing her preparations for him. Ironically, what she does would be totally appropriate in anticipation of presenting herself to her husband. It actually fits perfectly in the context of the Song of Solomon. But it is totally inappropriate outside the marriage covenant.

Chapter 8 continues the three-fold theme of wisdom, understanding, and truth. In 8:15–21, Solomon personifies these traits, declaring,

1. "By me kings reign"
2. "And princes decree justice"
3. "By me princes rule"
4. "And nobles [rule]"
5. "All the judges of the earth [rule]"
6. "Riches and honor are with me"
7. "I lead in the way of righteousness"

CHRIST IS REVEALED:

As the *Creator who prepared the heavens* – Proverbs 8:27–31 (Heb. 1:10; John 1:3)

52 WEEKS OF PURSUIT

WEEK 29, DAY 1: TODAY'S READING: PROVERBS 9-12

OVERVIEW:
Wisdom's invitation; the contrast between the righteous and the wicked; the contrast between the upright and the wicked.

HIGHLIGHTS & INSIGHTS:
One of the most incredible qualities of the Bible is its ability to transcend time and culture. Though it is thousands of years old, its relevancy and application to today is supernatural. The way the Holy Spirit designed and structured Proverbs makes it one of the easiest books in the entire Bible to apply to those of us living in the 21st century.

With that in mind, let's consider the big picture of the book of Proverbs. It has three divisions (2 Tim. 2:15), indicated by the three times Solomon identifies himself as the author of Proverbs.

- Division One – Proverbs 1–9
- Division Two – Proverbs 10–24
- Division Three – Proverbs 25–31

Chapter 9 is the final chapter in the first section of the book of Proverbs. It begins with a reference to wisdom's "seven pillars" (v. 1). These seven pillars are the seven manifestations of the Holy Spirit referred to in Revelation 4:5 as the "seven Spirits of God." (See Rev. 1:4; 3:1; 5:6.) These pillars, or manifestations, are specifically identified for us in Isaiah 11:2:

- The spirit of the Lord
- The spirit of wisdom
- The spirit of understanding
- The spirit of counsel
- The spirit of might
- The spirit of knowledge
- The spirit of the fear of the Lord

Throughout chapter 9, Solomon again personifies wisdom as a woman (9:1; 8:1–3), contrasting the *wise* woman and the *foolish* woman. Both extend an invitation to the simple, who is identified as one who "wanteth" (lacks) understanding (7:7; 9:4). And while both women offer similar invitations, they have very different motives—and results!

Both the wise and the foolish woman invite the simple one to a feast. Wisdom offers bread and wine (v. 5) which, coincidentally, are the same elements of the Lord's Supper (1 Cor. 10:16). Verse 17 describes the foolish woman's feast as "stolen waters" and "bread eaten in secret." Though her water is "sweet" and her bread is "pleasant," they are only temporarily satisfying! Ultimately, the feast of foolishness is a stinky pile of worms in the place where the fire is not quenched (Exod. 16:20; Isa. 66:24).

A key truth in the book of Proverbs is revealed in 9:9–10. To "increase in learning," we must possess the "fear of the Lord" and have the "knowledge of the holy" (Holy God, Holy Word, Holy Spirit, holy of holies, holy place, most holy place, etc.). Without this knowledge, we won't be able to make sense of the Bible or to tap into life's purpose. We'll have to come up with our own meaning and purpose for living, which will be foolish and completely irrational to the mind, will, and word of the Lord.

As we move into the second division of the book in chapter 10, it will be helpful to explain a bit about the form of ancient proverbs. There are actually 375 actual proverbs in this section (some extend for several verses) which take the form of one of three types of couplets.

- **Contrastive** couplets are normally identified by the word *but*. They catch your attention by pairing a truth with a striking contrast. "The lips of the righteous feed many: but fools die for want of wisdom" (Prov. 10:21).

- **Completive** couplets are identified by the word *and*. The second line of these proverbs agrees with the first, adding to or completing the idea. "In the fear of the Lord is strong confidence: and his children shall have a place of refuge" (Prov. 14:26).

- **Comparative** couplets are identified by the word *than*. They focus on what is actually the more excellent of two things being compared. "Better is a little with righteousness than great revenues without right" (Prov. 16:8).

CHRIST IS REVEALED:

As *One who hates lying* – Proverbs 12:22 ("He that sat upon the throne said … 'All liars, shall have their part in the lake which burneth with fire and brimstone: which is the second death.'" Rev. 21:5, 8)

52 WEEKS OF PURSUIT

WEEK 29, DAY 2: TODAY'S READING: PROVERBS 13-16

OVERVIEW:
The contrast of the upright and the wicked.

HIGHLIGHTS & INSIGHTS:
Chapter 13 begins, "A wise son heareth his father's instruction." Like any father, Solomon hoped that his son, Rehoboam, would follow his counsel, would actually hear and receive his instruction. For truth to be productive, it's not enough to merely *give* instruction—it must be received! Solomon longed for his own son to apply the truth that he was imparting to him so that his life would actually be *branded* by it!

Consider some of the wisdom and instruction in today's reading which Solomon was urging his son to hear and receive. And recognize that God inspired Solomon to write these things because He is, likewise, urging all of us to hear and receive them!

13:7 – It's possible to have *nothing*, and yet have *everything*! And it is possible to have *everything*, and yet, have *nothing*! Jesus wrote to the church in Smyrna, "I know thy ... poverty, (but thou art rich)" (Rev. 2:9). And to the church of the Laodiceans, Jesus said, "Thou sayest, I am rich ... and knowest not that thou art ... poor" (Rev. 3:17).

13:10 – Pride is the root of every "contention" in a marriage, a family, a friendship, a church, a neighborhood, or a community. The pride can exist in one party or both, but *all* contention is founded in pride! When we next find ourselves in a contentious situation, let's be sure to examine ourselves for pride first, before looking for it in others.

13:18 – Some people simply won't listen to anybody, and no amount of correcting them seems to do any good. Solomon lets us know that that path will lead us directly into "poverty and shame." If we "regard reproof," however, it will lead us directly into "honor." Today, let's consider how we respond when we are corrected!

13:20 – Where we end up in life is always affected by the friends we hang out with. If we choose wise friends, we will become wise. If we choose foolish friends, we will be destroyed right along with them.

13:24 – The wording of the first half of this verse sounds radical, but the point is not. Some parents think they love their children too much to see them affected by the results of corporal discipline. If they could see the result of *not* disciplining their children however, how it will ultimately affect their lifestyle and character, they would understand why God says they actually hate them!

14:12 – This is another verse that should be memorized! If you've memorized it already, you will be surprised how often you'll have occasion to use it in witnessing to the lost. (Notice the repetition of this verse in 16:25.)

14:15 – We can apply this verse in many avenues of life, but we must certainly apply it when listening to preaching or teaching! 1 John 4:1 echoes Solomon's sentiment in this verse: "Beloved, believe not every spirit, but try the spirits whether they are of God: because many false prophets are gone out into the world."

14:20 – You might think this situation would be a twenty-first century problem, not an ancient one! Some aspects of our depravity, however, transcend time and culture.

14:23 – There are two types of workers in the world: those who work and those who talk about working. Those who work will find *profit*. Those who talk about working will find *penury* (extreme poverty).

14:26 – Everyone is going to fear something! Those who fear the Lord will have a strong confidence and a place of refuge in typically fearful situations. Those who refuse to fear the Lord will find themselves without a refuge and fearful in many situations.

15:1 – This is another verse that you should memorize. We will all have ample opportunity to apply its wisdom over the course of our lifetime.

15:10, 12, 32 – Very few people can handle when others correct, reprove, or instruct them. That rebellious attitude, however, will cost them in the long run.

15:17 – Having few material possessions while surrounded by people who love you is a whole lot better than having many material possessions without love.

15:22 – Never forget the importance of seeking wise counsel and a lot of it! We'll never accomplish what we really want to accomplish without it.

15:23 – We never really know what people are dealing with internally. Sometimes God will use a simple word of encouragement to bless and refresh someone more than we will ever realize.

15:25a – What a strong warning! May God use it to humble us all today.

15:27 – If we're always looking for a way to make a fast buck, or looking for how to get something for nothing, our decisions will make life extremely difficult for our family.

15:28 – Think before you speak!

16:2 – Because of our human tendency to move through life without pausing to consider the real motives behind our actions, this is another verse that we can memorize to serve as a personal reminder to do so.

16:7 – This truth should serve as a great motivation for us to make certain that our ways always please the Lord!

16:9 – Having a heart for God and a passion for serving and pleasing Him is awesome and necessary, but we must be sure that *our* plan for our lives doesn't keep us from allowing the Lord to direct us step-by-step into *His* plan.

16:18 – When we see the manifestation of pride or a "haughty spirit," in ourselves or in others, just know that things are on the verge of collapsing!

16:19 – We must learn to surround ourselves with people with a "humble spirit."

16:32 – The only way to be "slow to anger" and "[rule] our spirit" is to be "*filled* with the *Spirit*" and "*walk* in the *Spirit*" (Eph. 5:18; Gal. 5:16).

CHRIST IS REVEALED:

As the *One who punishes the proud* – Proverbs 16:5 (Luke 14:11)

As the *Friend that sticks closer than a brother* – Proverbs 18:24 (John 15:14–15; Heb. 13:5)

52 WEEKS OF PURSUIT

WEEK 29, DAY 3: **TODAY'S READING: PROVERBS 17-20**

OVERVIEW:
The contrast between good and evil; warnings and instructions about life.

HIGHLIGHTS & INSIGHTS:

In *52 Weeks of Pursuit*, we've clearly seen that the Bible is filled with practical truths for living. In the book of Proverbs, those truths are especially recognizable. Proverbs is basically a collection of God's complex and diverse statements of what is *true* about life compared or contrasted with what is *not true*.

And we need these statements to be a functional part of our lives. On Week 28, Day 4, we suggested a daily schedule, reading the chapter of Proverbs that corresponds with the day's date. If we do that every month for the next 20 years, we will have read Proverbs 240 times! With that kind of repetition, the contrasts and parallels of God's truth would be fully loaded into the hard drive of our mind, providing us with moment by moment wisdom as the Holy Spirit guides us to walk in the way with the wise (Prov. 13:20).

One powerful statement in today's reading is Proverbs 17:1: "Better is a dry morsel, and quietness therewith, than an house full of sacrifices with strife." I completely agree! I'd much rather have my family all intact, living in peace in a shack with just enough food to get us by, than to live in a fat house, able to eat whatever we please, but have only strife in our relationships with each other (Prov. 21:9). But, in the pursuit of the "things on earth" (Col. 3:1–2), many Christians around the world live that way. They *got* what they *wanted*, but *lost* what they *had*! We must be wise. There are treasures in life far more valuable and precious than material wealth and monetary gain.

The first half of Proverbs 17:6 is tremendously powerful: "Children's children are the crown of old men." I know this is true, though you might have to become a grandfather to understand just how powerful those grandchildren are.

For those who are not yet grandparents, the second half of 17:6 contains a related, and equally powerful, truth. Solomon says, "The glory of children are their fathers." This is not just something we teach our children—this is a fact! By divine design, God places into a child's heart, even before they are born, a passionate desire to glorify the man they refer to as their father. It's why—totally unprovoked—little boys all over the world say to their friends, "My dad can beat up your dad." Or, "My dad is taller than your dad."

Some call this connection "Father-Power," and it's one of the most powerful forces in the entire world. More than environment or education, more than circumstances or socio-economic level, even more than a *mother*—humanly speaking, nothing has a more profound impact on who we are, what we are, and what we do than our *fathers*! Whether he was present or absent, living or dead, we feel his influence. Whether we knew him very well or not at all; whether we loved him, hated him, or somewhere "in-betweened" him; whether we like to admit it or not, all of us were deeply impacted by the man we call (or refuse to call) our father.

And that was God's design. God chose to give men, in their relationship with their children, the same title He reserved for Himself in His relationship with His children. Why? Because every earthly father is the primary model for God Himself in his child's life. What a huge blessing!

But at the same time, it's a huge stewardship. If a father displays the same character as the Father in heaven, if he raises his children "in the nurture and admonition of the Lord" (Eph. 6:4), then Father-Power becomes a positive force for good. As they grow and mature, those children are more able to connect intimately with their heavenly Father in a bond that will last of all eternity. But if a man breaks or misuses his Father-Power, it doesn't diminish his impact; it changes that influence into a negative force for evil. And in many cases, apart from God's grace and mercy, a child who has experienced negative Father-Power will struggle want to know the God who wants us to find Him and relate to Him in a Father-child relationship.

But negative Father-Power will destroy more than a child's perception of God. It can destroy the actual child! That's why God warns, "Ye fathers [not mothers or parents], provoke not your children to wrath" (Eph. 6:4). When a father "provokes" his child (misuses his Father-Power), the child will develop a rebellious "wrath" (Eph. 6:4) or a "discouraged" heart (Col. 3:21). *Rebellious wrath* can be seen in the gangs of young men living out their anger without any clue why they're angry in the first place. The *discouraged heart* is the broken young men who barely have enough fortitude to pick up their feet when they walk, much less find a job and become responsible, mature adults. Biblically, these are always the result of broken Father-Power. And this is why, at the heart of God's monumental declaration in Proverbs 17:6, is the inherent warning to fathers: "Don't break your Father-Power!"

To those of us prone to diarrhea of the mouth, Proverbs 17:27 says: "He that hath knowledge spareth his words: and a man of understanding is of an excellent spirit." This verse has spawned various catch phrases and quips, such as:

- "Blessed is the man who, having nothing to say, refuses to give evidence of it"
- "Silence is a hard argument to refute"
- "He can never speak well who cannot hold his peace"
- "As a man grows older and wiser, he talks less — but says more"

Clearly, many of us would do well to memorize this verse!

Chapter 18:1 says, "Through desire a man, having separated himself, seeketh and intermeddleth with all wisdom." To arrive at wisdom, we must possess a "desire" that is so intense we are willing to "separate" ourselves from anything and everything that would interfere with that pursuit. If you are looking for a reason to continue on in the *52 Weeks of Pursuit* (though I hope you don't need a reason!), this verse is a great one.

According to 18:2, the fool, on the other hand, has only one pursuit: "That his heart may discover itself." How many fools (God's identification, not mine) have *lost* themselves while trying to *find* themselves? Allowing our heart to "discover itself" is always an invitation to disaster! Instead, we have been instructed to "keep [our] heart with all diligence" (Prov. 4:23). Solomon is clear: we need to *guard* our heart, not to *find* it!

Proverbs 18:8 is extremely graphic: "The words of a talebearer are as wounds, and they go down into the innermost parts of the belly." If you've ever been on the receiving end of a talebearer's words, you understand just how perfect that description is. The talebearer is, in effect, a murderer! He slays a person's reputation or character with the sword of the tongue (Ps. 57:4; 64:3). Many hearts are bleeding today because they have been stabbed by someone's words. And though we can't stop others from doing it to us, we most certainly can keep from doing it ourselves! Once again, the heart of the matter is the matter of the heart. Jesus said in Matthew 12:34, "For out of the abundance of the heart the mouth speaketh." May God help us to "Keep [guard] our heart" today!

CHRIST IS REVEALED:

As *the King Who sits on the throne of judgment* – Proverbs 20:8 (John 5:22)

52 WEEKS OF PURSUIT

WEEK 29, DAY 4: TODAY'S READING: PROVERBS 21-24

OVERVIEW:
Warnings and instructions about life.

HIGHLIGHTS & INSIGHTS:
Solomon, the son of David, intended for his son, Rehoboam, to personally apply the wisdom, admonition, and instruction he was imparting when these proverbs were initially written. And our Lord Jesus Christ, the Son of David, intends the same for us, His "sons" (the New Testament identification of "sons" includes both males and females, John 1:12; 1 John 3:1–2; Php. 2:15). In today's chapters, we find key bits of wisdom, admonition, and instruction that the Son of David intends for us to apply personally, 3000 years after the son of David wrote them down!

Regarding Human Authority – 21:1
The Lord's authority trumps every earthly authority. However, the Lord works through human authorities, directing them as He wills, to accomplish His own purposes. A simple rule of thumb for us is to obey our human authorities until following them would cause us to disobey God's authority—what He has clearly revealed in His Word.

Regarding Self-Justification – 21:2
Solomon tells us, "Every way of a man is right in his own eyes." In other words, we have the dangerous ability to justify anything!

Regarding Choosing a Spouse – 21:9, 19
Simple instruction to the wise: "It is better to dwell in a corner of the housetop, than with a brawling woman in a wide house." And "It is better to dwell in the wilderness, than with a contentious and an angry woman."

Regarding Pleasing People – 21:10
Some people are just so evil, nothing we do will ever be enough to win their favor.

Regarding Treatment of the Poor – 21:13; 22:16, 22–23
How we deal with the poor is how the Lord will deal with us! If we mess with their souls, God will mess with ours.

Regarding the Tongue – 21:23
We need to learn not to say everything we think! Involving ourselves in other people's matters never works to our advantage.

Regarding Our Attitude Toward Preparation – 21:31
We need to work to be prepared, but at the same time, realize that without the Lord, we can do nothing (John 15:5).

Regarding Our Name – 22:1
We must protect our name from blot because we have been given Christ's "good name." We are "CHRIST-ians" or "CHRIST'S-ones." And it is better to receive Christ's "loving favor" than "silver and gold" (wealth).

Regarding Humility and the fear of the Lord – 22:4
Humility and the fear of the Lord go hand in hand. The only way to see ourselves for who we really are is to see the Lord for who He really is! Until we fear the Lord, we will be preoccupied with thoughts about self. As Andrew Murray said, "Humility is not thinking meanly of ourselves; it is not thinking of ourselves at all."

Regarding Child Training – 22:6
Every child is different, so God has a different "way" for each of them to go. A parent must so

understand the truth and wisdom of the Word of God—and the uniqueness of their children—that they are able, not only to direct them toward that way, but to train them in it. That is how God intends for them to remain in His way and focus on the unique way He desires to use them for their entire lives.

Regarding Borrowing Money – 22:7
The problem with *owing* people money is that they end up *owning* us!

Regarding Team Building – 22:10
Having the wrong people on the team will always keep things stirred up!

Regarding Laziness – 22:13
A lazy person always has an excuse for not doing what they ought to be doing.

Regarding Disciplining Children – 22:15
Only one thing can free a child from the foolishness that is bound in his heart—the "rod of correction"! Parents, psychologists, psychiatrists, and other experts will never invent or discover another successful alternative.

Regarding Choosing Friends – 22:24–25
Solomon instructs us not to hang out or be friends with an angry person because they will inevitably rub off on us! We'll start acting like them, and it will be a snare to our very soul. We must choose our friends wisely.

Regarding Co-signing – 22:26–27
As a general rule, we should not co-sign on loans for people. If we do, we must be prepared and willing to joyfully assume the entire debt as a gift. In other words, if we wouldn't give them the money, we shouldn't co-sign the loan!

Regarding Not Losing Sight of Our Familial and Spiritual Roots – 22:28; 23:10
Proverbs 22:28 says, "Remove not the ancient landmark, which thy fathers have set." And 23:10 agrees: "Remove not the old landmark; and enter not into the fields of the fatherless."

Regarding Alcohol – 23:19–21, 29–31
Solomon is clear about the dangers of alcohol. "Hear thou, my son, and be wise, and guide thine heart in the way. Be not among winebibbers; among riotous eaters of flesh: For the drunkard and the glutton shall come to poverty: and drowsiness shall clothe a man with rags" (23:19–21). And "Who hath woe? who hath sorrow? who hath contentions? who hath babbling? who hath wounds without cause? who hath redness of eyes? They that tarry long at the wine; they that go to seek mixed wine. Look not thou upon the wine when it is red, when it giveth his colour in the cup, when it moveth itself aright" (23:29–31).

Regarding Having a Home Blessed of the Lord – 24:3–4
There are three key components to having a home that is blessed of the Lord. It is built by *wisdom*. It is established by *understanding*. And it is "filled with all precious and pleasant riches" (the things money can't buy) by *knowledge*!

Regarding Seeking Wise Counsel – 24:6
Seeking wise counsel is imperative before making important decisions. The danger of our blind spots is removed when we have heard the wisdom and insight of a "multitude of counsellors."

Regarding Hard Work – 24:30–34
We can learn a lot from the man whose field is overtaken with thorns and weeds, and whose territorial wall is falling down. He illustrates perfectly that if we are only interested in sleeping and relaxing, we will inevitably come to poverty. God admonishes us to learn how to work hard.

CHRIST IS REVEALED:

As *He that is pure, whose work is right* – Proverbs 21:8 (John 4:34; 17:4)

52 WEEKS OF PURSUIT

WEEK 29, DAY 5: TODAY'S READING: PROVERBS 25-28

OVERVIEW:
Similitudes and instructions; warnings and instructions.

HIGHLIGHTS & INSIGHTS:
Today we enter the final section of the book of Proverbs, chapters 25–31. Each of the three sections of Proverbs is identified by the repetition of the words, "The proverbs of Solomon" (1:1; 10:1; 25:1).

The structure of chapters 25-27 is different than what we have encountered thus far in this book. Here the proverbs are not individual verses presenting a specific proverbial truth, but groups of verses on the same topic. The literary term for this is an *epigram*, "a brief, clever, pointed remark or observation typically marked by an antithesis." Then chapter 28 returns to the comparative, completive, or contrastive couplets used in the previous sections of the book.

The first part of chapter 25 reveals Solomon's wisdom about *kings* (monarchs, rulers, or presidents of nations):

- Kings like to "search out a matter" (25:2)
- A king's heart is "unsearchable" (25:3)
- Kings' thrones are "established in righteousness" (25:5)
- Kings reject people who praise themselves (25:6)
- Kings have no patience with people who vaunt themselves (25:7)

Chapter 26 begins with Solomon's discourse on *fools:*

- What fools really need is the rod of correction (26:1–3)
- The fool is unable to articulate the truth of a proverb (26:7)
- Giving honor to a fool is dangerous to him and to others (26:8)
- A parable in a fool's mouth is as a wound—he'll hurt you with it! (26:9)
- Any reward a fool receives comes from the God of all creation (26:10)
- The fool will inevitably return to his folly (26:11)
- There is more hope for a fool than for a self-proclaimed "wise man" (26:12)

Verses 4–5 contain what might look like a contradiction. Verse 4 instructs us *not to answer* a fool according to his folly lest we become like him. In verse 5, Solomon says *to answer* a fool according to his folly lest he become wise in his own conceit. So which is it? Are we supposed to answer a fool in his folly or not?

The key is that there are two types of fool. The fool in verse 4 is a *committed* fool. He is already "wise in his own conceit" (v. 5). He accepts wrong as right and persuades others to believe as he does. Answering this type of fool won't change his mind—it only drives him deeper into his folly. He is argumentative. He will twist our words to negatively influence new or immature Christians or to convince a simple fool that the truths we're communicating are wrong. This type of fool can only be ignored.

A *simple* fool, on the other hand, is reachable and teachable. He is foolish because he lacked the proper influences in his life to teach him about God's wisdom. He is looking for a role model and he will inevitably find one! He easily falls under the influence of "sinners" (1:10–19) or committed fools, but he doesn't have to. If we "answer [him] according to his folly" (26:5) and reach him with the gospel of salvation, we can introduce him to the ultimate role model, the Lord Jesus Christ (1 John 2:6), and become an earthly role model for him through a discipling relationship (1 Cor. 11:1).

Next, Solomon focuses our attention on *sluggards* in 26:13-16:

- The sluggard gives exaggerated reasons for not leaving his house (26:13)
- The sluggard has restless sleep (26:14)
- The sluggard doesn't even like to exert the energy to feed himself (26:15)
- The sluggard is very skilled in creating ways to avoid work (26:16)

Finally, chapters 27–28 are full of practical truths for living. I will highlight some here, though God may certainly emphasize different ones to you in your reading today.

- Proverbs 27:1 is another great verse to memorize. It's a vivid reminder not to presume upon the future, and we will be able to use it repeatedly as we witness to lost people.

- The wisdom of 27:2 should be a no-brainer—but it isn't! Whether blatantly or subtly, our speech reveals the "pride of life" (1 John 2:16) that makes us want others to recognize our greatness. The key to not praising ourselves is not controlling our tongue, however. It's in recognizing we are "nothing" (Gal. 6:3).

- As 27:6 suggests, a friend who loves us enough to speak hard truths to us, even at the risk of hurting our feelings, is a great treasure. Being willing to receive the rebuke of a friend should be our aim.

- Proverbs 27:10a reminds us of the value of cross-generational relationships with family friends.

- There is the obvious practical wisdom in Proverbs 27:12, but don't miss the Prophetic application for those of us living in the last days. The "day of evil" (Jer. 17:17–18) that Jesus called the "tribulation" (Matt. 24:21) is fast approaching. God has provided a hiding place in Christ (Col. 3:3), and the prudent will enter that refuge. But the "simple" will see the warning signs and continue headlong into the punishment that awaits the lost.

- In 27:17 we see that friendships that result in mutual spiritual stimulation and edification are imperative for our spiritual well-being.

- For every father and pastor, Proverbs 27:23 admonishes us to know what is happening or not happening in the spiritual lives of those under our care. May we be *diligent* to provide even greater loving oversight.

- Proverbs 27:26a reveals the actual animal that God used to clothe Adam and Eve after they sinned in the Garden. As you might expect, their covering required the shedding of blood and the death of a sacrificial lamb! (See John 1:29; Rev. 4:4.)

- In 28:6, we see that we are better off having no material possessions but great character, than having great possessions and no character.

- God certainly wants us to pray, but Proverbs 28:9 is a warning. If our lives reveal a disregard for God's word, He won't be blessed or impressed by our prayers. In fact, if we don't listen to Him, it is an abomination to assume that He will listen to us! Think of it this way: if we disregard how God has chosen to communicate to us, He will choose to disregard how we communicate with Him.

- Proverbs 28:13 implores us to take full responsibility for our sin. And while we sometimes try to hide our sins from God, we more often "cover [our] sins" by refusing to own the wrongs we do to other people. Getting right with people is imperative to being right with God!

- According to 28:21, we must treat every person with the same respect, regardless of their physical beauty, their position in the community, or their material wealth. When we elevate one person over another, Solomon says we will inevitably make compromises over the simplest

matters of life.
- God is clear in 28:20 and 22 that being rich is not wrong in and of itself. It is wrong, however, to desire to be rich because that desire will leave us impoverished in other key areas of our life.

CHRIST IS REVEALED:

As the *One who rewards those who repay evil with good* – Proverbs 25:21–22 (Rom. 12:20)

WEEK 30, DAY 1: **TODAY'S READING: PROVERBS 29-31**

OVERVIEW:
More warnings and instructions; the words of Agur; the words that Lemuel's mother taught him.

HIGHLIGHTS & INSIGHTS:
We'll conclude the book of Proverbs today with two powerful perspectives. First, while Psalms presents the *heart* of God, Proverbs presents His *mind*, or more specifically, the *mind of Christ* (1 Cor. 2:16). This book intricately reveals to us how God *thinks*. In Proverbs, we see God's viewpoint on virtually every issue of life. And if we would adopt God's viewpoint, as revealed in Proverbs, as our viewpoint, it wouldn't just *simplify* our lives, it would *revolutionize* them!

And, second, whereas Leviticus gives God's detailed instruction concerning the *physical* aspects of *Israel's* life, Proverbs details God's instruction concerning the *spiritual* aspects of a *believer's* life. We can trace any conflict we have—relational or financial, in our home, church, or community—to a violation of some spiritual truth God specifically revealed in the book of Proverbs. This book is that comprehensive and that practical!

Proverbs concludes with chapter 31, the infamous passage on the virtuous woman. Historically and Devotionally, chapter 31 lists qualities God wants every woman to aspire to possess. But from a Prophetic standpoint, there's a whole lot more going on! Chapter 31 describes a virtuous woman, but only one woman in Scripture is specifically called a virtuous woman. Do you know who?

It just happens to be Ruth (Ruth 2:3; 3:11). As we learned in our *52 Weeks of Pursuit*, Ruth is that member of a cursed race who, in a time of famine, heard the good news that there was bread in the city of Bethlehem. Upon hearing this news, she leaves her father and mother and all she holds dear in her homeland to partake of this bread. Having arrived in Bethlehem, she goes to work in the harvest field of her one and only Jewish kinsman redeemer until he called her up out of that field to be his bride.

Ruth is the greatest picture of the church (the Gentile bride of the Jewish kinsman redeemer from Bethlehem who is the Bread of Life) in the Old Testament, so Prophetically, the virtuous woman of Proverbs 31 is fulfilled in us, the Bride of Christ! And once we make that connection, this chapter takes on new significance, not just for ladies, but for every person who is "espoused" to Jesus Christ as their "one husband" (2 Cor. 11:2)!

Consider verse 28: "Her children arise up, and call her blessed; her husband also, and he praiseth her." One day, all of God's "children" will "arise up" at the rapture (1 Thess. 4:13–17). And after we are "caught up" (1 Thess. 4:17), we will appear before the judgment seat of Christ where those God has graciously permitted us to win to Christ (our spiritual "children") will call us blessed. What a joyful and humbling experience that will be! But the greatest joy on that day will be for our "husband," the Lord Jesus Christ, to praise us, saying, "Well done" (Matt. 25:21).

The question of Proverbs 31:10 is a good one: "Who can find a virtuous woman?" Sadly, in these last days of the Laodicean period, the answer is *not many*! She is extremely rare. She is almost extinct. But if we would make the book of Proverbs our wise and "Wonderful Counselor" (Is. 9:6) for living life by applying God's wisdom in the first thirty chapters, we will find that we have actually become the virtuous woman of chapter 31. Would our Lord consider you a virtuous woman?

CHRIST IS REVEALED:
As the *One who descended from and ascended to heaven* – Prov. 30:4 (John 3:13)

52 WEEKS OF PURSUIT

WEEK 30, DAY 2: **TODAY'S READING: ECCLESIASTES 1-6**

OVERVIEW:
The vanity or emptiness of life under the sun (apart from God); the vanity in life's cycles (chapter 1); the vanity in life's pursuits (chapter 2); the vanity of time (chapter 3); the vanity of social status (chapter 4); the vanity of religion and riches (chapter 5); the vanity of a long life (chapter 6).

HIGHLIGHTS & INSIGHTS:
The title of the book of Ecclesiastes comes from the Greek word *ecclesia* which means "a called-out assembly." This is also where we get the word *ecclesiology*, referring to the study of the church. Interestingly enough, the human author of this book repeatedly refers to himself as "the Preacher" (1:1–2, 12; 7:27; 12:8–10). From a Historical standpoint, then, and based on the other descriptive phrases he uses to refer to himself (1:1 – "son of David" and "king in Jerusalem"; 1:16 – the one who had "gotten more wisdom than all they that have been before me in Jerusalem"; and 12:9 – the one who had "set in order many proverbs"), we know that the author is Solomon.

But Prophetically, there is more going on. We have is an Old Testament book, written by the "son of David, king in Jerusalem," preaching, as it were, to a "called-out assembly." Could it be that our Lord Jesus Christ (the Son of David and King of Jerusalem) is actually preaching a message to those of us in His church about what is really important in life? And in these last days of the church age, one of the key difficulties (sins!) found in Christ's church is all the time we spend chasing things we think will give meaning to life—but which are, invariably, the wrong things! Yet they were the very things Solomon was chasing, too.

The context of Ecclesiastes is, of course, the other books of biblical wisdom. We've noted previously that the book of Psalms reveals the *heart* of *God*, and the book of Proverbs reveals the *mind* of *Christ*. Now, the book of Ecclesiastes reveals to us the *mind* of the *Spirit*. It shows the great contrast between the workings of the spirit of *man* and the Spirit of *God*.

Ecclesiastes is a book of warning. As an old man, King Solomon is reflecting on a life full of selfish living, worldly pursuits, and many regrets. Inspired by the Spirit, his intent is to spare us the bitterness of learning by our own experience that, apart from God, nothing "under the sun" (a phrase Solomon repeats twenty-nine times in twenty-seven verses) can satisfy the human heart. This small book offers undeniable evidence of our need for a Savior to give our lives meaning. Without Jesus Christ, and the mission He left us to accomplish, we would all be living the same empty life that Solomon so eloquently describes.

The basic theme of the book of Ecclesiastes can be summed up with Jeremiah 2:13: "For my people have committed two evils; they have forsaken me the fountain of living waters, and hewed them out cisterns, broken cisterns, that can hold no water." This is a perfect picture of Solomon's problem and the problem of many (dare we say, most) believers today. From this verse we learn three things about people in general:

1. They are *empty* (because they have no God)
2. They are *stubborn* (because they are determined to be filled with something)
3. They will ultimately be *disappointed* (because they cannot be filled)

Ecclesiastes describes in detail all the earthly things that do not satisfy, but which men in every generation pursue (See John 4:13). Solomon tried them all and found them wanting. His list included…

- Human wisdom (1:16–18)
- Pleasure (2:1–3)
- Superiority (2:15)

- Hard work/labor (2:19–21)
- Alcohol (2:3)
- Possessions (2:4-6)
- Power (2:7)
- Money (2:8–9, 5:10–11)
- Music (2:8)

Solomon was correct in his conclusion that "all is vanity" (Ecc. 1:2). Our life, our accomplishments, and our labor are completely meaningless. Without God, they're totally useless. Thankfully, Jesus came to meet our every need and to give us an eternal purpose for our lives on earth. 1 Corinthians 15:58 says, "Therefore, my beloved brethren, be ye stedfast, unmoveable, always abounding in the work of the Lord, forasmuch as ye know that your labour is not in vain in the Lord." May we spend our lives faithfully seeking our Lord Jesus Christ and passionately carrying out His mission!

CHRIST IS REVEALED:

As the *Son of David* – Ecclesiastes 1:1 (Matt. 1:1)

As the *King of Jerusalem* – Ecclesiastes 1:1 (Ps. 2:6)

52 WEEKS OF PURSUIT

WEEK 30, DAY 3: TODAY'S READING: ECCLESIASTES 7-12

OVERVIEW:

The vanity of wisdom apart from God (chapter 7); the vanity of hoping in government (chapter 8); the vanity of life's unfairness (chapter 9); the vanity of foolish living (chapter 10); the vanity of selfish living (chapter 11); the vanity of forgetting God (chapter 12); Solomon's conclusion of the whole matter.

HIGHLIGHTS & INSIGHTS:

Ecclesiastes 7 is the 666th chapter in the Bible. The number 666 belongs to the man that Revelation 13:18 refers to as "the beast," 2 Thessalonians 2:8 refers to as "that Wicked," and 1 John 2 refers to as the "Antichrist." This 666th chapter declares that "there is a wicked man that prolongeth his life in his wickedness" (7:15). And in Revelation 13 "that Wicked" man will receive a mortal head wound halfway through the Tribulation, but will prolong "his life in his wickedness" as Satan literally inhabits his body and continues his rampage for the last half of the Tribulation.

This 666th chapter also includes another familiar character from Proverbs: the strange woman. In Revelation 17 she is riding on the back of the beast (the wicked man). In other words, she is the harlot, the adulterous religious system that the Antichrist will use to unite the world religiously during the Tribulation Period (Rev. 17:3–6). And Ecclesiastes 7:26 warns us about her: "And I find more bitter than death the woman, whose heart is snares and nets, and her hands as bands: whoso pleaseth God shall escape from her; but the sinner shall be taken by her." This is a perfect description of what will take place religiously on this planet during the Tribulation!

Solomon is clear in Ecclesiasties 7:23 that wisdom acquired apart from God will not bring us fulfillment in life. While we are to seek wisdom (Prov. 2:2), real wisdom (God's wisdom, not "the wisdom of this world" 1 Cor. 1:20–21; 2:6; 3:19) doesn't come from seeking *wisdom*; it is a byproduct of seeking *God*! (See Ecc. 2:26; Eph. 1:17; James 1:5)

In chapter 8, Solomon warns against hoping in government or politics to make lasting change. A nation's laws and policies can change behavior, but only God has the power to change people's hearts through the new birth. No law on earth is perfect, but God's law is (Ps. 19:7). No human's judgments are always true and righteous, but God's are (Ps. 19:9). Lasting change will never come unless believers in Jesus Christ take seriously the privilege and responsibility of being trusted with the gospel (1 Thess. 2:4) and faithfully carry out our mission. Then we will see God, not government, change hearts, one at a time!

Ecclesiastes 8:11 says, "Because sentence against an evil work is not executed speedily, therefore the heart of the sons of men is fully set in them to do evil." This principle has a number of key applications.

1. *In a Nation* – This verse explains why the death penalty is not an effective deterrent to crime. In America, the average wait on death row is over 10 years! Not quite what you'd call "executed speedily," that's for sure!

2. *In a Home* – When disciplining your own children, parents must discipline as "speedily" as possible. Beware of giving idle threats about consequences while letting your own frustration build. Delaying punishment sets up our children's hearts to become "fully set in them to do evil."

3. *In a Church* – When some "evil work" seems to be present in the church, a pastor or leader must carefully assess what is actually going on. Acting hastily with wrong information will damage people and the pastor's continued leadership. However, once a situation has been biblically assessed to be an "evil work," that leader must deal with it "speedily," lest the problem fester and spread like a cancer throughout the fellowship.

Chapter 12 begins, "Remember now thy Creator in the days of thy youth, while the evil days come not, nor the years draw nigh, when thou shalt say, I have no pleasure in them." Many young people believe that, with their entire lives before them, they can live for themselves *now* and get serious about God and His mission *later*. Despite the warning of Proverbs 27:1, they are convinced they have time to do all the things they want to do—first. But how audacious it is, Solomon declares, to offer to the holy, Creator God our left-overs rather than our very best!

While we present ourselves to the Lord "in the days of our youth" (12:1a), as strapping and vivacious young people with unending promise, potential and possibility, Solomon describes us presenting ourselves for the Lord's use at a time in life when we are none of those things (in 12:1b–7). In our old age, we'll live a whole different experience:

- Life, itself, is a burden (12:1b)
- We have one health crisis after another (12:2)
- Our hands are shaking (12:3a), and our knees are bowing and weak (12:3b)
- Our teeth are falling out (12:3c)
- We're losing our sight (12:3d)
- We're losing our hearing (12:4a)
- We awaken from sleep at the slightest sound (12:4b)
- Our voice is deep and weak (12:4c)
- We become afraid of heights (12:5a), and all kinds of other minor things (12:5b)
- Our hair turns white just before turning loose! (12:5c)
- The smallest things become a hassle (12:5d)
- The desires that used to drive us are no longer there (12:5e) because we're about to die (12:5f)
- Our body, in general, is just falling apart, until it is thrown in the ground and returns to dust (12:6–7)

Through Solomon's words, God is calling to every young man and woman: "Remember now thy Creator in the days of thy youth!"

In light of all that Solomon experienced in his life "under the sun," Solomon concludes that everything in life all comes down to this: "Fear God and keep his commandments: for this is the whole duty of man" (12:13). After being born again, those two simple pieces of advice will take us far in our journey!

CHRIST IS REVEALED:
As the *poor wise man* – Ecclesiastes 9:14–16 (2 Cor. 8:9)

As the *Creator* – Ecclesiastes 12:1 (John 1:1–3, 14)

WEEK 30, DAY 4: TODAY'S READING: SONG OF SOLOMON 1-8

OVERVIEW:

The song of all songs that describes the love between a man and a woman (this is one of 1,005 songs written by Solomon — 1 Kings 4:32)

Scene 1: In the King's Palace (1:1–2:5); Scene 2: In the Young Maiden's Bedroom (2:6–3:5); Scene 3: The King's Entrance (3:6–11); Scene 4: In the Young Maiden's Bedroom (4:1–5:1); Scene 5: In the Presence of the King (5:2–7:13); Scene 6: In the Beloved Shepherd's Town (8:1–14).

HIGHLIGHTS & INSIGHTS:

We come today to the last of what is referred to in theological circles as the "Poetic Books" of the Old Testament: Job, Psalms, Proverbs, Ecclesiastes and Song of Solomon. Many have noted through the centuries that each of the Poetic Books reveal one of the basic, yet essential, elements of man:

- Job recording for us the cry of man's **spirit**

- Psalms, Proverbs, and Ecclesiastes recording the cry of man's **soul**
  (And if man's soul be defined as the mind, will and emotions, then the Psalms express man's emotions; Proverbs expresses man's will; and Ecclesiastes expresses man's mind)

- Song of Solomon records the cry of man's **body**
  (Revealing that the basic yearning of the body is for love that is expressed through physical intimacy)

It should be noted and realized that the Song of Solomon is at times a very graphic book in terms of its description of human love and intimacy. Because of the sometimes explicit nature of its contents, many 21st century pastors and leaders have actually forbidden the reading and/or teaching of this book in a public setting. It is my belief, however, that, as the Bible says of itself, "every word of God is pure" (Prov. 30:5) and in my mind it becomes a little spooky when a pastor or church suddenly begins to think and act as if they are more holy than our supremely holy God and His supremely holy word! It's reported that during the Dark Ages, as our Bible-believing brothers and sisters (and forefathers!) known as the Albigenses were being hunted like animals by the Roman Catholic Church because of their unshakable stance on the word of God and their dogmatic belief that salvation was by grace through faith—apart from baptism and other sacraments of the Roman Catholic Church—that they frequently read, quoted and referred to the Song of Solomon.1

In the "big picture" of the last two of the Poetic Books, it is important to note the contrast between Ecclesiastes and the Song of Solomon. The book of Ecclesiastes (which, though written after the Song of Solomon, but in God's sovereignty, appears chronologically in our Bibles before it) ends with the statement "vanity of vanities" (Ecc. 12:8). In a stark contrast, the Song of Solomon begins with the phrase "song of songs" (Son. 1:1). The simple and yet powerful point is that life apart from a personal relationship with Christ is the "vanity" of all "vanities" (the theme of Ecclesiastes)—but living life in the midst of a personal, meaningful, purposeful, and intimate love relationship with Christ places us in the very center of the joy and bliss of the "song of songs" (the theme of Song of Solomon).

When determining the three layers of application (Historical, Doctrinal/Prophetic, Devotional/Inspirational — See page 11 in the "Introduction" for a reminder of them) for any part of the Bible, typically the easiest application to uncover is the Historical Application. It is actually nothing more than laying out what actually happened in the particular text under consideration. Interestingly, I find that the Song of Solomon is unique in

that both the Doctrinal/Prophetic Application and the Devotional/Inspirational Application of this book seem quite clear and easily discovered, whereas the Historical Application seems rather difficult to determine.

From a Doctrinal/Prophetic standpoint, there are actually three applications. The Song of Solomon points to and pictures the love relationship between:

- God the Father and Israel
- The Messiah and Israel
- Christ and the church

From a Devotional/Inspirational standpoint, there are at least two tremendously significant applications:

- The Song of Solomon pictures the intimate, personal love relationship the individual believer is intended to enjoy with the Lord Jesus Christ
- The Song of Solomon is a "How-To Manual" for husbands and wives to live by so they might experience the blessing of an intimate, personal love relationship with one another

But, as mentioned above, it is actually the Historical Application that poses the most difficulty for me. The storyline of the song is somewhat difficult to follow in its written form, because it is often hard to distinguish which of the characters in the story is actually speaking. Were the characters actually singing this song, it would certainly be obvious.

There are many interpretations concerning who the two lovers in the Song of Solomon actually are, and what the storyline actually is. The two most plausible historical interpretations in my mind are these:

First, it may be that the two lovers in the story are Solomon and the Shulamite. If this is the correct interpretation, it would appear that in Solomon's quest to find out what it would be to just be a "normal guy" in Israel, he made a trip to northern Israel disguising himself as a shepherd. During this time, he fell madly in love with a beautiful "country girl," if you will, and she with him. But then, rather unannounced, Solomon went back to his palace. Sometime later, the Shulamite gets word that the king (Solomon), her unknown lover, has summoned her into his presence. It is only then she realizes that the one who has stolen her heart is actually the king of Israel. In the palace, he invites her to become his "number one" lady and lover, as it were. (Son. 6:8-9)

Personally, what is very appealing about this interpretation is that the book of Song of Solomon would most likely be the "song of songs" (1:1) sung by the King of kings and Lord of Lord's to His bride, the church, on the wedding day (Rev. 19:7).

What has caused others to question this interpretation is this whole thing of Solomon inviting the Shulamite to be his "number one" lady and lover... in his harem of 60 wives, 80 concubines and countless other women (Son. 6:8-9), on his way, nonetheless, to what would become 700 wives and 300 concubines (1 Kings 11:3)! Those who question this interpretation argue that if Solomon is a picture of Christ in this book, his invitation to the Shulamite, a clear picture of the church, doesn't appear to be consistent with Christ's character.

The second possible interpretation is that the song is actually a love story with three main characters. The first character is a beautiful young maiden (the "fairest among women" 1:8; 5:9; 6:1) who appears to come from an oppressive family (1:5–6). The second character is the man of her dreams, a simple shepherd (1:7), who despite a lowly estate is the maiden's "beloved" who has stolen her heart (1:13-14). The third character is the

wealthy and mighty King Solomon, who is renowned for his obsession with beautiful women—and for getting whomever he wished (1 Kings 11:3)!

In this interpretation, the story is basically this: On one of Solomon's journeys, he meets a beautiful young lady and is so smitten by her that he exercises his self-invented kingly privilege in taking her to his palace. The young maiden is not impressed with his wealth nor his words and has no interest whatsoever in having a relationship with the king. She is already madly in love with a young shepherd. Though the "daughters of Jerusalem" (2:7; 3:5; 8:4 – a nice way of referring to Solomon's harem) try to persuade her to turn her affection toward Solomon, she can only think of her true love and desires to be with him. On several occasions, Solomon seeks to win her affection, but to no avail. She is passionate only for her beloved. Finally, Solomon frees her to return to her family and the man of her dreams.

In this interpretation of this story, rather than being a picture of Christ, Solomon is actually a picture or type of the world, trying anything and everything to lure the young maiden ("bride-to-be", 2 Cor. 11:2) away from the beloved Shepherd. As believers, we are the bride of Christ and, like the young maiden, our affection for our Beloved should be so all-encompassing that we refuse to allow anything in this world to come between us. God commands us to love Him with all of our heart, soul, mind, and strength (Mark 12:30) and not to love the world or even be its friend (James 4:4; 1 John 2:15).

Which is the proper historical interpretation? I'll allow you to draw your own conclusion. Regardless of your conclusion, may we remember daily the faithfulness and love our beloved Savior-Shepherd has for and demonstrates to us—and return that same kind of faithfulness and love to Him!

CHRIST IS REVEALED:

As the *Shepherd* — Song of Solomon 1:7 (1 Pet. 2:25)

As the *Beloved* — Song of Solomon 1:14; 2:8; 8:5 (Matt. 3:17; 12:18)

---

[1] Stedman, Ray C. "Message: Song of Solomon: A Love Song and a Hymn." www.raystedman.org.

WEEK 30, DAY 5: **TODAY'S READING: ISAIAH 1–6**

OVERVIEW:
Israel's backslidden condition; Isaiah's exhortation for repentance; the coming of Christ's kingdom; Jerusalem's glorious future; God's judgment upon sinners; Isaiah's vision of God's holiness.

HIGHLIGHTS & INSIGHTS:
The book of Isaiah is one of the most intriguing books of the entire Bible. It contains either some very strange coincidences or some very incredible things God reveals to us through it!

- Is it mere coincidence that the Bible contains 66 books and Isaiah contains 66 chapters?
- Is it mere coincidence that Isaiah 1 begins as Genesis does, talking about the heavens and the earth? (v. 2; Gen. 1:1)
- Is it mere coincidence that Isaiah 40 contains the familiar words, "The voice of him that crieth in the wilderness, Prepare ye the way of the Lord, make straight in the desert a highway for our God" (v. 3), as does the 40th book of the Bible, the first book of the New Testament, the Gospel of Matthew (Matt 3:1–3)?
- Is it mere coincidence that Isaiah 66 talks about the "new heavens and the new earth" (v. 22), corresponding with the last chapter of the last (66) book of the Bible, Revelation 21 (Rev. 21:1)?
- Is it mere coincidence that the first 39 chapters of Isaiah (representing the Old Testament) are so different in content from the last 27 chapters (representing the New Testament) that many have insisted there are two authors of this book? The first 39 chapters, coincidently enough, point to man's tremendous need for salvation, and the last 27 chapters point to God's gracious provision of it!

Clearly, the book of Isaiah is a microcosm of the Bible. A microcosm is "a miniature, a small and yet perfect representation of the whole." New York City is called a microcosm of the world because it has residents from literally every nation on earth. The capstone of a pyramid is a microcosm of the pyramid itself—it's a miniature of the entire pyramid. That's the book of Isaiah—a perfect, miniature representation of the entire Bible!

Next, let's consider the book of Isaiah as a whole. Isaiah begins the section of the Bible called the Prophets (Luke 24:27, 44), which is divided into the Major Prophets and Minor Prophets. *Major* and *minor*, here, do not refer to significance, but to length. The Major Prophets are simply longer books than the Minor Prophets.

Isaiah prophesied around 814 to 769 BC, corresponding to 2 Kings 16–25, and he primarily addresses the two southern tribes. The theme of Isaiah, and of all of the prophetic books, is the Day of the Lord, or the second coming of Christ. No matter the situation that Israel faced, the sins Israel was committing, or the subject the prophet was preaching about—the prophetic books always end with or point to the Day of the Lord!

In chapter 1, Israel has, once again, spiraled downward into apostasy. In verse 4, Isaiah describes their backslidden state with seven different phrases. They are sinful, laden with iniquity, evildoers, and corrupters. They have forsaken the Lord, provoked the Holy One, and gone away backward. Spiritually, these people were a mess! But in contrast to God's graphic description in Isaiah 1:4, they thought they were doing okay. They were going through the motions, keeping all the feasts, the sacrifices, the new moons, and the sabbaths long after they had any meaning in their hearts or any bearing on their lives.

And, if I may paraphrase, God says to Israel in Isaiah 1:10–15: "I'm sick of all of your religiosity! Don't bring me any more of your vain oblations! I can't stand it! You're wearing me out with all of this stuff you're doing! I'm going to close my eyes so I don't even have to see any more of your hypocrisies! When you lift up your hands in prayer, all I see is all of the sinful things you've been doing with them! Spare Me!"

52 WEEKS OF PURSUIT

Interestingly, Isaiah 1 mirrors Revelation 3:14–22, our Lord's letter to the Laodiceans, which describes the spiritual condition of His church in our day. Now, too, God's people come to church looking the part, giving an offering, singing songs, taking notes, nodding or saying *amen* in all the right places, but our hearts are not in it! What we do on Sundays has little, if any, bearing on what happens in our lives Monday through Saturday!

And God's answer in Isaiah's day (and now) is, "Get your heart right! Then, get your heart into it!" God says, "Wash you, make you clean; put away the evil of your doings from before mine eyes; cease to do evil; Learn to do well; seek judgment, relieve the oppressed, judge the fatherless, plead for the widow. Come now, and let us reason together, saith the LORD: though your sins be as scarlet, they shall be as white as snow; though they be red like crimson, they shall be as wool. If ye be willing and obedient, ye shall eat the good of the land: But if ye refuse and rebel, ye shall be devoured with the sword: for the mouth of the LORD hath spoken it" (Is. 1:16–20). The parallel New Testament passage is, no doubt, 2 Corinthians 6:14–7:1.

A key phrase in Isaiah 1:19 is, "If ye be willing *and* obedient." Laodicean churches are filled with *willing* people. They're *willing* to serve in a children's class, *willing* to care for the facilities, *willing* to offer the Lord a gift of love on the first day of the week, *willing* to do many things. They just don't *do* them! *Willing*? Yes! *Obedient*? No!

On the other hand, Laodicea is also filled with *obedient* people. They would never think about missing a service (Heb. 10:25). They would never not participate in the offering (1 Cor. 16:2). They always take notes during the message on Sunday morning. They *do* a lot of things, but their *obedience* is strictly a matter of *duty*! It is ritualistic, legalistic, hypocritical. It's the result of self-disciplining and suppressing their real desires and cranking out spiritual-looking activity, rather than the joyous, passionate, heart-felt, Spirit-led response of a *willing* heart. God calls us to be both "willing and obedient."

Since the theme of the Prophets is the Day of the Lord, consider underlining in your Bible every specific reference to that Day that you see. Every day, I'll include a list with your reading, but it is more engaging and valuable if you find them yourself first. By doing this, you'll understand in a whole new way why the first day of our *52 Weeks of Pursuit* began by emphasizing that the Day of the Lord is the theme of the Bible!

SPECIFIC REFERENCES TO THE DAY OF THE LORD:
- 2:2 – "And it shall come to pass in the last days"
- 2:11 – "in that day"
- 2:12 – "For the Day of the Lord"
- 2:17 – "in that day"
- 2:19 – "when he ariseth to shake terribly the earth"
- 2:20 – "in that day"
- 2:21 – "when he ariseth to shake terribly the earth"
- 3:7 – "in that day"
- 3:18 – "in that day"
- 4:1 – "in that day"
- 4:2 – "in that day"
- 5:30 – "in that day"

CHRIST IS REVEALED:

As the *One who will judge the nations* – Isaiah 2:2–4 (2 Tim 4:1)

As the *Branch of the Lord, beautiful and glorious* – Isaiah 4:2 (Zech. 3:8; 6:12; Jer. 23:5; 33:15; Is. 11:1)

52 WEEKS OF PURSUIT

WEEK 31, DAY 1: **TODAY'S READING: ISAIAH 7-12**

OVERVIEW:
Isaiah's message for King Ahaz; Christ's birth and kingdom foretold; Assyria to be broken; the promise of Israel's restoration; Christ, the Branch.

HIGHLIGHTS & INSIGHTS:
Today's chapters are sometimes referred to as "The book of Immanuel" because of their clear prophecies concerning the Lord Jesus Christ.

Isaiah prophesied during the reigns of King Ahaz, Hezekiah, Manasseh, Amon, Josiah, Jehoahaz, Jehoiakim, Jehoiachin, and Zedekiah (2 Kings 16–25). Remember, after Solomon's death, the nation of Israel divided. The ten northern tribes were called Israel, and the two southern tribes, Judah. Israel's capital was Samaria; Judah's was Jerusalem. Isaiah's ministry centered in Jerusalem, but his messages influenced both kingdoms.

Chapter 7 begins with Judah under attack. The surrounding nations wanted to form a coalition to stand against Assyria, but King Ahaz of Judah refused to join. So Syria and Israel joined forces to attack Judah to try to force her to cooperate with them (7:1–2). (We learn in 2 Kings 16:1–9 that rather than trusting the Lord to help, Ahaz was secretly negotiating with Assyria to protect him.) In Isaiah 7:3–9, God sent Isaiah and his son Shearjashub (meaning "the remnant shall return") to meet Ahaz while he was inspecting the water supply and give him a message of confidence and hope. They tell him not to fear because Israel and Syria would both be broken within sixty-five years. In the fulfillment of the prophecy, Assyria defeated Syria (Damascus) in 732 BC, and defeated Israel in 721 BC.

In 7:10–16, God told Ahaz to ask for a sign to confirm the prophecy, but Ahaz piously refused. So the Lord gave a sign to the entire "house of David" (7:13): "Therefore the Lord himself shall give you a sign; Behold, a virgin shall conceive, and bear a son, and shall call his name Immanuel" (7:14). This, like many prophecies in the Old Testament, involved what's called a double fulfillment. In other words, to affirm and confirm that the prophecy would be fulfilled in the future, God would often give a partial fulfillment of the prophecy in the immediate present. Isaiah 7:14 is an obvious reference to virgin birth of Jesus Christ (Luke 1:31–35). But the partial fulfillment of the prophecy was that Isaiah's wife would have a child (Is. 8:1–8).

Isaiah's first wife, the mother of Shearjashub, had died, and Isaiah had taken a new wife shortly after giving this prophecy, and the virgin he took to wife gave birth to a child which they named Mahershalalhashbaz (meaning, "speed to the spoil, haste to the prey") within the next year. Chapters 7:17–10:34 is a warning to apostate Israel that Assyria would come and completely annihilate them. It was at this very juncture that Mahershalalhashbaz was born, his name pointing to the impending destruction of Samaria and Syria (8:4).

In chapter 9:1–7, we find a second prophecy concerning the coming Messiah. (Compare with Matt. 4:13–16.) And in 9:8–10:34, Isaiah continues to warn Israel of her impending ruin. At the same time, he warns Assyria not to become proud of her victories, recognizing that she would simply be a tool in the hand of God and that she too would soon be defeated.

We can also see in this section that Assyria is a type of the Antichrist ("The Assyrian" – 14:25; 19:23; 30:31; 31:8; 52:4; Ezek. 31:3; Hos. 5:13; 11:5; Mic. 5:5–6) who will gather the nations of the world together in battle against Israel at Armageddon at the end of the Great Tribulation!

In chapters 11 and 12, Isaiah prophesies that Israel and Judah will unite in the kingdom.

SPECIFIC REFERENCES TO THE DAY OF THE LORD:

7:18 – "in that day"

7:21 – "in that day"

7:23 – "in that day"

9:7 – "and upon his kingdom, to order it, and to establish it"

9:14 – "in one day"

10:3 – "in the day of visitation"

10:17 – "in one day"

10:20 – "in that day"

10:27 – "in that day"

10:32 – "that day"

11:10 – "in that day"

11:11 – "in that day"

11:16 – "in that day"

12:1 – "in that day"

12:4 – "in that day"

CHRIST IS REVEALED:

In the *Son who is born of a virgin, called Immanuel* – Isaiah 7:14 (Matt.1:23; Luke 1:26-35)

In the *Child born unto us, and the government shall be upon his shoulder* – Isaiah 9:6 (Rev. 11:15)

WEEK 31, DAY 2: **TODAY'S READING: ISAIAH 13-18**

OVERVIEW:
The judgment of Babylon; the judgment of Assyria; the judgment of Philistia; the judgment of Moab; the judgment of Damascus; the judgment of Ethiopia.

HIGHLIGHTS & INSIGHTS:
Chapter 13 is a transition chapter. Whereas Isaiah 1–12 dealt with judgments specifically related to Judah and Israel, chapters 13–23 broaden the prophecies of judgment to include the Gentile nations.

Since Babylon was the nation that destroyed Jerusalem and took the people of Judah captive in 586 BC, it is not surprising that she is at the top of God's list of the Gentile nations to receive His judgment. In 13:5, God declares that those who would actually wield His judgment would "come from a far country." Historically, these were the people of Persia, a nation about 350 miles east of Babylon. In a Prophetic sense, those who will "come from a far country" to execute judgment will be the Lord Jesus Christ and the armies of heaven (Rev. 19:11–16), and they will come "in that day"—the Day of the Lord (13:6, 9, 13).

Once God has executed His judgment "in that day," Isaiah says to the nation of Israel, "And it shall come to pass in the day that the LORD shall give thee rest from thy sorrow, and from thy fear, and from the hard bondage wherein thou wast made to serve" (14:3). This is the peace and rest Israel will experience during the millennial reign of the Lord Jesus Christ. And when His kingdom has finally been established, God says, "The whole earth is at rest, and is quiet: they break forth into singing" (14:7). What a day that is going to be! May we say with the Apostle John, "Even so, come, Lord Jesus" (Rev. 22:20).

Isaiah 14:8–23 certainly has application to the king of Babylon, but there is much more going on. God is also speaking to the satanic power working behind and through that earthly king—Lucifer himself. God does a similar thing in Ezekiel 28:11–17, addressing himself to the King of Tyrus. But in both cases, what we really get is vital information about Lucifer's fall. In Isaiah 14:13–14, God records for us Lucifer's infamous five "I will" statements:

- "I will ascend into heaven"
- "I will exalt my throne above the stars of God"
- "I will sit also upon the mount of the congregation, in the sides of the north"
- "I will ascend above the heights of the clouds"
- "I will be like the most High"

These blasphemous declarations are tremendously significant, teaching us about the location of heaven and the position Lucifer once held. We learn that the presence of our Lord in heaven is a northerly direction (Psalm 75:6; 48:2; Job 26:7; 37:22), far "above the heights of the clouds" and "above the stars of God." We learn that Lucifer had a throne, which was in "Eden, the garden of God" (Ezek. 28:13). Hmmmm.

Lucifer's fifth "I will" is especially important. From the beginning, Satan had the same mode of operation that he still uses today. For all of human history, he was and is a deceiver! Revelation 12:9 says he "deceiveth the whole world"! Satan is not successful because he presents himself as Satan in order to turn the world into a bunch of Satan worshippers. Nor does he try to get all the inhabitants of the earth to hate God or to set themselves against God. No, he seeks to *counterfeit* God by actually *posing as God*. And through *religion*, he deceives people into thinking that they are following God and loving God and obeying God, when they aren't! We must be very discerning in these last days (1 Tim. 4:1; 1 John 2:18). Satan has always wanted to "be *like* the most High" (emphasis added)!

And if you think Satan isn't serious about this, he is. In recent days, Satan has masterfully written himself right out of almost every church history book on the market. And even worse, he's written himself out of almost every Bible on the market! In some Bibles, Isaiah 14:12 refers to him, not as "Lucifer, son of the morning," but as the "morning star." And some even cross reference this phrase to 2 Peter 1:19 and to Revelation 22:16, where the "morning star" is specifically identified as our very Lord Jesus Christ Himself! Again, we must be discerning and aware of how the Bible says Satan operates.

Isaiah 14:27 says, "For the Lord of hosts hath purposed, and who shall disannul it? And his hand is stretched out, and who shall turn it back?" Obviously, in context, this is talking about God's purposes concerning Babylon and Israel. Devotionally, however, it also applies to anything and everything God has promised that is in accordance with His purposes for us as New Testament believers.

In chapters 15–16, Isaiah prophesies the destruction of Moab. He is certainly describing what would happen in his own time, but his words also refer to what would happen in the distant future! One day Moab will seek refuge in Judah (16:3–4), and rescue will come from the Lord Jesus Christ as He rises to His throne at His second coming, "judging, and seeking judgment, and hasting righteousness" (16:5; See also 9:7; 11:4; 28:6; 32:16; 33:5; 42:1, 3–4; 51:5). And though what this verse describes was in *distant future* for Isaiah and those living in *his* time, its ultimate fulfillment will, no doubt, be in the *near future* for those living in *this* time!

Chapters 17 and 18 prophesy the destruction of both Damascus and Ethiopia, but they are filled with verbal icons, powerful descriptions of Christ's second coming and the beginning of His millennial reign. (17:4, 7, 9, 11; 18:4)

SPECIFIC REFERENCES TO THE DAY OF THE LORD:

13:6 – "the Day of the Lord"

13:9 – "the Day of the Lord"

13:13 – "in the day"

14:3 – "in the day"

17:4 – "in that day"

17:7 – "at that day"

17:9 – "in that day"

17:11 – "in the day"

18:4 – "I will take my rest"

CHRIST IS REVEALED:

As the *One who will sit on the throne of David* – Isaiah 16:5 (Luke 1:32–33)

WEEK 31, DAY 3: TODAY'S READING: ISAIAH 19-25

OVERVIEW:
The judgment of Egypt; the judgment of Babylon; the judgment of Edom; the judgment of Arabia; the judgment of Jerusalem; the judgment of Tyre; the establishment of the millennial kingdom; the blessings of the millennial kingdom.

HIGHLIGHTS & INSIGHTS:
In chapters 19–20, Isaiah prophesies about the judgment of Egypt. He describes the "Lord [riding] upon a swift cloud" (19:1), wreaking such havoc that it sends Egypt into a massive civil war (19:2). Again, the Assyrian judgment of Egypt is a picture of the judgment our Lord will execute upon Egypt on the Day of the Lord! In his prophecy, Isaiah sees a time when the land of Judah is preeminent in the world (19:17). Both the Egyptians and the Assyrians will be subject to Israel's Messiah and worship Him (19:18–23). At that time (during the millennium), Isaiah prophesies that these former enemies, Israel, Egypt and Assyria, will live in harmony, blessed of the Lord (19:24–25).

In chapter 20, God uses Isaiah as an object lesson to warn the people of Judah who were seeking an alliance with Egypt against Assyria. God instructed Isaiah to remove his outer garment and his sandals to picture what would become of the Egyptians and Ethiopians: they would be humiliated and destitute (naked and barefooted). He says that the Assyrians would expose the "buttocks" of the Egyptians (20:4), and because Judah had sought an alliance with them, they would also be ashamed. Rather than putting their trust in Egypt, they should have trusted the Lord!

The phrase in chapter 21, "the desert of the sea," refers to the Babylonian plain by the Tigris and Euphrates Rivers. Babylon is identified in 21:9 as the object of this prophecy, and once again, there is both a historic and prophetic fulfillment. The words "Babylon is fallen, is fallen" (21:9) are repeated in Revelation 14:8 and 18:2 at the time of Christ's Second Coming. Isaiah 21:10 says that Babylon's destruction will spell freedom for God's people, Israel, who will have been *threshed* (beaten down or afflicted). The remainder of chapter 21 deals with the judgment of Edom (21:11–12) and the judgment of Arabia (21:13–17).

Having prophesied God's judgment on the nations surrounding Jerusalem, in chapter 22, Isaiah prophesies God's judgment upon Jerusalem. It is called "the valley of vision" in verse 1 because Jerusalem was surrounded by valleys on three sides. From a historic standpoint, this is the judgment found in 2 Kings 25, as Babylon invaded Jerusalem under Nebuchadnezzar in 588–586 BC. But we see the promise of a future fulfillment "in that day" (at the Second Coming of Christ) in Isaiah 22:8, 12, 20, 25.

In chapter 23, Isaiah prophesies that Tyre, the commercial trading center of the Mediterranean world would be destroyed because of her pride. Historically, Alexander the Great conquered Tyre in 332 BC.

Chapter 24 begins with "Behold," a word which always points to a future event in Scripture. Isaiah is describing the establishment of the millennial kingdom. The first six verses describe a universal judgment of the entire earth. The terms Isaiah uses in verse 1 are tremendously graphic: "Behold, the LORD maketh the earth empty, and maketh it waste, and turneth it upside down, and scattereth abroad the inhabitants thereof." In verses 13–16, Isaiah says the godly remnant that survives the Tribulation will praise the Lord for His righteous judgments. The Apostle John sees the same fulfillment in Revelation 7:1–10; 15:3–4; 16:5, 7; 19:2. The remainder of the world will be judged in a horrific fashion, as described in Isaiah 24:17–23.

Chapter 25 depicts the millennium as a feast. Isaiah describes a banquet at which Gentiles from all over the] world will bow their knee and worship Israel's king who sits on His throne in Jerusalem, or "in this mountain" (25:6–7, 10).

SPECIFIC REFERENCES TO THE DAY OF THE LORD:

19:16 – "in that day"

19:18 – "in that day"

19:19 – "in that day"

19:21 – "in that day"

19:23 – "in that day"

19:24 – "in that day"

20:6 – "in that day"

22:5 – "it is a day of trouble"

22:8 – "in that day"

22:12 – "in that day"

22:20 – "in that day"

22:25 – "in that day"

23:15 – "in that day"

24:21 – "in that day"

25:9 – "in that day"

CHRIST IS REVEALED:

In *Eliakim, the master of Hezekiah's household* – Isaiah 22:20–22 (Christ is over the household of faith and has the "key of David," Rev. 3:7; Heb. 3:6; Gal. 6:10)

WEEK 31, DAY 4: **TODAY'S READING: ISAIAH 26-31**

OVERVIEW:
Worship in the millennial kingdom; praise for the preservation of Israel; woe against the drunkards of Ephraim; woe against Jerusalem; woe against the schemers; woe against those who trust in Egypt; woe against those who trust in Egypt's military defense.

HIGHLIGHTS & INSIGHTS:
Chapters 26 and 27 describe the worship that will be taking place in the millennial kingdom. Chapter 26 begins, "In that day shall this song be sung in the land of Judah" and then gives us the actual words of the song! It is a song of praise to the Lord for His glorious protection. The godly will enter into the "strong city" of Jerusalem, but be aware: the strength of the city is not in her physical walls but in the spiritual walls of salvation the Lord Himself imparts to its occupants (26:1–2). Because they trust in and meditate on the Lord, He blesses them with "perfect peace" (v. 3). But verse 3 is also a biblical prescription for experiencing that kind of peace now! When our minds are totally and passionately "stayed on" the Lord, we will totally and passionately trust in the Lord (26:3–4).

The song continues in verses 5–11 with praise for the Lord's judgment against His enemies. Verses 12–15 declare praise for God's permanent victory over His enemies. And verses 16-21 declare praise for the Lord's deliverance from suffering, specifically Israel's suffering in the Tribulation. Isaiah then gives them the glorious promise of resurrection (26:19).

In chapter 27, the song praises God for the slaying of Leviathan. This slithering creature, described as a "serpent" and a "dragon" (27:1), pictures Israel's enemies. In Job 41, we saw that Leviathan is that seven-headed, red dragon (Ps. 74:13–14; Rev. 12:3) who is "that old serpent, called the Devil and Satan" (Rev. 12:9). Israel's enemies in the Tribulation are the nations, but God is clear that the power working through these nations is Satan himself! In fact, until the birth of Christ, Satan relentlessly persecuted the seed (Gen. 3:15) that would become the nation of Israel because He would come from her (Rev. 12). Since the birth of Christ, he has mercilessly and relentlessly persecuted the nation of Israel because He did come from her. And Revelation 12 reveals that the persecution against the nation of Israel will only be heightened during the Tribulation, until, as Isaiah describes, the Lord steps in to defeat Leviathan (Satan).

Chapter 27 praises the Lord for His judgment against the Gentile nations that have been used by Satan to afflict Israel and ends with Israel worshipping "the Lord in the holy mount at Jerusalem" (27:12–13). This is no small thing! It is exactly what the Father has intended His Son to receive (Ps. 66:4; Phil. 2:9–11). Praise the Lord, it is going to happen sooner, rather than later!

In chapters 28–31, Isaiah pronounces five of six woes upon those who scoff at God's Word—in 28:1; 29:1; 29:15; 30:1; 31:1. The sixth woe is in 33:1. God is indicting Israel and Judah for trusting in their wealth and their alliances with foreign nations, rather than trusting Him.

- The first woe is against Ephraim, the large tribe that represented the Northern Kingdom. It anticipates the Assyrian invasion and the fall of Israel in 722 BC. But it also looks ahead to the Day of the Lord ("in that day" 28:5) when the remnant of Israel would repent and receive a "crown of glory" and a "diadem of beauty," descriptions of our Lord Jesus Christ when He returns to the earth to establish His millennial reign.

- The second woe is against "Ariel, the city where David dwelt!" (Jerusalem 29:1). It prophesies the invasion of the Assyrian army under Sennacherib and describes, both Historically as well as Prophetically, how the nations that hunger and thirst for Israel's destruction will themselves be destroyed.

- The third woe appears in 29:15–24, against those who seek to scheme against the Lord, who foolishly think He doesn't see them. That may just be the epitome of what we might call delusional!

52 WEEKS OF PURSUIT

- Isaiah 30:1 is the fourth woe, directed against Judah for their rebellion against the Lord, specifically for trusting in Egypt rather than the Lord. Chapter 30 then describes how the alliance with Egypt would fail and how Judah would be chastened of the Lord. In verse 18, God points, once again, to that time when the chastening would end, when He would destroy the nations of the world that set themselves against Israel and bring Israel into the blessings of the Messiah when He rules in His kingdom.

- The fifth woe, in chapter 31, continues the condemnation against Judah for looking to Egypt for military help against the Assyrians. The chapter ends with God's declaration that Assyria would ultimately be defeated, not by *man*, but by *Him* and that they would be defeated, not by *man's sword*, but by *God's*! And you are holding that very Sword in your hands right now. It can defeat all of the worldliness that is afflicting your life today!

SPECIFIC REFERENCES TO "THE DAY OF THE LORD":

26:1 – "in that day"

27:1 – "in that day"

27:2 – "in that day"

27:12 – "in that day"

27:13 – "in that day"

28:5 – "in that day"

29:18 – "in that day"

30:23 – "in that day"

30:25 – "in the day"

30:25 – "in the day of the great slaughter"

30:26 – "in the day"

31:7 – "in that day"

CHRIST IS REVEALED:

As the *Precious (chief) Cornerstone, a sure foundation* – Isaiah 28:16 (Eph. 2:20–21; Matt. 21:42; Acts 4:10–12; Rom. 9:33; 1 Pet. 2:6–8)

WEEK 31, DAY 5: **TODAY'S READING: ISAIAH 32-39**

OVERVIEW:
Israel's deliverance through Messiah's reign; woe against Assyria; destruction of the Gentile nations; blessings in the millennial kingdom; the invasion of the Babylonians under Sennacherib; Hezekiah's consultation with Isaiah; Hezekiah's dependence and trust in the Lord; Hezekiah's illness and recovery; Hezekiah's foolish reception of the Babylonian messengers; Israel's captivity into Babylon foretold.

HIGHLIGHTS & INSIGHTS:
Chapter 32 begins, "Behold, a king shall reign in righteousness, and princes shall rule in judgment" (v. 1). This is the glorious time in the millennium that John described in Revelation: "[Thou] hast made us unto our God kings and priests: and we shall reign on the earth" (5:10); and "They shall be priests of God and of Christ, and shall reign with him a thousand years" (20:6). Isaiah's prophecy that "the spirit be poured upon us from on high" (32:15) refers to the *last days*, which began with a partial fulfillment of the prophecy on the Day of Pentecost in Acts 2 (see Acts 2:16–17 specifically), but were put on hold after the stoning of Stephen in Acts 7. They will pick up again during the Tribulation after the parenthesis of the church age. (See Is. 44:3; Ezek. 36:25–27; Joel 2:28–32.)

In chapter 33, the sixth and final "woe" is pronounced on Assyria. Isaiah prophesies that the Assyrians, under Sennacherib, would bring Judah into subjection, forcing them to pay tribute (taxes) while demanding their total surrender. The Lord promises deliverance from the Assyrians and uses the occasion, once again, to point to the millennial kingdom when the nations of the world will never threaten Israel again. The righteous will live in peace with their Messiah: "For the Lord is our judge, the Lord is our lawgiver, the Lord is our king: he will save us" (33:22).

In chapters 34–35, as in chapters 24–27, the Lord describes the universal judgment of the Gentile nations which will be fulfilled at Armageddon (Rev. 19:11–21) using words such as *nations*, *people*, *earth*, and *world* (34:1). Isaiah points to the physical (35:3–6) and spiritual (35:7–10) changes that will take place when the Lord Jesus Christ returns at the Second Coming and establishes His millennial kingdom on the earth. Verse 8 says, "And an highway shall be there." It's called "The way of holiness," and only "the redeemed [those who have been bought by the blood of the King of kings, the Lord Jesus Christ] shall walk there" (35:9).

Chapter 36:1–38:8 parallels the events of 2 Kings 18:17–20:11. When threatened by the Assyrians, King Hezekiah looked to Isaiah, God's man, and to God Himself for help (37:1–2). The proud Assyrians warned Hezekiah in a letter not to trust the Lord to deliver them. But Hezekiah "received the letter from the hand of the messengers, and read it: and Hezekiah went up unto the house of the Lord, and spread it before the Lord. And Hezekiah prayed unto the Lord" (37:14–15). Because of Hezekiah's dependence and trust in God, He promised to protect Jerusalem and deliver His believing remnant. That night, the Lord destroyed 185,000 Assyrian soldiers, and Sennacherib (the boastful "intimidator") went back home with his tail between his legs!

Wow! Let's consider how the Devil may be seeking to intimidate us today, and carefully follow Hezekiah's example! Let's do what Paul described in Philippians 4:6–7: "Be careful for nothing; but in every thing by prayer and supplication with thanksgiving let your requests be made known unto God. And the peace of God, which passeth all understanding, shall keep your hearts and minds through Christ Jesus."

When Hezekiah got sick (38:1), he prayed that the Lord would spare his life. The Lord answered his prayer, granting him fifteen more years. When the Babylonians heard that he had recovered from his sickness (39:1), they sent messengers and a present to him. Hezekiah foolishly received them and showed them all of the immensity and glory of the treasures in Solomon's Temple. As a result, Isaiah prophesied that they would return and carry away all of the treasures they had seen, along with all of God's people, into Babylonian captivity.

One final note: Isaiah 38–39 actually precede chapters 36–37 chronologically. They're placed there because they anticipate the Babylonian captivity, which is the subject matter in chapters 40–66. Also remember, Isaiah is a microcosm of the Bible, so chapter 39 ends the section representing the thirty-nine books of the Old Testament.

SPECIFIC REFERENCES TO THE DAY OF THE LORD:

34:8 – "the Day of the Lord's vengeance"

34:8 – "the year of recompense for the controversy of Zion"

35:4 – "God will come with vengeance"

35:4 – "God [will come] with a recompense"

37:3 – "a day of trouble"

38:1 – "in those days" (more specifically, the Tribulation Period)

CHRIST IS REVEALED:

As the *One who wields "the sword of the Lord" in judgment* – Isaiah 34:6 (Rev. 19:15)

52 WEEKS OF PURSUIT

WEEK 32, DAY 1: TODAY'S READING: ISAIAH 40-45

OVERVIEW:
Judah's future captivity in Babylon and promise of deliverance (40:1–11); God's omnipotence (40:12–26); God's sustaining power (40:27–31); God's sovereignty in history (41:1–7); God's protection of Israel (41:8–20); God's challenge to the idols (41:21–29); the Servant of the Lord (42:1–25); the assurance of Israel's restoration (43:1–44:5); the witness of the restored nation (44:6–23); the fulfillment of restoration (44:24–45:25).

HIGHLIGHTS & INSIGHTS:
Chapter 40 begins the second section of the book of Isaiah, representing the New Testament. In fact, Isaiah begins this section as Matthew does, with "The voice of him that crieth in the wilderness, Prepare ye the way of the Lord, make straight in the desert a highway for our God" (40:3; Matt. 3:1–3). And to help you keep your bearings in these twenty-seven chapters, each day's overview will provide a more detailed outline.

Isaiah 40:3 is a key passage I use when I engage Jehovah's *False* Witnesses outside my house (2 John 7–10 tells us not to let them in our house!), just before I lovingly, but matter-of-factly, tell them they are of an "antichrist spirit" (2 John 7). Why this verse? In this prophecy—which Jehovah's *False* Witnesses readily agree refers to John the Baptist—Isaiah says that he (John the Baptist) will prepare "the way of the Lord." In the Old Testament, the word Lord (capital L and small capital ord) always means the Hebrew word *Jehovah*. It's even translated *Jehovah* in the "Bible" (I use the term extremely loosely) that Jehovah's *False* Witnesses use. And when Isaiah's prophecy is fulfilled in Matthew 3:1–3, John the Baptist is referring to the Lord Jesus Christ! Isaiah 6:5 reveals the same incredible truth. Isaiah saw Jehovah ("the Lord of hosts") in all His glory, and in John 12:37–41, the Holy Spirit moved John to write that Isaiah was seeing *Christ's* glory and was speaking of *Christ*! Jesus Christ *is* Jehovah!

Isaiah's words regularly disprove the claims of Jehovah's *False* Witnesses. In chapter 42:8, God clearly says that glory belongs to Jehovah alone: "I am the Lord: that is my name: and my glory will I not give to another." John 1:14 says, "And the Word was made flesh, and dwelt among us, (and we beheld his glory, the glory as of the only begotten of the Father,) full of grace and truth." According to Isaiah 42:8, glory belongs only to Jehovah, so if Jesus Christ isn't Jehovah, how did he get glory? And in John 17:5, as Jesus prayed to Jehovah, His Father, He prayed, "And now, O Father, glorify thou me with thine own self with the glory which I had with thee before the world was." In light of Isaiah 42:8, why would Jesus ask for something Jehovah doesn't give?

Isaiah 43 also contradicts Jehovah's *False* Witnesses' claims. God refers in verse 10 to His "witnesses." We might call them Jehovah's *True* Witnesses! In verse 11, God clearly says that there is only one Jehovah, and He is the *only saviour*: "I, even I, am the LORD; and beside me there is no saviour." But check out Titus 2:13: "Looking for that blessed hope, and the glorious appearing of the great God and our *Saviour* Jesus Christ." Paul here refers to Jesus Christ as the "saviour" and as "the great God." Not *a* God, like the Jehovah's *False* Witnesses' "Bible" says in John 1:1, but *the* God. Doesn't that just make you wanna shout a big hearty Amen!

Isaiah 44:6 says that Jehovah (Lord) is the *only* eternal God. Only Jehovah God is the "first" and the "last." And in Revelation 1:10–11, John says, "I was in the Spirit on the Lord's day, and heard behind me a great voice [in context, it's the voice of Jesus Christ], as of a trumpet, Saying, I am Alpha and Omega, *the first and the last*." Hallelujah!

Finally, Isaiah 44:24 says that Jehovah (Lord) made "all things" by Himself ("myself"). And John 1:3 says, "All things were made by him [by the Word, who is the Lord Jesus Christ, v.1]; and without him was not any thing made that was made." And Colossians 1:16 says, "For by him [the "Son," the Lord Jesus Christ, v. 13] were all things created that are in heaven, and that are in earth, visible and invisible, whether they be thrones, or dominions, or principalities, or powers: all things were created by him, and for him." Biblically, Jesus Christ, the Son of God, is Jehovah!

SPECIFIC REFERENCES TO THE DAY OF THE LORD:

40:10 – "the Lord God will come with strong hand, and his arm shall rule for him"

42:4 – "till he have set judgment in the earth"

42:13 – "The Lord shall go forth as a mighty man"

CHRIST IS REVEALED:

As *Jehovah* – Isaiah 40:3; 42:8; 43:10–11; 44:6; 44:24

As *Shepherd* – Isaiah 40:11 (John 10:11)

As *Creator* – Isaiah 40:28 (John 1:1–3; Col. 1:16)

As *Redeemer* – Isaiah 41:14 (Gal. 3:13; 1 Pet. 1:18–19; Rev. 5:9)

As *He to whom every knee shall bow and every tongue swear (confess)* – Isaiah 45:23 (Phil. 2:10)

52 WEEKS OF **PURSUIT**

WEEK 32, DAY 2: **TODAY'S READING: ISAIAH 46–52**

OVERVIEW:

Israel's preservation and restoration from Babylon (46:1–47:15); admonition to the restored nation (48:1–22); the mission of the Servant (Messiah) (49:1–26); the submission of the Servant (50:1–11); the provision of the Servant (51:1–52:12).

HIGHLIGHTS & INSIGHTS:

In chapter 45:1, the Lord promised to raise up Cyrus, the Persian King, to conquer the Babylonians and set the captives of Israel free, enabling them to return to their land. Of course, Cyrus prefigures the Lord's "anointed," the Lord Jesus Christ, who will one day (soon!) establish His millennial kingdom and restore Israel to her homeland. On "that day," all of the Gentile nations of the world will submit to the rule of Israel's King, and "every knee shall bow, every tongue shall swear" (45:23; Phil. 2:10–11).

In chapters 46 and 47, Isaiah details the collapse of Babylon and her gods. God declares that those gods are powerless to rescue Babylon from His impending judgment and destruction. Just as God raised up Cyrus from the east to conquer Israel's oppressor (46:11), the Lord Jesus Christ will also rise from the east as the "Sun of righteousness" to deliver the Nation of Israel on the Day of the Lord (Mal. 4:1–2).

In chapter 48, like many in Laodicea (Rev. 3:14–22), the Lord indicts those who confess His name "but not in truth," whose lives don't reflect his "righteousness" (48:1). The Lord would discipline Israel for her stubbornness ("thy neck is an iron sinew, and thy brow brass" v. 4) by allowing Babylon to take them captive. But He also promises to bring them back. Praise the Lord for His marvelous grace and mercy; in our stubbornness, we need both as surely as Israel did and does!

Throughout the next few chapters, the Lord introduces his Servant, the Messiah. In chapter 49, the Lord reveals His Servant and how He will restore Israel physically and spiritually in the Promised Land. Though "Zion said, The Lord hast forsaken me, and my Lord hath forgotten me" (49:14), the Lord promises that He will not forsake or forget them! Even though they rejected Him (John 1:11), the Servant will fulfill His purposes and promises to them, blessing Israel and the Gentile nations of the world in the millennium (49:22, 25–26). Chapter 50 contrasts Israel's disobedience with the Servant's obedience.

In chapters 51–52, the Nation of Israel is exhorted to look through the eyes of the faith into the future (51:1–2) when the Lord, the Comforter of Zion (51:3), will rescue Israel. He will bring them into their land and the blessing of Messiah's rule in the millennial kingdom where they will no longer be afflicted by the Gentile nations (52:1). In light of His promise of deliverance, Israel is exhorted to "Break forth into joy, sing together, ye waste places of Jerusalem: for the LORD hath comforted his people, he hath redeemed Jerusalem. The LORD hath made bare his holy arm in the eyes of all the nations; and all the ends of the earth shall see the salvation of our God" (52:9–10).

May we be filled with a passion for the suffering Servant ("his visage was so marred more than any man, and his form more than the sons of men," 52:14) to "be exalted and extolled, and be very high" (52:13), when "the kings [of the nations] shall shut their mouths at him" (52:15). And, once again, may we all cry out with the Apostle John, "Even so, come, Lord Jesus" (Rev. 22:20).

SPECIFIC REFERENCES TO THE DAY OF THE LORD:

46:13 – "I will place salvation in Zion for Israel my glory"

51:3 – "the Lord shall comfort Zion"

51:11 – "the redeemed of the Lord shall return, and come with singing unto Zion"

52:6 – "in that day"

52:8 – "when the Lord shall bring again Zion"

52:10 – "The Lord hath made bare his holy arm in the eyes of all the nations"

52:10 – "all the ends of the earth shall see the salvation of our God"

CHRIST IS REVEALED:

As the *First and the Last* – Isaiah 48:12 (Rev. 1:11; 2:8; 22:13)

As the *Savior and Redeemer* – Isaiah 49:26 (Titus 2:13–14; 2 Pet. 1:1; 1 Cor. 6:20; Gal. 4:4–5; 1 Pet. 1:18–19)

52 WEEKS OF **PURSUIT**

WEEK 32, DAY 3: **TODAY'S READING: ISAIAH 53-59**

OVERVIEW:

The humiliation of the Servant (Messiah) (53:1–12); the blessings of the Servant (54:1–55:13); the blessing of God upon the Gentiles (56:1–8); the condemnation of God upon the wicked (56:9–57:21); the restoration of true worship (58:1–14); the transgression of Israel (59:1–8); the confession of Israel (59:9–15a); the Lord's deliverance of Israel (59:15b–21).

HIGHLIGHTS & INSIGHTS:

Isaiah 53 is one of the most incredible chapters in the entire Bible. On a desert road in Acts 8, the Ethiopian eunuch was struggling to understand this very chapter. The Lord prompted Philip to ask him if he understood what he was reading. When the eunuch responded, "How can I, except some man should guide me?" (v. 31), the Scripture says, "Then Philip opened his mouth, and began at the same scripture, and preached unto Him Jesus" (v. 35). Philip used this passage to lead the Ethiopian dignitary to Christ, and it is commonly believed that through his conversion the gospel first made its way into the continent of Africa in the first century. Isaiah 53 is the most comprehensive, yet concise passage in the Bible concerning the life and death of the Lord Jesus Christ. Because of its significance, we will devote most of our attention to this chapter of today's reading.

In verses 1–3, Isaiah prophesies the rejection that our Lord would endure. John 1:11 says, "He came unto his own, and his own received him not." But why did Israel reject Him? By the time the Lord Jesus Christ was born, the Jews were being oppressed by Rome. Obviously, they hated it! Therefore, the Messiah they were looking for was a political revolutionary, a warrior who would overthrow Rome. They expected Him to establish His own kingdom on the earth, one in which the Jews would be preeminent.

Instead, Isaiah declared that, the Jews would not believe that the "arm of the Lord" (the Lord Jesus Christ) was revealed because of how He made His entrance into this world. He came as a humble bush ("tender plant"), not as a stalwart tree. He didn't come on the scene displaying the physical power and majesty that would attract them to Him ("he hath no form nor comeliness; and when we shall see him, there is no beauty that we should desire him," v. 2). He came offering life to the parched soil of their lives, but it wasn't the life they were looking for.

"Dry ground" (vs. 2) is a reference to how spiritually barren Israel would be when He was revealed. They failed to grasp that the physical oppression by Rome was just a picture of their spiritual oppression as they were held in the snare of this world by the will of Satan himself (2 Tim. 2:26; Eph. 2:2). They failed to realize that, for their Messiah and King to have citizens in His kingdom, He had to deal with the sin issue that resulted in their spiritual death (Gen. 2:17; Rom 5:12) and that, to qualify for citizenship in His kingdom, they needed to experience a supernatural spiritual birth by calling upon the name of the Lord. They failed to realize that their Messiah would take up a *cross* before He would take up His *crown*, that there would be *humiliation* before His *exaltation*, that there would be *suffering* before there would be *glory*.

As a result, the Jews "despised and rejected" God's glorious Servant, their promised Messiah. The King of kings became "a man of sorrows." The One to whom belongs all glory was "acquainted with grief." They hid their "faces from him," the One who offered life and forgiveness to all who would look to Him. The One who should have been lauded and honored was "despised" and not "esteemed" (Is. 53:3). He came to bear the "griefs" and "sorrows" man had inflicted upon himself through the choice of sin, but He was treated as a common criminal, as if He was worthy of the treatment He received (v. 4).

Isaiah 53:5 describes Christ's crucifixion: He was "wounded" and "bruised." He experienced "chastisement" and "stripes" (referring to His back being scourged with whips). Isaiah also tells us the reason for such brutality. It was "for our transgressions" and "for our iniquities." He then reveals the result of His crucifixion: "our peace," with God and, thus, with ourselves. It was so we could be "healed"! Obviously, Isaiah is not referring to our physical healing, but the healing our soul and spirit needed because every one of us had "gone astray," turning from God "to [our] own way" (v. 6) God reveals through Isaiah that He was providing His only begotten Son to die a substitutionary death for our sin: "the Lord hast laid on him the iniquity of us all" (v. 6).

In verses 7–9, Isaiah's prophecy reveals that through the entire unfair trial and merciless crucifixion, our Lord Jesus Christ "opened not his mouth." And when Christ died, it would be with "the wicked" (He was crucified between two thieves), but also with "the rich" (Matt. 27:57 says was laid in the tomb of a rich man named Joseph of Arimithea).

And though the details of Isaiah's prophecy are humanly tragic and horrific, verses 10–12 let us know that every single detail of this entire ordeal was purposed and planned by God Himself! It is the same incomprehensible truth Peter preached on the Day of Pentecost: that Christ was "delivered [to His tormentors] by the determinate counsel and foreknowledge of God" (Acts 2:23).

While we can use the Overview to keep our bearings in today's reading, we can all stand to "lose our bearings" in the wonder of our glorious Savior and His willingness to offer Himself as ou sacrifice as described in Isaiah 53. Let us also pray that, like Philip, God will allow us to use this chapter to preach Jesus to some needy soul today.

CHRIST IS REVEALED:

As the *One who was rejected by His own* – Isaiah 53:3 (John 1:11; Luke 23:18)

As the *One who remained silent though falsely accused* – Isaiah 53:7 (Mark 15:3–5)

As the *One who was buried with the rich* – Isaiah 53:9 (Matt. 27:57–60)

As the *One who was crucified with sinners* – Isaiah 53:12 (Mark 15:27–28)

WEEK 32, DAY 4: **TODAY'S READING: ISAIAH 60-66**

OVERVIEW:

The exaltation of Jerusalem in the Day of the Lord (60:1–22); the mission of the Messiah in His first coming (61:1–2a); the mission of the Messiah in His second coming (61:2b–11); the restoration of Zion (62:1–63:6); the petition of Israel (63:7–64:12); God's response to Israel's prayer (65:1–25); the blessing of God in the millennial kingdom (66:1–24).

HIGHLIGHTS & INSIGHTS:

Throughout the book of Isaiah, and in today's chapters specifically, God points to that incredible day when the Lord Jesus Christ will establish His millennial kingdom. When the remnant of Israel returned after the Babylonian captivity, the city of Jerusalem—its walls, gates, and temple—was in shambles ("laid waste," 64:10–11). It was anything but glorious. But Isaiah looks ahead to a time when the Lord Jesus Christ will have made it all abundantly glorious. In fact, the word *glory* (or glorify, glorified, glorious) appears twenty-three times in these seven chapters alone!

In Isaiah 60:1–2, Isaiah prophesies: "Arise, shine; for the Lord is risen upon thee. For, behold, the darkness shall cover the earth, and gross darkness the people: but the Lord shall arise upon thee, and his glory shall be seen upon thee." In fact, we are living, right now, in that biblical *nighttime*.

Jesus said in John 9:5, "As long as I am in the world, I am the light of the world." So in Acts 1:9 when Jesus ascended back to the right hand of His Father, the "Sun" went down, so to speak, and it became *nighttime* as far as God is concerned (Rom. 13:12; 1 Thess. 5:5–7; Phil 2:15). We now await the moment when the "Sun of righteousness [will] arise" (Mal. 4:1–2) and the light will again shine on this planet because it will be the *Day* of the Lord!

And in that day, according to 60:3–9, the Gentile nations will come in peace to Jerusalem, offering gifts to "the Holy One of Israel," the Lord Jesus Christ. At that time, Isaiah describes how the walls of the nation will be rebuilt (v. 10), and the "gates shall be open continually; they shall not be shut day nor night" (v. 11), implying that there will no longer be the threat of an invading nation or nations (60:10–22).

The Lord Jesus Christ read Isaiah 61:1–2 in His home synagogue in Nazareth in Luke 4:16–21, concluding with "This day is this scripture fulfilled in your ears." Interestingly, Jesus very purposely stopped in the middle of Isaiah 61:2, before the phrase: "and the day of vengeance of our God." At that point in Christ's ministry, the fulfillment of that phrase still depended on the Nation of Israel's response to Him! When Israel refused His final offer of the kingdom at the stoning of Stephen, God inserted the parenthesis of the church age. Now "the day of vengeance of our God" (the Tribulation and Second Coming) will not begin until God's plan for the church has been accomplished, and we are living in what God calls "the acceptable year of the Lord" (61:2). We must, therefore, "walk in wisdom toward them that are without, redeeming the time" (Col. 4:5). Isaiah 61:2 concludes that, following the Tribulation and Second Coming ("the day of vengeance"), the Lord will "comfort all that mourn" (the millennium), turning Israel's suffering and affliction into blessing and rejoicing.

In Isaiah's day Israel was God's "forsaken" wife, left "desolate" because of her whoredoms (62:4). But when the Lord Jesus Christ establishes His kingdom, Israel will be called *Hephzibah* ("my delight is in her") and *Beulah* ("married"), as she will again be married to Jehovah and He will delight in her. (See Hosea 2:16–17.) Remember Israel is the bride of the Father; we (the church) are the bride of Christ (2 Cor. 11:2; Rev. 21:9).

Isaiah 63 gives the promise of coming vengeance. While we are presently living at a time when God is pouring out His love, mercy and grace, justice will be served on this planet! Often, Christians show only the side of the coin that is stamped with Christ's love. The other side of the coin, however, is stamped with His wrath (Rev. 15–16). And His wrath is just as far-reaching and powerful as His love. Perhaps our focus on the love of God, to the exclusion of His wrath, is why those who are not saved, and many who are, do not fear the Lord as Scripture repeatedly admonishes us to do (2 Cor. 7:1).

Isaiah 63 pictures Christ as a bloody warrior. At His first coming, His enemies stained Him with His own blood. In this passage, Isaiah sees Him at His second coming, once again stained with blood—not His own blood this time, but the blood of His enemies (63:1–4)! He who was the Prince of Peace in His first coming (Isa. 9:6) will be a Man of War at His second coming (Exod. 15:3; Rev. 14:17–20; Isa. 63:1–4).

Chapter 65 records the Lord's response to the prayer of His remnant, and chapter 66 describes the true worship of the Messiah in His millennial kingdom. As we conclude the book of Isaiah, we see that chapter 66 covers the same ground as the 66th book of the Bible, the book of Revelation, including the Tribulation, the Second Coming, the millennium, and the new heaven and new earth.

SPECIFIC REFERENCES TO THE DAY OF THE LORD:

60:1 – "the glory of the Lord is risen upon thee"

60:2 – "the Lord shall arise upon thee, and his glory shall be seen upon thee"

60:7 – "I will glorify the house of my glory"

60:13 – "I will make the place of my feet glorious"

60:20 – "the days of thy mourning shall be ended"

61:2 – "the day of vengeance of our God"

63:4 – "the day of vengeance"

63:4 – "the year of my redeemed"

66:15 – "the Lord will come with fire"

66:18 – "I will gather all nations and tongues; and they shall come, and see my glory"

CHRIST IS REVEALED:

As the *Anointed One preaching good tidings* – Isaiah 61:1 (Luke 4:16–22)

As the *Creator of new heavens and new earth* – Isaiah 65:17; 66:2 (John 1:1–3; 2 Pet. 3:13; Rev. 21:1)

As the *One whose glory will be witnessed by all the nations* – Isaiah 66:18–19 (Rev. 5:12–13)

52 WEEKS OF **PURSUIT**

WEEK 32, DAY 5: **TODAY'S READING: JEREMIAH 1-4**

OVERVIEW:
God's call of Jeremiah (1:1–19); God's explanation that Israel was an unfaithful spouse (2:1–3:5); God's explanation that there was still time for Israel to repent (3:6–4:4); God's warning of judgment for Israel's refusal to repent (4:5–31).

HIGHLIGHTS & INSIGHTS:
God used Jeremiah to prophesy in Judah during the Southern Kingdom's final forty years. Assyria had destroyed the Northern Kingdom (Israel) one hundred years earlier, but had eventually been overthrown by the Babylonians.

According to 1:2–3, Jeremiah's ministry spanned about 40 years (approx. 627–587 BC). He began to prophesy in the thirteenth year of Judah's last *righteous* king, Josiah (640–609 BC) and continued through the wicked reigns of Jehoahaz, Jehoiakim, Jehoiachin, and Judah's last *actual* king, Zedekiah (597–587 BC) and "the carrying away of Jerusalem captive" in 586 BC (2 Chron. 36; 2 Kings 23–25).

Jeremiah is sometimes referred to as the Weeping Prophet (See 9:1; 13:17; 14:17; 15:17–18; Lam. 1:2; 2:11, 18) His tears flowed out of his passion for God's glory (13:15–17) and Israel's backsliding from her God. *Backsliding* is the key word in the book (2:19; 3:6, 8, 11–12, 22; 5:6; 8:5; 14:7), and the prophet calls for the people to repent for this sin eleven times. Though repentance was Jeremiah's continual message, Judah refused, and no Old Testament prophet suffered more opposition than Jeremiah. (See 2:8, 27; 4:9; 5:31; 6:14; 14:13–16; 18:18; 23:9–40; 26:8–19; 27:9–16; chapters 28–29)

The book of Jeremiah is not arranged in chronological order, but by subject matter. This arrangement helps us to see more clearly the tragic results of sin. Perhaps the simplest breakdown of the book is as follows:

- Chapters 1–33: The Fate of Judah
- Chapters 34–45: The Fate of Jerusalem
- Chapters 46–52: The Fate of the Gentile Nations

Biblically, there is no doubt that life begins *before* our actual *birth* (Ps. 139:14–15) and continues on *after* our actual *death* (Heb. 9:27). In Jeremiah 1:5, God tells the prophet that, even before forming him in his mother's womb, He "knew" him. Before he was born, He "sanctified" and "ordained" Jeremiah to be "a prophet unto the nations." God had a purpose for Jeremiah before his birth, and the same is true for our lives!

Just as Moses did in Exodus 3, Jeremiah's initial response to God's call was to point out his own inadequacies and inabilities (Jer. 1:6). And in verses 7–10, just like Moses, God reminded Jeremiah that His call was not about who Jeremiah was; it was about who God is. He was sending Jeremiah. He would tell Jeremiah what to say: "I have put my words in thy mouth" (v.9). And when the people didn't like it, God promised that "I am with thee to deliver thee" and "I have this day set thee over the nations and over the kingdoms" (v. 8, 10).

In verse 10, Jeremiah's actual ministry was to be six-fold: 1) "To root out" 2) "To pull down" 3) "To destroy" 4) "To throw down" 5) "To build" 6) "To plant." God told Jeremiah that two-thirds of his preaching was to be negative! This is why we must understand what a prophet was actually called to do. In the Bible, a prophet was a man that God raised up to take His side against the people who had turned away from Him. Obviously, that's a bit simplistic, but that's it in a nutshell! And the people in Jeremiah's day were far from God's side, so it was no wonder Jeremiah had it so tough.

Interestingly, the ministry of the New Testament preacher is surprisingly similar to that of an Old Testament prophet. In 2 Timothy 4:2, Paul said that a preacher of the Word must "reprove," "rebuke," and "exhort with all longsuffering and doctrine." That's also two-thirds negative! And just like

52 WEEKS OF PURSUIT

Jeremiah, it's no wonder those who preach the Word have it so tough in our day! In the Laodicean Church Period (1901–rapture), God's side is a far cry from His people's side (Rev. 3:14–22).

In 1:17–19, God warned Jeremiah that his task would be very intimidating ("be not dismayed at their faces," v. 17) and that it would be a constant battle ("they shall fight against thee," v. 19). Despite the difficulty, however, God commanded Jeremiah to "Man up!" ("gird up thy loins," v. 17) and promised His abiding presence and power ("I am with thee, saith the Lord, to deliver thee," v. 19). With a promise like that, surely we all could endure immense difficulty and adversity! And the reality is, we have the same promise. Jesus said in Matthew 28:18–20: "All power is given unto me in heaven and in earth. Go ye therefore [He is going to empower us with His power!] … and, lo, I am with you always, even unto the end of the world!"

In 2:1–3:5, God has some strong words for Jeremiah about His people. He likens them to an adulterous spouse, in contrast to God's constant faithfulness and goodness to them. In 2:1–3, He tells Jeremiah that Israel had forgotten her youthful devotion to Him (when God had first delivered them out of Egypt— her "first love," Rev. 2:4). He continues with a litany of complaints: she had become ungrateful (2:4–8); she had changed her God (2:9–13); she had ignored God's discipline (2:14–19); she had denied any wrongdoing (2:20–28); she had mistreated the poor (2:29–37); and, spiritually speaking, she had been sleeping around (3:1–5). In spite of Judah's sin, however, God tells Jeremiah that He is merciful and that He is willing to forgive her if she will simply return to Him, having put away her other lovers (3:6–4:4). What an incredibly merciful and gracious God we serve!

In 4:5–31, God tells Jeremiah that though Israel has time to repent, it's only a small window of opportunity. He warns that if they refuse to return to Him, He will send an army to annihilate their nation.

SPECIFIC REFERENCES TO THE DAY OF THE LORD:

3:16 – "in those days" (specifically, the Tribulation Period)

3:17 – "At that time they shall call Jerusalem the throne of the Lord"

3:18 – "in those days" (specifically, the Tribulation Period)

4:9 – "at that day"

CHRIST IS REVEALED:

As the *Fountain of Living Waters* – Jeremiah 2:13 (John 7:37; John 4:1–26)

52 WEEKS OF **PURSUIT**

WEEK 33, DAY 1: **TODAY'S READING: JEREMIAH 5-8**

OVERVIEW:

God's instruction for Jeremiah to search for the righteous (5:1–9); God's promise to judge the wicked (5:10–6:30); Jeremiah's first message to the people concerning their faith in the temple and external religion (7:1–8:3); Jeremiah's message concerning rejecting the truth of God's Word (8:4–22).

HIGHLIGHTS & INSIGHTS:

Before God actually begins to *empower* Jeremiah to preach against the sin of the people in chapter 7, He takes the events recorded in the first six chapters to *impassion* him. As chapter 5 begins, God doesn't send Jeremiah on a search-and-destroy mission. It's a search-so-I-won't-destroy mission! God wants Jeremiah to understand the depths to which His people had apostatized and why His judgment against them was so deserved. Just as God told Ezekiel in his day to search for one single man to "make up the hedge, and stand in the gap" (Ezek. 22:30), God tells Jeremiah to see if he, too, could just find one man somewhere in the land who simply sought truth and executed judgment (5:1). But just as Ezekiel's search ended with the pitiful words, "But I found none," Jeremiah's search produced the same empty result. The people were so incredibly perverted in their thinking, they even viewed God's mercy as weakness (vs. 11–13). Through the fiery preaching of Jeremiah (5:14), God promises the invasion of a mighty army to destroy them.

Jeremiah 5:31 should not only introduce you to the horrific spiritual climate of Jeremiah's day, but also remind you of the horrific spiritual climate of our own day: "The prophets prophesy falsely, and the priest bear rule by their means; and my people love to have it so." God said something strangely similar to Timothy through the Apostle Paul concerning our day: "After their own lusts shall they heap to themselves teachers, having itching ears; And they shall turn away their ears from the truth, and shall be turned unto fables" (2 Tim. 4:3–4).

In chapter 6, God reveals why Judah had become so debauched that "from the least of them even to the greatest of them every one is given to covetousness; and from the prophet even unto the priest every one dealeth falsely" (6:13). The key is in verse 10: the Word of God held no delight or significance in the people's hearts. The reason our world has gotten to the place it has is the same for us. Even in our churches, week after week, from the pulpit and in the lives of the people, truth sits forsaken. And that is the whole goal of our *52 Weeks of Pursuit*. We read, not simply to go through the Word of God, but to so delight ourselves in the God of the Word that His Word finds a resting place everywhere as it reproves, rebukes, and exhorts us (2 Tim. 4:2).

Having revealed these truths in chapters 1–6, in chapter 7, God turns Jeremiah loose to fulfill the six-fold ministry He had given him (1:10). God strategically places Jeremiah at the entrance to the temple (7:1), confronting those who believed they were doing fine spiritually because of their great temple and their involvement there (7:4). We must never confuse *blessings* and *busyness at church* with spirituality! God's words here challenge us, as well as Israel: "For if ye thoroughly amend your ways and your doings; if ye thoroughly execute judgment between a man and his neighbour; If ye oppress not the stranger, the fatherless, and the widow, and shed not innocent blood in this place, neither walk after other gods to your hurt: Then will I cause you to dwell in this place, in the land that I gave to your fathers, for ever and ever" (7:5–7). Our personal and holy God is not impressed with, or even interested in, external religion (2 Cor. 7:1).

In chapter 8, Jeremiah preaches a similar message as he does in chapter 7. In this case, however, their sense of spiritual superiority came not from the temple (7:4), but because they possessed the Law of Moses (8:8). Again, God reminds them, and us, that He wants more than for us to simply attend church services and read our Bible. Obviously those things have their place, but God wants to hold His rightful place as Lord in our lives!

Of the many applications of Jeremiah's words to those of us living in the last days (2 Tim. 3:1–6), the centrality of God's Word is one of the most valuable. Judah's spiritual leaders did not properly proclaim the truth of God's Word (Jer. 8:8–12). Their prophets turned the truth of God into lies (2 Tim. 4:4), telling the people that God was okay with the way they were living. Today, we still need "Jeremiahs" who will unashamedly, lovingly, and dogmatically proclaim the truth of God's Word regardless of the consequences.

CHRIST IS REVEALED:

As the *One who demanded a cleansed temple* – Jeremiah 7:1–11 (Mark 11:17)

52 WEEKS OF PURSUIT

WEEK 33, DAY 2: **TODAY'S READING: JEREMIAH 9-12**

OVERVIEW:
Jeremiah's life amid a deceitful people (9:1–9); Jeremiah's grief over Judah (9:10–26); Judah's idolatry and exile (10:1–25); Israel's history of covenant breaking (11:1–17); Jeremiah's enemies plot against him (11:18–23); Jeremiah's complaint concerning the wicked (12:1–4); God's challenge to Jeremiah (12:5–13); God's promise to restore Israel (12:14–17).

HIGHLIGHTS & INSIGHTS:
Jeremiah was definitely the right man for the job! God's people needed a prophet who would clearly communicate God's *message* and His *heart*! Jeremiah gave them both. In chapter 8, God revealed his heart through Jeremiah, who cried out, unable to find comfort for the sorrow and pain in his heart over Judah's refusal of her King and Healer (8:18–22). Today, in chapter 9, we hear Jeremiah's cry: "Oh that my head were waters, and mine eyes a fountain of tears, that I might weep day and night for the slain of the daughter of my people" (v. 1). What Jeremiah provided the people of Judah—God's message and God's heart—is exactly what Laodicea needs of its pastors. Sadly, it is, most generally, one extreme or the other. Either a pastor is all heart and no truth or all truth and no heart. Pray earnestly that God will allow your pastor to have both, that he will declare the message just as God gave it— with God's heart! Pray that, although he must reprove and rebuke in these Laodicean days, he will also preach with a heart that loves and breaks for the people ("exhort with all longsuffering," 2 Tim. 4:2).

The more Jeremiah began to understand just how devastating God's judgment would be (9:9–26), the more earnestly he preached and the more he longed for God's people to repent. He cries out, "Thus saith the LORD, Let not the wise man glory in his wisdom, neither let the mighty man glory in his might, let not the rich man glory in his riches: But let him that glorieth glory in this, that he understandeth and knoweth me, that I am the LORD which exercise lovingkindness, judgment, and righteousness, in the earth: for in these things I delight, saith the LORD" (Jer. 9:23–24). In context, these verses reveal that God's judgment could have been stayed if the people, rather than glory in everything but God, had simply sought to understand and know Him! And we, too, must stand in awe of the glorious wonder of our God! That's why Paul said, "But God forbid that I should glory, save in the cross of our Lord Jesus Christ" (Gal. 6:14). It is only through the cross of our Lord Jesus Christ that we can understand anything about God or know Him at all (1 Cor. 2:14). It was through the cross that our Lord exercised "lovingkindness, judgment, and righteousness, in the earth" (Jer. 9:24).

As Jeremiah preaches his heart out in chapter 10, he declares the greatness of the one "true God" (v. 10) saying, "There is none like unto thee, O Lord; thou art great, and thy name is great in might" (v. 6). He confronts Israel with the fact that God is not just their national deity, but the Creator, the only "living God," the "everlasting King," and the One who will unleash His judgment upon the whole world (vs. 10–12). And when God's people bow to the gods of other nations, the Lord will turn them over to be consumed by those nations (v. 25).

In chapters 11 and 12, even though God warned Jeremiah of the opposition and adversity that would inevitably come his way (1:17–19; 9:1–3), Jeremiah apparently thought it might happen otherwise. In 11:18–2, the Lord reveals to Jeremiah that the men of his hometown were plotting to take his life and then tells Jeremiah to prepare for even worse times (12:5–13). And we are the same. Though God clearly said, "In the world ye shall have tribulation" (John 16:33), and "Yea, all that will live godly in Christ Jesus shall suffer persecution" (2 Tim. 3:12), we're caught off guard when it happens to us. Despite God's warning, "Beloved, think it not strange concerning the fiery trial which is to try you, as though some strange thing happened unto you" (1 Pet. 4:12), we are amazed when trials unfold in our lives!

Despite all of God's warnings, however, one of the beautiful things that surfaces throughout Jeremiah is that God's ultimate purpose behind exercising His judgment is to restore and renew. Chapter 12 ends with the compassion of the Lord and His willingness to not only deliver Israel, but all nations (vs. 14–17).

SPECIFIC REFERENCES TO THE DAY OF THE LORD:

10:10 – "at his wrath the earth shall tremble, and the nations shall not be able to abide his indignation"

11:11 – "I will bring evil upon them, which they shall not be able to escape"

11:12 – "the time of their trouble"

12:12 – "the sword of the Lord shall devour from the one end of the land even to the other end of the land"

CHRIST IS REVEALED:

In the *One whose judgment is inescapable* – Jeremiah 11:11 (2 Thess. 1:7–9)

As the *One who will devour with His sword* – Jeremiah 12:12 (Rev. 19:19–21)

52 WEEKS OF PURSUIT

WEEK 33, DAY 3: **TODAY'S READING: JEREMIAH 13-17**

OVERVIEW:
The object lesson of the ruin of Judah (13:1–11); Israel described as a drunken nation (13:12–14); Jeremiah pleading to the nation (13:15–27); Judah's drought and Jeremiah's intercession (14:1–22); God's refusal to answer Jeremiah's prayers (15:1–9); Jeremiah's complaint against God (15:10–18); God's call for Jeremiah's repentance (15:19–21); Jeremiah's personal renewal (16:1–17:18); God's message through Jeremiah concerning the Sabbath (17:19–27).

HIGHLIGHTS & INSIGHTS:
Chapter 13 begins with an object lesson. God instructs Jeremiah to get a "linen girdle" (a belt or waistband) and put it around his "loins" or his waist. He then told Jeremiah to remove it and hide it in a hole in a rock near the Euphrates. After many days, God told him to go back to retrieve it, and he found that the belt was totally ruined. God explained that, like the belt, Judah would become "good for nothing" because of her pride, her refusal to hear the Word of God, her wicked imagination, and her idolatry (vs. 9–10). God wanted Judah "for a people, and for a name, and for a praise, and for a glory," but "they would not hear" (v. 11). As God's people in a different dispensation, He also wants us "for a people, and for a name, and for a praise, and for a glory." Are we hearing Him?

Even after God revealed all of this to Jeremiah concerning Judah's inevitable fate, Jeremiah still pleaded, wept, and yearned for Judah to repent and give glory to God once again. Would to God that we had Jeremiah's passion for the glory of God and the souls of men!

God's first punishment is described in 14:1—a terrible "dearth" or drought. Jeremiah asked God to be merciful and remove the drought, but God said they were getting what they deserved (v. 10). He even told Jeremiah to stop praying for them (v. 11)! Still, Jeremiah continued to pray on their behalf. In 15:1, God tells Jeremiah that even if Moses or Samuel were praying on the people's behalf (and that's some pretty major props for those two fellas!), His judgment was going to be unleashed.

In 15:10–18, Jeremiah gets upset with God. He complains that all he had ever done was what God wanted him to do, but all it had ever gotten him was pain and heartache (vs. 15–18a). He even suggests that God is a liar (v. 18)! Jeremiah was actually beginning to sound much like the people to whom he was called to minister. In verses 19–21, God tells Jeremiah that he better sort out his head and his heart and get back to the task God had intended for him. Jeremiah was simply going to have to find a way to carry out his mission, even though he would never receive any encouragement from the people to whom he was seeking to minister. Imagine, in Jeremiah's entire ministry, a 40 year span (627-587 BC), he never saw one convert! Bless his heart!

Chapter 16:1–8 is another object lesson. God makes His point by giving Jeremiah three strange commands. First, he instructs him not to marry (vs. 1–4) because his wife and children would only be mercilessly killed by the armies God would use to punish Israel's sin. Second, God tells Jeremiah not to mourn for the dead (vs. 5–7) because, in light of what was about to happen in Judah, they would be better off than the living. And third, he was not to participate in any feasts because all they produced was wishful thinking in a land without hope (16:8). God tells Jeremiah that these three things would provide him the opportunity to warn the people of the impending judgment to come and the need to repent. At the end of the chapter (16:14–18), God points to a time following His judgment upon them, when He would deliver Israel out of her oppression and bondage, just like He did in delivering them out of Egypt.

In 17:1, God reaffirms to Jeremiah that Israel's idolatry was etched in their hearts with "a pen of iron, and with the point of a diamond." Because of their unfaithfulness to Him, God warns Jeremiah against trusting them for anything and urges him to trust in Him alone. Verse 9 is a classic: "The heart is deceitful above all things, and desperately wicked: who can know it?" May we all meditate on that for about the next 20 years!

In 17:12–18, Jeremiah offers an incredibly humble and powerful prayer for renewal, asking God for spiritual healing, deliverance from his oppressors, and for courage. Immediately, God charges Jeremiah to stand at the gates, where all who came into or out of Jerusalem could hear, and confront them about their observance of the Sabbath—or lack thereof! He tells them that if they don't stop carrying things in and out of the city on the Sabbath, God would allow an invading army to see to it that all activity in the city ceased!

CHRIST IS REVEALED:

As the *Hope of Israel* – Jeremiah 14:8 (Titus 2:13)

WEEK 33, DAY 4: **TODAY'S READING: JEREMIAH 18-22**

OVERVIEW:
God's lesson to Jeremiah at the potter's house (18:1–10); Jeremiah's message to Judah based on the lessons from the potter (18:11–17); Israel's opposition to Jeremiah (18:18–23); Jeremiah fights his calling (19:1–20:18); Jeremiah's message of opposition to kings (21:1–22:30).

HIGHLIGHTS & INSIGHTS:
God is most certainly the Master Illustrator. He uses His physical creation to teach us spiritual truth, just as Romans 1:20 says He does. Chapter 18 is another brilliant example of God employing this technique in the ministry of Jeremiah (13:1–7; 16:1–9). This time, God takes Jeremiah on a little field trip to the potter's house to show Jeremiah that He (God) is as the Potter and Israel is as the clay. And like a potter, He can do with Israel whatever He jolly-well wants! Even more to the point, if Israel would repent, He would fashion them into a beautiful and usable vessel, but if they chose to remain rebellious and obstinate, He could mar them in an instant, right in His powerful hands. And as the Potter, it would be perfectly within His right to do so!

Based on this object lesson in 18:1–10, God tells Jeremiah to get out there and call the nation to repentance (v. 11). Obviously, recognizing God's sovereignty ("as seemed good to the potter to make it," 18:4) and God's omnipotence ("as the clay is in the potter's hand, so are ye in mine hand," 18:6) puts a whole different "oomph!" behind a preacher's message! But in 18:18, the "oomph!" of the message wasn't well received. As consistently happened throughout Jeremiah's ministry, it only brought more hatred and opposition from the people. At the end of chapter 18, Jeremiah is fed up with the people and calls upon God to give them what they deserved.

In chapter 19, God uses a similar object lesson to make His point to the people. He tells Jeremiah to take "a potter's earthen bottle" (v. 1) and go preach to Judah's king and the inhabitants of Jerusalem. He was to preach a strong message about God's judgment that would come upon them because of their idolatry and rebellion. In effect, Jeremiah said, "You're kind of like this jar," smashed it right in front of them, and continued, "And God is going to smash you into a million tiny pieces just like that, and you won't be able to glue yourself back together!" (19:10–12).

Needless to say, the message didn't go over well with the supposed religious leaders or the people in general! In chapter 20, Pashur, "chief governor in the house of the Lord," smacks Jeremiah in the face and slams him into stocks in the city jail (v. 1). Jeremiah tells him, "Just for that, God has changed your name from Pashur (meaning "freedom") to Magormissabib" (meaning "terror on every side"), and Jeremiah prophesied the "terror" that would soon come upon Pashur and all those who believed his lies (20:4–6).

But once again, the opposition of the people was wearing on Jeremiah. In the second half of chapter 20, he registers his complaint against God for calling him to such a long, difficult, and painful ministry. He felt like God had deceived him and tells God, "You're stronger than me so You can take it, but I just can't do it anymore" (20:7–8). He even vows never to preach again or even mention the name of the Lord to anybody (20:9). But Jeremiah found that God's Word was so deeply embedded in him that it burned like a fire in his bones and the only way to find relief was to preach. May God's Word would be that deeply embedded in us!

So, Jeremiah preached on. He had come to grips with the fact that it was the right thing to do, even though being right didn't make it easy. In fact, biblically, it might be better to say, if it's right—it won't be easy! Paul, most certainly, could vouch for that (2 Cor. 11:24–28).

In chapters 21 and 22, it becomes apparent that Jeremiah had nailed some things in his relationship with God and the ministry to which he had been called. He has matured as a believer and a prophet. And just as God told Jeremiah that he would preach to and receive opposition from kings, princes, priests, and the people of the land (1:17–19), in this next section, Jeremiah preaches to each of these groups of people, receiving the retaliation God had prophesied from each (chapters 21–29). Each time, however, the more seasoned and mature Jeremiah is able to hand the opposition over to God, rather than blame Him for it.

CHRIST IS REVEALED:

As the *One who pronounces judgment upon those who refuse to obey His word* – Jeremiah 19:15 (John 5:22)

WEEK 33, DAY 5: **TODAY'S READING: JEREMIAH 23–26**

OVERVIEW:

Jeremiah preaches about the righteous King who would rise to the throne (23:1–8); Jeremiah preaches against the false prophets (23:9–40); Jeremiah preaches against the people (24:1–25:38); Jeremiah preaches against false worship and false prophecy (26:1–29:32).

HIGHLIGHTS & INSIGHTS:

In chapters 21–29, Jeremiah preaches to the exact groups God declared in 1:17–19: "kings, princes, priests, and the people of the land." From 21:1–23:8, Jeremiah preaches against the kings. Though God pronounced woe upon these wretched shepherds ("pastors") who were leading Judah to destruction, God also points to a different day when a righteous King from David's line would rise to the throne: "Behold, the days come, saith the Lord that I will raise unto David a righteous Branch, and a King shall reign and prosper, and shall execute judgment and justice in the earth. In his days Judah shall be saved, and Israel shall dwell safely: and this is his name whereby he shall be called, THE LORD OUR RIGHTEOUSNESS" (23:5–6). Of course, that righteous Lord and King from David's Branch (his line or ancestry) is the King of kings Himself, the Lord Jesus Christ! Little did Jeremiah or those who heard him preach realize that he was describing what will happen two thousand years after our Lord's first coming (1 Pet. 1:10–12).

In 23:9–40, Jeremiah turns from preaching against the kings to preaching against the prophets. So much of what Jeremiah preached against the prophets of his day, he could come and preach against many of the preachers in our day! Jeremiah says: "Thus saith the Lord of hosts, Hearken not unto the words of the prophets that prophesy unto you: they make you vain: they speak a vision of their own heart, and not out of the mouth of the Lord. They say still unto them that despise me, The Lord hath said, Ye shall have peace; and they say unto every one that walketh after the imagination of his own heart, No evil shall come upon you" (23:16–17). Likewise, in Laodicea, the words that are spoken in the name of the Lord, or in the name of preaching, leave people void of God's truth (2 Tim. 4:4).

The message from the prophets in Jeremiah's day, like many of the preachers in our day, was void of the message of God's impending judgment. The people were told they were going to be all right ("No evil shall come upon you"), even though they willfully and blatantly lived for self, self-satisfaction, and self-gratification ("after the imagination of his own heart," 23:17). But preachers must preach a message "out of the mouth of the Lord" (the Word of God), not out "of their own heart" (23:16). God already gave His commentary on men's hearts: they are so deceitful and desperately wicked it is impossible to even know what's actually going on in them (17:9)! Preachers, spare us the message you feel the Lord has laid on your heart and give us the Lord's heart as revealed in His Word!

In 23:22, God says that if those prophets would have "stood in his counsel," so that the people would have actually heard the Words of the Lord, the people would have turned from "their evil way, and from the evil of their doings." In this verse, God reveals that evil is not just about our actions ("the evil of their doings"). Evil is also a way (a way of life or the "course of this world," Eph. 2:2). And may every preacher in Laodicea read Jeremiah 23:31 just before they walk out to preach: "Behold, I am against the prophets, saith the Lord, that use their tongues, and say, He saith." Woah! Or, maybe better stated, Woe!

In chapters 24 and 25, Jeremiah turns his preaching against the people. And even though the people had horrific spiritual leadership, God still held them responsible for their actions. We must recognize that, at the Judgment Seat of Christ, God will not receive the argument, "But my pastor didn't preach the Word!" That may be true, but God has not only given us His Word, He has even placed the resident Truth Teacher (the Holy Spirit) inside each one of us (1 John 2:27). We will all be held personally responsible for our stewardship of God's Word and God's Spirit.

And just like in Laodicea, one of the reasons Judah had such terrible spiritual leadership is that the people didn't want godly counsel or leadership. The way Jeremiah was treated is more than proof of that. God says of our day that the people do "not endure sound doctrine, but after their own lusts shall they heap to themselves teachers, having itching ears; And they shall turn away their ears from the truth, and shall be turned unto fables" (2 Tim. 4:3-4).

In chapter 26, Jeremiah begins to preach, finally, against the priests. In 26:2–8, we see that carrying out the Lord's perfect will comes with a very significant cost! The priests and the prophets actually call for Jeremiah's death (vs. 7–15). The Bible is very clear on this point: "Yea, and all that will live godly in Christ Jesus shall suffer persecution" (2 Tim. 3:12). Yes, following God's will costs us—but the rewards are out of this world! Literally!

SPECIFIC REFERENCES TO THE DAY OF THE LORD:

25:29 – "For I will call for a sword upon all the inhabitants of the earth"

25:30 – "The Lord shall roar from on high"

25:31 – "He will give them that are wicked to the sword"

25:33 – "At that day"

CHRIST IS REVEALED:

As the *King raised unto David a righteous Branch* – Jeremiah 23:5 (Matt. 2:1; Matt. 1:1; Luke 1:31–33)

As the *Lord our Righteousness* – Jeremiah 23:6 (1 Cor. 1:30; 2 Cor. 5:21)

WEEK 34, DAY 1: **TODAY'S READING: JEREMIAH 27-30**

OVERVIEW:
Jeremiah's cry to reject the false prophets and false prophecy concerning Babylon (27:1–22); Jeremiah's cry to reject the false prophets and false prophecy concerning the Babylonian captivity (28:1–17); Jeremiah's letter to those already taken into captivity urging them to reject the false prophets and to seek the Lord (29:1–32); Jeremiah's message about Israel's future restoration (30:1–24).

HIGHLIGHTS & INSIGHTS:
At the beginning of King Zedekiah's reign, the Lord prophesied that Babylon, under Nebuchadnezzar's leadership, would overthrow Judah and that Judah would serve the one He had used to discipline them (27:8). But the prophets of Judah, along with the diviners, dreamers, enchanters and sorcerers (27:9), told the people they wouldn't serve the king of Babylon. Jeremiah passionately warns Judah not to hearken to their lies (vs. 9, 14, 16); God would send them into captivity, but He would ultimately restore them (v. 22).

In both Jeremiah 27 and 2 Timothy 4:2–4 we see that what we call a negative sermon may actually be a powerful and positive word of God. Many preachers' so-called positive messages feel better on the ears than negative messages. But God's negative messages will always have more powerful ramifications in our lives than those supposed positive ones! Jesus said to those of us living in this Laodicean Period, "As many as I love, I rebuke and chasten" (Rev. 3:19). In other words, negativity from those who preach the Word of God is actually a very positive thing!

In that same year, Jeremiah was addressed in the temple by Hananiah (chapter 28). Hananiah must have been a big-name prophet in Judah. Claiming to speak for "the Lord of hosts, the God of Israel," he declared that God had broken Babylon's power over Judah, and that within two years, all of the vessels that had been taken out of the temple would be returned, along with all of the exiles (vs. 2–3). It was certainly a positive message. Unfortunately, it wasn't true! Through Jeremiah, God tells Hananiah that Babylon's yoke was a yoke of iron, not an easily broken yoke of wood, and that he was a liar (28:13–15). Jeremiah then prophesied Hananiah's death for his sin of misleading the people, and he died that same year, verifying which one of them was truly speaking for the Lord. Even so, the people refused to listen to the words of the Lord through Jeremiah.

Chapter 29 records the letter Jeremiah wrote to the Jewish people who had already been taken into captivity. He tells them not to listen to the false prophets who have been prophesying their quick release. The captivity was going to last seventy years, so they should make the best of it by building houses, planting gardens, and strengthening their families because most of them would die in that place. Our gracious God even promised that, if they would refuse to listen to the false prophets and seek Him, their lives in captivity in Babylon would be better than those who lived in the freedom of Judah! And once again, they refused to listen to Him.

In chapter 30, Jeremiah's message turns in a more positive direction. Though the message referred to a future time, (the Great Tribulation and Second Coming of Christ when God will restore the nation of Israel to her homeland and to her Messiah), the break from negativity had to be refreshing for Jeremiah. The events taking place in the Middle East today are setting the stage for what God prophesied through Jeremiah in this chapter. It is an exciting time to be alive if for no other reason than that! Lift up your head, my brothers and sisters; our redemption draweth nigh!

SPECIFIC REFERENCES TO THE DAY OF THE LORD:

30:7a – "That day is great, so that none is like it"

30:7b – "The time of Jacob's trouble" (Specifically, the Tribulation)

30:8 – "In that day"

30:24 – "In the latter days"

CHRIST IS REVEALED:

As the *Lord who will be raised up as David their King* – Jeremiah 30:9 (Matt. 2:2; 1:1; Luke 1:31–33)

52 WEEKS OF PURSUIT

WEEK 34, DAY 2: **TODAY'S READING: JEREMIAH 31-33**

OVERVIEW:

God's promise that Israel will be His people (31:1–14); God's promise of mercy to weary Israel (31:15–26); God's promise to make Israel secure (31:27–30); God's promise of a New Covenant with Israel (31:31–40); God's instruction to Jeremiah to buy a field (32:1–15); God's explanation to Jeremiah (32:16–35); God's promise to bring the exiles home (32:36–44); God's promise to keep His promises (33:1–26).

HIGHLIGHTS & INSIGHTS:

Jeremiah continues his positive message for Israel in chapter 31, though, as we discussed yesterday, the ultimate fulfillment of his prophecy won't be until the Second Coming of Christ. God says through Jeremiah, "And it shall come to pass, that like as I have watched over them, to pluck up, and to break down, and to throw down, and to destroy, and to afflict; so will I watch over them, to build, and to plant, saith the Lord" (v.28). In other words, just as God was careful to *punish* Israel, He will be just as careful to *bless* them.

Jeremiah 31:31 is very significant because God speaks of a new covenant that He would make with Israel and Judah. Throughout the Old Testament, we have seen God make at least three major covenants.

The first was the Abrahamic Covenant in Genesis 17:7-8: "And I will establish my covenant between me and thee and thy seed after thee in their generations for an everlasting covenant, to be a God unto thee, and to thy seed after thee. And I will give unto thee, and to thy seed after thee, the land wherein thou art a stranger, all the land of Canaan, for an everlasting possession; and I will be their God." When combined with Genesis 12:2–3, the Lord promised Abraham heirs, a great name, a homeland, fame, protection, and the blessing of all nations through him.

God made the second major covenant with Israel at Mount Sinai (Exod. 20; Lev. 27). We refer to it as the Mosaic Covenant because this covenant was mediated by Moses. Unlike the Abrahamic Covenant, this was not an unconditional and everlasting covenant.

The third major covenant, the Davidic Covenant, was God's promise to David of an everlasting kingdom. Through Nathan the prophet the Lord told David, "And when thy days be fulfilled, and thou shalt sleep with thy fathers, I will set up thy seed after thee, which shall proceed out of thy bowels, and I will establish his kingdom. He shall build an house for my name, and I will stablish the throne of his kingdom for ever" (2 Sam. 7:12–13). Jeremiah repeated in chapter 23:5 that the coming King of Israel, the Messiah, the one whose kingdom would be eternal, would come through the kingly line of David.

God's promise of a new covenant in Jeremiah 31:31–34 would not negate the everlasting covenants that He had made with Abraham and David. This covenant would participate with and work in conjunction with them. One of the tremendous beauties of this new covenant is that, while in the Mosaic Covenant God was constantly saying, "Thou shalt," this covenant is filled with God saying, "I will." What a blessed contrast! (To see for yourself, count God's "I will" statements in 31:31–40 and 32:36–44!) And please recognize that, although this is an everlasting covenant God made specifically with Israel and Judah, we have been permitted to participate in the blessing of this new covenant by God's sovereign plan and grace. Paul said in Romans 11:17 that we, "being a wild olive tree, wert grafted in among them, and with them partakest of the root and fatness of the olive tree."

After these glorious promises in chapters 30–31, God returns to Jeremiah's present situation and His impending judgment on Israel and Judah in chapter 32. Just before Babylon's final siege of Jerusalem, God tells Jeremiah to do something strange: he was to buy some land. Purchasing property just before your city is overtaken by a foreign enemy is not exactly a wise business deal, to say the least! But God was once again using an object lesson to make His point. This time, He was telling His people, through Jeremiah, that though judgment would come, He would restore the people to their homeland. He repeats the fact that there is nothing too hard for Him (32:17, 27). He would bring the people back to their land where they would enjoy the blessing of His new covenant. Again, these promises will be fulfilled during the Great Tribulation as Israel turns to her Messiah and will be enjoyed by the Nation of Israel as He returns at the end of the Tribulation to establish His millennial kingdom.

Chapter 33 is a joyous chapter that focuses on God's character. It reminds us that the truth of God's Word is grounded in the trustworthiness of His person. He will perform every single thing He has ever promised (33:14). It will be fulfilled just as He said, right when He said, just how He said. It is true for Israel and Judah and, praise the Lord, it's just as true for you and me!

SPECIFIC REFERENCES TO THE DAY OF THE LORD:

31:29 – "In those days" (The Tribulation)

31:31 – "Behold, the days come"

31:33 – "After those days"

31:38 – "Behold, the days come"

33:15 – "In those days, and at that time"

33:16 – "In those days"

CHRIST IS REVEALED:

As the *One who forgives sins* – Jeremiah 31:34 (Matt. 9:6; John 8:10–11)

By *Jeremiah, who acted as a kinsman-redeemer in purchasing the land of his cousin* – Jeremiah 32:6–14 (Lev. 25:25, 44; Ruth 2:20; 3:12–13; Gal. 4:4–5; Titus 2:13–14)

As *the Branch* – Jeremiah 33:15 (Zech. 3:8; 6:12; Jer. 23:5; Isa. 11:1)

52 WEEKS OF PURSUIT

WEEK 34, DAY 3: TODAY'S READING: JEREMIAH 34-38

OVERVIEW:
God's faithfulness to the Davidic Covenant (34:1–10); Israel's unfaithfulness to their fellow countrymen (34:11–22); Israel's unfaithfulness to their God (35:1–19); Israel's rejection of God's Word (36:1–32); Jeremiah preaches against a false sense of security and self-deception (37:1–10); Jeremiah is imprisoned (37:11–21); Jeremiah is delivered (38:1– 16); Jeremiah presents Zedekiah alternatives (38:17–28).

HIGHLIGHTS & INSIGHTS:
Today, we will read the second section of the book of Jeremiah and begin the third. The first section, the first thirty-three chapters, detailed the fate of Judah. Chapters 34 and 35 detail the fate of Jerusalem, and the third section, chapter 36 to the end of the book, details the fate of the Gentile nations. God declared this would be Jeremiah's focus when He first called him: "Before I formed thee in the belly ... I ordained thee a prophet unto the nations ... See, I have this day set thee over the nations and over the kingdoms, to root out, and to pull down, and to destroy, and to throw down, to build, and to plant" (1:5, 10).

As chapter 34 opens, Babylon is about to conquer Jerusalem. God sends Jeremiah to tell King Zedekiah that the city would fall to the Babylonians, but that he would not be killed in the invasion. That God was willing to spare this wicked king's life is not only a testimony of His incredible mercy and grace, but also a testimony of His faithfulness to keep His promises. In the Davidic Covenant, God promised that David's lineage would survive. Although the covenant was obscured as David's kingly line lived in exile, it was not revoked.

In 34:12–22, God reveals that Israel had not been faithful to one another by obeying His plan to release in the seventh year anyone who, for financial reasons, had sold themselves into slavery. In chapter 35, He compares the faithfulness of the Rechabite family to Israel's unfaithfulness to Him. As the family of Rechab stood as a shining light in the darkness of Jeremiah's day, may our families likewise bring glory to God against the lukewarmness and apostasy of our day (Rev. 3:16; 1 Tim. 4:1).

Chapter 36 is a profound and important story. In it, we see the divisive nature of the Word of God and its utter indestructibility! Because Jeremiah had been forbidden to enter the Temple (36:5), he dictated the words of the Lord to Baruch, the scribe. Baruch wrote a scroll and delivered it to the leaders of Israel, once again calling for Israel's repentance. The words were so powerful that the temple officials sent them to the king. But before Jehudi, who was reading the scroll to the king, got to the fourth page, the king grabbed it, cut it with his penknife, and threw it into the fire! It's a very interesting story and very easy to follow. But there is more here than meets the eye.

This story actually provides one of the clearest explanations in the Bible about the process of the inspiration and preservation of Scripture! Jeremiah 36:4 says, "Then Jeremiah called Baruch the son of Neriah: and Baruch wrote from the mouth of Jeremiah all the words of the Lord, which he had spoken unto him, upon a roll of a book." The process of inspiration as described here, interestingly enough, is precisely how 2 Peter 1:21 says it happened: "For the prophecy came not in old time by the will of man: but holy men of God spake as they were moved by the Holy Ghost." Jeremiah *spoke* his words to Baruch the scribe, but the words Baruch wrote weren't just *Jeremiah's words*. They were the very "words of the Lord" (36:4). In fact, Jeremiah restates the process in 36:6 as he says to Baruch: "Go thou, and read in the roll, which thou hast written from my mouth, the words of the Lord."

And through this story, God is making sure we understand how the actual process of inspiration and preservation works. In verse 17, the Temple leaders ask Baruch: "Tell us now, How didst thou write all these words at his mouth?" Baruch replies, "He pronounced all these words unto me with his mouth, and I wrote them with ink in the book" (v.18). In other words, what Baruch had in written form were the very words of God—what those in theological circles refer to as the "original manuscripts." And what happened to Jeremiah's original manuscript here also happened to all of the original manuscripts in history. They were totally destroyed! But God did not only *inspire* His Word and words; He also promised to *preserve* them (Ps. 12:6–7; Matt. 5:18). And although Jeremiah's original manuscript was gone, God had no problem remembering exactly what they said, and He certainly had no problem producing a copy that contained "all the words of the book which Jehoiakim king of Judah had burned in the fire" (Jer. 36:32).

This story is significant because many people today balk at the idea that the Bible we hold in our hands (as opposed to the original manuscripts which have been destroyed) is the very Word and words of God, just as He intended them. However, it stands to reason that if God went to the trouble of inspiring His words in original manuscripts (which He obviously did not intend to keep in existence or we'd have them!), it certainly is no trouble for Him to preserve them in a book that we can actually wrap our hands and our lives around.

Another issue people raise has to do with the italicized words in the King James Bible. Before we address that concern, let's consider how those words got there. The original manuscripts of the Old Testament were written in Hebrew; the New Testament was written in Greek and Aramaic. These original languages, then, were the basis for later translations into other languages. But there is no such thing as a word-for-word translation simply because some words do not have a corresponding equivalent. So as the King James translators were translating the Bible into English, the italicized words were used to convey the meaning of the original language when there was no English equivalent. So then, some argue, how can we believe that we hold in our hands "every word of God" (Prov. 30:5), if there are words that have been added? But that is not the right question. Instead we need to ask ourselves whether that is uncharacteristic of how God has previously worked in the process of inspiring and preserving His Word? And it is not. Jeremiah 36:32 says that the copy God produced contained every single word of the original, "and there were added besides unto them [besides the words written in the original scroll] many like words."

In chapters 37–38, Jeremiah continues to hammer the message of Jerusalem's destruction as God told him to do, and he is cast into prison for carrying out God's will. For a detailed unfolding of chapters 37 and 38, refer to the outline provided in today's Overview section above.

CHRIST IS REVEALED:

By *Jeremiah, who stood as a faithful witness to the revealed will of God* – Jeremiah 38:2–10 (Matt. 26:59)

52 WEEKS OF PURSUIT

WEEK 34, DAY 4: TODAY'S READING: JEREMIAH 39-43

OVERVIEW:

The destruction of Jerusalem (39:1–10); God's deliverance of Jeremiah and Ebedmelech (39:11–18); Jeremiah's release (40:1–16); the plot against Gedaliah (41:1– 10); the hostages taken by Ishmael are rescued (41:11–18); the Jews request a word from God through Jeremiah (42:1–6); Jeremiah delivers God's word (42:7–22); the people reject God's word (43:1–7); God's rejection of the people (43:8–13).

HIGHLIGHTS & INSIGHTS:

The day which Jeremiah had prophesied finally arrived. Verse 1 of chapter 39 says that Nebuchadnezzar and "all his army" came against Jerusalem, "and they besieged it." Those whom God had called to be His holy people, blessed with a holy standing before Him, with a holy temple in a holy land, had desecrated their holy calling. King Zedekiah escaped through a secret passage in the middle of the night, but was overtaken and brought before Nebuchadnezzar (39:4–5). He killed Zedekiah's sons in front of him and then "put out Zedekiah's eyes" (39:6–7). Imagine having the slaughter of your children be the last thing you ever see, knowing for the rest of your life that it was because of your own sin! It is an amazing phenomenon that parents can be so willfully blinded to how our precious children will bear the consequences of our sinful choices. Sadly, Zedekiah's selfishness and cluelessness in this regard represents the rule, rather than the exception, right up to this present day (Gal. 6:7–8).

Just as God promised Jeremiah when He first called him (1:17–19), Jeremiah's life was spared in the whole demise of the nation (39:11–18). Ironically, the king of Babylon showed Jeremiah more kindness than the four previous kings of Judah! In chapter 40, Jeremiah is freed by the Babylonians. They give him the option of being provided for in Babylon or remaining with the remnant that was permitted to stay in the land (40:4). In the spirit and tradition of Moses, Jeremiah chose "to suffer affliction with the people of God", rather than "to enjoy the pleasures of sin … in Egypt" (Heb. 11:24–26). Or, in this case, Babylon!

In 40:5–6, the king of Babylon appoints Gedaliah as governor over the people who remained in the land. Gedaliah encouraged the people to quietly and respectfully serve Babylon, assuring them that if they did, things would go well with them (40:9). Unfortunately, a plot was devised against Gedaliah, and in chapter 41, Ishmael murdered him and many who were with him, taking many hostages as well. Ishmael's plan was to flee to the city of Ammon, leaving the Jews around Jerusalem to suffer the wrath of the Babylonians. At that point, the people had two options: flee to Egypt and trust them for help against the Babylonians, or remain where God had placed them and trust Him for help. The decision they should have made is an absolute no-brainer, but in a moment of difficulty or trial, it is often much easier to trust the world's (Egypt) solution, instead of trusting God. In the moment, it doesn't always feel like such a no-brainer! We need God's wisdom and discernment to see our choices as He sees them.

Surprisingly, the people of Judah sought Jeremiah's counsel about what they should do (42:1–4), pledging that whatever God said through him, regardless of what it was, they would obey it (42:5–6). What a switch!

God told them that, if they would remain in the land, He would protect them and bless them, but if they went to Egypt for help, they would be completely destroyed (42:7–18). Jeremiah suspected that they were full of talk, but no walk—full of show, but no go (42:19–22). And in chapter 43, his hunch proved right. Rather than obey Jeremiah's words (which is to say, God's words), they accuse Jeremiah of setting them up to fall to the Babylonians. Clearly, they had planned to do what they wanted to do all along; they had just hoped that God's will lined up with theirs. The same empty promises are constantly made in our day, promises of surrender to God's will that will only be carried out if it's what we already want to do (2 Tim. 3:1–5). As the old saying goes, "The more things change, the more they stay the same." Chapter 43 ends with another of God's object lessons. This time, He reveals that Babylon would conquer Egypt just as they had Judah.

SPECIFIC REFERENCES TO THE DAY OF THE LORD:

39:16 – "In that day"

39:17 – "In that day"

CHRIST IS REVEALED:

Through *Gedaliah*, who instructed the Jews to pay homage to the heathen nation that ruled over them – Jeremiah 40:9 (Matt. 22:21)

WEEK 34, DAY 5: **TODAY'S READING: JEREMIAH 44-49**

OVERVIEW:

God's condemnation through Jeremiah of the remnant's idolatry in Egypt (44:1–14); the people blatantly confess their affection for idols (44:15–19); God's last word concerning the faithless remnant (44:20–30); God's exhortation to Baruch (45:1–5); God's judgment upon Egypt (46:1–28); God's judgment upon Philistia (47:1–7); God's judgment upon Moab (48:1–47); God's judgment upon Ammon (49:1–6); God's judgment upon Edom (49:7–22); God's judgment upon Damascus (49:23–27); God's judgment upon the lesser nations (49:28–33); God's judgment upon Elam (49:34-39).

HIGHLIGHTS & INSIGHTS:

At the end of chapter 34, the remnant had chosen to rebel against the word of the Lord through Jeremiah in spite of their extravagant promises to obey. They went to Egypt hoping to find a place of refuge against the wrath of the Babylonians. Not content to simply go themselves, they forced Jeremiah and Baruch to go with them. Perhaps they thought that God would not exercise judgment against them if these men of God were with them. Regardless of what they thought, Jeremiah's preaching against them wasn't over. And neither was God's judgment! Jeremiah walked them through the wickedness and idolatry of Judah, despite God's cry to them through the prophets, "Oh, do not this abominable thing that I hate" (44:4). Jeremiah promised that, just as surely as God's "fury" was poured out on their cities and in the streets of Jerusalem, leaving them "desolate" (v. 6), God's judgment would fall upon them in Egypt. Even after watching the painful effects of sin as people incur and endure the chastisement of Almighty God, we so easily deceive ourselves that "it'll be different for us" or "we'll be the exception."

Hearing Jeremiah's message did not cause the people to repent. Instead they decided they had not served other gods enough! Ya know, there's stupid, and then there's stooooooopid! They went back to worshipping the "queen of heaven" (Ashtoreth), reasoning that their lives had turned for the worse when they stopped worshipping her (44:17–19). Have I mentioned how utterly stooooooopid sin can make us?

And lest we think this idolatry "shoe" doesn't fit us, in the New Testament, God identifies covetousness as idolatry (Col. 3:5). He doesn't say that it is *like* idolatry, He says that it *is* idolatry! And at least three times in the New Testament, covetousness specifically refers to the desire for illicit sexual fulfillment. What happens in the whole world of sexual sin is no different than what was happening to the remnant in Egypt. People know how sexual sin has destroyed thousands and tens of thousands of homes before them, but they think it won't destroy theirs. Oh God, deliver us from ourselves!

Chapter 45 is a short chapter where God speaks to Baruch through Jeremiah. Baruch was one of only two people (Ebedmelech being the other one) in Jeremiah's forty-year ministry who responded to his preaching in any positive way. But, God says, Baruch's sadness about how things had shaken out for Jerusalem was because of how it had affected *him*, instead of how it had affected *God*! The chief characteristic of our day is that we are "lovers of [our] own selves" (2 Tim. 3:1–2). We must be careful not to deceive ourselves into thinking we're spiritual because we're repulsed by the condition of our country or the world. Do we hurt because God hurts, or do we hurt because of how the sin of the world has affected and is affecting our lives?

In the remaining chapters in today's reading, God details His judgment upon the Gentile nations:

- His judgment upon Egypt (46:1–28)
- His judgment upon Philisita (47:1–7)
- His judgment upon Moab (48:1–47)
- His judgment upon Ammon (49:1–6)

52 WEEKS OF PURSUIT

- His judgment upon Edom (49:7–22)
- His judgment upon Damascus (49:23–27)
- His judgment upon the lesser nations (49:28–33)
- His judgment upon Elam (49:34–39)

These nations basically encompassed all of the known world at that time. God's message through Jeremiah was that there is no nation who can defy Him and not incur His judgment upon themselves. If that is true, our nation is on a collision course with disaster!

SPECIFIC REFERENCES TO THE DAY OF THE LORD:

46:10 – "The Day of the Lord God of host, a day of vengeance"

48:41 – "At that day"

48:47 – "In the latter days"

49:22 – "At that day"

49:39 – "In the latter days"

CHRIST IS REVEALED:

Through *God's servants, the prophets* – Jeremiah 44:4 (Matt. 12:17–18; Acts 3:20–21)

WEEK 35, DAY 1: TODAY'S READING: JEREMIAH 50-52

OVERVIEW:

God's judgment upon Babylon (50:1–51:64); the fall of Jerusalem and Zedekiah's torment (52:1–11); the Babylonians destroy the Temple (52:12–23); the people are exiled (52:24–30); God has not forgotten and will not forsake David's descendants (52:31–34).

HIGHLIGHTS & INSIGHTS:

Up to this point, God has used Babylon as His tool to mete out judgment upon the nations addressed in chapters 44–49. In chapter 50, however, Jeremiah prophesies God's judgment upon Babylon and her many gods.

After Babylon's defeat, God's chosen people would once again be gathered to their homeland. This was partially fulfilled in 538 BC when Cyrus made a decree permitting the Jews to return to Jerusalem. The context, however, points to the complete fulfillment of these promises during the Great Tribulation. (Notice all of the references to the Tribulation and Second Coming of Christ in this passage: "in those days," 50:4; "it is the vengeance of the Lord," 50:15; "in those days," 50:20; "the vengeance of the LORD our God," 50:28; "in that day," 50:30.) The references to future fulfillment continue in chapter 51, as Jeremiah details Babylon's judgment, and his picture is very similar to what the Apostle John describes in Revelation 17–18.

In chapter 51, God also points to Israel's restoration in the last days. Despite all of her defiance, God still loves Israel and intends to bless her. Though the conflict in the Middle East rages today, Jeremiah (not to mention John, Isaiah, Ezekiel—really, all the prophets!) points to the fact that, in the very near future, the conflict will be over, and Israel will be sitting on top! Obviously, not everything Israel does today is right, but we cannot overlook the *everlasting* Abrahamic Covenant: "And I will bless them that bless thee [Abraham, or Israel], and curse him that curseth thee" (Gen. 12:3). Non-Christians may think that is a fatalistic viewpoint, but it is a settled fact. Israel is going to end up on top, and her Messiah and King (and ours, hallelujah!) will rule the entire world from His throne in Jerusalem. America has made some incredibly sinful and stupid decisions in the last half of a century (or more!). Perhaps God has not unleashed His judgment upon us because our faithfulness to bless Israel. If (or when) we curse them, I'm afraid we'll finally seal our own doom!

In 51:59–64, God gives one final object lesson through Jeremiah. The prophet "wrote in a book all the evil that should come upon Babylon" (51:60) and told Seraiah to take it and read it in Babylon. After reading it, he was to take the scroll, tie it to a rock and cast it into the Euphrates, explaining to the people that that's exactly what God was going to do to them!

The book of Jeremiah concludes in chapter 52 with a somewhat lengthy explanation about the fall of Jerusalem. It is almost word for word what is written in 2 Kings 25 and very similar to what was detailed in Jeremiah 39:1–18. It recounts the city's fall, Zedekiah's attempt to escape, his capture, and the murder of his sons "before his eyes" (52:20) just before he lost his physical sight.

Back in 1 Kings 9:1–9, after Solomon built the Temple, God promised to keep His name there as long as they served only Him. "But," He said, "if ye shall at all turn from following me, ye or your children, and will not keep my commandments and my statutes which I have set before you, but go and serve other gods, and worship them: Then will I cut off Israel out of the land which I have given them; and this house, which I have hallowed for my name, will I cast out of my sight; and Israel shall be a proverb and a byword among all people" (1 Kings 9:6–7). The people did not live up to their end of the bargain, but as you might imagine, God most certainly lived up to His! Jeremiah 52:12–30 is the fulfillment of God's warning to Israel in 1 Kings 9:6–7.

The book of Jeremiah ends, however, with just a flicker of hope. After thirty-seven years of being exiled in Babylon, Jehoiachin, king of Judah, is shown preferential treatment (52:31-34). It is a reminder that God has not forgotten the Davidic Covenant, and as Jeremiah 30–33 makes clear, God will ultimately fulfill His promises to bless Israel.

SPECIFIC REFERENCES TO THE DAY OF THE LORD:

51:2 – "In the day of trouble"

51:6 – "The time of the Lord's vengeance"

51:11 – "It is the vengeance of the Lord"

CHRIST IS REVEALED:

As the *Redeemer who pleads our cause* – Jeremiah 50:34 (Luke 1:68; Rom. 8:34)

As the *Creator of the universe* – Jeremiah 51:15 (Col. 1:16)

WEEK 35, DAY 2: TODAY'S READING: LAMENTATIONS 1-5

OVERVIEW:
Jeremiah's lamentation over Jerusalem's destruction (chapter 1); God's justifiable wrath (chapter 2); God's incredible mercy (chapter 3); God's anger against Jerusalem (chapter 4); a plea for restoration (chapter 5).

HIGHLIGHTS & INSIGHTS:
The Lamentations of Jeremiah, as the title states, is the expression of Jeremiah's incredible sorrow over the sins of God's people that had resulted in the destruction of the temple in Jerusalem and the entire kingdom of Judah. These five chapters are more or less a postscript to the book of Jeremiah. They are a separate book in our English Bible, but in the Hebrew Bible, they are contained in the third section called the Writings. This book employs acrostic poetry, much like we saw in Psalm 119. In chapters 1, 2 and 4, each succeeding verse begins with the next letter of the Hebrew alphabet. Chapter 3 actually contains three acrostic poems.

From a Historical standpoint, the book of Lamentations deals with the fall of Jerusalem in 586 BC. From a Doctrinal (Prophetic) standpoint, the book deals with the events during and surrounding the Tribulation Period.

In chapter 1, Jeremiah likens the city of Jerusalem to a grieving widow. He describes the fact that once she was a princess, but has now become a "tributary," or slave (1:1). At one time she was surrounded by friends and lovers (1:2), but everyone has forsaken her, leaving her to grieve and weep alone. In verse 4 of chapter 1, Jeremiah even personifies the roads leading to Jerusalem: "the ways of Zion do mourn." At one time, they had been filled with incoming worshippers, but now they were totally desolate. The picture Jeremiah describes in this chapter is heartbreaking and pitiful. Having to put the reality of Jerusalem's condition into words becomes more than Jeremiah can handle. By the time he gets to verse 16, he says: "For these things I weep; mine eye, mine eye runneth down with water." May our hearts break and our eyes leak, as did Jeremiah's, for the similar condition of the church of the Lord Jesus Christ in the last days of the Laodicean church period (Rev. 3:14–22).

When God called His son, Israel, out of Egypt (Hos. 11:1), He led them with the cloud of His glory. At this point in their history, the Lord once again covered them with a cloud, not of His glory, but of "his anger" (2:1). In times past, the Lord fought on Israel's behalf against their enemies, but now the Lord fought against Israel (2:2–5). Again, Jeremiah *laments* as he describes Israel's awful condition: "Mine eyes do fail with tears, my bowels are troubled, my liver is poured upon the earth, for the destruction of the daughter of my people" (2:11). Jeremiah recognized, however, that they had gotten exactly what they deserved (2:17) because they listened to their false prophets (2:14) and stubbornly refused to repent of their idolatry.

Lamentations 2:15 is perhaps the saddest verse in the entire book: "All that pass by clap their hands at thee; they hiss and wag their head at the daughter of Jerusalem, saying, Is this the city that men call The perfection of beauty, The joy of the whole earth?" Applied to our Laodicean condition, many Christians are "whooping it up" about all of the so-called spiritual things that are taking place, but we have to wonder if the world isn't looking at the church and saying, "Is this the glorious church of the Lord Jesus Christ, the beautiful, chaste virgin Bride that is without spot or blemish or any such thing?" (Eph. 5:27; 2 Cor. 11:2). May God give us Jeremiahs in these last days who will lament our grievous condition.

In the middle of chapter 3, after two and a half chapters of focusing on the pitiful condition in the land, Jeremiah lifts his eyes to the Lord. In the midst of the sorrow and ruin, he is reminded of the mercy and compassion of the Lord, the incredible fact that "his compassions fail not" and "are new every morning" (3:22–23). In response, Jeremiah declares, "Great is thy faithfulness!" In other words, he says, "We have certainly failed You, O God, but You will not fail us." May we, too, praise the Lord today for His marvelous, infinite, matchless mercy and grace! In the remainder of chapter 3, Jeremiah calls upon the people to stop their whining, search their hearts, confess their sin, and get right with God! He then calls upon God to punish those He used as the instrument of His wrath against Jerusalem.

Chapter 4 reveals just how horrendous the situation in Jerusalem had actually gotten. Children were being mistreated and abused by their parents. Things were so desperate that some mothers were actually eating their own children! God says that His punishment against this city would even be greater than His punishment of Sodom!

Chapter 5 continues the description of the deplorable situation in Zion and ends with Jeremiah crying out to God, "Turn thou us unto thee, O Lord, and we shall be turned; renew our days as of old" (5:21). The good news is that, in the very near future, God is finally going to answer Jeremiah's prayer!

SPECIFIC REFERENCES TO THE DAY OF THE LORD:

2:1 – "In the day of his anger"

2:22 – "In the day of the Lord's anger"

CHRIST IS REVEALED:

Through *Jeremiah's sorrow over Jerusalem* – Lamentations 1:12–22 (Matt. 23:37; Luke 13:34)

As the *Merciful Savior* – Lamentations 3:22 (Jude v. 21)

52 WEEKS OF PURSUIT

WEEK 35, DAY 3: TODAY'S READING: EZEKIEL 1–5

OVERVIEW:
Ezekiel receives a vision of God's glory (chapter 1); Ezekiel receives his commission (chapter 2); Ezekiel is instructed to physically typify the siege and judgment of Jerusalem (chapters 3–5).

HIGHLIGHTS & INSIGHTS:
We begin today with some basic information about the book of Ezekiel to help us get our bearings in this powerful book. Ezekiel's name means "strengthened by God." Along with Jeremiah and Daniel, he was called by God to prophesy against Israel during the time of exile. Ezekiel 1:1–2 provide the historical context of the book.

To understand the actual tone of Ezekiel's message, we must understand how Ezekiel fits into the story of the Old Testament. The Old Testament breaks down into six natural chronological divisions:

- Genesis – Begins with the creation of the world and ends with Jacob's sons in Egypt.
- Exodus – Begins with Jacob's sons in Egypt and ends with Joshua leading the nation of Israel to possess the Promised Land.
- Judges – Covers the period in Israel's history when a variety of judges ruled.
- Kings – Covers all the kings who ruled Israel from Saul until both kingdoms fell to conquering nations. The Northern Kingdom (Israel) was defeated by Assyria and carried away captive in 722 BC. Judah, the Southern Kingdom, was defeated by Babylon and carried away captive in 606 BC.
- Exile – The nation of Israel's seventy years of exile.
- Return – The time of Israel's return to their homeland, when both the temple and Jerusalem were rebuilt under the leadership of Zerubbabel, Ezra, and Nehemiah.

The exile had been prophesied as far back as Moses (Deut. 28) and as recently as the prophet Jeremiah (Jer. 25:11–12). Israel's disobedience culminated in their failure to keep the Sabbath for the land (2 Chron. 36:21). God had kept track of Israel's refusal to let the land rest and exiled Israel for seventy years to provide the land that rest. This is a chilling reminder of the consequences of sin. There is no doubt that Israel had grown accustomed to ignoring the Sabbath for the land. But God knew! God will not ignore sin (Gal. 6:7).

Judah had temporarily turned to God under the reign of Josiah (640–609 BC). After Josiah was killed by the Egyptian army, however, the Southern Kingdom plunged back into sin under their four remaining kings:

- Jehoahaz (609 BC)
- Jehoiakim (609–598 BC) – Daniel was taken captive during his reign
- Jehoiachin (598–597 BC) – Ezekiel was taken captive during his reign
- Zedekiah (597–586 BC) – A puppet king under the reign of Nebuchadnezzar

The exile had begun in 606 BC and ended in 536 BC. During those seventy years, both Daniel and Ezekiel were taken captive to Babylon. Eventually, Babylon, under the leadership of Nebuchadnezzar, would burn the temple and destroy Jerusalem.

Ezekiel and his wife were among the 10,000 Jews taken into captivity along with king Jehoiachin in 597 BC (2 Kings 24:11–18). He was 25 years old when he was taken to Babylon and 30 years old when his ministry began (Ezek. 1:1). He ministered for 22 years (until 570 BC). The exiled Jews were more colonists than captives. They were permitted to farm tracts of land under somewhat favorable conditions. Ezekiel even had his own house. But we must grasp that Ezekiel was already in captivity while he prophesied to the Jews who had not been taken captive.

Chapter 1 records one of the most incredible visions in the Word of God. It includes four living creatures flying through the air like a flash of lightning, a crystal sea, creatures with multiple eyes and faces ushering in a throne, and an appearance of the pre-incarnate Christ. Ezekiel is brought into the presence of the Lord for a glimpse of the Second Advent. Just like Isaiah (Isa. 6:1–8) and the Apostle John (Rev. 4–5), Ezekiel is so overwhelmed by the revelation of Christ in His glory that the most comfortable position he could find was on his face! And, in contrast to the nonchalant way many Christians approach the Lord Jesus Christ today, every person will respond that way when they see Christ in His glory (Rom. 14:11). There is no room for pride or selfishness in the presence of God Almighty.

In chapters 2 and 3, God commissions Ezekiel to prophesy to the nation of Israel during the seventy-year exile. One of the key applications of this passage is that Ezekiel is a picture for every preacher—and every Christian—of what it really means to be entrusted with the stewardship of the Word of God. It begins with having an encounter with Christ. In chapter 1, Ezekiel came face to face with Christ, but his encounter didn't just about what Ezekiel saw, but also what he heard. Speaking in the first person, Ezekiel says, "I heard a voice of one that spake" (1:28). And more than just hearing words, Ezekiel records that "the spirit entered into me when he spake" (2:2). Like Ezekiel, our effectiveness as a steward of the Word of God must begin with a daily encounter with Christ that results in our hearing His voice and being filled with His Spirit (Eph. 5:18).

But how can we possibly have an encounter with Christ, knowing that He doesn't (and won't) appear to us in a vision like Ezekiel's? We encounter Christ by yielding ourselves to Him as we position ourselves before Him through the pages of His holy Word. Through the written revelation of the Word of God, we too get a glimpse of Christ in all of His glory (Eph. 1:18) and hear, as it were, His voice.

And yet, it isn't enough for us to just hear God's words. God instructed Ezekiel, "All my words that I shall speak unto thee receive in thine heart" (3:10). We must receive God's words into our heart to such a degree that they change the way we think, speak, act and react. Even more, God tells Ezekiel to receive *all* His words. Over the course of his ministry, God is going to give Ezekiel some very difficult things to say and do. But when it comes to God's Word, we can't pick and choose what we will obey and what we won't. Sometimes the Word will be sweet; sometimes it will be bitter. Sometimes it will comfort; sometimes it will sting. We are only responsible to receive it—all of it!

Next, God instructed Ezekiel to speak His words. And just as he was to receive all of them, he was also responsible to speak all of them. God commanded him to "speak my words unto them" (whether the people liked it or not, 2:7) and "when I speak with thee, I will open thy mouth, and thou shalt say unto them, Thus saith the Lord God" (3:27). These are the steps I wish every pastor and believer in the world would use in their mission—to allow God to speak His word to us and receive it so we are filled with the Spirit, having applied it in our own lives. And then, to join the Apostle Paul in saying, "I have not shunned to declare unto you all the counsel of God" (Acts 20:27). Instead of declaring to others conclusions based on our own life experiences and opinions, we are responsible for declaring the Word of God.

Finally, Ezekiel's actions mirrored his words. God repeatedly asks Ezekiel to demonstrate His truth to Israel by the way he lives (the sign of the tile, shaving, burning hair, lying on each side, and imprisonment). Our life must reflect the truth of God. Our actions must speak even louder than our words!

And now, at last, you would think that Ezekiel was ready to go speak to the people. But no. God knew that if he would truly be effective in imparting His words to them, there was still more that would need to take place. Ezekiel would first need to identify with the people. That's why Ezekiel "sat where they sat" (3:15). Before Ezekiel spoke a word to the people, he sat quietly for seven days with those who would be the recipients of God's message. May we learn from Ezekiel's example. We must be willing to spend time with people and listen to them before we expect them to listen to us. How can we expect to share the love of Christ with people with whom we are unwilling to identify? The old cliché is so true: "People don't care how much you know until they know how much you care."

Finally, God gives Ezekiel a warning. Ezekiel had to realize that he would be held accountable for the mission God had assigned to him. He would not be held accountable for the response of the people. But he was responsible to hear, receive, and speak the words of God (3:15–21). At the Judgment Seat of Christ, we will be held accountable for the mission God has assigned to us (Rom. 14:12; 2 Cor. 5:10). God will not hold us accountable for how people responded to our message, but we will give account for whether or not we heard the Word of Christ, received the Word of Christ, and shared the Word of Christ (Col. 3:16; 1 Tim. 4:16).

That is the picture Ezekiel provides. Let us use his experiences to assess our own lives and ministries.

- Are we encountering Christ daily by surrendering ourselves before Him through the pages of His Word?
- Are we actually listening to His words and receiving them in our hearts?
- Do our lives give evidence of the filling of the Spirit?
- Are we actively and purposefully seeking to identify with those around us, so we might be effective in communicating God's truth to them?
- Are they able to see and hear God's truth by observing it in how we live our lives?

CHRIST IS REVEALED:

As the *Appearance of a Man upon the throne* – Ezekiel 1:26 (Rev. 1:13–17)

WEEK 35, DAY 4: **TODAY'S READING: EZEKIEL 6-11**

OVERVIEW:

God judges Israel for their idolatry (chapter 6); the severity of God's judgment (chapter 7); the vision of Jerusalem's sin (chapter 8); the vision of God's judgment on Jerusalem (chapter 9); the vision of the cherubim and God's glory (chapter 10); Israel is warned about the false security of Jerusalem (chapter 11).

HIGHLIGHTS & INSIGHTS:

Ezekiel uses the title "Son of Man" some 93 times, nearly half the total times it appears in the entire Bible. The prophet Daniel uses it to refer to the promised Messiah (Dan. 7:13), which is why it appears 84 times in the New Testament in reference to our Lord Jesus Christ. Given the Jews' reaction to our Lord referring to Himself by that title, they understood that this title had specific Messianic implications. Luke 22:66–71 says:

> And as soon as it was day, the elders of the people and the chief priests and the scribes came together, and led him into their council, saying, Art thou the Christ? tell us. And he said unto them, If I tell you, ye will not believe: And if I also ask you, ye will not answer me, nor let me go. Hereafter shall the Son of man sit on the right hand of the power of God. Then said they all, Art thou then the Son of God? And he said unto them, Ye say that I am. And they said, What need we any further witness? for we ourselves have heard of his own mouth.

We should also note that Ezekiel himself is a type of our Lord Jesus Christ. Ezekiel ministered to the nation of Israel as a prophet and a priest during the time of exile, just as our Lord will minister to Israel as a prophet and a priest during the Tribulation. And the period of judgment and restoration pictured in Ezekiel foreshadows the judgment and restoration of Israel during the Tribulation and the millennial reign of Christ.

Another key phrase we find repeated throughout the book of Ezekiel is "know that I am the Lord." Of the 77 times this phrase appears in the Bible, 63 of them are in this book. It is repeated so often because Israel, during Ezekiel's ministry, *didn't know the Lord*! They had forgotten who God was. Israel had turned to idolatry, having replaced God with man-made images (6:4; 8:5–16). They had trusted in their wealth (7:19) and in the walls of Jerusalem (11:3) for security. Their exile and eventual restoration was intended to remind Israel that He is the Lord!

Ezekiel's visions of God's judgment are precise and severe. Since Israel's idolatry had begun at the temple, causing God to remove His presence (8:6), God's judgment would also begin at His temple (9:6). Throughout the Old Testament, Satan desired to destroy the place where God's glory was intended to dwell. He succeeded during the exile when Nebuchadnezzar burned the temple in 586 BC. The temple was rebuilt, only to be destroyed again by Rome in 70 AD. Let this be both a reminder and a warning to us because God's glory is currently intended to dwell in us! Just like in Ezekiel's day, the enemy wants us to turn to other gods through covetousness (idolatry) and turn away from God to find security in material riches and self-made "walls." In order to prevent God's judgment on our own temple (our heart), as happened in Ezekiel's time, we must evaluate whether we, like Israel, have forgotten who God is. Perhaps we need to be reminded to "know that I am the Lord!" God Himself is the only One who can keep us safe. We must recognize that He is the Lord!

God appears to Ezekiel for the third time at the beginning of chapter 10. It is during this encounter that God reveals to Ezekiel that Israel would one day be restored (11:17–20). This final restoration will usher in the millennial reign of Christ. And how awesome it is that, even in the midst of tribulation, God promises deliverance.

SPECIFIC REFERENCES TO THE DAY OF THE LORD:

7:7 – "The day of trouble is near"

7:10 – "Behold the day"

7:12 – "The day draweth near"

7:19 – "The day of the wrath of the Lord"

CHRIST IS REVEALED:

As the *One Man clothed with linen* – Ezekiel 9:2 (Rev. 1:13)

52 WEEKS OF PURSUIT

WEEK 35, DAY 5: TODAY'S READING: EZEKIEL 12-16

OVERVIEW:

Ezekiel's actions illustrate the exile (chapter 12); God warns the false prophets (chapter 13); God warns Israel that judgment is inevitable (chapters 14–15); God reminds Israel of His grace in saving them and their decision to forsake Him (chapter 16).

HIGHLIGHTS & INSIGHTS:

In the book of Jeremiah, God repeatedly used object lessons to make His point. In Ezekiel, He called the prophet not only to speak His truth, but also to illustrate it through outward demonstrations. Leaving with his stuff through the wall in 12:1–16 illustrates the captivity of Israel's king, Zedekiah (2 Kings 25:1–10). Ezekiel's trembling in 12:17–20 illustrates the desolation that Israel will experience during the exile.

And what God was asking Ezekiel to do in declaring His message is exactly what He asks us to do. Whether for good or for evil, we not only speak with our lips, we also speak with our lives. In the New Testament, this truth is wrapped up in the word *conversation*. Simply put, it means "the way we live our lives." Paul tells us in Philippians 1:27: "Only let your conversation be as it becometh the gospel of Christ." In other words, our conversation should reflect that we have been transformed by the power of the gospel. And in 1 Timothy 4:12, Paul tells Timothy to be "an example of the believers, in word, in conversation, in charity, in spirit, in faith, in purity." Obviously, our words are what we say with our lips; our conversation is what we say through our life! This is the point of the the old adage, "Your life is speaking is so loudly, I can't hear the words you're saying." In light of these truths, we would do well to examine ourselves:

- What message am I communicating to my Savior through the life He sees me living?
- What message am I communicating to my family through the life they see me live in our home?
- What message is my life communicating to those in my sphere of influence who are lost?

Even though Ezekiel passionately warns Israel of impending judgment, there are still those who refuse to take God seriously. Some of the Jews had adopted a proverb that I'll paraphrase this way: "With the passing of time, every warning of Ezekiel has proven false" (12:22). Fed up with their smart mouths and pompous attitude, God tells Ezekiel in 12:23–25:

> Tell them therefore, Thus saith the Lord God; I will make this proverb to cease, and they shall no more use it as a proverb in Israel; but say unto them, The days are at hand, and the effect of every vision. For there shall be no more any vain vision nor flattering divination within the house of Israel. For I am the Lord: I will speak, and the word that I shall speak shall come to pass; it shall be no more prolonged: for in your days, O rebellious house, will I say the word, and will perform it, saith the Lord God.

In other words, brace for impact, because the hammer is about to fall! Every generation somehow convinces itself that they can live their lives like they want, that there won't be consequences for their sin. The Bible is clear, however, sin always has a payday (Gal. 6:7; Num. 32:23). We must be careful not to think God's longsuffering is apathy towards sin.

While Ezekiel was barking about the coming judgment of God upon their nation, the other so-called prophets in the land were prophesying peace and safety (Ezek. 13:10, 16; 14:9). The people chose to believe their message, further demonstrating Israel's arrogance. We see the same thing in our time, as Paul described in 2 Timothy 4:3–4: "For the time will come when they will not endure sound doctrine; but after their own lusts shall they heap to themselves teachers, having itching ears; And they shall turn away their ears from the truth, and shall be turned unto fables."

The prophets in Israel also foreshadow the Antichrist, who will come to power at the beginning of the

Tribulation, proclaiming a message of peace and safety at a time when God will be about to release His vengeance and wrath on the earth (1 Thess. 5:3; Rev. 6:2; Dan. 8:25). Just as God's judgment was inevitable during the ministry of Ezekiel, so His judgment will be inevitable during the coming Tribulation.

Chapter 16 is one of the most brutally descriptive images of our sinful condition—and His grace! This chapter is so graphic and so powerfully indicting upon the Jews that some of the ancient rabbis did not allow it to be read publicly! God likens Israel to an abandoned child who was born of the wrong parents and left for dead in a field (16:3–5). God sees Israel lying in her own blood and says, "Live" (16:6). God blesses Israel with beauty (holiness), clothing (righteousness), and jewels/crown (rewards). He anoints Israel with oil (a type of the Holy Spirit) and makes her His bride (16:7–14). But despite God's amazing grace, Israel prostitutes herself to other nations and other gods. She continuously involves herself in spiritual adultery (16:15–59).

Ezekiel 16:60 contains one of the most powerful and beautiful words in the entire Bible: "Nevertheless." Despite Israel's broken promises and spiritual adultery, God still remembers His *everlasting* covenant. What a beautiful yet solemn picture of the reality of our life. God does not keep His word to us because of our goodness or obedience. It is because of His grace. Like Israel, we continually forsake our God—nevertheless! (See Eph. 1:11–14; 4:30.)

SPECIFIC REFERENCES TO THE DAY OF THE LORD:

13:5 – "In the day of the Lord"

CHRIST IS REVEALED:

As the *Bridegroom* – Ezekiel 16 (Matt. 9:15; John 3:29)

52 WEEKS OF PURSUIT

WEEK 36, DAY 1: TODAY'S READING: EZEKIEL 17–20

OVERVIEW:
The parable of the eagles (chapter 17); man's responsibility for sin (chapter 18); God's lamentation for Israel's captivity (chapter 19); God refuses inquisition (chapter 20).

HIGHLIGHTS & INSIGHTS:
In Ezekiel 17, God instructs Ezekiel to speak a parable to the house of Israel using the figure of eagles. The first eagle represents Nebuchadnezzar who came to Jerusalem and took away the king's seed (the twigs) and planted them again in Babylon. The highest branch of the cedar tree represents king Jehoiachin, the king of Judah who was exiled in 597 BC.

Nebuchadnezzar replaced Jehoiachin with a native Judean prince, Zedekiah, instead of a foreign ruler. By ensuring that Zedekiah prospered in his reign, Nebuchadnezzar intended for the kingdom of Judah to stay dependent on him, but it was not to be. The second eagle in Ezekiel's parable represents Egypt, specifically Pharaoh-hophra to whom Zedekiah looked for help. Jeremiah had warned Zedekiah not to make an alliance with Egypt (Jer. 37:5–7; 44:30), but the king ignored Jeremiah's counsel (Ezek. 17:15). Although Egypt offered temporary relief from the oppression of Nebuchadnezzar, in the end, Babylon defeated Egypt and put Zedekiah to death. Had Zedekiah simply obeyed God's counsel to him through Jeremiah, he would have been fine.

May we learn from Zedekiah's tragic mistake! Like Zedekiah, we often find ourselves in trials and temptations that threaten our safety or well-being. In those times, we can listen to the voice of God revealed in His Word, or we can seek to escape adversity by looking to worldly alternatives (Egypt). By God's grace, we must tenaciously hold to what the Word of God says and completely trust God with the outcome. Our worldly scheming will never produce a positive result.

Ezekiel 17:22–24 is a messianic prophecy. "Of the highest branch" refers to Christ who, unlike Zedekiah, will overshadow a mighty kingdom. Note the surety of God's Word in verse 24: "I the Lord have spoken and have done it." God is referring to a future event as if it were history. God's Word is certain. What He has declared is completely sure, whether He's talking about the past or the future! May that truth give us confidence in His holy Word today.

Chapter 18 begins with a proverb that is a warning to those who blame others for their problems. In 18:2, Israel claimed their forefathers had "eaten sour grapes," setting their children's teeth "on edge," or causing them to suffer the sharpness of exile. But God flatly rejects their blame-shifting. Many people in our time have fallen into the same trap, blaming others for their circumstances or for their being the way they are. "My Dad this..." or "My Mom that..." or "If I would have had a different upbringing..." are among the many excuses we hear. But God is clear that we must take responsibility for our own actions. We didn't get to choose our parents, and we can't always control our circumstances, but we can always control our attitudes, choices, actions, and reactions. God would have shown the children of Israel mercy if they had repented. Instead, they committed the same sins as their forefathers, then blamed them for the outcome! We must take responsibility for our lives. There will be no blame-shifting or finger-pointing when we give account before Him at the judgment seat of Christ. God reminds Israel that His heart's desire is always for repentance (18:32). May we learn to take responsibility for our sin and repent of it with godly sorrow and godly repentance (2 Cor. 7:10).

In chapter 19, Ezekiel records "a lamentation for the princes of Israel" (v. 1). The word *lamentation* means a "loud cry." It is poetic song (usually three beats, followed by two beats) that expresses deep emotion. This lamentation is for king Jehoahaz, who languished in an Egyptian prison (2 Kings 23:31–33) and for king Jehoiakim, who was taken captive to Babylon (2 Kings 24:1–12). They are depicted as lion's whelps (19:2, 5). The lamentation ends with a summary of Israel's current state (19:10–14). Her exile is pictured as a plant in a dry and thirsty ground. Ezekiel 19:14 states that Israel has no "sceptre to rule" and ends with the strange phrase: "This is a lamentation and shall be for a lamentation." In other words, this is a lamentation for Israel's immediate condition as well as a future lamentation for her suffering during the Great Tribulation. That lamentation will end with Israel's Messiah, our Lord Jesus Christ, reigning over the earth from His throne in Jerusalem, and He will rule with a sceptre made of an iron rod (Rev. 19:15).

In chapter 20, the leadership of Israel ("the elders") come to Ezekiel to enquire of the Lord. God, obviously knowing their real motives, responds that He "will not be inquired of by you" (v. 3). He reminds them that under their so-called leadership, Israel had not only been disobedient, but were still living in disobedience. The chapter ends with a vivid picture of God's judgment with fire (20:45–49). The leaders of Israel reply by spiritualizing Ezekiel's message, and instead of taking it literally, they accuse Ezekiel of speaking in parables. Even today, many people and denominations spiritualize what God intends to be taken literally and take literally what God intends to be understood spiritually.

CHRIST IS REVEALED:

As the *Tender One planted upon a high mountain* – Ezekiel 17:22

52 WEEKS OF PURSUIT

WEEK 36, DAY 2: TODAY'S READING: EZEKIEL 21-23

OVERVIEW:

Judgment pronounced against Jerusalem (chapter 21); Jerusalem's sin (chapter 22); Jerusalem's seduction (chapter 23).

HIGHLIGHTS & INSIGHTS:

In chapter 21, God instructs Ezekiel to sigh in the midst of the people (v. 6). When they ask the reason for his bitter anguish, he is to remind them that God's judgment is imminent and will affect every person in Israel. God describes his judgment as a sharp sword being removed from its sheath. In the Historical context, the sword represents the king of Babylon (21:19). Prophetically, this sword foreshadows the day Christ will come in judgment upon this earth with a sword that proceeds out of His mouth which, of course, is the Word of God (Rev. 19:15).

Beginning in verse 18, God tells Ezekiel to make a map and trace on it two routes for the king of Babylon to follow. One route goes to Jerusalem; the other will take him to Rabbath of the Ammonites, which had conspired with Judah to rebel against Babylon in 593 BC. Ezekiel records how the king of Babylon would use three types of magic to call upon his gods to decide which city to attack. First, he would use arrows. The arrows would be marked with a name, put in a quiver, and whirled about. The first one to fall out would reflect the decision of the god. The next form of magic would be "images" or teraphims. From the record of history, we learn that these images were actually the mummified heads of children! The third, and most common, form of magic was the "liver." Judgment was made based on the color of a sacrificed lamb's liver. Having heard from his gods, Nebuchadnezzar would attack Jerusalem.

The Jews were skeptical of Ezekiel's continual prophecies against Judah and Jerusalem. They doubted that the king's "magic" would lead him to target Jerusalem or that he would be able to take the city (21:23). Although the king of Babylon was using magic as His guide, Proverbs 21:1 teaches us that his heart was in the hand of the Lord. God would use the king's magic to bring judgment against His people.

From a Historical standpoint, the "wicked prince of Israel" is Zedekiah (21:25–27). From a Prophetic standpoint, however, Zedekiah typifies the coming Antichrist. Then, in verse 26, God instructs Israel to "remove the diadem" worn by the priests and "take off the crown" worn by the kings. In verse 27, God says: "I will overturn, overturn, overturn, it: and it shall be no more, until he come whose right it is; and I will give it him." God repeats *overturn* three times to express the most severe judgment against these offices (priest and king) and declares that, after their captivity, neither office would be restored until our Lord Jesus Christ comes. And look how God the Father refers to his beloved Son: He is the only One "whose right it is" to be called Priest and King!

In chapter 22, Ezekiel chronicles Jerusalem's sins. Once again, God begins by judging the leadership. He specifically mentions the prophets, priests and princes (vs. 25–28). The priests violated the law by not distinguishing that which was holy from that which was profane (v. 26). The sin of the princes was their desire to make money at the expense of people (v. 27). The prophets flat-out lied about what God had said (v. 28).

God looked for a man among the leadership to stand in the gap (22:30). Sadly, He found none. Even the great prophets Ezekiel and Jeremiah were unable to turn the heart of a single man in Israel to repentance. There would be a man 400 years later, however, who would stand in the gap for all mankind—the God-Man, our Lord Jesus Christ!

In chapter 23 the capital city of the Northern Kingdom (Samaria) and the capital city of the Southern Kingdom (Jerusalem) are likened to two sisters who are seduced into adultery by their lovers. The elder sister, Aholah, represents Samaria, and the younger sister, Aholibah, represents Jerusalem. Samaria was seduced by Assyria (Isa. 7:17–20; 10:5–11), and Judah was seduced by Egypt. Israel is repeatedly warned in Scripture not to go to Egypt for help. But Israel continually disobeyed God's instruction, culminating in Zedekiah's formation of an alliance with Egypt against Babylon (Ezek. 17:15).

The illustration of these two harlot sisters in chapter 23 provides one of the most vivid descriptions of the seduction of sin in the Bible. Sin always follows a specific pattern or process which can be summed up in four steps:

- Desire (23:5–7; James 1:14) – Sin becomes "desirable" (23:6) to us
- Delivered (23:9; James 1:15a) – God allows us to be "delivered" to the passions we are allowing to control us
- Defiled (23:13, 17; James 1:15b) – Acting upon our passions causes us to be "defiled"
- Destroyed (23:22–49; James 1:15c) – God allows our sin to run its destructive course in our lives. Both Samaria and Jerusalem got what they wanted, but it ended up destroying them both (Rom. 6:23)!

The seduction of sin is a real and powerful influence that we must guard against. Though we may think we are immune, chapter 23 offers several other key principles worth noting:

- Lust for what we see will eventually lead to actions (23:14–16)
- What we see can destroy our mind (23:17)
- Those who seduce us in the name of "love" will eventually hate us (23:22, 28)

Sin will destroy us if we give in to its seduction. We are not immune to its temptations in any area, but we must be especially watchful in the realm of sexual sin, including viewing pornography or coveting wrong relationships. Let us be on our guard against the four-step seduction of sin!

SPECIFIC REFERENCES TO THE DAY OF THE LORD

21:29 – "Whose day is come, when their iniquity shall have an end"

22:24 – "In the day of indignation"

CHRIST IS REVEALED:

As the *One who has the "right" to be both Priest and King* – Ezekiel 21:27

As the *One who will stand in the gap* – Ezekiel 22:30

52 WEEKS OF PURSUIT

WEEK 36, DAY 3: TODAY'S READING: EZEKIEL 24-27

OVERVIEW:
God's purging of Jerusalem (chapter 24); God's judgment against Gentile nations (chapter 25); God's judgment against Tyre (chapter 26–27).

HIGHLIGHTS & INSIGHTS:
In chapter 24, God tells Ezekiel to write down a parable about a bloody stew that represents Jerusalem. Twice Ezekiel repeats the Lord's warning: "Woe to the bloody city" (24:6, 9). Many times, the Word of God promises God's vengeance on those who shed "innocent blood" (Deut. 19:10; 1 Sam. 19:5; 1 Kings 2:31) because it pictures *the* innocent blood that would one day be shed at Calvary (Matt. 27:4). The innocent blood of our Lord Jesus Christ redeemed us from sin, but those who do not accept God's gift of grace will be held accountable for the death of God's only Son and will suffer the judgment of God's righteous wrath. How God must love us to have allowed the innocent blood of His beloved Son to be shed for our sin!

Ezekiel is instructed not to mourn when his wife dies (24:15–18), picturing that there would be no time to mourn when God's judgment came on Jerusalem. It also foreshadows the swift and calamitous judgment that will come on the Day of the Lord. However, even in God's judgment, there is mercy. In 24:25–27, Ezekiel speaks to certain Jews who will escape the judgment of Jerusalem and come to Babylon. Historically, this is fulfilled in Ezekiel 33:21, but Prophetically, it points to those who will be saved from the judgment of the Tribulation.

In chapter 25, Ezekiel prophesies against Gentile nations who rejoiced when Israel was chastened by God (25:3, 6, 8) and took vengeance on Israel when she was weak (25:12, 15). God does not take kindly to people rejoicing when Israel is chastened! Much of the world rejoices when bad news is broadcasted about Israel; many others look forward to the day Israel will suffer during the Tribulation. God will use the nations to execute His sovereign plan to bring judgment against Israel, but after God has used them, He will bring His judgment upon them! And from a Devotional perspective, we should never rejoice when we see God's chastening on others either (Prov. 24:17).

Chapters 26–28 is a three-chapter judgment against Tyre, a lamentation of a glorious and great trade ship destroyed by the high seas (26:17). An ancient Phoenician city, Tyre first appears in the Bible in Joshua 19:29. Tyre was a great commercial city. During the reigns of David and Solomon, Tyre exercised great influence on the commercial, political, and even religious life of Israel. Hiram, king of Tyre, was a devoted friend of David (2 Sam. 5:11) who helped both kings in their building projects (1 Kings 5:1–12; 1 Chron. 14:1; 2 Chron. 2:3, 11), but the two kingdoms later drifted apart. The Tyrians sold Jews as slaves to the Greeks and to the Edomites (Joel 3:4–8; Amos 1:9–10).

The eleventh year in 26:1 is the eleventh year of Jehoiachin's reign—586 BC, when Jerusalem was captured. In 26:7, we learn that God will use Nebuchadnezzar to bring judgment on Tyre. He is called "a king of kings," making him a type of the Antichrist. As Nebuchadnezzar ruled the kings of the ancient world, the Antichrist will stand in authority, ruling the world until the true King of kings arrives, making quick work of him (Gen. 3:15; Rev. 20:1–3).

The prophecies in chapters 26–28 were fulfilled literally and with unmistakable clarity (Isaiah 23; Jer. 47:4), reminding us that everything in the Word of God will come to pass. What a blessed promise and a stern warning!

SPECIFIC REFERENCES TO THE DAY OF THE LORD:

24:25– "In the day when I take from them their strength"

24:26– "That he that escapeth in that day shall come unto thee"

24:27– "In that day shall thy mouth be opened to him which is escaped"

26:18– "Now shall the isles tremble in the day of thy fall"

26:20– "I shall set glory in the land of the living"

27:27– "In the day of thy ruin"

CHRIST IS REVEALED:

As the *One who "shall set glory in the land of the living"* – Ezekiel 26:20

52 WEEKS OF PURSUIT

WEEK 36, DAY 4: TODAY'S READING: EZEKIEL 28-32

OVERVIEW:
God's judgment upon the prince of Tyrus (chapter 28); God's judgment upon Pharaoh (chapter 29); God's judgment upon Egypt (chapter 30); the fall of Assyria (chapter 31); a lamentation for Pharoah/Egypt (chapter 32).

HIGHLIGHTS & INSIGHTS:
Chapter 28 concludes God's judgment against Tyre. The passage has been dated shortly before the siege of Tyre by Nebuchadnezzar (585–573 BC). The prince of Tyre was Ithobal II, whose arrogance is demonstrated by the fact that he actually considered himself to be God (28:2). But there are several other interesting facts revealed in this passage.

- If the pride of this prince sounds familiar, it should. It was being fueled by the same being who at one time said, "I will be like the most high" (Isa. 14:12–14; Ezek. 28:16–17). The specific imagery and wording in this passage reveals that the judgment applies not only to the historical rule of Tyre, but also to Lucifer himself! See more on this below.

- Ezekiel mentions that this prince was "wiser than Daniel" (28:3), which indicates that some supernatural power was obviously enabling him. But it also indicates that Daniel was well-known throughout the world by this time. When Ezekiel made this statement, Daniel would have already served in Nebuchadnezzar's court for about 25 years.

- Ezekiel states that this "prince" has been successful in accumulating wealth, but also reveals that it was his pride that brought about God's judgment (28:6). The prince's death is prophesied in 28:10: "Thou shalt die the deaths of the uncircumcised by the hand of strangers: for I have spoken it, saith the Lord God." The invasion of Tyre by Babylon was also prophesied in Jeremiah 27:1–7.

"Moreover" (28:11) marks a transition in this account, revealing that Ezekiel is about to go further in his condemnation of the ruler who is referred to as "the king" in 28:12, rather than "the prince" (28:2). While *king* and *prince* are often used interchangeably in Scripture, secular history does not record a king of Tyre, only a prince. Why the distinction? Why did Ezekiel change terms? Because of who this king actually is.

He is said to be "full of wisdom, and perfect in beauty" (28:12). While this description could refer to a mortal man in some sense, the next phrase cannot. This earthly king had not and could not have been "in Eden the garden of God" (v. 13). Some scholars suggest that Ezekiel simply meant a garden so beautiful it could be compared to Eden. But that is not what the text says. This king to whom the Lord was speaking had literally been in Eden! It is apparent the Lord is no longer speaking to *the physical ruler of* Tyre, but to the *spiritual ruler* who was working through him! Through Ezekiel, He is speaking to someone who actually had been in Eden over 3,000 years earlier—King Lucifer (Satan) himself! And this is not the only time in Scripture when the Lord spoke "to Satan" as he was speaking to a literal, physical man! Looking directly at Peter and responding to what Peter had just said, Jesus said, "Get thee behind me, Satan" (Matt. 16:22–23). Obviously, Peter had not at that moment turned into Satan incarnate; rather, Jesus was speaking to the spiritual power that was operating through him at that moment. This is what is happening in Ezekiel 28.

Ezekiel 28:11–17 provides a very enlightening description of Lucifer (his name means "light-bearer") before his fall. God had created him with precious stones and musical instruments woven into his very being (v. 13). The precious stones obviously allowed him to fulfill his role as "light-bearer," reflecting and refracting the light of God into a rainbow of color throughout the universe. The musical instruments were apparently given so that he might fulfill his role as the worship leader of the sons of God. He provided the music as the sons of God would sing in praise to the Lord (Job 38:7).

Verse 14 also refers to Lucifer as the "anointed cherub," the epitome of perfection until iniquity was found in him. In Isaiah 14:13–14, we saw that his iniquity was expressed through five "I Will" statements:

- "I will ascend into heaven"
- "I will exalt my throne above the stars of God"
- "I will sit also upon the mount of the congregation, in the sides of the north"
- "I will ascend above the heights of the clouds"
- "I will be like the most High"

But this ruler of Tyre not only pictures Lucifer; he is also a type of the coming Antichrist. He is described as a man (28:2), a prophet (28:3), a king (28:2, 12), and a priest, symbolized by the precious stones which the priests wore in the Old Testament (28:13). This ruler represents the presence of Satan (who was once in Eden), personified through a man who will seek to counterfeit the offices of a prophet, priest, and king. In 28:17–19, the judgment upon this man is also revealed. God will bring "fire from the midst of thee" to devour him, and he will be reduced to ashes and scattered for the world to see (v. 18). God declares, "Never shalt thou be anymore" (28:19). The Man who is the rightful Prophet, Priest, and King—the very God-Man Himself—will defeat him! This chapter ends with a promise to Israel concerning the millennial reign of this Man, our glorious Lord Jesus Christ (28:25–26).

Chapters 29–32 record God's judgment against the nation of Egypt. Contrary to God's instruction, Israel had turned to Egypt for help against Babylon (Jer. 42:14–22; 43:7–11). Egypt had succeeded in causing the Babylonians to lift the siege against Jerusalem (Jer. 37:5–7), but in time, Egypt returned to their homeland, and Jerusalem was invaded and burned (Jer. 37:8–10).

In 29:17–20, God once again condemns Egypt and uses Nebuchadnezzar to accomplish His will. Historically, Nebuchadnezzar was running out of resources as he waged war against Tyre (29:18). God empowered him to conquer the land of Egypt, and Nebuchadnezzar used the spoils to pay his army to continue to fight. Chapter 29 ends with a prophecy concerning the Lord Jesus Christ, describing Him as "the horn of the house of Israel" that would "bud forth" (29:21).

In chapter 31, God again addresses Satan by speaking to a man. This time, the man was Pharaoh (31:1–9). In this passage, God likens Satan to a tree in Eden that stood above all of the other trees (31:5) and talks about how the other trees of Eden envied him (31:8–9). During this same time period, Daniel also uses the metaphor of a tree to describe Nebuchadnezzar, who is a type of the Antichrist (Dan. 4:10).

God speaks to Satan by addressing the Gentile leaders of these Gentile nations (Tyre, Babylon, Egypt) because the Antichrist's kingdom will be a conglomeration of Gentile nations united during the Tribulation to destroy Israel and rule this world (Ps. 2:2–3; Rev. 12). God is continually reminding him (Satan) that one day, both he and his kingdom will be destroyed. As a preview of Satan's future judgment, God does what He says He will do, bringing each of these Gentile nations to ashes. The entire Bible is all about a battle for a kingdom, and God continues to remind Satan, and us, of exactly how the story is going to end!

SPECIFIC REFERENCES TO THE DAY OF THE LORD:

29:21– "In that day will I cause the horn of the house of Israel to bud forth"

30:2– "Howl ye, Woe worth the day!"

30:3– "For the day is near, even the day of the Lord is near, a cloudy day"

30:9– "In that day shall messengers go forth from me"

30:18– "The day shall be darkened, when I shall break there the yokes of Egypt"

32:10– "In the day of thy fall"

CHRIST IS REVEALED:

As the *Horn of the house of Israel* – Ezekiel 29:21

52 WEEKS OF PURSUIT

WEEK 36, DAY 5: TODAY'S READING: EZEKIEL 33-36

OVERVIEW:
The responsibility of the watchman and the fall of Jerusalem (chapter 33); wicked shepherds and God's Shepherd (chapter 34); judgment against Edom (chapter 35); the restoration of Israel (chapter 36).

HIGHLIGHTS & INSIGHTS:
God told Ezekiel, "So thou, O son of man, I have set thee a watchman unto the house of Israel" (33:7). A watchman's job was to warn the people. If they did not listen, they were responsible for the outcome. But if the watchman did not do his duty, he would be held accountable. God is reminding Ezekiel that it is not up to him to change the hearts of the people. It is, however, his responsibility to proclaim His truth.

Because of Ezekiel's warning, the children of Israel considered their situation hopeless. However, God still offered mercy. Reading all of Jeremiah's and Ezekiel's prophecies against Israel, it may seem that God takes pleasure in inflicting judgment on His people. Nothing could be further from the truth! God reminds Ezekiel (and us) that He takes no pleasure in the death of the wicked. He desires the wicked would repent and live (33:10–11).

We must also recognize our responsibility to our lost friends and neighbors. Like Ezekiel, we are seated on the wall of a city, as it were, knowing God's judgment is imminent. Those asleep in the city are our family, friends, neighbors, and co-workers. God forbid that we would be silent. We are to warn those on a collision course with God's wrath to turn from their sin to Christ (1 Thess. 1:9–10) and begin walking in the statutes of life and live (Ezek. 33:11–16). Who have we warned of God's impending judgment this week? With whom have we shared the incredible message of God's mercy and grace through the gospel of Christ?

Chapter 33 also reveals the unfathomable depths of man's pride. Rather than responding to Ezekiel's message in repentance, the children of Israel had the audacity to question God's fairness in how He exercises judgment (33:17–20). This is a typical response of man to the reproof of God's message. To this day, we hear questions such as "How could a loving God send people to hell?" Such questions are man's attempt to refuse responsibility for his own sin. God makes clear that, despite their criticism of Him, every man will be judged after his own ways (33:20).

For years, Ezekiel had warned that Jerusalem would eventually fall to Babylon. In 33:21, a refugee from Jerusalem notified Ezekiel that it had finally happened. Before the messenger arrived, however, Ezekiel knew that Jerusalem had fallen. The night before the messenger arrived, God had revealed this truth to Ezekiel (33:22–29). Ezekiel then warns those who were spared in the destruction of Jerusalem and scattered in the land that they were still in the path of God's impending judgment (33:27–28).

Chapter 33 ends with God revealing to Ezekiel that the people were talking against him (v. 30). God essentially tells Ezekiel, "Sure, multitudes all flock together to be in your presence. And it looks like they're hanging on every word. And it looks like something wonderful is taking place. But they're not going to do a single thing you tell 'em!" God explains, "Oh, they talk a big game about how much they love, but their hearts have no interest whatsoever in following Me or My ways. Their only desire is following after their own covetousness. The only thing they really love is themselves!" Basically, Ezekiel is entertainment for them; nothing he said would change the way the people lived. I know it sounds negative, but what God is describing sounds like what happens to many pastors in these last days! Still, God tells Ezekiel, once His judgment comes to pass, His people would know a prophet had been among them (33:31–33).

In chapter 34, Ezekiel condemns Israel's leaders. Instead of protecting and providing for God's people, they had only served themselves. They had failed to care for God's people and meet their needs (34:2–6), and as a result, the children of Israel had been scattered (vs. 5–6). But God says that He would personally seek out His lost sheep and save them (34:11–16; Matt. 9:36). There is still a future restoration for the children of Israel. God promises that He will set up "one shepherd ... even my servant David" (34:23–24). This refers to the Shepherd who would come from David's lineage, our Lord Jesus Christ (John 10:11), specifically to Christ's ministry during His millennial reign.

Chapter 35 is a prophecy against Edom or Seir (Gen. 32:3). Mount Seir is the mountainous area settled by the Edomites. This prophecy has already been fulfilled. Edom was defeated by Babylon, then by Medo-Persia, and finally in 126 BC by John Hyrcanus, the Hasmonean, who compelled the Edomites to become Jewish proselytes. Since that time, there has been no trace of the Edomites.

Chapter 36 speaks to the restoration of Israel. Even in the midst of their exile and judgment, God asks creation to remember His promise to them (36:1). Because of their disobedience, Israel would be scattered, but after that, He would gather the children of Israel out of all of the countries of the world and bring them again into their own land (36:24). This was fulfilled in 1948 when the Jews returned to their homeland after World War II. Prior to 1948, many scholars scoffed at the idea that Israel would be physically gathered together again, but after 1948, it isn't hard to see at all. In the history of civilization, no people, except the Jews, has been able to maintain their identity without a homeland. The Jews were miraculously able to do it, however, so that this specific prophecy could be fulfilled! The restoration of Israel is one of the greatest proofs that the Bible is, in fact, God's Word.

Ezekiel 36:25–38 speaks to the restoration of Israel in the millennium. Recognize that we are presently living in that tiny space between Ezekiel 36:24 and 36:25. "But this I say, brethren, the time is short" (1 Cor. 7:29).

SPECIFIC REFERENCES TO THE DAY OF THE LORD

34:12– "In the day that he is among his sheep that are scattered"

36:33– "In the day that I shall have cleansed you from all your iniquities"

CHRIST IS REVEALED:

As the *One Shepherd* – Ezekiel 34:23–24 (1 Pet. 5:4)

52 WEEKS OF PURSUIT

WEEK 37, DAY 1: TODAY'S READING: EZEKIEL 37-40

OVERVIEW:
The resurrection of Israel (Chapter 37); God's Judgment against Gog (chapters 38–39); Ezekiel's vision of the millennial temple (chapter 40).

HIGHLIGHTS & INSIGHTS:
Chapter 37 continues a series of prophecies given to Ezekiel the night before the messenger in Ezekiel 33:21–22 arrived. God knew that Israel's heart would faint once they knew that Jerusalem had been destroyed and the temple burned. God takes Ezekiel to a valley full of dry bones and asks if the bones can live again. (If the children of Israel didn't believe in an individual resurrection, as some liberal scholars suggest, this vision would have no meaning.) Ezekiel is commanded to prophesy to the bones (v. 4) and to the wind (v. 9), and after he does, the bones are resurrected before his very eyes. God explains the meaning of the vision in 37:11–14. These bones represent the whole house of Israel being resurrected as a nation.

The Jews were cut off from their homeland, defeated and without hope. Nevertheless, God gives Israel hope. He gives them His Word. He promises that Israel, as a nation, will be resurrected (Isa. 66:8). God tells Ezekiel to join together sticks on which he has written the names of the parts of Israel, illustrating that Israel will be one nation (37:15–19). The rest of the chapter looks forward to the millennium.

Chapters 38–39 tell of a northern confederacy of nations (38:6, 15) who will invade the Promised Land and wage war against Israel (38:16). The phrases "after many days" and "latter years" (38:8) indicate that this prophecy is tied to the Second Coming of Christ (39:11). The nations will be led by the Antichrist (Rev. 12:1-3) and will receive God's fury and wrath (Ezek. 38:18–23). It will take Israel seven months to bury the dead (39:12)! God also tells Ezekiel to call the carrion birds and carnivorous animals to consume the fallen flesh (39:17; Rev. 19:21). Chapter 39 ends with God's promise to never hide His face from Israel again (v. 29), a reference to the beginning of the millennial kingdom.

Introduction to Ezekiel 40-48

The last section of Ezekiel contains specific details about Christ's millennial reign, more than all other Old Testament prophecies combined. The vivid descriptions of the millennial temple and reinstated rituals and sacrifices must be approached as we have approached the rest of the book—literally! Ezekiel, a priest, is speaking of a literal temple and literal sacrifices in a literal future kingdom. Of course, the reinstatement of the temple and sacrifices doesn't nullify or diminish the finished work of Christ on the cross. Just as the Old Testament sacrifices pointed forward to the cross, the millennial sacrifices will point back to the cross. These last nine chapters break down as follows:

- The New Temple (40:1–43:12)
- The New Worship (43:13–47:12)
- The New Appointment of Land (47:13–48:35)

Ezekiel began with a vision of Christ at the Second Coming and ends with a vision of Christ in the millennial kingdom.

SPECIFIC REFERENCES TO THE DAY OF THE LORD

38:14– "In that day when my people of Israel dwelleth safely"

39:8– "This is the day whereof I have spoken"

39:11– "And it shall come to pass in that day"

CHRIST IS REVEALED:
The *Man* – Ezekiel 40:3.

52 WEEKS OF PURSUIT

WEEK 37, DAY 2: **TODAY'S READING: EZEKIEL 41-44**

OVERVIEW:
Measurements of millennial temple (chapter 41); measurements of the temple chambers (chapter 42); God's glory returns to the temple (chapter 43); the priests (chapter 44).

HIGHLIGHTS & INSIGHTS:
Chapters 41 and 42 describe the specific measurements of the temple. Note that it is Christ alone, not Ezekiel, who enters the most holy place of the temple (41:3–4), just as it was Christ alone who entered the most holy place to make atonement for our sin (Heb. 9:8, 12; 10:19).

The side chambers will be the priest's quarters in the millennial temple (41:5–11), a reminder of the priesthood of all believers, a key New Testament doctrine. In the Old Testament, only a select group of men offered sacrifices as Levitical priests in accordance with the law. Those priests were pictures of our great High Priest, the Lord Jesus Christ, who by His one sacrifice for sin ended the need for a Levitical priesthood. In the New Testament, because of Christ's sacrifice, He has now made those of us who have called upon His name for salvation part of a new priesthood—the priesthood of all believers.

Peter said in 1 Peter 2:9: "But ye are a chosen generation, a royal priesthood, an holy nation, a peculiar people; that ye should shew forth the praises of him who hath called you out of darkness into his marvellous light." In Revelation 1:5–6, John said: "Unto him that loved us, and washed us from our sins in his own blood, And hath made us kings and priests unto God and his Father." Peter said that we are Christ's "holy priesthood, to offer up spiritual sacrifices, acceptable to God by Jesus Christ" (1 Pet. 2:5). And there are at least seven spiritual sacrifices referred to in Scripture:

1. The sacrifice of praise (Heb. 13:15; Ps. 54:6; Jer. 33:11)
2. The sacrifice of thanksgiving (Ps. 107:22; 116:17; Heb. 13:15)
3. The sacrifice of doing good and communicating to other's needs (Heb. 13:16)
4. The sacrifice of our body (Rom. 12:1)
5. The sacrifice of a broken spirit (Ps. 51:17)
6. The sacrifice of righteousness (Ps. 4:5; 51:19; Deut. 33:19)
7. The sacrifice of faith (Phil. 2:17)

In light of these sacrifices, we must ask ourselves, "Am I fulfilling my role in bringing glory to God as a New Testament priest?"

The galleries mentioned in Ezekiel 41:15–20 were buildings decorated with palm trees and cherubim. Between the palm trees was a cherub with two faces: the face of a man and the face of a lion. These faces obviously represent both the *humanity* and *kingship* of our Lord Jesus Christ who was one hundred percent *man* and one hundred percent *God*! The altar of incense is described in Ezekiel 41:21–26 (Exod. 30:1–3). The incense represents the prayers of God's people (Ps. 141:2).

There is no reference to the Ark of the Covenant in the millennial temple. This is a direct fulfillment of Jeremiah 3:16–17: "And it shall come to pass, when ye be multiplied and increased in the land, in those days, saith the Lord, they shall say no more, The ark of the covenant of the Lord: neither shall it come to mind: neither shall they remember it; neither shall they visit it; neither shall that be done any more. At that time they shall call Jerusalem the throne of the Lord; and all the nations shall be gathered unto it, to the name of the Lord, to Jerusalem: neither shall they walk any more after the imagination of their evil heart." There will be no need for the Ark as a type of Christ in the temple, for Christ Himself will be sitting on the throne of His glory in the temple during the millennium!

Chapter 42 contains specific measurements of the court temple chambers (vs. 1–12), details concerning the use of the chambers by the priests (vs. 13–14), and the measurement of the outer wall and entire complex (vs.15–20). The walls in the millennial temple will be about one mile on each side, which means that the millennial temple will not fit on the current Mount Moriah (where Solomon's temple stood). This will require a modification of the land. Zechariah prophesied about this change: "And the Lord shall be king over all the earth: in that day shall there be one Lord, and his name one. All the land shall be turned as a plain from Geba to Rimmon south of Jerusalem" (Zech. 14:9–10).

Chapter 43 must be understood in the context of Ezekiel's previous prophecy. Earlier in the book, God's glory had departed from the temple (10:19; 11:23). Here, God's glory returns to a future physical temple (43:1–5). Praise God for His mercy and grace and His passion for the glory of His own name! (See Ezek. 20:9, 14, 22, 44; 36:23; 39:7, 25.)

As we said in Week 35, Day 4, God always intended for his name to dwell in all of its glory in the temple and, therefore, God's enemy (and ours) has always hated it. The enemy hated Solomon's temple; it was ultimately burned by Babylon. The enemy hated Herod's temple; it was ultimately burned by Rome. The enemy hated Christ, who was the personification of the temple (Matt. 12:6; John 2:19), and He was crucified by Rome. God has now made us His temple where He has set His name (1 Cor. 6:19–20), so now we are the enemy's target. Satan seeks to devour us (1 Pet. 5:8) because he wants to devour the glory that God is worthy of receiving from the temple of our lives. At times, he may even be successful! But just as God's glory will return to the physical temple, God can restore the lives that the enemy has destroyed—for His glory! And unlike the physical temples of the Old Testament, God will never leave us (Heb. 13:5; Eph. 4:30).

Chapter 44 deals with regulations for the priests who will serve in the millennial temple. Once again, as the priesthood of believers, we find numerous pictures of how we should minister in our priesthood.

"The prince" is referred to at least fourteen times in chapters 44–47. He is permitted to enter through the porch of the eastern gate, the same gate through which the Messiah has entered! He cannot be the Messiah, however, since he offers a sacrifice for his own sin (45:22; Heb. 4:15). We cannot be sure about his identity. He is most likely a descendant of David. Some believe he may even be David himself! We can only speculate.

Will there be sin in the millennium? This is often a confusing question for believers. At the end of the millennium, there will be another sinful rebellion against God (Rev. 20:7–9). Who will these rebels be? They will certainly not be us! Believers in Christ from the church age will carry out our existence in the millennial kingdom in a glorified body that will be exactly like Christ's glorified body, a body incapable of committing sin (Phil. 3:21; 1 Cor. 15:53–54; Col 3:4; Rom. 8:23). Hallelujah! But there will also be Tribulation saints who will "endure to the end" of the Tribulation (Mat. 24:13), enter the millennial kingdom in mortal bodies, and will continue to have children and further populate the millennial kingdom. These will be born with a sin nature and must willingly choose to receive Christ. When Satan is loosed for that little season at the end of the millennium, they will make their choice. Sadly, and might I add, unbelievably, there will be those who will ultimately reject Christ. Why? For the same reason people reject Christ today. They simply refuse to submit to Christ's Lordship (Luke 19:14).

CHRIST IS REVEALED:

As the *One who enters the most holy place* – Ezekiel 41:3–4 (Heb. 9:8, 12)

52 WEEKS OF **PURSUIT**

WEEK 37, DAY 3: **TODAY'S READING: EZEKIEL 45–48**

OVERVIEW:
The allotment of land for the priests and the millennial temple (chapter 45); offerings and sacrifices during the millennium (chapter 46); the waters of the land healed and the land divided (chapters 47–48).

HIGHLIGHTS & INSIGHTS:
Chapter 45 begins with an allotment of land to be offered to the Lord during the millennium (45:1–8). This land will cover about eight square miles. A rectangle of 25,000 x 10,000 cubits in the middle will be for the temple and the dwelling place for the priests. A similar rectangle to the north will be for the Levites, and on the south, a rectangle of 25,000 x 5,000 cubits will be reserved for the city itself. (A "cubit" is an ancient linear unit based on the length of the forearm from the elbow to the tip of the middle finger. It is usually given as 17–21 inches, or 43–53 cm.)

Ezekiel's description makes it clear that the temple will be the focal point of the land. It will be surrounded by an area for the priests on the east and west, an area for the Levites on the north, with the city located to the south. An area for the prince (discussed in yesterday's reading) will exist outside the domain of the priests. After detailing the layout of the land, Ezekiel admonishes the priests of his day to execute judgment and justice by ceasing to take advantage of the people (45:9–12). The sinful conduct to which the priests had grown accustomed will certainly have no place in the millennial kingdom.

Ezekiel 45:13–17 records the offerings Israel will give to the prince. The prince in turn will make provision for the sacrifices for public worship. The remainder of the chapter (45:18–20) records the institution of a new festival to start the new year with an emphasis on holiness, as well as the reinstitution of the Passover and the Feast of Tabernacles (45:21–25). The offerings in the millennial temple will be much richer and more abundant than those under the law.

Chapter 46 deals with the offerings and sacrifices to be offered during the millennium as well as the reinstitution of the Sabbath (46:1). The Sabbath is an entirely Jewish observance—it was never intended to be kept by anyone other than a Jew (Rev. 2:9b). God clearly reveals that it was a sign that He instituted specifically and exclusively between Himself and the nation of Israel (Ezek. 20:12; Deut. 5:14–15). As people who comprise the Lord's church, for us to try to incorporate the Sabbath into our worship makes us false worshippers (John 4:23). It will be on the Sabbath when the prince will enter through the eastern gate of the inner court to lead the children of Israel in worship (46:12).

Ezekiel 46:16–17 teaches that if the prince gives an inheritance to his sons it is permanent, but a gift given to a servant lasts only to the year of Jubilee. What an incredible picture that paints for us because, praise God, His Prince (our Lord Jesus Christ, Acts 3:15; 5:31) deals with us as sons and not as servants (Gal. 4:7; Rom. 8:14).

Ezekiel is now escorted once again to the door of the temple (47:1). Waters issue forth from the entrance, symbolizing that all blessings flow from the presence of the Lord (James 1:17). God then heals and transforms the waters of the Dead Sea, a body of water formerly unable to support life, into a living sea of fresh water (47:6–12). It is an incredible picture that we were once a body incapable of supporting life, but now we have been spiritually healed and transformed by the power of God, no longer dead in trespasses and sins (Eph. 2:1).

The remainder of this chapter (47:13–23) and chapter 48 deal with the dividing of the land. In chapter 47, the strangers (non-Jews) living during the millennium are included (47:21–23). The Mosaic Law did not permit the stranger to acquire land, but it will be permissible during the millennium. The right is extended to those who will settle permanently in the land of promise, having children there. Again, there will be children born during the millennium.

In chapter 48 we see the distribution of the Promised Land for the millennial age. All the tribal portions extend across the breadth of the land. All the tribes are west of the Jordan, with a central tract of land separated for the temple, the city, and the prince's land (discussed in chapter 45).

Dan is the first tribe mentioned in regard to the distribution of the land. But when the Apostle John lists the 12,000 from each of the 12 tribes of Israel that will comprise the 144,000 witnesses of Jehovah during the Tribulation, the tribe of Dan had been written out of the list of tribes because of their idolatry (Rev. 7:5–8). In the millennium, however, God in His grace and mercy will restore the tribe of Dan. What a beautiful truth. Our God restores what has been lost. He repairs what has been broken. He sees past our failures. Our God is all about restoration.

The book of Ezekiel began with much of Israel in exile. Nebuchadnezzar was the king of the world. Over the course of Ezekiel's life, the glory of the Lord departed from the temple, and the temple and Jerusalem were burned and destroyed. In these last nine chapters, however, God gave Ezekiel a glimpse of Israel's future. The book of Ezekiel ends with a new city, and the name of that city is "The Lord is there" (48:35). Hallelujah!

SPECIFIC REFERENCES TO THE DAY OF THE LORD

45:22– "And upon that day"

48:35– "The name of the city from that day shall be, The Lord is there"

CHRIST IS REVEALED:

As *Waters of life coming forth form the presence of God* – Ezekiel 47:1 (John 4:14)

WEEK 37, DAY 4: **TODAY'S READING: DANIEL 1-3**

OVERVIEW:
Daniel and his friends are taken captive in Babylon away from their families (chapter 1); Nebuchadnezzar's dream and Daniel's interpretation (chapter 2); the image of gold erected by Nebuchadnezzar and the refusal of Daniel's three friends to bow down and worship it (chapter 3).

HIGHLIGHTS & INSIGHTS:
Since the Jews refused to heed Jeremiah's passionate call to repent and follow the Lord in obedience, the Babylonian army came and conquered their land just as Jeremiah had warned. In those days, it was customary for a conquering nation to take the very best and most promising youth from the conquered land to be trained in the king's court. Since Daniel and his three teenage friends were all princes of the royal family (1:3), they were snatched from their homes in Jerusalem and taken to the king of Babylon's palace. The goal was to conform them to the ways of Babylon, that they might serve in his kingdom for the rest of their lives. As Daniel 1:4b–7 describes, this process involved a new home, new knowledge, new diets, and new names. Satan's strategy is still the same today! He is bent on conforming God's people (especially young people!) to the kingdom of this present evil world's system that they might serve his purposes for the rest of their lives (Rom. 12:1–2; 2 Tim. 2:26).

Showing unbelievable courage and maturity, Daniel and his friends purposed in their heart that they would not defile themselves with the king's meat (1:8). They dared to stand for what they believed to be true and right even though it meant possible death. Of course, risking their own lives was one thing. But their decision also risked the life of Melzar, the king's steward who controlled the diets of the Hebrew children. If their physical appearance indicated they were not following the king's directions, it would mean his neck as well as theirs (1:10). Daniel believed God would honor their refusal to eat the king's meat. He asked Melzar, in whom he had found favor, for a ten-day trial of eating vegetables and water to prove that God would step up on their behalf. Ten days later, their countenances were much healthier than those who ate the king's prescribed diet. We often talk about the law of sowing and reaping (Gal. 6:7–8) from a negative standpoint; this is a positive example of the principle! Because of the great faith these young men sowed at this point in their life, they reaped God's promotion and protection in the worldly kingdom of Babylon throughout the remainder of their lives!

In chapter 2, Nebuchadnezzar has a dream. He demands that his wise men interpret it, after telling him what the dream actually was! None knew the dream, of course, so Nebuchadnezzar ordered all the wise men to be slain. Daniel asks the king for time, and that night, God revealed the dream and its interpretation to Daniel. He tells the king the dream, sparing the lives of the wise men from certain death. Nebuchadnezzar is impressed and pleased with Daniel, and to show his appreciation, he promotes Daniel and his three friends to key positions of authority in his kingdom. The dream that Daniel interpreted was actually a prophetic outline of world history. It describes the kingdoms and governments that would rule the world from Babylon all the way to this present day (2:28). Without the prophecies in the book of Daniel, it would be impossible to interpret the book of Revelation. The two books go hand in hand (1 Cor. 2:13).

Chapter 3 takes place about twenty years after Nebuchadnezzar's dream. While Nebuchadnezzar had acknowledged that Jehovah God is the "God of gods, and a Lord of kings" (2:47), he evidently suffered a major lapse in memory in that intervening years. In this chapter he sets up a golden image of himself and requires every person in the entire kingdom to bow before it and worship it. This poses a major problem for Shadrach, Meshach, and Abednego (the Babylonian names of Daniel's three Hebrew friends). If they were so surrendered to God's Word that they refused to eat the king's meat, they certainly would have no part in bowing down before the king's image! (Daniel must have been away from the kingdom at the time the image was set up because his uncompromising and godly character most certainly proves that he would have been among those who refused to bow down to the image!) They refused to bow to his golden image, and Nebuchadnezzar cast them into the fiery furnace. In the midst of the furnace, there is an incredible pre-incarnate appearance of the Lord Jesus Christ, the fourth man in the fire, who protected them not only from the flames, but from the very smell of smoke! Nebuchadnezzar was again reminded of the power of Jehovah God and made a decree stating that it was illegal for anyone to speak against Him! He also promoted these three men in his kingdom.

CHRIST IS REVEALED:

As the *Stone* – Daniel 2:35, 45 (Eph. 2:20; 1 Pet. 2:6–7; Rom. 9:31–33)

As the *Fourth Man in the fire* – Daniel 3:25

52 WEEKS OF PURSUIT

WEEK 37, DAY 5: **TODAY'S READING: DANIEL 4-6**

OVERVIEW:
Nebuchadnezzar's tree dream and Daniel's interpretation (chapter 4); Belshazzar and the handwriting of God on the wall (chapter 5); Daniel and the lion's den (chapter 6).

HIGHLIGHTS & INSIGHTS:
In chapter 4, Nebuchadnezzar has another dream. This time he dreamed about a huge tree overshadowing the entire earth before an angelic voice ordered it to be cut down. Once again, the king summoned his wise men to interpret the dream, but none could, so once again, Daniel, the man of God, provides the interpretation. After hearing the dream, Daniel was reluctant to declare the troubling interpretation, sitting in complete silence for a solid hour. The dream dealt with some pretty disconcerting things the king would be encountering in his near future.

The dream's interpretation was not difficult. The tree represented Nebuchadnezzar and his mighty kingdom, and the tree would be cut down because Nebuchadnezzar did not give God the glory even after beholding all of the things God had done. Not only would Nebuchadnezzar lose his position, but he would be forced to live like a beast of the field for seven years. Those seven horrific years were intended to teach Nebuchadnezzar humility, but even after hearing and believing the interpretation, he continued with his prideful boasting (4:30).

While his boastful words were still in his mouth, the interpretation began to be fulfilled. For seven years he lived as a beast. After those seven long years, he finally "lifted up [his] eyes unto heaven ... and blessed the most high" (4:34). Though it took drastic measures to finally flush out Nebuchadnezzar's pride, this chapter is essentially the story of Nebuchadnezzar's conversion! Our God is, indeed, merciful!

Nebuchadnezzar's powerful statement in 4:37 serves as a practical warning: "Those that walk in pride [God] is able to abase." But don't miss that this chapter is also a preview of what will befall the nations of the world in the latter days. As the nations boast of their greatness and glory, God will send seven years of judgment upon them, bringing them extremely low. Then, at the end of the Tribulation, Christ will return to the earth to establish His millennial kingdom. The nations that have trusted Him will enter into the glorious kingdom while the others will be abased.

In chapter 5, Daniel is about eighty years old, and Belshazzar, Nebuchadnezzar's grandson, is now king. Apparently, Belshazzar did not worship the one true God of heaven, as we find him throwing a party in honor of one of the Babylonian gods. He was not content to simply drink wine in honor of his gods; he also feels the need to blaspheme the God of the Jews (and the whole earth) by using the sacred temple vessels in his idolatrous and blasphemous feast (5:3–4). Just then, a mysterious hand appeared and wrote a secret message on the wall, causing Belshazzar to shake uncontrollably in fear (5:6). Again, the king's experts could not interpret the message, and the king was even more freaked out (5:9).

The queen hears that God had crashed her wicked husband's party and tells him that Daniel could most certainly interpret the writing. Obviously, Belshazzar was oblivious to both Daniel and his God! Daniel is summoned, and as we'd expect, he uses his God-given spiritual wisdom to provide the interpretation. Three key words—numbered, weighed, divided—summarize God's message to Belshazzar in the infamous "handwriting on the wall" (a phrase that to this day refers to imminent disaster). Belshazzar's days were *numbered*, and his time was up! He had been *weighed* on God's scales and found wanting! And his kingdom would be taken from him and *divided* by the Medes and Persians.

There is no evidence that Belshazzar actually believed Daniel or repented or showed concern, for that matter! He did keep his promise to Daniel, promoting him to third in command, as if his kingdom would continue forever. That same night, Belshazzar was slain, and the Medes and Persians took the kingdom just as God had said (5:30–31).

Chapter 6 deals with a day in the life of Daniel, the prime minister of the Medo-Persian empire. God had honored Daniel's faithfulness through many different kings and kingdoms. But ever since Cain and Abel, the wicked have hated the righteous, a fact proven again by the events in this chapter. The other leaders of the land manipulate the king to pass a law prohibiting any man from petitioning no god or man except the king for a period of thirty days. This was a trap specifically designed to ensnare Daniel. They knew he prayed to his God three times every day, and they knew he would continue regardless of the law, choosing to obey God rather than men (6:10; Acts 5:29). After hearing of this new law, just as His conspirators suspected, Daniel fearlessly continued his pattern of prayer just as before! Though the king loved and respected Daniel, because of the law, he was forced to cast Daniel into the lion's den, even against his own inner desires (6:14). The law simply could not be reversed, even by the king himself (6:15).

Daniel was placed into the lion's den. King Darius spent a sleepless night of fasting (6:16–18). When morning finally arrived, much to the king's delight, Daniel's God had miraculously spared him from the mouths of the lions (6:19–23). The men who had accused Daniel were cast into the lion's den and killed (6:24). The king then made a decree stating that Daniel's God was the one true God and that He was to feared and followed (6:25–27). Daniel went on to prosper in the kingdom throughout the reign of Darius and Cyrus (6:28).

CHRIST IS REVEALED:

As *God's Angel sent to shut the lion's mouths* – Daniel 6:22 (Rev. 20:3; 1 Pet. 5:8; Heb. 11:33)

WEEK 38, DAY 1: **TODAY'S READING: DANIEL 7-9**

OVERVIEW:
Daniel's vision of the four great beasts (chapter 7); Daniel's vision of the ram and the he-goat (chapter 8); Daniel's 70 weeks (chapter 9).

HIGHLIGHTS & INSIGHTS:
Until now, Daniel has been interpreting dreams for others. In chapter 7, God gives him extraordinary visions of his own. His first vision is of four great beasts that came up from the sea. An angel explains this dream to Daniel. Each beast represented a kingdom:

- **The Lion with wings:** the Babylonian empire (7:4). Babylon was ruling at this time, but in just a few years, the empire would fall (chapter 5).

- **The Bear with ribs:** the Medo-Persion empire (7:5). The three ribs represent the three empires already defeated in history (Egypt, Babylonia, Libya). The bear stood "raised up on one side," indicating that one half of the empire (Persia) was stronger and more honorable than the other half (the Medes).

- **The four-headed, winged Leopard:** the Grecian empire (7:6). The Grecian empire was led by Alexander the Great who swiftly conquered the world, defeating the Persians in about 331 BC. Alexander died, however, in 323 BC, and his vast kingdom was divided into four parts (thus the four heads). Four of his generals took parts of the kingdom and ruled them as monarchs.

- **The terrible Beast:** the Roman empire (7:7–8, 17–27). This picture seems to go beyond history into the "latter days." We see the ten horns on the beast which parallel the ten toes of the image in chapter 2, the revived Roman Empire of the last days. Verses 8 and 20 tell us that a "little horn" (ruler) will appear and defeat three of the ten kingdoms represented by the ten horns and toes. This little horn will then become a world ruler, the Antichrist! His mouth will speak great things, and he will persecute the saints for three and a half years (7:25). God will send judgment (7:9–14, 26–28) in the person of Jesus Christ to slay this beast and set up His kingdom forever!

This vision in chapter 7 complements and supplements the one from chapter 2. Chapter 2 provides the vision of the nations from *man's* vantage point (precious metals), while the vision of chapter 7 provides the vision of the nations from *God's* vantage point (ferocious beasts). The vision in chapter 8 is actually an amplification of 7:6, explaining how Greece will conquer Medo-Persia.

Chapter 9 is the prophecy concerning Daniel's seventy weeks. While Daniel was praying, confessing his own sins and the sins of his nation, the angel Gabriel touched him and give him this prophecy concerning Jerusalem. It is a time period of seventy weeks of years (70 x 7 or 490 years). The event that begins the countdown of these 490 years is a decree that the Jews may rebuild Jerusalem (v. 25). That decree was issued by Artaxerxes in 445 BC, about one hundred years after Daniel received this prophecy (Neh. 2). Gabriel said there would be "seven weeks and threescore and two weeks" (69 x 7 or 483 years) between the decree and the coming of the Messiah. Prophetic years in the Bible are 360 days, not 365 days, so we can calculate that exactly 173,880 days (483 x 360) after the decree was issued, Jesus rode into Jerusalem on Palm Sunday! (See the book *The Coming Prince* by Sir Robert Anderson for a thorough treatment of this prophecy.) Since Messiah was rejected and cut-off as was prophesied, there remains yet one week of years to be fulfilled. This week of years is what the Bible refers to as the seven-year Tribulation or the time of Jacob's trouble. It is detailed for us in Revelation 6–19 and ends with Christ's return to take His rightful place as King of the whole earth. Amen!

CHRIST IS REVEALED:

As the *Ancient of Days* – Daniel 7:9 (John 1:1–3, 14)

As the *Son of Man* – Daniel 7:13 (Mark 10:45; Luke 6:5)

As *Messiah* – Daniel 9:25 (Matt. 16:16; 1 John 5:1)

52 WEEKS OF PURSUIT

WEEK 38, DAY 2: **TODAY'S READING: DANIEL 10-12**

OVERVIEW:
Daniel's prayer answered by God's messenger who was detained for twenty-one days by the Prince of Persia (chapter 10); prophecy of the kingdoms from Daniel's time to the Antichrist (chapter 11); the Great Tribulation (chapter 12).

HIGHLIGHTS & INSIGHTS:
The first half of the book of Daniel relates the prophet's personal historic experiences. The second half focuses on his prophetic visions. God's people, the Jews, a major political and military force among the Gentiles since the days of Joshua, now find themselves under Gentile domination. But even world powers do not rise and fall without the consent of Almighty God! In a remarkable collection of prophecies, Daniel sets forth both the near and distant future of God's chosen people—a future filled with purifying judgment and blessing.

In 2 Corinthians 4:18, Paul distinguishes between two realities: the *temporal* realm (what we can see with our physical eyes) and the *eternal* realm (what we can't see). It is this realm which Elisha prayed would be revealed to his servant in 2 Kings 6:15–17. And it is this unseen realm, according to Daniel 10, where much of our spiritual warfare takes place. Daniel had been waiting for twenty-one days for an answer to his prayer. In 10:13, the angel tells Daniel that "the prince of the kingdom of Persia withstood" him, preventing him from bringing God's answer to Daniel. This "prince of Persia," one of the "principalities … powers … rulers of the darkness of this world … [and] spiritual wickedness in high places" mentioned in Ephesians 6:12, was specifically set above and against the nation of Persia (10:13, 20). Evidently, these demonic spiritual forces are highly regimented and intricately networked in their battle against God's purposes and people around the globe. Considering the reality of the warfare going on above Daniel's head during those three weeks, we have to wonder what might have happened had Daniel not fasted and prayed? And how many answers to prayer have we forfeited because of our lack of faithfulness and importunity?

The history of the Greek Empire is detailed in chapter 11. This is truly one of the most remarkable prophecies in the entire Bible. In perfect sequence, Daniel chronicled a number of future events:

- The coming of Alexander the Great
- The division of his empire into four parts
- The conflicts between Syria and Egypt
- Israel's miseries as the pawn between these two rival powers (called the "king of the north and the king of the south")
- The dark days of the tyrant, Antiochus Epiphanes. (A picture of the Antichrist)
- The intervention of Rome in the affairs of Palestine

Daniel then speaks of the last days and the coming Antichrist. Verse 20 reveals that he will be a "raiser of taxes," and many believe that verse 37 suggests that he may be a homosexual ("neither shall he regard … the desire of women"). We cannot say with absolute certainty, but, if he is a homosexual, this would appear to be the only mention of it in Scripture. We must also consider that the verse says that he will not regard the "desire *of* women," not the "desire *for* women." Certainly, *of* and *for* can be used interchangeably, but a key cross reference we pick up from the verbiage in Daniel 11:37 is Luke 1:28, when the angel Gabriel greets Mary as "thou that art highly favoured … among women," and Luke 1:42, when Elisabeth, filled with the Spirit, says, "Blessed art thou among women." It would appear that it was the desire of every Jewish maiden to be the one chosen to give birth to the Messiah. So, Daniel 11:37 may be a prophecy that the Antichrist will have no regard for the Lord Jesus Christ, the One who was "the desire of women." But again, we cannot say with absolute certainty.

In chapter 12, Daniel writes prophetically concerning the Great Tribulation, though even he doesn't understand the meaning of what he's writing (12:8). As he asks God to help him to understand, God says that the words he was writing under the inspiration of the Holy Spirit "are closed up and sealed till the time of the end" (v. 9). Which just happens to be the very time in which we are now living! In other words, we have the ability to understand the prophecies in the book of Daniel, even more than the human author of the book himself!

Regarding the "time of the end," Daniel 12:4 says that "many shall run to and fro, and knowledge shall be increased." This is an amazing prophecy considering our access to transportation (cars, trains, airplanes, space shuttles) and information (computers, cell phones, the internet) is exponentially more than what was available in Daniel's time or even 150 years ago! We are truly living in "the time of the end" (12:9). Let us purify ourselves as we await our Lord's coming (1 John 3:3), and may there be a passion in our souls to get the gospel to the lost while we still have time (Rom. 1:16; Matt. 28:19–20).

CHRIST IS REVEALED:

As the *One who lives forever* – Daniel 12:7 (John 8:58; Rev. 1:8; 4:8)

52 WEEKS OF PURSUIT

WEEK 38, DAY 3: TODAY'S READING: HOSEA 1-6

OVERVIEW:
Israel compared to an unfaithful wife (chapter 1); God seeks reconciliation with Israel (chapter 2); Hosea's reconciliation with his wife (chapter 3); God's controversy with his people (chapters 4–6).

HIGHLIGHTS & INSIGHTS:
The next section of the Old Testament is the Minor Prophets. As we have mentioned, they are minor not in content, but in length. The books of the Bible written by these twelve prophets are simply shorter than the writings of Isaiah, Jeremiah, Ezekiel, and Daniel.

A prophet was someone God called to take His side against nations and peoples ("A prophet speaketh in the name of the Lord," Deut. 18:22). For no prophet was this more true than Hosea. God asked him to do the unthinkable—marry a wife God knew would break his heart by her unfaithfulness (Hos. 1:2).

Why would God do such a thing? First, because it was a graphic *illustration*. God told Hosea, whose name means "Jehovah" or "God is salvation" (like Joshua in the Old Testament and Jesus in the New Testament), to take a wife of whoredoms to depict the unfaithfulness of Israel to the Lord, her "husband." (See Ezek. 16:8–15.)

Secondly, faithful Hosea taking an unfaithful wife was a graphic *realization*. God wanted Hosea to preach to unfaithful Israel, feeling in his heart what God felt in His. Perhaps the only way Hosea could really preach "in the name of the Lord," with the Lord's passion and compassion, was to live through the same hurt with his lover, Gomer, that God felt with His lover, Israel.

In fact, our hurts are a profound opportunity for us to do the same. Many times, God allows the circumstances of our lives to unfold as they do, not only because they fit perfectly into His sovereign plan for our lives, but to allow us to feel in our hearts what He feels in His! Putting into words what we have experienced and felt can help us recognize how what we feel is exactly what God says in His Word that He feels. The New Testament calls this "the fellowship of his sufferings" (Phil. 3:10) which, by "being made conformable unto his death," allows us to "know him, and the power of his resurrection." Unfortunately, most Christians never connect the dots between the pain they experience and what our Lord experienced ("His suffering"). They use their circumstances to justify a vengeful, angry, or bitter spirit, instead of allowing them to develop a deeper fellowship with our Lord! Though we desire to be people "after His own heart," who know Him, love Him and manifest His power (1 Sam. 13:14), we overlook the very circumstances that God would use to transform us into that exact kind of people (Rom. 8:28–29).

And finally, Gomer is a very graphic and extremely sad picture of us. When we "love the world" (1 John 2:15) or justify our "friendship [with] the world" (James 4:4), our "husband" (2 Cor. 11:2) and God of our salvation, the Lord Jesus Christ, views it as adultery (Jam. 4:4).

In chapter 1, God uses Hosea's three children to preach to Israel.

- God named his first child Jezreel, meaning "God sows" or "God scatters," to depict that God was about to scatter the nation of Israel.

- His second child, God named Loruhamah, meaning "no mercy" or "unpitied," because God would no longer extend His mercy to Israel and she (Israel) would be taken into captivity.

- The third child, God named Loammi, meaning "not my people," indicating that He no longer recognized Israel as His children. It is possible that Loammi was not Hosea's child, but a child of Gomer's whoredoms.

It would be difficult to get away from your calling if your children's names represented God's perspective on the very people you were ministering to. It would be like God asking twenty-first-century preachers to name our children *Laodicea* (meaning "the rights of the people" and "lukewarm") to depict the state of His church and His people and *Selfish* to reveal the real love of His people—"their own selves" (2 Tim. 3:2). Can you even imagine?

However, in Hosea 2:1, the Lord points to a time when the "Lo" (meaning "no" or "not" or "without") would be removed, and Israel would once again be Ammi ("my people") and Ruhamah ("having obtained mercy"). In that day, Jezreel will no longer mean "God scatters," but "God sows." God says, "And I will sow her unto me in the earth; and I will have mercy … and I will say to them which were not my people, Thou art my people; and they shall say, Thou art my God" (2:23). This will happen during the Great Tribulation, culminating with the Second Coming of Christ and the establishment of His millennial kingdom.

SPECIFIC REFERENCES TO THE DAY OF THE LORD

1:5– "And it shall come to pass at that day"

1:11– "For great shall be the day of Jezreel"

2:16– "And it shall be at that day"

2:18– "And in that day will I make a covenant"

2:21– "And it shall come to pass in that day"

5:9– "In the day of rebuke"

6:2– After two days will he revive us: in the third day he will raise us up"

CHRIST IS REVEALED:

Through *Hosea's love for his unworthy, sinful wife* – Hosea 3:1–5 (Rom. 5:8; 8:32; 2 Pet. 1:3)

52 WEEKS OF PURSUIT

WEEK 38, DAY 4: TODAY'S READING: HOSEA 7-14

OVERVIEW:
Israel's sin rebuked (chapter 7); Israel's judgment foretold (chapters 8–10); Israel's restoration promised (chapters 11–14).

HIGHLIGHTS & INSIGHTS:
Just as God had predicted, Hosea's wife, Gomer, deserted her faithful husband for other lovers, providing a painful and graphic illustration of Israel's unfaithfulness to her husband, God Himself. In chapter 3, Gomer ends up on the slave block, and God commands Hosea to go redeem her ("buy her back") and restore her as his wife. He does (and all I can say is, "What a guy!"), but remember, Hosea is a simply a picture of God, His love for Israel, and His plan to restore her as His wife. And so I say, "What a God!"

The people of Israel knew who Hosea was and what his wife had done. They, no doubt, pointed the finger at her and her many sins. They didn't realize, however, that they were pointing the finger at themselves! In 4:1–2, Hosea begins to lay out their sin, their own unfaithfulness to their Husband! Hosea describes them with several pictures:

1) A morning cloud (6:4) – As in, here one minute and gone the next.
2) A cake not turned (7:8) – We might say half-baked. In other words, their spirituality was superficial.
3) Gray hairs (7:9) – Gradually losing their strength, but unaware of the change.
4) A silly dove (7:11) – Extremely fickle, here, there, and everywhere.
5) A deceitful bow (7:16) – Appearing ready to fulfill its purpose, but unable to hit the target.

Before we are too hard on Israel, however, let's consider how many of these pictures our Lord might use to describe our relationship with Him. It is amazing how the more things change, the more things stay the same!

In chapter 8, Hosea declares that the Assyrians would come to take Israel into captivity in the near future. He likens God's judgment to the circling of an eagle (8:1), the devastation of a whirlwind (8:7), and the burning of a fire (8:14). We have seen, in the *52 Weeks of Pursuit*, the Galatians 6:7–8 principle that we reap according to what we've sown. But we actually reap *more* than we have sown! The few seeds a farmer sows multiply into a huge harvest. Israel sowed the wind, yet reaped a whirlwind (8:7; 10:13). Do we really want to reap (and in abundance) what we're presently sowing in our lives? May we learn from Israel's mistakes, just as 1 Corinthians 10:6 and 11 admonish us to do.

Chapter 9 reviews some key locations of Israel's past sins. Hosea references the deep corruption at Gibeah (9:9), the "shame" and "abominations" at Baalpeor (9:10), and the "wickedness" at Gilgal. (9:15) A life of sin leaves a trail that tells the story of how we ended up where we did.

Praise the Lord the book of Hosea doesn't end on a negative note! Just as Hosea never lost his love or his heart for his wife in spite of her unfaithfulness, God did not lose His love or His heart for Israel in spite of theirs! Just as Hosea bought his wife out of slavery to be restored in their relationship, God points to the time when He would redeem Israel out of their slavery and restore her to relationship with Him.

God reveals His heart for Israel in chapter 11. He reminds them of how He loved them from the very beginning of their relationship when He called them out of Egypt and how, from the very beginning of His marriage to them, they were "bent to backsliding" (11:7). God "drew them with … bands of love" (11:4), but they saw those bands as restrictive and wanted to be free of Him.

In chapter 14, God cries out to His wife to return to Him (14:1), saying, "I will heal their backsliding, I will love them freely: for mine anger is turned away from him" (14:4). He points to a time when the nation will be as a beautiful lily, a fruitful olive tree, and flourish as a vine (14:5–9). Again, this points to the Second Coming of Christ when our Lord Jesus Christ establishes His millennial kingdom.

SPECIFIC REFERENCES TO THE DAY OF THE LORD

9:5– "In the solemn day, and in the day of the feast of the Lord"

10:14– "In the day of battle"

CHRIST IS REVEALED:

In *Israel*, as the *Son who was called out of Egypt* – Hosea 11:1 (Matt. 2:14–15)

52 WEEKS OF PURSUIT

WEEK 38, DAY 5: **TODAY'S READING: JOEL 1–3**

OVERVIEW:
The plague of locusts; Joel's call to repentance; the great Day of the Lord; the Holy Spirit; the restoration of Israel; the judgment of the nations.

HIGHLIGHTS & INSIGHTS:
The book of Joel begins, "The word of the Lord that came to Joel the son of Pethuel" (1:1). The name Joel means "Jehovah is God," and the name Pethuel means "the sincerity of God" or "godly simplicity." The breakdown of the book of Joel is quite simple: The Day of the Lord (chapter 1), The Day of the Lord (chapter 2), The Day of the Lord (chapter 3). Clearly, we'll need to exert great mental energy to keep that outline straight.

God begins with a question: "Hath this been in your days, or even in the days of your fathers?" (1:2b). The inferred answer, of course, is no. The "days" Joel is about to describe are so devastating that no one had ever seen anything like it. Jesus said the same thing concerning the Great Tribulation: "For then shall be great tribulation, such as was not since the beginning of the world to this time, no, nor ever shall be" (Matt. 24:21).

Joel's prophecy concerning those days is a message God wanted to be handed down through each generation of a family (1:3). The first generation (1:2b) was to tell their children (second generation, 1:3a), and they were to tell their children (third generation, 1:3b), who were to tell their children (fourth generation, 1:3c). Again the Bible reminds us that, whether we want them to or not, our lives are going to impact the next four generations—negatively, as in Exodus 20:5 and 34:7, or positively, as in Psalm 78:4–7. The good news is we get to choose which it will be!

Joel 1:4 warns of the "pests" that worm their way into our lives and, slowly but surely, eat away the important things. He describes the cycle this way: What the palmerworm doesn't eat, the locust will. What the locust doesn't eat, the cankerworm will. And what the cankerworm doesn't eat, the caterpillar will. God is calling Israel (and us) to wake up and sober up (1:5) so that we can recognize the pests in our lives before it's too late and before the adversary devours the next four generations of our family (1 Pet. 5:8).

And even if we've been sleeping on our watch or have become drunk spiritually (1 Thess. 5:6–7), if we'll obey Joel 1:5 and both wake up and sober up, God can and will "restore to [us] the years that the locusts hath eaten, the cankerworm, and the caterpillar, and the palmerworm" (2:25). This is the clear Devotional application of these verses. Historically, Joel is preaching these truths to the people of Judah. Using the destruction caused by a recent locust plague as a comparison, he declares that their only escape from the judgment God was about to unleash through an invading army from the north (the Assyrians) was through repentance.

But remember, Doctrinally, the book of Joel is about the days of the Great Tribulation ("those days," 2:29; 3:1) which will lead up to "the Day of the Lord" ("that day," 1:15; 2:1–2, 11; 3:14, 18). Joel is prophesying about the judgment of God during the Tribulation when a northern confederacy of nations converges on Israel just prior to her restoration "in that day" when the Nation of Israel will finally repent and the Lord Jesus Christ will establish His millennial kingdom.

Distinguishing the three layers of application will keep us "between the lines" as we navigate this book. That is vital because a lot of false teaching is propagated out of this little book! Most of the false doctrine results because Peter quotes Joel chapter 2 when he was preaching on the Day of Pentecost in Acts 2. Peter basically says, "*This*" (the events taking place at Pentecost in Acts 2) "was *that*" (the events Joel was prophesying in Joel 2).

By failing to "rightly [divide] the word of truth" (2 Tim. 2:15), both in Joel 2 and Acts 2, however, these two chapters have been used to give credence to the modern tongues movement. That movement actually has nothing whatever to do with Joel's prophecy or the events of Acts 2 and everything to do with some crazy stuff taking place at Bethel Bible College in Topeka, Kansas, in 1901 and at the Azusa Street Mission in Los Angeles in 1906!

There are a few key things we need to make sure that we are taking note of in these two extremely misunderstood and controversial chapters...

- In Acts 2, Peter is very careful *not* to say that the speaking in tongues on the day of Pentecost was the *fulfillment* of the things Joel prophesied! He only said that Joel had *spoken* of it.
- On the day of Pentecost in Acts 2, the Spirit was *not* poured out "upon all flesh" (Joel 2:28).
- Joel doesn't mention *anything* about tongues anywhere in chapter 2!
- None of the wonders that Joel does mention in Joel 2:28 took place on the Day of Pentecost.

Had the nation of Israel exercised a national repentance on the Day of Pentecost, even up to Stephen's audience with and message to the ruling counsel of Israel in Acts 7, what took place at Pentecost could have become the fulfillment of Joel's prophecy! Because of Israel's refusal to repent, however, Joel's prophecy was put on hold and won't pick up again until the Tribulation.

SPECIFIC REFERENCES TO THE DAY OF THE LORD

1:15– "Alas for the day! for the day of the Lord is at hand"

2:1– "For the day of the Lord cometh"

2:2– "A day of darkness and of gloominess, a day of clouds and of thick darkness"

2:11– "For the day of the Lord is great and very terrible"

2:31– "Before the great and the terrible day of the Lord come"

3:14– "For the day of the Lord is near in the valley of decision"

3:18– "And it shall come to pass in that day"

CHRIST IS REVEALED:

As the *One who said, "I will pour out my spirit upon all flesh"* – Joel 2:28 (Zech. 12:10; Isa. 54:13; Ezek. 39:29)

52 WEEKS OF PURSUIT

WEEK 39, DAY 1: TODAY'S READING: AMOS 1-6

OVERVIEW:
God's judgment upon eight nations (chapters 1–2); the guilt and punishment of Israel (chapters 3–6).

HIGHLIGHTS & INSIGHTS:
One of the most beautiful things about the book of Amos was the man God chose to write it. Amos was a common, ordinary guy of average intelligence. He didn't come from a well-to-do or noble family, so there is no family pedigree in the introduction (Amos, the son of...). In fact, Amos described himself as a "herdman [sheep-breeder], and a gatherer of sycamore fruit" (7:14) to highlight that God hadn't chosen him because he was something special. Yet, God used this common, ordinary, very average man in an uncommon, extraordinary, and above-average way!

In fact, all throughout history, God has been a champion for the common man! Speaking of Jesus, Mark said, "And the common people heard him gladly" (Mark 12:37). It was the nobility and intelligencia who refused to believe and follow Jesus; they contended with Him and, ultimately, put Him to death! As Paul reminds us in 1 Corinthians 1:26: "For ye see your calling, brethren, how that not many wise men after the flesh, not many mighty, not many noble, are called." Instead, God has always taken great pleasure "[choosing] the weak things of the world to confound the things which are mighty; and the base things of the world, and things which are despised, hath God chosen, yea, and things which are not, to bring to nought things that are" (1 Cor. 1:27–28). Of course, we cannot take this principle further than God does. He doesn't say "Not *any* wise, mighty and noble are called," but "Not *many* wise, mighty and noble are called." There are some—there just aren't many!

Still, may we recognize today that God wants to do the same uncommon, extraordinary, above-average thing He did with Amos with common, ordinary, average folks like me and you! And while this point doesn't help us understand the book of Amos itself, it will help us to understand how incredibly God wants to use each of us.

Chapter 1 of the book of Amos indicates that Amos prophesied during the days when Uzziah was king in Judah and Jeroboam was king in Israel (v. 1). He was a contemporary of Hosea and his prophetic ministry happened somewhere between 783–753 BC. During this time historically, the Northern Kingdom appeared to be going extremely well. Businesses flourished, the economy was good, and the government was stable. Spiritually, however, the entire kingdom was full of idolatry, greed, injustice, immorality, pride, and hypocrisy.

In the first two chapters, Amos pronounces judgment on eight nations: Damascus of Syria (1:3), Gaza (1:6), Tyrus (1:9), Edom (1:11), Ammon (1:13), Moab (2:1), Judah (2:4), and Israel (2:6). He says that God will attack them as a "roaring lion" (1:2; 3:8) and a "consuming fire." Notice the repetition:

- "But I will send a fire..." (1:4)
- "But I will send a fire..." (1:7)
- "But I will send a fire..." (1:10)
- "But I will send a fire..." (1:12)
- "But I will kindle a fire..." (1:14)

He also repeats the phrase, "For three transgressions, and for four" (1:3, 6, 9, 11, 13; 2:1, 4, 6). Very simply, three plus four equals seven, the number of completion. God had reached the top, as it were, with the transgressions of these nations, and He was about to execute His complete judgment upon them!

In 2:6–16, Amos identifies the specific sins that had prompted God's promise of judgment upon Israel: bribery, greed, adultery, immorality, selfishness, ungratefulness, drunkenness (even forcing the

Nazarites to drink, 2:12), and rejecting God's Word. Sounds like a perfect description of the spiritual climate in our day!

In chapters 3–6, Amos delivers three sermons to identify God's purposes in this judgment. Each sermon begins the same way: "Hear this word" (3:1; 4:1; 5:1).

- In the sermon in 3:1–15, he tells the people the reason for God's judgment upon Israel.

- In his sermon in 4:1–13, Amos lists all the things God had already sought to do to get Israel to repent, to no avail. (Note the fierceness of Amos's preaching in 4:12: "Prepare to meet thy God, O Israel!")

- In chapter 5:1–6:14, Amos preaches a message of lamentation for Israel's fallen condition. In 5:3, he declares that unless there is a national repentance, ninety percent of Israel will die. Amos calls for the people to seek the Lord (5:4, 6, 8, 14) and not just religious activity ("But seek not Bethel," 5:5).

All three messages have tremendous Devotional application to us and Doctrinal application for Israel in the future.

SPECIFIC REFERENCES TO THE DAY OF THE LORD

1:14– "With shouting in the day of battle, with a tempest in the day of the whirlwind"

2:16– "In that day"

3:14– "That in the day that I shall visit the transgressions of Israel upon him"

5:18– "Woe unto you that desire the day of the Lord… the day of the Lord is darkness, and not light"

5:20– "Shall not the day of the Lord be darkness, and not light?

6:3– "The evil day"

CHRIST IS REVEALED:

As the *Creator of the universe* – Amos 5:8 (Heb. 1:2–3; Rev. 4:11)

52 WEEKS OF PURSUIT

WEEK 39, DAY 2: TODAY'S READING: AMOS 7-9; OBADIAH 1

OVERVIEW:
The five visions symbolizing the approaching judgment: the plague of locusts, the devouring fire, the plumbline (Amos 7), the basket of summer fruit (Amos 8), the altar (Amos 9); the abasement of Edom's pride (Obad. 1:1–4); the destruction of Edom (Obad. 1:5–16); the restoration of Israel and Judah and the extinction of Edom (Obad. 1:17–21).

HIGHLIGHTS & INSIGHTS:
In chapter 6, AMOS had concluded the third of three sermons giving the reason God's judgment was about to come upon the people of Israel. They seemed to have so many spiritual things in place. They observed the feast days. They made sacrifices and gave their offerings. They sang songs to the Lord (5:21–25). Like many people and churches today, they thought they were worshiping. But God wasn't looking at their appearance; He was looking at their hearts (1 Sam. 16:7; 2 Cor. 5:12). Though they had all the correct *outward actions*, their *inward attitudes* were corrupt. "He that hath ears to hear, let him hear!"

In 6:1–6, Amos challenges those who have developed a false sense of security ("them that are at ease in Zion") and trust in everything but God ("the mountain of Samaria," or money, homes, their ivory beds) to beware God's impending judgment. Then, in chapters 7–9, God gives Amos a series of visions to illustrate His judgment.

Chapter 7 covers the first three visions. In 7:1, Amos sees locusts ("grasshoppers") coming and stripping the land of all of its vegetation. He intercedes on Israel's behalf, and the Lord stays the plague of locusts (7:2–3). We must never underestimate the power of intercessory prayer. God responded to Amos and to Elijah (James 5:16–17), and He will respond in our day as well. Is there someone for whom God would have you intercede today?

The second vision is almost the same as the first, but rather than locusts destroying the land, Amos sees it being destroyed by fire after a severe drought (7:4). Again, Amos intercedes on Israel's behalf, and God chooses to deliver the land (7:5–6).

In the third vision in 7:7–9, Amos sees the Lord holding a plumbline and standing by a wall that was perfectly plumb. This time, God was inspecting Israel to see if they were out of line, if they measured up. We would do well to consider whether we would measure up if God held the plumbline of His perfect Word next to our life today. Is any area of our life out of line? Unlike the first two visions, however, Amos offers no intercession, and God offers no retraction of His plan to judge them. In the remainder of chapter 7, Amaziah, who was the state priest, as it were, tells Amos to go to Judah (7:12) and do his little prophesying there! Amos tells him, "Listen pal, I was minding my own business tending sheep and picking fruit when God called me to prophesy on His behalf and there ain't anybody, including you, that's gonna get me to stop! And while I'm at it, I just happen to have a prophecy for you! Your wife is going to become a streetwalker and your entire family is going to die by the sword because of your sin and compromise" (7:14–17, [my paraphrase]). Go Amos!

In chapter 8, God gives Amos a fourth vision: a basket of summer fruit (8:1–3). Israel, like summer fruit, was ripe for judgment, and the end was near. Amos spends the rest of chapter 8 identifying the sins for which the judgment was coming.

In chapter 9, Amos receives the fifth and final vision. He sees the Lord Himself standing at the altar (9:1–10). God is revealing the inescapability of His judgment. Regardless of where Israel goes, God will find them. The book of Amos doesn't end on a negative note, however. In 9:11–15, God promises the future restoration of Israel which will unfold "in that day." What day? The Day of the Lord—the Second Coming of our Lord Jesus Christ!

OBADIAH

The book of Obadiah is only twenty-one verses long. Obadiah, whose name means "servant of the Lord," prophesied between 587–580 BC. As with every prophetic book of the Old Testament, the theme is the Second Coming of Christ, or "the Day of the Lord." This book is unique in that it is the only book of the Bible written against a particular nation of people: the Edomites. Though most of the Old Testament books address the Jews (Israel), Obadiah actually addresses Gentiles.

The Edomites are the descendants of Esau, a group of people who have consistently caused Israel problems. In 1 Chronicles 18:14 they become servants to Israel, but in 2 Chronicles 21:8–10, they revolt and continue to cause Israel problems. They eventually allied with Sennacherib and Nebuchadnezzar and caused Israel's downfall. Simply put, God hates the Edomites! Why? Because He said, "And I will bless them that bless thee, and curse them that curseth thee" (Gen. 12:3). The Edomite nation cursed Israel, and thus, God curses them.

This little book provides great insight into Romans 9:13 where many good people lose their way. God says, "Jacob have I loved, but Esau have I hated." Some (Calvinists, Hyper-calvinists) conclude, based on that statement, that God chooses who goes to heaven and who goes to hell. If we go back to Genesis 25, however, God specifically said that there were two nations in Rebekah's womb. This is about *nations*, not *individuals*! The descendants of Esau, the Edomite nation, hated Israel, and because of that, God hated them!

And the Edomites are still in the Middle East today; we just know them by different names today. Their game plan, however, is still the same as it ever was: do anything and everything possible to cause Israel grief! In fact, Psalm 83:4–6 lists the Edomites with the ten confederated nations of the Antichrist (Ps. 83). That certainly provides great insight into current events in the Middle East!

SPECIFIC REFERENCES TO THE DAY OF THE LORD

Amos

8:3– "And the songs of the temple shall be howlings in that day"

8:9– "And it shall come to pass in that day"

8:13– "In that day"

9:11– "In that day will I raise up the tabernacle of David that is fallen"

Obadiah

1:8– "Shall I not in that day… even destroy the wise men out of Edom"

1:12– "In the day of distress"

1:13– "In the day of their calamity"

1:14– "In the day of distress"

1:15– "For the day of the Lord is near upon all the heathen"

CHRIST IS REVEALED:

As the *Plumbline* – Amos 7:7–8 (The Lord Jesus Christ alone is the perfect standard, qualified to walk in the midst of His people, measuring good and evil and true and false, Rev. 2–3)

52 WEEKS OF PURSUIT

WEEK 39, DAY 3: TODAY'S READING: JONAH 1-4

OVERVIEW:
Jonah's call and rebellion (chapter 1); Jonah's chastening and repentance (chapter 2); Jonah's second call and obedience (chapter 3); Jonah's rebellion and God's rebuke (chapter 4).

HIGHLIGHTS & INSIGHTS:
There may be no more important prophetic book of the Old Testament than the little book of Jonah. This book prophesies and teaches us about the death, burial, and resurrection of Jesus Christ. In fact, Jesus said, "An evil and adulterous generation seeketh after a sign; and there shall no sign be given to it, but the sign of the prophet Jonas [Jonah]: For as Jonas was three days and three nights in the whale's belly; so shall the Son of man be three days and three nights in the heart of the earth" (Matt. 12:39–40). This is why the book of Jonah has been more "spoken against" (Luke 2:34) than any other Old Testament book.

The attacks come in different forms. The unsaved world claims that the events in this book are just fiction, that Jonah is merely another example of similar stories in mythology: Andromeda, Orion, and Hercules, who was in the belly of a sea creature for three days and three nights. This is the work of the devil who always has a counterfeit. He wants the book of Jonah to be seen as fiction, just like all of his fictitious stories in mythology. Obviously, though, the devil's attack isn't against the facts of Jonah's tale; it's an attack against Christ and His death, burial, and resurrection! Remember, Jesus said, "As was Jonah, so was the Son of Man" (Matt. 12:39–40). If Jonah is fictitious, so was Christ's death, burial and resurrection! Or, more simply, if the book of Jonah is a *lie*, than Jesus was a *liar*!

Another key attack comes from scholars in the saved world. They believe that the events happened, but not that Jonah was dead in the belly of that "great fish" (1:17) or "whale" (Matt. 12:40). Again, "As was Jonah, so was Jesus!" If Jonah didn't actually die and resurrect from the belly of the whale, then Jesus didn't actually die (enter the "swoon theory") and resurrect from the heart (belly) of the earth! Jonah was the only sign given of the resurrection, and I didn't say that: Jesus did (Matt. 12:39). It doesn't matter that we can't figure it out physiologically, scientifically, practically or any other way. If Jesus said Jonah was a picture of the resurrection, then Jonah had to die, and that's where we submit ourselves to Romans 3:4: "Let God be true, but every man a liar"! Interestingly, the book of Jonah begins, "Now the word of the Lord came unto Jonah the son of Amittai" (1:1a) The name Jonah means "the dove," and the name Amittai means "truth" or "truth telling." A dove is a biblical type of the Holy Spirit (Matt. 3:16), and truth is specifically defined in Scripture as Jesus (John 14:6) and as the Word of God (John 17:17). We could say, then, that the book of Jonah is by the Spirit of God (2 Pet. 1:21) to give us the truth about Jesus, and leave it at that!

Historically, Jonah was a prominent prophet in the Northern Kingdom (Israel) during the reign of Jeroboam (793– 753 BC), with the specific events of this book taking place around 760 BC. As revealed in these four chapters, his real ministry is to preach to Gentiles, who do respond to his message with repentance, marking the greatest revival in the history of mankind! Ninevah was a city of almost a million people, certainly qualifying it as a "great city" (1:2; 3:2–3; 4:11). And every single person in the city responded to the call to repent (3:5).

From a Prophetic standpoint, Jonah is a type of the 144,000 in Revelation 7:4–9 who preach to Gentiles when the world experiences the greatest revival in the history of mankind.

Some interesting details may help us understand both the importance of the book of Jonah and its placement in the canon of Scripture as well as its big picture.

- Ninevah is the capital city of Assyria, the dominant world power of that time. Jonah knew that two things were true: (1) The wickedness of Assyria had come up to God (1:2), and God was about to blast 'em! And (2) Assyria was about to blast the Nation of Israel! If God judges

Assyria for their sin first, Israel will be spared. If Jonah preaches to Ninevah and they repent, he is not only signing his own death warrant, but the death warrant of his entire nation. Suddenly it makes more sense why Jonah goes in the opposite direction when he's called to preach to Ninevah and why he's so ticked off when a million sinners repent (See Jer. 18:7–8).

- Jonah went to Whale University.

- Everyone in the entire book of Jonah obeyed God except the man of God for whom the book is named. The storm, the dice (casting of lots), the sailors, the fish, the Ninevites (again, every last one of them!), the east wind, the gourd, the worm—absolutely everyone and everything obeyed, except the one we would expect.

- Jonah shows us that it is very possible to serve the Lord and not love people. Throughout the book, God makes it very clear He loves and has pity for lost souls (4:2, 11). But Jonah had more love and pity for himself, and for the lousy gourd (4:10–11), than he did for the lost multitudes in the city. As we read this incredible book, we would do well to ask ourselves: "Do I care more about myself than I do God's will or the lost? With what is my life more consumed than the salvations of lost people on this planet?"

CHRIST IS REVEALED:

As the *One who would die, be buried, and rise from the dead after three days* – Jonah 1:7–2:10 (Matt. 12:39–41)

52 WEEKS OF PURSUIT

WEEK 39, DAY 4: TODAY'S READING: MICAH 1-7

OVERVIEW:
Micah prophesies of God's wrath (chapter 1); God's attitude toward oppression (chapter 2); God's judgment on Israel's leaders (chapter 3); the restoration of Israel (chapter 4); Christ foretold (chapter 5); the Lord's controversy (chapter 6); more concerning Israel's restoration (chapter 7).

HIGHLIGHTS & INSIGHTS:
Micah, whose name means "Who is like Jehovah," was a country boy from the foothills of Judah. He prophesied to the nation of Israel for twenty-five years between 735–710 BC. His ministry spanned the reigns of Jotham (750–731 BC), Ahaz (731–715 BC), and Hezekiah (715–686 BC). Most of his prophecy is directed toward Judah (the Southern Kingdom) since the Northern Kingdom was about to fall to Assyria. He was a contemporary of Hosea and Isaiah.

The book begins with God's word to Micah concerning Jerusalem, Judah's capital, and Samaria, Israel's capital. Micah's heart for the Lord and His people is so tender that his message literally brings him to tears and mourning (1:8–9). His prophecy is partially fulfilled when Israel is taken captive by Assyria in 722 BC and Judah is taken captive by Babylon in 605 BC. However, when taken literally, the passage points to a future time when Israel (as a nation) will once again be judged. The reference to the "Lord [coming] forth out of his place ... [to] tread upon the high places of the earth" (1:3) refers to the Tribulation which culminates with the Day of the Lord, the Second Coming of Christ.

In chapter 1, God addresses one of Israel's key sins: idolatry. In chapter 2, God singles out injustice, another of Israel's key sins, specifically those who devise ways to oppress their neighbor (2:2). God says repeatedly in the Bible that He will repay those who oppress the less fortunate, especially the fatherless and widows (Jer. 7:5–7; 23:3–5; Ezek. 22:7; Zech. 7:10–12; Mal. 3:5). Having compassion on the fatherless and widows by visiting them in their affliction has always been a priority for God (James 1:27; Isa. 1:17; Exod. 22:22; Deut. 10:17–18; 14:29; 16:11, 14; 24:19–21; 26:12–13; Ps. 68:5; 146:9). May we share our Lord's compassion by seeking opportunities to minister to those who are oppressed and afflicted in our churches, our communities, and the world. God's heart for the vulnerable compels us to minister to widows, single moms, those whose fathers have died or abandoned them, and others. Real ministry means really sacrificing to meet real needs!

Micah 2:10 warns Israel about the coming captivity and against prophets who were saying the captivity wouldn't happen. Micah points out that they will only follow the prophets who tell them positive things, regardless of how ridiculous their prophecies were (2:11). It's an important warning: a preacher's popularity in no way indicates that preacher's accuracy! The Bible repeatedly depicts how easily people will follow preachers who scratch them where they itch! Paul says this will be a primary characteristic of our time (2 Tim. 4:2–4). We must be discerning!

In chapter 3, God warns that He will hold the leaders of Israel accountable for how they abused His people, failing to care for them, protect them, and lead them. Just as the Antichrist will proclaim peace before the Tribulation (Dan. 8:25), the leaders of Israel were proclaiming peace before the coming captivity, and God promises His judgment upon them (3:5–7). In fact, God's judgment always begins at His house and with His leaders (1 Pet. 4:17).

In chapter 4, which parallels Ezekiel 44–48, Micah prophesies of the coming millennium. Verse 1 provides a beautiful description of life during Christ's millennial reign, as the Lord's people "flow" into His glorious presence! The Lord will reign over all the nations of the earth (4:7), and nations will finally be at peace with other nations (4:3–5). In this present time, world leaders work tenaciously to bring peace on earth, but there will be never be peace on this earth apart from Christ. And this principle applies to our personal walk as well. Everyone on this planet wants their hearts, minds, and lives to be shrouded in peace. But few want Christ. Only when we daily surrender every aspect of our lives to the Lordship of Christ and allow His kingdom, with its power and glory, to be established in us, we will discover His glorious and lasting peace.

Micah 5:2 is one of the most well-known prophecies concerning Christ, describing Bethlehem, the city of His birth. Micah also reveals the magnificence of Christ's kingdom as it is established on the earth at His second coming (5:4ff). "The Assyrian" in this chapter is a specific reference to the coming Antichrist (5:5–6).

In chapter 6, Micah records a trial where the Lord presents His legal case ("controversy," 6:2) against His people. He calls on nature to serve as the jury (6:1) and Micah to act as His prosecuting attorney. He reminds Israel of His goodness to them, specifically in the leaders He had provided for them in Moses, Aaron and Miriam (6:3–5). From a Devotional standpoint, this reference to these specific leaders is awesome because all three were imperfect. Aaron and Miriam are most often remembered for their failures (the golden calf and questioning Moses's authority). Still, God reminds Israel that they were His chosen leaders and, thus, are a sign of His goodness. What an encouragement to all of us who have failed as a leader or have failed to properly follow God's designated leaders in our lives!

The outcome God desired for this trial was for Israel to rise above religious ceremony to gain a genuine relationship with Him. And even though we live in a different dispensation, Micah 6:8 provides a simple, but comprehensive, overview of how God intends for all of His people to live: "He hath shewed thee, O man, what is good; and what doth the Lord require of thee, but to do justly, and to love mercy, and to walk humbly with thy God." He wants us to walk *with Him*. And He wants us to do what is right, even as we show mercy to those who don't.

The book of Micah ends with a prophecy regarding the eventual restoration of Israel (7:12–20). It is certainly an incredible reality for the nation of Israel, but from a Devotional standpoint, it is also an incredible reminder to us that God delights in mercy (7:18), He has compassion on us (7:19a), He pardons our iniquity (7:19b), and He has cast all of our sins into the deepest sea (7:19c).

SPECIFIC REFERENCES TO THE DAY OF THE LORD

2:4– "In that day shall one take up a parable against you"

4:6– "In that day… will I assemble her that halteth"

5:10– "And it shall come to pass in that day"

7:4– "The day of thy watchmen and thy visitation cometh"

7:11– "In that day shall the decree be far removed"

7:12– "In that day also he shall come even to thee from Assyria"

CHRIST IS REVEALED:

As the *Ruler in Israel who was born in Bethlehem* – Micah 5:2 (Luke 1:32–33; 2:4–6)

52 WEEKS OF PURSUIT

WEEK 39, DAY 5: TODAY'S READING: NAHUM–HABAKKUK

OVERVIEW:
Nahum, whose name means "comforter," comforts God's people by revealing God's plan to take vengeance on the wickedness of Assyria and her capital city, Nineveh (Nah. 1–3); Habakkuk's difficult questions for God (Hab. 1–2); Habakkuk's praise to God for answering his questions (Hab. 3).

HIGHLIGHTS & INSIGHTS:

NAHUM

The Old Testament is primarily written to and by Israelites, God's chosen people. Any Old Testament book written to a nation other than Israel, then, is certainly significant in the plan and revelation of God. Only three prophets (of sixteen) address Gentile nations: Obadiah prophesied to Edom, and Jonah and Nahum prophesied to Nineveh, the capital city of Assyria.

Both Edom and Nineveh were Gentile nations who worshipped false gods and were used by Satan to persecute the nation of Israel. And God doesn't take either of these offenses lightly (1:14; 3:19). Only 150 years before, God had sent Jonah to warn Ninevah of coming judgment, proving that He is "good, and ready to forgive; and plenteous in mercy unto all them that call upon [him]" (Ps. 86:5). A revival broke out as the people heeded Jonah's words and repented! The Ninevites failed to make disciples, apparently, because in the book of Nahum, God is once again about to pour out His wrath upon them (1:2–6).

Nahum describes how God will "make an utter end" of the city of Nineveh (1:8–9). There would be "an overrunning flood" (1:8) as the "gates of the rivers shall be opened, and the palace shall be dissolved" (2:6). Enemy invaders would ravage and spoil the fortressed city (3:1–7). Eighteen years after Nahum's prophecy, Nabopolassar, king of Babylon, unsuccessfully besieged Nineveh for three years. The siege broke when the Tigris River suddenly overflowed, washing a hole in the city wall, and the Babylonian army entered, murdering the people and pillaging their goods. The destruction was so complete (1:9) that Alexander the Great marched over the former city without seeing any evidence of a previous civilization and archaeologists didn't begin excavating the city until 1845 AD.

The moral of Ninevah's story is this: God is long-suffering, but He isn't a doormat! When you worship false gods (our modern-day false gods are things like wealth, self, and sex) and mess with God's people, God will make a complete and utter end of you (2 Thess. 1:7–9). Those who have placed their faith in the Lord Jesus Christ, however, will be safe in the day of judgment (Nahum 1:7).

Also in Nahum, God addresses a man (1:11) and a woman (3:4–19) whose full identities are revealed in Revelation: the Antichrist and Mystery Babylon (Rev. 17–18). Nineveh and her king are types of these end time characters.

HABAKKUK

While the moral of Nahum's message is that God is not a doormat, the moral of Habakkuk's message is "God sure seems to be a doormat!" Nahum is the prophet of God's *wrath* realized; Habakkuk is the prophet of God's *patience* realized. In chapter 1, Habakkuk is struggling with two of the most common questions of life: "Why doesn't God answer my prayers?" (1:2) and "If God is good and all powerful, why does He allow evil and suffering in the world?"

The first verse describes Habakkuk as an indignant prophet pinned under the unbearable burden of life's injustices. The man of God has suppressed his frustration and confusion until he can no longer take it. Habakkuk unleashes his pent up anger, puts God on trial, and asks Him why the wicked are allowed to evade judgment and prosper. God leads Habakkuk up a specific path to the only possible answer: God knows what He's doing—so relax (3:17–19). The path is as follows: It begins with a "burden" (1:1); the burden is transformed into a "vision" (2:1–4); the vision becomes a "prayer" (3:1); and the path ends with "rejoicing" and confidence (3:18–19). If we look back, we will see that all of our wrestling matches with God have followed this same path and what we thought at the beginning was an obstacle was actually a stairway leading us high above the nagging questions and issues of life. May our feet, indeed, be as hinds' feet (3:19).

Historically, Habakkuk predicts the Babylonian captivity (1:5–11). Prophetically, chapter 3 describes events surrounding the return of Jesus Christ.

SPECIFIC REFERENCES TO THE DAY OF THE LORD

Nahum

1:7– "The Lord is good, a strong hold in the day of trouble"

2:3– "In the day of his preparation"

Habakkuk

3:16– That I might rest in the day of trouble"

CHRIST IS REVEALED:

As the *Stronghold of the faithful in the day of trouble* – Nahum 1:7 (John 16:33)

As the *Holy One* – Habakkuk 3:3 (Mark 1:24; Acts 2:27; 3:14; 13:35)

As the *Coming Savior of Israel* – Habakkuk 3:4–6, 18 (Acts 13:23)

52 WEEKS OF PURSUIT

WEEK 40, DAY 1: TODAY'S READING: ZEPHANIAH–HAGGAI

OVERVIEW:
God's judgment of Judah (Zeph. 1:1–2:3); God's judgment of the Gentile nations (Zeph. 2:4–3:7); God's restoration of His people (Zeph. 3:8–20); a call to build (Hag. 1:1–15); a promise of glory (Hag. 2:1–9); a problem of defilement (Hag. 2:10–19); a promise to a servant (Hag. 2:20–23).

HIGHLIGHTS & INSIGHTS:
ZEPHANIAH

Zephaniah is one of the strongest preachers in the Bible. After a brief mention of his background and historical context (1:1), he goes straight for the jugular: "I will utterly consume all things from off the land, saith the Lord" (1:2). Zephaniah's message is a message of judgment. In fifty-three total verses, there are at least twenty references to the Day of the Lord. Look for phrases such as *day of the Lord*, *that day*, *the day*, *same day*, or *at that time*.

The Day of the Lord is a two-edged sword. On one side, it is a horrendous day for evildoers. Zephaniah says, "That day is a day of wrath, a day of trouble and distress, a day of wasteness and desolation, a day of darkness and gloominess, a day of clouds and thick darkness" (1:15). The earth's mightiest men shall "cry bitterly" (1:14), and the wealth of the earth's richest men will be unable to "deliver them in the Day of the Lord's wrath" (1:18).

On the other side, though, the Day of the Lord is a glorious day for the Lord's faithful. Zephaniah exhorts, "Sing, O daughter of Zion; shout, O Israel: be glad and rejoice with all the heart" (3:14). In 3:17, Zephaniah adds, "The Lord thy God in the midst of thee is mighty; he will save, he will rejoice over thee with joy; he will rest in his love, he will joy over thee with singing." Paul also describes this two-fold reality in 2 Thessalonians 1:7–10: "And to you who are troubled rest with us, when the Lord Jesus shall be revealed from heaven with his mighty angels, In flaming fire taking vengeance on them that know not God, and that obey not the gospel of our Lord Jesus Christ: Who shall be punished with everlasting destruction from the presence of the Lord, and from the glory of his power; When he shall come to be glorified in his saints, and to be admired in all them that believe (because our testimony among you was believed) in that day." While those who "know not God" will receive His vengeance and punishment, on that very same day, those of us who have believed will joyfully ensure the Lord is both "glorified" and "admired."

Though Zephaniah focuses on the Day of the Lord, another key word in the book is *remnant*. The actual theme of the book is "the salvation of Israel's remnant." Interestingly, Zephaniah means "Jehovah hides" or "Jehovah protects/treasures." That is exactly what God will do with Israel's believing remnant during the outpouring of His incredible wrath in the Day of the Lord (Rev. 12:13–17).

A brief breakdown of the book is as follows:

- In 1:1–2:3, Zephaniah reveals God's judgment of Judah. In 1:4–6, Judah, like Laodicea, had three kinds of sinners: Those who have totally forsaken God and worship idols; those who worship (or think they worship) both God and idols; those who at one time followed the Lord, but have totally and openly forsaken Him and want nothing to do with Him.

- In 2:4–3:7, Zephaniah reveals God's judgment of the Gentile nations. After describing this judgment, God appeals to Israel in 3:1–7, saying, in effect, "If I will judge the heathen nations for their sins, how much more will I judge this sin of the nation that I separated out of all the nations of the world to be holy unto Me?"

- In 3:8–20, Zephaniah reveals God's restoration of His people. The book ends with the incredible promise that God will one day punish the Gentiles and restore Israel and Judah to Himself and to the land. Zephaniah 3:8 describes the battle of Armageddon, when the Lord Jesus Christ will return out of heaven to rescue Israel from the Gentile nations who gather against her and to establish His millennial kingdom (Rev. 19:11–12: Zeph. 3:8, 15). The Lord's final message to Israel is, "At that time will I bring you again, even in the time that I gather you:

for I will make you a name and a praise among all people of the earth, when I turn back your captivity before your eyes, saith the Lord" (3:20). That promise will certainly be in the very near future!

HAGGAI

The book of Haggai is the second shortest book of the Old Testament, only two chapters long. Haggai is the first of three prophets (Haggai, Zechariah and Malachi) who prophesied after the exile in 520 BC. Their books are referred to as post-exilic books.

Historically, in 536 BC, Ezra led about 50,000 Jews back into their land after the Babylonian captivity. Under Ezra's leadership, they rebuilt the altar, reinstated the sacrifices, and in 535 BC, laid the foundation for rebuilding the temple. Because of the incredible opposition they faced, work on the temple ceased. The work eventually continued and was ultimately brought to completion through four godly men: Zerubbabel, the governor; Joshua, the high priest; and Haggai and Zechariah, the prophets.

Haggai begins his prophecy (1:1) on September 1, 520 BC. Sixteen years had passed since the temple foundation was laid, and it was covered with weeds, not walls. And while God's house lay desolate, the people had found the time and money to complete their own houses! Haggai's message to Zerubbabel and Joshua was, "The people have made a priority out of their own houses and careers, and it's time priority is given to the Lord's house and His cause!"

The book of Haggai breaks down into four sections. Each section is a sermon Haggai preached, prefaced by the date on which it was delivered (1:1; 2:1; 2:10; 2:20). In each sermon, Haggai points out a particular sin that keeps God's people from fulfilling His will and accomplishing His work.

1) Making self a priority instead of the Lord (1:1–15; 2 Tim. 3:1–2)
2) Looking back instead of looking ahead (2:1–9; Phil. 3:13–14)
3) Failing to be cleansed of sin (2:10–19; 2 Cor. 7:1)
4) Unbelief (2:20–23; Heb. 3:12–4:2)

Let's ask ourselves today: "What work has God called me to accomplish that I haven't finished? (See 1 Cor. 15:58.)

SPECIFIC REFERENCES TO THE DAY OF THE LORD

Zephaniah

1:7– "For the day of the Lord is at hand"

1:8– "In the day of the Lord's sacrifice"

1:9– "In the same day also will I punish all those that leap on the threshold"

1:10– "And it shall come to pass in that day"

1:14– "The great day of the Lord is near… even the voice of the day of the Lord"

1:15– "That day is a day of wrath… trouble… distress… wasteness… desolation… darkness… gloominess… clouds and thick darkness"

1:16– "A day of the trumpet and alarm"

1:18– "In the day of the Lord's wrath"

2:2– "Before the day of the Lord's anger come upon you"

2:3– "In the day of the Lord's anger"

3:8– "The day that I rise up to the prey"

3:11– "In that day"

3:16– "In that day"

Haggai

2:23– "In that day"

CHRIST IS REVEALED:

As the *King of Israel, even the Lord* – Zephaniah 3:15 (John 1:49)

52 WEEKS OF **PURSUIT**

WEEK 40, DAY 2: **TODAY'S READING: ZECHARIAH 1–8**

OVERVIEW:
A call for repentance and exhortation to fathers (1:1–6); the eight visions designed to encourage the people to rebuild the temple (1:7–6:8); Joshua is crowned the high priest (6:9–15); Jews from Bethel inquire concerning the continuance of fasting (7:1–8:23).

HIGHLIGHTS & INSIGHTS:
Because of their content and length, it is unsurprising that Genesis, Psalms, and Isaiah are often quoted books in the New Testament. But surprisingly the book of Zechariah is quoted almost forty times in the New Testament! Easily the most Christ-centered of all of the Minor Prophets, Zechariah contains more messianic prophecies than perhaps any other Old Testament book.

Zechariah and Haggai were contemporaries who ministered to the same people, even though their lives, their ministries, and their books are filled with contrasts. Haggai was an old man, Zechariah was a young man (2:4). Haggai preached sermons, Zechariah shared visions. Haggai's ministry was marked by admonition, Zechariah's ministry was marked by encouragement.

The book begins, "The word of the Lord unto Zechariah, the son of Berechiah, the son of Iddo" (1:1). Zechariah means "Jehovah remembers." Berechiah means "Jehovah blesses," and Iddo, means "His time." All together, these three names state, "Jehovah remembers and blesses in His time." While we should be encouraged by that truth today (Prov. 15:23; 25:11), the Historic and Prophetic significance has to do with the Jews and Jerusalem. In fact, Jerusalem is mentioned thirty-nine times in the book. Zechariah 1:14–17 offers an overview of the book's theme: God, the great I AM, is jealous for Jerusalem; He remembers what the heathen did to His city, and one day He will bless Jerusalem with prosperity and peace.

Zechariah's prophecy begins with a powerful exhortation to fathers in 1:1–6. In 1:2 with a statement that could just as easily be made in our day: "The Lord hath been sore displeased with your fathers." The devil's all-out war on fathers is one of the most horrific aspects of the Laodicean Period. He has attacked fathers because God gave them a title He uses for Himself in our relationship with Him. As fathers, we must be vigilant to fulfill our seven biblical responsibilities to our children so that, if the Lord were to comment on our fathering as He did in Zechariah 1:2, He would be able to say He was pleased with us, instead of being "sore displeased," as in their case. Even more, may we heed the admonition and promise of verse 3: "Turn ye unto me, saith the Lord of hosts, and I will turn unto you!"

The Old Testament makes clear that, unless something supernatural takes place in a man's life, he invariably becomes like his father. And since that isn't often a good thing (1:2), Zechariah warns: "Be not as your fathers" (1:4). Though the prophets were crying out to the fathers to turn from their "evil ways" and "evil doings," they paid absolutely no attention whatsoever to them! In verse 5, God asks, "Where are they [now]?" In other words, "How'd that work out for 'em?" Zechariah states that, had they taken hold of God's words and statutes, His words and statutes would have taken hold of them (v. 6). They could have received blessing from the Lord, but because they refused to listen and turn, they willfully chose cursing. Fathers, we may miss some things from Zechariah's visions in the first six chapters, but we cannot afford to miss the message in the first six verses!

What follows is a series of eight visions that Zechariah received and was commanded to share with the people. God designed the eight visions (1:7–6:8) to encourage the people to rebuild the temple. Each one is introduced with a reference to sight such as, "I saw," "I lifted up my eyes and looked," and "He showed me." Here is a short summary of each vision and its message:

1) The Man Riding on a Red Horse (1:7–17) - God is displeased with the Gentiles who are at ease while His people are afflicted. He will punish the nations and restore His people.

2) The Four Horns and Four Carpenters (1:18–21) – God will destroy the four Gentile world

powers.

3) The Man with a Measuring Line (2:1–13) – God will restore Jerusalem.

4) Joshua the High Priest (3:1–10) – God will cleanse and restore the priesthood, which represents the nation.

5) The Golden Candlestick and Two Olive Trees (4:1–14) – Israel, God's light-bearer, will rebuild the temple by the power of the Spirit of God (pictured by oil) under the leadership of Joshua and Zerubbabel.

6) The Flying Roll (Scroll) (5:1–4) – God will judge the sin in the land.

7) The Woman Sitting in the Ephah (a basket used for measuring) (5:5–11) – Wickedness (the woman) will be carried from the land back to the land of its origination—Babylon.

8) The Four Chariots (6:1–8) – God controls the nations. His enemies have been shut down, and Jerusalem is safe.

In 6:9–15, the word of the Lord comes to Zechariah not in the form of a vision. Joshua is a type of the Lord Jesus Christ, a "priest-king" referred to as The BRANCH who would build the temple and sit on the throne.

Chapters 7 and 8 form an interlude in the book where God addresses the subject of fasting. The only required fast in the Old Testament was the fast on the Day of Atonement, but the Jews had included fasts to remember the fall of Jerusalem. (We might equate it with remembering the fall of the Twin Towers on 9/11.) Zechariah uses this as an opportunity to teach about God's intention through fasting.

SPECIFIC REFERENCES TO THE DAY OF THE LORD

2:11– "And many nations shall be joined to the Lord in that day"

3:9– "And I will remove the iniquity of that land in one day"

3:10– "In that day"

CHRIST IS REVEALED:

As the *Branch* – Zechariah 3:8; 6:12 (Isa. 11:1; Jer. 23:5; 33:15)

As the *Stone that removes sin* – Zechariah 3:9 (Rom. 9:31–33)

As *Joshua* (the Hebrew name for Jesus) *the Priest-King* – Zechariah 6:11–13

52 WEEKS OF PURSUIT

WEEK 40, DAY 3: **TODAY'S READING: ZECHARIAH 9-14**

OVERVIEW:
Zechariah's first "burden" or oracle, emphasizing Christ's first coming (9:1–11:17); Zechariah's second "burden" or oracle, emphasizing Christ's second coming (12:1–14:21).

HIGHLIGHTS & INSIGHTS:
The Bible is the most incredible history book the world has ever seen. While it's obviously much more than just that, in terms of history, it is in a class totally by itself. No other history book in the world would even dare to write about events that haven't yet taken place! (See Isaiah 42:9; 46:9–10.)

In the 20th and 21st centuries, the world seems to vacillate in its concern of world domination between Great Britain, the United States, Germany, Russia, China, Iran, and Korea—or all of the above. From a biblical standpoint, however, the only nation the world truly needs to concern itself with is Israel! And as the prophet Zechariah reveals, even if all the nations of the world combined military forces and converged upon Israel (which is exactly what will happen at the Battle of Armageddon!), it still wouldn't (won't) be enough to stop them! Not because Israel's military power and prowess is so great, but because Israel's coming King is so great and so infinitely powerful!

People in the 21st century spend a lot of time wondering:

- What will ultimately come of the conflict in the Middle East between the Arabs and Jews?
- Will the Jews actually be able to hold their land and their beloved city of Jerusalem?
- What nation—the U.S.? Russia? China?—will ultimately be the world power when all of the turmoil in the world has been settled and the war on terror is over?

The answers are clearly found in the prophecies revealed through Zechariah: Jerusalem will stay in the hands of the Jews, God will establish Israel's borders according to His specific design, and after the military rampage of the Lord Jesus Christ at His second coming, Israel will dominate the world under the rule of their Messiah and King! At that time, Isaiah 9:7 will be a glorious reality: "Of the increase of his government and peace there shall be no end, upon the throne of David, and upon his kingdom, to order it, and to established it with judgment and with justice from henceforth even for ever. The zeal of the Lord of hosts will perform this." (Also see Luke 1:32b–33.)

Chapters 9–14 divide into two oracles that God calls "burdens" (9:1; 12:1) against specific nations. In 9:1–8, the prophet describes the judgment that would come against Israel's neighbors. This passage is actually describing the conquest of the Alexander the Great. Though he conquered many cities, he did not destroy Jerusalem!

In contrast to the judgment pronounced on Israel's neighbors, God promised His people a King whose reign would establish the world in peace (9:8–10). Rather than entering Jerusalem on a regal charger (at his first coming), Zechariah saw this King on a lowly donkey (Matt. 21:4–5; John 12:12–16). Zechariah tells us He would be sold for the price of a slave (11:12; Matt. 27:3–10); He would be arrested and smitten (Zech. 13:7; Matt. 26:31); He would be wounded in the house of His friends (Zech. 13:6; Matt. 26:47–50); and He would be pierced on the cross (Zech. 12:10; John 19:32–37). Ironically, Jerusalem, the city of Peace, crucified its King, the Prince of Peace.

Zechariah prophesied a full five hundred years before Christ's first coming, but every detail of Zechariah's prophecy came to pass exactly the way he said they would. So we can assume that Zechariah's prophecies concerning Christ's second coming will come to pass with the same impeccable precision!

The glory that Zechariah describes as he concludes his prophecy is hard to put into words. He provides an awe-inspiring panorama of what God has in store for Israel "in that day" (that phrase appears fifteen times in chapters 12–14 alone).

From a topographical standpoint, Zechariah says the Mount of Olives will split in two when Christ sets foot on it at His second coming (Zech. 14:4; Matt. 24:3). From a military standpoint, Zechariah says that all the nations that mess with Israel will be obliterated (Zech. 12:9; Rev. 16:14–16; 19:19–21). From a spiritual standpoint, all of the godless idols, false prophets, and spirits will be removed from the land (Zech. 13:2–3). And from a political standpoint, the Lord Jesus Christ alone will be King of the entire earth (Zech. 14:9). That, my friend, is why it is called the Day of the Lord! It's *the day* the Lord set apart unto Himself and blessed way back in Genesis 2:1–3 and *the day* to which all of history has been and is pointing! On that "glorious day," God's Son will finally receive the glory due His name!

SPECIFIC REFERENCES TO THE DAY OF THE LORD

9:16– "And the Lord their God shall save them in that day"

11:11– "And it was broken in that day"

12:3– "And in that day will I make Jerusalem a burdensome stone for all people"

12:4– "In that day"

12:6– "In that day"

12:8– "In that day"

12:9– "And it shall come to pass in that day"

12:11– "In that day"

13:1– "In that day"

13:2– "And it shall come to pass in that day"

14:1– "Behold, the day of the Lord cometh"

14:4– "And his feet shall stand in that day upon the mount of Olives"

14:6– "And it shall come to pass in that day"

14:7– "But it shall be one day which shall be known to the Lord"

14:8– "And it shall be in that day"

14:9– "In that day shall there be one Lord, and his name one"

14:13– "And it shall come to pass in that day"

14:20– "In that day"

14:21– "And in that day there shall be no more the Canaanite in the house of the Lord of hosts"

CHRIST IS REVEALED:

The *Coming King* – Zechariah 9:9 (Matt. 21:4–5)

The *One sold for thirty pieces of silver* – Zechariah 11:12 (Matt. 27:3–10)

The *One wounded by his friend* – Zechariah 13:6 (Matt. 26:47–50)

The *One who was pierced* – Zechariah 12:10 (John 19:32–37)

The *Smitten Shepherd* – Zechariah 13:7 (Matt. 26:31)

The *Lord who will return to the Mount of Olives* – Zechariah 14:4 (Matt. 24:3)

52 WEEKS OF PURSUIT

WEEK 40, DAY 4: TODAY'S READING: MALACHI 1-4

OVERVIEW:
Introduction (1:1); Israel questions God's love (1:2–5); the priests dishonor God (1:6–2:9); God's people dealing treacherously with one another (2:10–16); Israel's perversion of good and evil (2:17); the promise of the messenger of the covenant (3:1–7); Israel robs God (3:8–12); Israel's arrogant words against God (3:13–15); God's message of reassurance (3:16–4:3); exhortation to remember the law of Moses (4:4); the promise of Elijah's return before the Day of the Lord (4:5–6).

HIGHLIGHTS & INSIGHTS:
With today's reading, we will have read the last of the 929 chapters, 23,214 verses, 592,439 words, and 2,728,100 letters (approximately!) that comprise the Old Testament. Of course, the goal of the *52 Weeks of Pursuit* isn't simply to get through the Word of God, but for the Word of God to get through us. Still, this is a major accomplishment!

The book of Malachi is unique for five reasons.

First, we don't know the exact date this book was written. Most scholars believe that Malachi lived about one hundred years after Haggai and Zechariah, placing him around the time of the reforms of Ezra and Nehemiah. To help place him historically, let's review a few dates. A remnant returned from captivity in 536 BC. Under Haggai and Zechariah's leadership, the temple was rebuilt betwen 520–516 BC. Sixty years later (457 BC), Ezra arrived to reestablish the nation spiritually, and thirteen years after that (444 BC), God used Nehemiah to rebuild the wall. Malachi is most likely a contemporary of Nehemiah because they faced the same exact spiritual problems:

- A profane priesthood (Mal. 2:1–9; Neh. 13:27–30)
- Mixed marriages with the heathen (Mal. 2:10–16; Neh. 13:23–29)
- The withholding of tithes from God's house (Mal. 3:8–12; Neh. 13:10–13)
- An overall spiritual apathy in the hearts of God's people

So, while we don't know for sure, the date of the book is usually placed at between 450–400 BC.

Second, the book of Malachi has a unique style. Using a question-answer format, Malachi reveals the people's spiritual cluelessness due to their arrogance and apathy. There are at least 25 questions recorded in these four brief chapters!

Third, this book is unique in that 47 of the 55 verses are actually spoken by God—the highest percentage of any of the books of the prophets.

Fourth, the book of Malachi ends on a note of condemnation and judgment, rather than restoration and hope. God chose a surprising and revealing word to conclude the Old Testament. (Take a second to look it up.) It points us to the reality of man's sinful condition and makes us long for a remedy that will satisfy God's justice and holiness. Can you think of one? See 1 John 2:2!

Finally, this book is unique because, after Malachi penned the final word in 4:6, God gave no new revelation for a period of about 400 years, what we call "the four hundred years of silence." Still, we might say the last book of the Old Testament foreshadows the first book of the New Testament, when John the Baptist breaks the silence by declaring, "Prepare ye the way of the Lord." (Read Malachi 3:1, followed by Matthew 3:1–2!)

SPECIFIC REFERENCES TO THE DAY OF THE LORD

3:2– "But who may abide the day of his coming?"

3:17– "In that day when I make up my jewels"

4:1– "For, behold, the day cometh, that shall burn as an oven"

4:3– "In the day that I shall do this"

4:5– "The coming of the great and dreadful day of the Lord"

CHRIST IS REVEALED:

As the *Lord, whom ye seek, (who) shall suddenly come to His temple* – Malachi 3:1 (Mark 11:15–17)

As the *Sun of righteousness* – Malachi 4:2 (John 9:5)

WEEK 40, DAY 5: **TODAY'S READING: MATTHEW 1-4**

OVERVIEW:
The Genealogy of the King (chapter 1); the Birth of the King (chapter 2); the Announcement of the King (chapter 3); the Testing of the King (chapter 4).

HIGHLIGHTS & INSIGHTS:
As we leave the Old Testament and come into the New Testament today, four hundred years have passed. Four hundred years may not seem like a long period of time. To help to put it in perspective, however, four hundred years ago, most English-speaking people didn't even own a copy of the Bible! Four hundred years is a long time!

And in those four hundred years, God had remained completely silent. There had been no new revelation. God hadn't spoken to a single soul by direct revelation (Gen. 3:8), through the Angel of the Lord (Judg. 6:12), out of a cloud (Exod. 34:5–7), from a burning bush (Exod. 3:4), from the mouth of a donkey (Num. 22:28), from the mouth of a prophet (Deut. 18:18), or by any other means. But though He had been silent in the world, He certainly hadn't been absent! During those four hundred years, God was orchestrating all of history to prepare the world for the coming of His only begotten Son. Remember, Galatians 4:4 says, "But when the fulness of time was come, God sent forth his Son, made of a woman, made under the law."

But also understand that the world had changed in those four hundred years. By this time, Hebrew had become a dead language, and Greek and Aramaic were the languages of communication and commerce. There were also at least five different sects on the scene in Israel that were influencing the world religiously, socially and politically.

- The Scribes – These men were highly regarded by the Jews as the interpreters and teachers of Scripture. Ezra was perhaps the first of this sect, but by the time of Christ, they had degenerated greatly from Ezra's character and godliness. They constantly opposed Christ, and some of Christ's most harsh words were directed to the Scribes and the Pharisees (our next sect).

- The Pharisees – Also highly regarded by the Jews, these men saw themselves as holy and zealous guardians of the law. They were ultra-conservative in all aspects of their beliefs and external behavior. They, too, opposed the Lord Jesus Christ and were frequently denounced by Him.

- The Sadducees – If the Pharisees were the religious "right," the Sadducees were the religious "left." They were mostly part of the wealthy, influential, priestly parties and were rationalistic and liberal in their beliefs, denying the immortality of the soul as well as the resurrection.

- The Herodians – This was not a religious group, but a political party which took its name from Herod. Because of their zealousness for the Roman government, they viewed Christ as a threat to Rome's authority, as merely another political revolutionary.

- The Zealots – These were extreme and radical defenders of a theocratic form of government (God-Rule) and committed acts of violence against the Roman government to champion their cause.

We will run into these sects repeatedly throughout the four gospels and understanding who they were is vital to grasp the social, political, and religious world of the New Testament.

MATTHEW
As the events of the book of Matthew are easily understood, we will begin with an analysis of the book as a whole.

52 WEEKS OF PURSUIT

1. **INFORMATION ABOUT THE AUTHOR**

    His name: Matthew.
    His name means: Gift of Jehovah
    He is also called Levi (Mark 2:13–14; Luke 5:27–29)
    He was a Publican (Matt. 10:3; 17:24–27; Rom. 13:1–7)
    He was born a Jew (Mark 2:14; Luke 5:27)
    He was the son of Alphaeus (Mark 2:14)
    He had two brothers, James and Judas (Mark 3:18; Luke 6:16)
    He was chosen to be one of the 12 disciples (Luke 6:12–16; Matt. 10:1–4; Mark 3:13–19)

2. **FACTS ABOUT MATTHEW'S GOSPEL**

    Approximate date of writing: 64–66 AD
    Written from: Jerusalem
    Dates of the recorded events: 4 BC–33 AD
    Theme: Christ, the King of the Jews
    Christ is seen as: The Promised King
    Key Verse: Matthew 27:37
    Key Word: Kingdom (56 times)
    Chapters: 28
    Verses: 1,071
    Words: 24,755

3. **FEATURES OF MATTHEW'S GOSPEL**

    This is the only gospel that uses the phrase "kingdom of heaven" (32 times).
    This is the only gospel that uses the phrase "that it might be fulfilled which was spoken" (9 times)
    This gospel contains 60 references to the Old Testament.
    This gospel contains 25 fulfilled prophecies.

4. **A SIMPLE OUTLINE OF MATTHEW'S GOSPEL**

    Two Rejections:

    - Rejection #1 - The rejection of the Kingdom (Chapters 1–12)

    - Rejection #2 - The rejection of the King (Chapters 13–28)

52 WEEKS OF PURSUIT

WEEK 41, DAY 1: TODAY'S READING: MATTHEW 5-7

OVERVIEW:
The constitution of the King and His kingdom.

HIGHLIGHTS & INSIGHTS:
There are several things we must keep in the forefront of our thinking that will help to keep us from going out of bounds in the Gospel of Matthew.

First, understand that Matthew is not written from a chronological standpoint, as are the Gospels of Mark and Luke. I like the way John Phillips explains Matthew's approach:

> He tends to group his material in order to produce a cumulative effect for the point he is making that Jesus is the Messiah of the Jews. For example, beginning in chapter 5 (today's reading), we have the Sermon on the Mount – what Jesus taught. This is followed by a series of miracles in chapters 8 to 9, by no means in the order of occurrence, but which show what Jesus wrought. These miracles are followed in turn by a series of reactions to Jesus, illustrating what people thought. It seems clear that Matthew's material is arranged so that it can be easily remembered and certainly the contents of his gospel are more easily remembered than the contents of the other synoptics.

Second, keep in mind the specific Jewish nature of this Gospel. Proverbs talks about the importance of identifying landmarks. Proverbs 22:28 says, "Remove not the ancient landmark, which thy fathers have set." Proverbs 23:10 adds, "Remove not the old landmark; and enter not into the fields of the fatherless." Obviously, from a Historical standpoint, these verses describe the importance of identifying land boundaries and keeping them in place. However, from a Devotional standpoint, we could say that *the Jew* is the "ancient landmark" of the Bible that we must never lose sight of or remove! Once we lose sight of the Jew when interpreting the Bible, we will find ourselves in "the fields of the fatherless." Specifically, there are four books of the Bible where people often get doctrinally discombobulated: Matthew, Acts, Hebrews, and James. Nearly every doctrinal controversy and division in the body of Christ comes out of a verse, passage, or chapter in one of those four books. And all four of them are specifically related to the Jew!

Once we lose the "ancient landmark" of the Jew in these books, we might well end up in the doctrinal equivalent of "the fields of the fatherless": believing in works for salvation; or that baptism is a requirement for salvation; or that you can lose your salvation; or that tongues and healing are for today, and more. All of those false doctrines are propagated today because somebody lost sight of the Jew in these books!

Recognizing the place of the Jew is vital today as we come to Matthew's record of the first sermon Jesus ever preached, the Sermon on the Mount. All the way through the Old Testament, God had been promising a kingdom to the Jews. They understood that kingdom to be a literal, earthly kingdom where God's ruler (God's "anointed" in Hebrew; God's "Messiah" in Greek) would sit on the throne of David. That kingdom is what the book of Matthew is all about. Matthew calls it the kingdom of heaven, and his Gospel, the only one to use the phrase, refers to it thirty-two times! Matthew's Gospel presents Christ as King of the kingdom of heaven. (It is also referred to as the "kingdom of Israel" in Acts 1:6.)

In yesterday's reading, the King appears (chapter 2). In chapter 3, He is heralded, and in 5:1, He sits and delivers the constitution for the kingdom. But the subject of His sermon isn't heaven; it's the kingdom of heaven (Matt. 5:3, 10, 19–20; 7:21). And the sermon isn't directed to the Gentiles, or to God's church, but to Jews (1 Cor. 10:32). Someone might say, "But it's in the New Testament!" And it is. But the context of the book, along with this sermon, is strictly Jewish!

One of the biblical realities many people seem to overlook when reading the Gospels is that we don't officially enter into the New Testament, according to the Bible's definition, until the death of Christ, which in Matthew's Gospel isn't until chapter 27! Hebrews 9:16–17 says, "For where a testament is, there must also of necessity be the death of the testator. For a testament is of force [is only enforced] after men are dead: otherwise it is of no strength at all while the testator liveth." In the strictest sense of the word, that means we don't actually enter the New Testament until the very end of each of the Gospels—at the death of Christ. More will be said about this tomorrow.

As we read the Sermon on the Mount today, our Lord's audience is Old Testament Hebrews who at that time were still under the law. In His sermon, He presents the real intent of the law and the principles of the millennial kingdom (the kingdom of heaven). There are truths that Gentiles in the church age can apply Devotionally to our lives, but it has no application whatsoever to how people are saved in our dispensation.

WEEK 41, DAY 2: **TODAY'S READING: MATTHEW 8-10**

OVERVIEW:
Christ presents Himself as Israel's King by fulfilling the signs and wonders prophesied of the Messiah in the Old Testament (chapters 8–9); the Twelve are "sent forth" to preach the "Gospel of the kingdom" (chapter 10).

HIGHLIGHTS & INSIGHTS:
Christians tend to make several overarching errors that just about ensure that their biblical interpretation and application will not be correct. One of the most critical mistakes is thinking that the Bible is a Christian book that primarily has to do with us—as in Christians. You say, "How in the world could you say that? Do you mean to tell me that the Bible *isn't* a Christian book and that it *doesn't* primarily have to do with Christians?" Exactly!

If we're ever really going to understand the Bible, we must face the fact that the Bible is a *Jewish* book that has to do with a *Jewish King* and a *kingdom* that has been promised to *Jews*! How very stereotypical of Laodiceans (believers in the last days whose chief characteristic is to be "lovers of their own selves," 2 Tim. 3:1–2; Rev. 3:14–22) to think that the Bible is all about us! We get the idea that the theme of the Bible is our salvation (Gentiles) and "how nice, thoughtful, and unbelievably gracious it will be of God to allow the poor Jews in the last days to have a part in it all." No, no, no! A thousand times, no! No wonder we get messed up!

The Bible is predominantly about a seven-thousand-year period in which those of us who comprise His church are merely a two-thousand-year parenthesis! It is certainly a glorious parenthesis that includes us and benefits us and is obviously part of a plan that God ordained before the foundation of the world. But to view the parenthesis of the church age as the theme of the Bible, or to interpret the Old Testament and, specifically, the Gospel of Matthew through Christian "glasses" is a grave error that will ultimately take the most sincere student of the Bible down the path to false doctrine.

At least 95% of *false* doctrine is really just *true* Bible doctrine applied to the wrong group of people or to the wrong period of time (dispensation). That's why, yesterday, we discussed the Jew, in a Devotional sense, being the "ancient landmark" in the Bible, and how that when that distinction is moved or removed, we make a doctrinal beeline into "the fields of the fatherless" (Prov. 22:28; 23:10).

Much of the problem, particularly in Matthew's Gospel, is that Christians fail to recognize that this Gospel is written to the *Jews*, to present Christ as *their* Messiah-King over the kingdom promised to *them* in the Old Testament. Just about every commentator in Christianity will talk about the Jewish nature of this Gospel, but will immediately begin to apply the teaching of Matthew's Gospel to Christians living in the church age! The Gospel of Matthew wasn't written to teach us about the church age, so we must be careful about applying it to us—at least until after the death of the Testator (chapter 27).

This Gospel is about the kingdom of heaven. It has to do with God's intention to establish a *literal* kingdom in Israel over which His Son will preside and over which He will rule the whole world from a *literal* throne in the *literal* rebuilt temple in the *literal* earthly Jerusalem.

And contrary to what most commentators say, the kingdom of heaven is not the same as the kingdom of God (a phrase found repeatedly in the other three Gospels), and the two phrases are not used interchangeably in the New Testament. That would be as absurd as saying that "God" and "heaven" are the same thing or that those two terms are used interchangeably in the Bible. (More will be said about this distinction tomorrow.)

But in light of that distinction, applying much of the teaching in Matthew to the parenthesis of the church age is not only poor hermeneutics, it is an invitation to false doctrine. A great case in point is 8:12. If we lose sight of the fact that the subject is the kingdom of heaven, we might end up believing

52 WEEKS OF PURSUIT

something as biblically ludicrous and ridiculous as someone who has been born again can wind in hell!

A few pithy comments about some of the verses in today's reading:

- 8:14 – How interesting that the so-called first Pope had a wife!
- 8:16 – Nobody in line to be healed by Jesus went away unhealed because of their lack of faith.
- 8:21 – The concepts represented by "Lord" and "me first" in this verse are mutually exclusive! Still, calling Jesus "Lord," but telling Him "me first," does characterize the church in the last days (2 Tim. 2:1–2).
- 8:26–27 –The wind and the sea recognize the voice of the One who spoke them into existence and obey! Oh, that humans would have that kind of discernment.
- 8:29 – Demons make an identification that the religious leaders of Jesus' day (the Scribes and Pharisees) were never able to make: Jesus is the Son of God!
- 8:32 – The pigs do a "swine dive" off the cliff and commit "sooey–cide." (Sorry!)
- 8:34 – The people were more freaked out by Jesus in their midst than by those who were demon possessed in their midst!
- 9:2 – There is a great practical lesson in this verse about doing whatever we can to bring the lost to Jesus!
- 9:11 – Jesus has time for sinful people like me!
- 9:27 – Even blind people could see what the Pharisees couldn't—that Jesus is the promised Messiah!
- 9:35 – The "gospel of the kingdom" is not the same gospel Paul preached or that he identified in 1 Corinthians 15:3–4.
- 9:37–38 – Though we are in a different dispensation, these verses are extremely true!
- 10:1 – To this point, the Twelve are referred to as disciples. As they are "sent forth" (10:5), they become apostles (10:2). The word *apostle* means "sent one." In Latin the word is *missio* from which we get our word missionary to refer to ones who are "sent forth."
- 10:5–6 – How about these verses to prove the Jewish nature of this gospel?
- 10:22 – This verse is a doctrinal back-breaker unless you keep it in the context of the kingdom of heaven.

WEEK 41, DAY 3: **TODAY'S READING: MATTHEW 11-13**

OVERVIEW:
The refusal of the King and the kingdom of heaven (chapter 11); the official rejection of the King by the leaders of the Nation of Israel (chapter 12); the kingdom is hidden in the form of parables (chapter 13).

HIGHLIGHTS & INSIGHTS:
To get our doctrinal bearings in the Gospel of Matthew, we must keep our eye on the Jew and the Jewish audience in this book. Regardless of popular teaching, the church has not replaced Israel, and the book of Revelation has some pretty strong things to say about "them which say they are Jews, and are not" (Rev. 2:9b; 3:9a). We are the parenthesis!

Daniel's prophecy of the seventy weeks of years (70 x 7=490) is particularly relevant here. Historically, the Jews "cut off" (crucified) their Messiah who had come to bring in the promised kingdom after sixty-nine weeks of years (483 years) had been completed. That means there is still one more week of years (7 years) remaining. We now refer to that week of years as the Tribulation. The parenthesis of the church age began after the stoning of Stephen—the Nation of Israel's final rejection of the kingdom—and will close at the rapture of the church. Indeed, the Old Testament prophecies saw no intervening period between the "sufferings of Christ and the glory that should follow" (1 Pet. 1:10–11). So once the parenthesis concludes, the final week of years will kick back in, and God will fulfill all of His Old Testament promises to the Jews and the Nation of Israel regarding the kingdom of heaven.

The kingdom of heaven is found only in the Gospel written to the Jews (Matthew). It is also called the "kingdom of Israel" in Acts 1:6. And, as was mentioned yesterday, almost every commentator will say that the kingdom of heaven is the same as the kingdom of God. Nothing could be further from the truth! This is why we cannot leave the Bible in forming our definitions. Running to the Greek for our definition of these "kingdoms" is a key way of insuring that we will never really understand them biblically. But if we let the Bible be the Bible and provide its own definitions, we'll discover the kingdom that was promised to the Nation of Israel. It is a literal, physical, governmental, Davidic, Messianic kingdom on the *earth*. It is this kingdom that Matthew emphasizes and identifies as the kingdom of heaven. It may seem confusing to call a literal, physical kingdom the "kingdom of HEAVEN," but from God's vantage point, the earth is actually the capital of His heavens and the place where He has chosen His plan for the universe to be enacted.

On the other hand, by biblical definition, the kingdom of God is something altogether different. We can make a biblical composite of this kingdom:

- Luke 17:20–21 – It doesn't come "with observation." You can't necessarily observe it or say "here it is" or "there it is" because it is "within you."

- Romans 14:17 – "It is not meat and drink, but righteousness, peace, and joy." (Though we can't observe the kingdom of God, we can observe its effects in the lives of people—righteousness, peace and joy.)

- 1 Corinthians 4:20 – "It is not in word, but in power."

- 1 Corinthians 15:50 – "Flesh and blood cannot inherit it." (Because it's not a *physical* kingdom!)

- John 3:3 – You enter it by a spiritual birth. (Because it is a *spiritual* kingdom!)

Much of the confusion concerning these two kingdoms is because in the parallel accounts, Matthew often uses kingdom of heaven when the other Gospels use the phrase kingdom of God. Rather than presumptuously concluding that they are the same thing, however, we must recognize that Jesus Christ is the embodiment of both kingdoms, so while He was on the earth, both kingdoms were present at the same time.

One of the reasons this distinction is so vital is that it affects the message that we preach! We preach the kingdom of God (Acts 8:12). The Jewish message of the kingdom of heaven was put on hold after Stephen's final offer to the Nation of Israel in Acts 7. It is a different message with different ramifications and promises that will be preached once again on this earth during Daniel's seventieth week (the Tribulation), once we have been removed.

A few pithy comments about some verses in today's reading:

- 11:5 – This verse explains why Matthew recorded the healing ministry of Jesus in chapters 8–9. Such things were how God told Israel in the Old Testament they would recognize their Messiah-King (Isa. 53:5–6; 61:1).

- 11:14 – Malachi 4:5 prophesied that Elijah would come before the establishment of the Day of the Lord (the kingdom of heaven). But had Israel received her King, the parenthesis of the church age would have been non-existent. That's why the church was in a mystery form in the Old Testament. Jesus lets us know that had the Nation of Israel received her Messiah, John the Baptist would have been the fulfillment of the prophecy concerning Elijah's coming. (All of the other Old Testament prophecies concerning the Day of the Lord could have and would have been fulfilled.) As it stands, Elijah himself will return during the Tribulation along with Moses (Moses = the Law, Elijah = the Prophets).

- 12:23 – The people recognize Jesus is the Messiah ("the son of David").

- 12:24 – The Pharisees don't recognize Jesus as the Messiah and attribute the power by which He performed His miracles to Satan!

- 12:31–32 – Here, Jesus describes the so-called unpardonable sin. There are four criteria to committing it:

    1. You must be a Jew.

    2. Jesus Christ must be publicly manifest in bodily form, performing signs and wonders.

    3. You, as a Jew, are an eyewitness of the events in #2.

    4. Your mind becomes so spiritually disoriented and perverted, and your heart so hardened, that you attribute the power through which Christ worked to Satan.

    In verse 32, Jesus gives two specific times that all four criteria can be fulfilled: "in this world" and "in the world to come." The first was during the earthly ministry of Jesus from 30–33 AD. The second is during the millennium ("the kingdom of heaven"). Clearly you haven't, won't, and can't commit the unpardonable sin!

- 13:1 – This marks a major shift in Jesus's ministry. *House* is a term used to refer to Israel. *Sea* is a term used to refer to Gentiles. The kingdom of heaven now goes into a parable form. Contrary to popular Laodicean teaching, a parable is *not* an earthly story that *reveals* a heavenly truth. It's a heavenly truth wrapped in an earthly story for the purpose of *hiding* the truth from those who don't really want it anyway (13:11–17).

- 13:55–56 – So much for Mary's perpetual virginity!

52 WEEKS OF **PURSUIT**

WEEK 41, DAY 4: **TODAY'S READING: MATTHEW 14-16**

OVERVIEW:
The feeding of the five thousand (chapter 14); the condemnation of false prophets (chapter 15); the great confession (chapter 16).

HIGHLIGHTS & INSIGHTS:
So far, in our reading of Matthew, we have sought to lay down some foundational understandings to keep us in-bounds doctrinally. We focused on the importance of identifying the Jew and the Jewish nature of this Gospel, as well as distinguishing between the kingdom of heaven and the kingdom of God. Now let's make sure we see how all of the pieces fit together to form the big picture.

The theme of the Bible focuses on a kingdom. The Bible begins with a struggle over a throne (Isa. 14:13), it ends with Someone sitting on a throne (Rev. 11:15), and everything between is God moving to put His Son on that throne while the devil does everything in his power, not only to stop Him, but to put himself on that throne (2 Thess. 2:4).

The kingdom, as it is defined in Scripture, has two distinct dimensions. These are delineated through the phrases the kingdom of God and the kingdom of heaven. And understanding what and where these kingdoms are as history unfolds through the Bible is, quite simply, the difference between sound doctrine and false doctrine.

The kingdom of heaven, sometimes referred to as the "kingdom of Israel" (Hos. 1:4; Acts 1:6), is a literal, physical kingdom with a literal, physical king sitting on a literal, physical throne in literal, physical Jerusalem and reigning governmentally over the entire literal, physical earth. (This literal earthly kingdom is referred to as the kingdom of heaven because God chose the *earth*, which is in the midst of the *heavens*, as the capital of the universe.) This is the kingdom Isaiah prophesied would be established by the promised Messiah, the Lord Jesus Christ (Isa. 9:6–7). The *only* time the kingdom of heaven is mentioned by name in the New Testament is in the Gospel of Matthew which was written to the Jews, a fact which must arrest our attention to the Jewish scope of its fulfillment.

The kingdom of God, on the other hand, is not a *physical* kingdom. As the Bible defines it, we find that "it is not meat and drink" (Rom. 14:17), it is not "flesh and blood" (1 Cor. 15:50), it does not come "with observation" (Luke 17:20), we cannot say "here it is" or "there it is" (Luke 17:21), and it is not even something that is expressed with "words," but with "power" (1 Cor. 4:20). This kingdom is a *spiritual* kingdom that is entered by a spiritual birth (John 3:3–5) and is placed within us (Luke 17:21).

Distinguishing between the kingdom of God and the kingdom of heaven is paramount, because as Jesus sent forth the apostles in Matthew 10, He sent them to "preach that the kingdom of heaven is at hand" (10:7). They were, therefore, sent to preach a kingdom-of-heaven message intended specifically for the Jews (the Nation of Israel). In fact, they were specifically instructed *not* to carry this message to the Samaritans (half Jew/half Gentile) nor to the Gentiles (10:5).

Interestingly, the Nation of Israel received their final offer of the kingdom of heaven through Stephen's incredible discourse to the ruling council of Israel in Acts 7. And in the very next chapter, Philip is led by the Spirit to preach to the Samaritans! That is where the transition in the book of Acts begins and where the New Testament message switched from the kingdom of heaven to the kingdom of God (Acts 8:5, 12).

What this reveals to us is that we must be very careful concerning the message we preach today. We must not proclaim a kingdom-of-heaven message in this dispensation so we avoid the blasphemy Jesus warned about in Revelation 2:9 (functioning like Jews when we aren't Jews). Likewise, we must be careful not to pattern our methods as we proclaim the kingdom of God after those who went proclaiming the kingdom of heaven. In this dispensation, we do not follow the model of the Twelve, the Seventy, or even the church in Jerusalem (Acts 2). We follow the model of the church at Antioch (Acts 13). The church at Antioch proclaimed the kingdom of God (the spiritual kingdom), sent out missionaries, and established local churches because the local church is the vehicle in this dispensation through which our Lord is carrying out His plan to bring worshippers into His spiritual kingdom and, ultimately, into the physical one!

A few comments about some of the verses in today's reading:

- 14:1 – Herod, like many in positions of power and authority today, fears everything he *shouldn't* and nothing he *should*. He fears John (14:4), the multitude (14:5), and embarrassment (14:9). He doesn't fear *God*!
- 14:14 – As we behold the sin-sick multitudes all around us, may we also be moved with compassion!
- 14:24–25 – The storms of life that threaten to overwhelm us, consume us, and destroy us are no problem for Jesus. In the context of the story, we could say, "What threatens to be over our head is under Jesus's feet!"
- 16:15–19 – This is a highly controversial passage, and historically has been a breeding ground for much false doctrine.
    - "The church" to which Jesus is referring in this passage is built upon *the* Rock—not Peter, but the Lord Jesus Christ!
    - The "keys" that Peter, the Apostle to the Jews, actually received in this passage were the "keys of the kingdom of heaven" (16:19). And when we move into the early chapters of the book of Acts, it is still the kingdom of heaven message that is being preached, so Peter, with the keys to the kingdom, is the predominant voice.
    - After the final offer of the kingdom was made to the Jewish ruling council through Stephen in Acts 7, however, God immediately makes the transition to the "half Jew/half Gentile" Samaritans in Acts 8. Then, in chapter 9, God calls out the Apostle to the Gentiles (Saul, who would become Paul), and in chapter 10, Saul (Paul) preaches a kingdom-of-God message to Gentiles like you and me. For the rest of the book of Acts, Paul, the Apostle to the Gentiles is the predominant voice.

52 WEEKS OF PURSUIT

WEEK 41, DAY 5: **TODAY'S READING: MATTHEW 17-20**

OVERVIEW:
The King's glory (chapter 17); the King's rebuke (chapter 18); the King's instructions (19:1–15); the King's demands (19:16–20:34).

HIGHLIGHTS & INSIGHTS:
We've discussed the importance of keeping your eye on the Jew when dealing with the New Testament. This often confuses people because they assume that since "all scripture is given by inspiration of God, and is profitable for doctrine, for reproof, for correction, for instruction in righteousness," that it all applies directly to them. We could say it this way, however: "Though all of the Bible is written *for* us, not all of the Bible is written *to* us."

I like the illustration Jeff Adams uses to make this point. Suppose I let you read a letter my grandfather wrote to me in which he offered the wisdom and insight he had gleaned through his life on the earth. When you come to a part in the letter where my grandfather talks about leaving me $100,000 in his will, you stop reading, look at me, and ask, "When do we collect our money?" I would quickly remind you that the letter was addressed to me and intended for me and that I was simply allowing you to glean from what my grandfather was seeking to teach me!

I think you get the point. When dealing with the Old Testament and some New Testament books, we as Gentiles living in the parenthesis of the church age must be careful to keep in mind that we are reading someone else's mail. We are the church, so we get our doctrine from the books of the Bible that are addressed to the church (church epistles) or those that are addressed to men who hold positions of leadership in the church (pastoral epistles).

Now, that doesn't mean that we can't glean many things from Matthew, or Hebrews (who do you think that book is addressed to?), or James (which is specifically addressed to "the twelve tribes"). We absolutely can find many things to apply to our lives in a Devotional sense. But we must make certain that we have "rightly divided the Word of truth" (2 Tim. 2:15). Matthew, Mark, Luke, John and Acts (at least until chapter 7) provide a historical perspective of the first coming of Christ from the standpoint of the Nation of Israel. Once the Nation of Israel rejects their King and His kingdom one final time in Acts 7, a transition takes place in the book of Acts:

- From an *Old Testament* structure to a *New Testament* structure.
- From God dealing with the *Nation of Israel*, to dealing with the *church*.
- From God working primarily with the *Jew*, to God working primarily with the *Gentile*.
- From a kingdom of heaven message, to a kingdom of God message.
- From the ministry of *Peter*, the apostle to the Jews (Acts 1–12), to the ministry of *Paul*, the apostle to the Gentiles (Acts 13–28).
- From God's base of operation being in *Jerusalem*, to His base in *Antioch*.

By the time these transitions are made and we get to the end of the book of Acts, the church is firmly established, and we move right into the letters written by Paul to the church. In those books, we are safe. They are written to us and lay out for us doctrine intended specifically for those of us living in this dispensation.

So, how do we know what to apply from the New Testament books written to Jews? Whatever we are applying needs to line up with what God revealed through Paul. Because of who Paul is (the apostle to the Gentiles) and because of who received his letters (churches and pastors of churches), we can be sure that anything God wants us to apply will be repeated in Paul's books. This principle resulted in some groups in church history being referred to as Paulicians.[1] They understood the importance of "rightly dividing the Word of truth" (2 Tim. 2:15) and not applying to us something God promised or intended for the Jews or the Nation of Israel.[2]

Keeping these things in mind in today's reading will be helpful. They will help you make the distinction between the things that apply only to the Jews and the Nation of Israel and those things that also apply to us because they are repeated in the Pauline epistles.

A few comments about the Transfiguration (Matt. 17:1–8).

- 17:1 – Peter, James, and John are the fulfillment of the strange statement the Lord made at the end of chapter 16, that there were some of the people that were listening to Him there who would be eyewitnesses of the Second Coming.

- 17:1 – This Second Coming pre-fulfillment actually took place "after six days." If we take those six days and plug them into the equation God laid out in 2 Peter 3:8, we discover that the Second Coming (which this passage is foreshadowing) will be after six thousand years of human history (6 days x 1000). Some astute folks will balk at such reasoning, citing Luke's account of the Transfiguration which says it was "about eight days" (Luke 9:28). I'm not the sharpest knife in the drawer, but I think that the number that is after six and about eight just might be seven! (Just like it is laid out in Genesis 2:1–3!)

- 17:2 – The word *transfigured* indicates that Christ's "figure" was "transformed." When He came to this earth, He couldn't be anything other than what He was—the very glory of the Father (John 1:16). That glory, however, was veiled in a body of flesh. At the Transfiguration Christ rolled back His flesh revealing the "glory of His Father" (16:27) that will be His when He returns to the earth at His second coming. (See Peter's comments about this in his incredible statement in 2 Pet. 1:16–18.)

- 17:3 – This is actually the first time Moses stepped foot in the Promised Land! What a thrill that must have been for him!

- 17:1–5 – In this "perfect" and "complete" picture of the Second Coming, there are seven that are in attendance: Jesus, Peter, James, John, Moses, Elijah, and God the Father.

---

[1] *Encyclopedia Britannica Online*, s.v. "Paulician," August 7, 2013, https://www.britannica.com/topic/Paulicians.
[2] Jack W. Langford, "The Paulicians (As They we're Called by Their Enemies)," SeparationTruth.com, September 4, 2018, http://separationtruth.com/resources/Paulicians+new.pdf, 5–6.

WEEK 42, DAY 1: **TODAY'S READING: MATTHEW 21-23**

OVERVIEW:
The King's judgments (21:1–22:14); the King's defense (22:15–46); the King's denunciation (chapter 23).

HIGHLIGHTS & INSIGHTS:
Between Matthew 13 and Matthew 25, there are a total of twelve parables on the kingdom of heaven, corresponding to the twelve tribes of Israel. They all deal with Israel's rejection of her Messiah and, from a Doctrinal standpoint, have no application to a Christian in the church age. Chapter 21 begins with three signs given to the Nation of Israel (21:1–22) which are followed by three parables (21:23–22:14).

- The *Coming* of the *King* (21:1–11)

The first sign is the Triumphal Entry, which fulfilled Zechariah's prophecy: "Rejoice greatly, O daughter of Zion; shout, O daughter of Jerusalem: behold, thy King cometh unto thee: he is just, and having salvation; lowly, and riding upon an ass, and upon a colt the foal of an ass" (9:9). In response, the people quote Psalm 118:26: "Blessed be he that cometh in the name of the Lord." This passage is a picture of what will take place at Christ's second coming, and at the Triumphal Entry, all of the Old Testament conditions and promises could have been fulfilled without the parenthesis of the church age. Through this sign, our Lord revealed Israel's *spiritual blindness*.

- The *Cleansing* of the *Temple* (21:12–16).

This was Christ's first act after the Triumphal Entry and the second sign to Israel. That the Temple had become a place of merchandise reveals Israel's spiritual condition at that time. In God's eyes, Israel had become a "den of thieves" (21:13). Jesus is quoting Isaiah 56:7 here, calling the Temple "my house," a tremendous claim of His deity. And when the chief priests and scribes accuse Him of receiving the accolades intended for the Messiah, Jesus quotes Psalm 8:2, a messianic psalm. In this sign, our Lord revealed Israel's inward *spiritual corruption*.

- The *Cursing* of the *Fig Tree* (21:17–22).

In this third sign, the fig tree pictures Israel (Matt. 24:32–33; Luke 13:6–10). This particular fig tree had leaves, but no fruit. The parallel passage in Luke 13:6–10 reveals that the tree actually had three years to bear fruit, but didn't. By this time in His ministry, Jesus had also revealed Himself to Israel for three years, but they had only an outward show of religion (leaves) and no reality (fruit). In this sign, our Lord revealed Israel's *outward fruitlessness*.

In 21:23–29, the chief priests and elders interrupt Jesus's teaching to question His authority. He answers with a question about John the Baptist's authority. They understood that if they said John's authority was from heaven, Jesus would ask them why they didn't get baptized. If they said that John's authority was from men, the people would have beat the devil out of them (which is exactly what they needed!). They refuse to answer, so Jesus refused to answer them.

Instead, He begins to teach three parables concerning the Nation of Israel.

- The Parable of the Two Sons (21:28–32) teaches that Israel rejected God the *Father*.
- The Parable of the Vineyard and the Husbandman (21:33–46) teaches that Israel rejected God the *Son*.

We do see, however, the future reality in 21:37: "They will reverence my Son"! Philippians 2:10–11 says, "That at the name of Jesus every knee should bow … and that every tongue should confess that Jesus Christ is Lord to the glory of God the Father."

- The Parable of the Marriage Feast (22:1–14) teaches that Israel rejected God the *Holy Spirit*. (See Acts 7:51.)

The remainder of chapter 22 (vs.15–46) can be broken down by four key questions that are asked:

- A *political* question about *taxes* (22:15–22).
- A *doctrinal* question about the *resurrection* (22:23–33).
- An *ethical* question about the *law* (22:34–40).
- A *personal* question about the *Messiah* (22:41–46).

In chapter 23, Jesus explain some things about the scribes and Pharisees. He talks first to His disciples and the multitude (vs. 1–12) with the scribes and Pharisees sitting right there! Then in verses 13–33, He speaks directly to them. And, when you read what He says to them, brace for impact! He delivers a series of eight woes or judgments against them. These woes easily compare with the eight Beatitudes Christ laid down in the Sermon on the Mount.

- Woe #1 (23:13) – The proud "shut up" the kingdom.
    - Beatitude #1 (5:3) – The "poor in spirit" inherit the kingdom.
- Woe #2 (23:14) – "Devourers" receive "damnation."
    - Beatitude #2 (5:4) – "Mourners" receive "comfort."
- Woe #3 (23:15) – The proud send people to "hell."
    - Beatitude #3 (5:5) – The meek inherit the "earth."
- Woe #4 (23:16–22) – Those who hunger and thirst for material gain are found empty.
    - Beatitude #4 (5:6) – Those who hunger and thirst for righteousness are filled.
- Woe #5 (23:23–24) – The proud reject mercy because of insignificant details and are judged ("woe").
    - Beatitude #5 (5:7) – The merciful shall obtain mercy.
- Woe #6 (23:25–28) – The outwardly pure but inwardly rotten will be judged.
    - Beatitude #6 (5:8) – The inwardly pure ("pure in heart") "shall see God."
- Woe # 7 and #8 (23:29–33) – Murderers and persecutors of the righteous are "children of them which killed the prophets" (the devil!).
    - Beatitude #7 and #8 (5:9–12) – Peacemakers and those who are persecuted for righteousness are called "children of God."

Chapter 23 closes with Jesus's heartfelt lamentation over Jerusalem. And check out that last verse: "For I say unto you, Ye shall not see me henceforth, till ye shall say, Blessed is he that cometh in the name of the Lord" (v. 39). In other words, as a nation, they won't see Him again until the time of Jacob's trouble (Dan. 12:1; Jer. 30:7), when in one day (Hos. 6:1–3; Isa. 26:12–21), the nation of Israel will be converted and healed (Rom. 11:26–27; Heb. 8:8–12) as they recognize that He is, in fact, the Messiah (Acts 2:36) and will cry out for His return (Psalm 44, 68, 74, 79, 83).

52 WEEKS OF **PURSUIT**

WEEK 42, DAY 2: **TODAY'S READING: MATTHEW 24-26**

OVERVIEW:
The King's return (chapters 24–25); the King's preparation (26:1–56); the King's trial (26:57–27:26).

HIGHLIGHTS & INSIGHTS:
The first verse in today's reading is tremendously significant: "And Jesus went out, and departed from the temple: and his disciples came to him for to show him the buildings of the temple" (24:1). We could say that, once Jesus (the "glory" of the Father, John 1:14) "departed" out of the temple, He would not return again and that the temple was doomed for destruction. Just as in 1 Samuel 4:19–22, it's as if Jesus had written "Ichabod" over the door, which means "the glory is departed." Jesus walks out and immediately begins to talk about the Temple's destruction (24:2).

Verse 3 of chapter 24 is also significant. After leaving the Temple, Jesus and His disciples make their way to the Mount of Olives, where they ask Him a very important question: "Tell us, when shall these things be? and what shall be the sign of thy coming, and of the end of the world?" It's incredible because, as they ask this question about the time of the second coming, Jesus is sitting in the exact place where His foot will first touch when He comes! (See Zech. 14:4.) Does God have a sense of humor or what?

Chapter 24 is a key place in Matthew where people can get spiritually disoriented and doctrinally discombobulated. But the context here has nothing to do with the church. By the time these events take place, the church will already be raptured out (1 Thess. 4:13–17), and Daniel's seventieth week has kicked in. The events described in chapters 24–25 will be fulfilled during the Tribulation, the time of Jacob's Trouble (Dan 12:1; Jer. 30:7). In fact, the signs Jesus describes here are listed in this exact order during the opening of the first six of the seven seals in Revelation 6:1–16, which also describes the Tribulation.

- 1st Sign (Matt. 24:5) – False Christ = 1st Seal (Rev. 6:1–2).
- 2nd Sign (Matt. 24:6) – War = 2nd Seal (Rev. 6:3–4).
- 3rd Sign (Matt. 24:7) – Famine = 3rd Seal (Rev. 6:5–6).
- 4th Sign (Matt. 24:7) – Pestilence = 4th Seal (Rev. 6:7–8).
- 5th Sign (Matt. 24:8–9) – Martyrdom = 5th Seal (Rev. 6:9–11).
- 6th Sign (Matt. 24:29) – Changes in Sun, Moon, & Stars = 6th Seal (Rev. 6:12–16).

Once we identify the context of Matthew 24, some verses start making a whole lot more sense. For example:

- 24:13 – "But he that shall endure unto the end, the same shall be saved."

    God will be dealing with believers differently in the Tribulation than He did in the church age. Those who call upon the name of the Lord during the Tribulation will not be sealed with the Holy Spirit as they are in this dispensation (Eph. 1:10–14). Believers in the Tribulation must endure to the end in order to be saved. That is, if they take the "mark of the beast" (Rev. 13:11–18), their destiny in the lake of fire will be forever sealed.

- 24:14 – "And this gospel of the kingdom shall be preached in all the world for a witness unto all nations; and then shall the end come."

    We hear this one a lot! People will say, "The sooner we get the gospel to all of the nations of the world, we'll bring the kingdom in." First of all, we don't preach the gospel of the kingdom in this dispensation, and if we did, we'd be asking for a curse according to Galatians 1:7–9! Secondly, the church has already been raptured by the time the 144,000 will fulfill this prophecy in the Tribulation.

- 24:31 – "And he shall send his angels with a great sound of a trumpet, and they shall gather together his elect from the four winds, from one end of heaven to the other."

    This verse is certainly referring to a rapture, but it is not the rapture of the church (1 Thess. 4:13–17). This is a rapture of Jewish saints (Ps. 50:2–5) at the end of the Tribulation (Rev. 11:11–12), just before the Battle of Armageddon (Isa. 26:20–21).

- 25:1–12 – Some will use this passage to teach that a believer in the body of Christ can lose their salvation. A few simple observations can help. The context (clearly stated in verse 1) is the kingdom of heaven. By that statement alone, we know we're dealing with a strictly Jewish context. Those involved here are virgins (plural), not a virgin (singular). "Virgins" are found in the Tribulation, not the church age (Rev. 14:1–6). The Bride of Christ is a "virgin" (2 Cor. 11:1–13) and is always referred to as one collective virgin, never virgins. Lastly, the virgins in this passage do not marry anyone, they go to meet someone, and the someone they go to meet is already married (Luke 12:36)! Note in verse 13 that it is the Son of man coming as a married bridegroom, not the Son of God coming for His bride!

Most of chapter 26 is familiar and self-explanatory. As you read it, however, let it minister to you in a fresh, new way.

52 WEEKS OF **PURSUIT**

WEEK 42, DAY 3: **TODAY'S READING: MATTHEW 27-28**

OVERVIEW:
The King's trial (26:57–27:26); the King's suffering and death (27:27–66); the King's victory (chapter 28).

HIGHLIGHTS & INSIGHTS:
Based on Hebrews 9:16–17, we will actually enter the New Testament in our reading today: "For where a testament is, there must also of necessity be the death of the testator. For a testament is of force after men are dead: otherwise it is of no strength at all while the testator liveth." Though it's an unusual way to think about the Gospels, applying this biblical principle is key to keeping our bearings in the New Testament.

Obviously, today's reading is rich and full of things worthy of commentary. You can make most of those comments yourself, so today we'll discuss the time factors involved in the last week of our Savior's life on the earth.

Traditionally, most have taught that Jesus died on what we call Good Friday. However, that tradition was handed down through the Roman Catholic Church. That, by itself, does not necessarily make it wrong (they also believe and teach concerning the virgin birth, the deity of Christ, and His bodily resurrection)—but anything handed down through that church should always raise about ten trillion red flags!

Now, I have to go on record that I absolutely love Roman Catholics, but I absolutely hate their church! A full one-sixth of the world's population professes to be Roman Catholic. While this system is called Christian (*catholic* indicates "universal Christianity"), they propagate what 2 Corinthians 11:4 calls "another Jesus … another spirit … another gospel." The Roman Catholic Church damns people's souls to hell while its members think they are following the Jesus of the Bible. This church is damnably deceptive, which is the reason for such strong, harsh-sounding statements. (See how Jesus commends the church in Ephesus in Revelation 2:1–2 for their harsh stance against false teaching!) Our hearts truly should break for people trapped in that system, and we must constantly be looking and praying for opportunities to love them past the blinders (2 Cor. 4:4) the enemy is using to hold them captive in his snare (2 Tim. 2:26).

But in regards to the issue of the death of Christ taking place on Good Friday, Jesus said in Matthew 12:40, "For as Jonas (Jonah) was three days and three nights in the whale's belly; so shall the Son of man be three days and three nights in the heart of the earth." (See also Matt. 16:21; 17:23; 20:19; 27:63; Mark 8:31; 9:31; 10:34; Luke 9:22; 13:32; 18:33; 24:46; John 2:19.) If Christ died on Friday afternoon at 3:00 p.m. and was in the grave before 6:00 p.m., there is not enough time for Him to have been in the grave for three days and three nights. Most well-meaning people who love God certainly as much as I do (and honestly are much more intelligent than me!) get around this by saying that in the Jewish mind of that day, any portion of a day was considered the whole. That may be the case, and may have been what Jesus had in mind, but I've always had a hard time with how specific Jesus was. He said "three days and three nights"!

So, instead of Good Friday, let's consider a Bad Wednesday, which fits the biblical timeline far better. (Don't worry, I'm didn't invent this line of reasoning. Many others agree with this timeline which has been suggested by Warren Wiersbe and others.)

The Jewish day began at sundown the previous day ("the evening and the morning were the first day," Gen. 1:5). So as we walk through these final days of Jesus's life, this is the timeline we have:

- Friday: Jesus came to Bethany six days before Passover (John 12:1).
- Saturday: Triumphal Entry (John 12:12–19, "on the next day")
- Sunday: Temple cleansed; fig tree cursed (Mark 11:12–18)

- Monday: Parables; questions; Olivet discourse (Matt. 21:23–25:46)
- Tuesday: Preparation for Passover (Matt. 26:2, "after two days")
- Wednesday: Upper room events; Gethsemane; arrest and trials; crucifixion (Matt. 26:20–27:58)
- Thursday: In tomb; the Passover Sabbath, "an high day" (John 19:31)
- Friday: Women brought spices when Passover Sabbath was past (Mark 16:1)
- Saturday: The regular weekly Sabbath
- Sunday: Christ arose sometime after sunset Saturday evening ("evening and the morning"), and the empty tomb is discovered early Sunday morning.

Certainly, the most important thing is not what we believe about *when* Christ died, but *that* we believe Christ died for our sins, was buried, and rose again the third day. But this question surfaces every Easter. Hopefully, this timeline will help.

We've mentioned that the Friday timeline was passed down through Roman Catholic tradition, but be careful of another related false teaching. Seventh Day Adventists claim that moving the day of worship from Saturday (the Sabbath—the seventh day of the week) to Sunday (the first day of the week) was also a tradition passed down through that false system, so God never intended Christians to worship on Sunday.

That God has ordained the first day of the week as the day of worship for Christians can be easily substantiated biblically:

1) Because we're Christians and not Jews (Exod. 31:13, the Sabbath is a sign between God and Israel)
2) The Lord rose from the dead on the first day of the week (Matt. 28:1)
3) The Holy Spirit came down on the first day of the week (Acts 2)
4) The disciples met on the first day of the week (Acts 20:7)
5) New Testament giving is to be brought on the first day of the week (1 Cor. 16:1–2)

WEEK 42, DAY 4: **TODAY'S READING: MARK 1-3**

OVERVIEW:
The Servant presented (chapter 1); the Servant in action (chapter 2); the Servant assisted (chapter 3).

HIGHLIGHTS & INSIGHTS:
The Gospel of Matthew was written to *Jews* to present Jesus Christ as the *King*. In perfect contrast, the Gospel of Mark was written to *Gentiles* to present Jesus Christ as a *Servant*. Because the Gospel of Mark is written to Gentiles, it has several distinctive features:

1. It does not begin with a genealogy. Gentiles are not typically preoccupied with Jesus's lineage because they have no blood connection with Abraham or David.

2. Mark does not quote from or reference the Old Testament as much as did Matthew because Gentiles are typically unfamiliar with the Old Testament. Matthew built his case on signs and Scripture, while Mark uses the most powerful kind of evidence in a Gentile court—eyewitnesses (Mark 10:46; 14:3; 15:21; 16:1). Mark's is also the only Gospel that explains the Jewish customs and teachings that a Gentile might not be familiar with (Mark 7:3-4; 12:18; 14:12; 15:42).

3. It is the shortest Gospel because God knows that Gentiles typically have a short attention span and are more interested in action than words. (Action movies are popular not because of their plot, but their action. Romans went to the Coliseum to watch the gladiators—it's action!) Likewise, Mark emphasizes Jesus's actions more than His teachings. Whereas Matthew took three chapters to record the Sermon on the Mount (Matt. 5-7), Mark skips the sermon, which chronologically would have taken place in chapter 1, and goes directly to the action that followed the sermon.

4. It moves quickly and directly to the main event of the book—the death, burial, and resurrection of Christ—which is the main purpose for a Gentile reader. About 40% of this Mark's Gospel deals with the last eight days of Jesus's life. Mark emphasizes being a citizen of the kingdom of God, not the kingdom of heaven.

The Gospel of Mark also presents Jesus Christ as a Servant, so it has several distinctive features that reflect that emphasis:

- No genealogy is included, not only because of the Gentile audience, but because the birth of a servant is unimportant.

- The key words in this gospel are "straightway" (19 times) and "immediately" (17 times), words that describe the actions of a servant. A servant does *what* he is told, *when* he is told. And a servant's *words* pale in comparison to his *works*. Also, it is only in the Gospel of Mark that the hands of Jesus are prominent (1:31; 6:2; 8:23, 25: 9:27). Hands are symbolic of the work of a servant.

- The key verse in the book, Mark 10:45, portrays Christ's servanthood: "For even the Son of man came not to be ministered unto, but to minister and to give his life a ransom for many." This verse also provides a perfect outline of the book:
  - The Servant's Work (chapters 1-10)
  - The Servant's Sacrifice (chapters 11-16)

Though Mark clearly presents Christ as a Servant, the Holy Spirit also directed Mark to emphasize the deity of Christ. At least five times the "Servant of all" (Mark 10:43-44) is referred to as "Son of God," "Son of the most high God," and "Christ, the Son of the Blessed" (Mark 1:1; 3:11; 5:7; 14:61; 15:39). To confirm His deity, Mark records over twenty of Christ's miracles, demonstrating His supreme power and authority over demons, disease, death, and nature. (See 1:21-28; 1:29-31; 1:32-34; 1:40-45; 2:3-12; 3:1-6; 4:35-41; 5:1-20; 5:22-24, 35-43; 5:25-34; 6:31-44; 6:45-50; 6:51-54; 7:24-30; 7:31-37; 8:1-9; 8:22-26; 9:2-10; 9:14-29; 10:46-52; 11:12-14, 20-26; 16:1-11; 16:19-20.)

52 WEEKS OF PURSUIT

WEEK 42, DAY 5: **TODAY'S READING: MARK 4-6**

OVERVIEW:
The Servant conquers a storm (chapter 4); the Servant conquers demons (chapter 5); the Servant sends out His disciples (chapter 6).

HIGHLIGHTS & INSIGHTS:
Since the narrative structure of the Gospels makes them relatively easy to understand, we focused yesterday on the big picture of Mark's Gospel. It clearly fits into God's plan to present the Lord Jesus Christ "to the Jew first [Gospel of Matthew], and also to the Gentile [Gospel of Mark]" (Rom. 2:10). Today we will consider the unique authorship of this Gospel.

As in Matthew, no specific verse states that Mark is the author of this Gospel. God did promise, however, to preserve His words, and that certainly would include the titles of the books. Very simply, we know that Mark is the author because God said that this is "The Gospel According To St. Mark"! Based on the testimony of Papias, one of the very early church fathers, it is commonly believed that Mark received the eyewitness information from the Apostle Peter who, according to 1 Peter 5:13, had won Mark to Christ and discipled him.

Mark is the actually the author's surname. His first name is John (Acts 12:12, 25; 15:37). John Mark came from a Christian family; he is first mentioned in connection with his mother, Mary, who had opened her home for prayer when Peter was imprisoned by Herod (Acts 12:1–2). His mother's brother was Barnabas, which makes John Mark his nephew (Col. 4:10).

When Barnabas and Saul (soon to be Paul) returned from Jerusalem in Acts 12, John Mark accompanied them to Antioch (Acts 12:25). Later, when Barnabas and Saul were sent out of the church of Antioch on their first missionary journey, John Mark was part of their missionary team (Acts 13:4–5). Not long into their journey, however, John Mark had had enough and headed back home (Acts 13:13).

The Scripture doesn't say why he went home. Perhaps it was tougher than he thought it was going to be. Maybe the pace was too fast, the persecution too intense, and the demonic activity too freaky. Maybe he was just plain old homesick! For whatever reason, though, he went home.

Later, when Paul and Barnabas were about to depart on their second missionary journey, Barnabas wanted John Mark to accompany them again (Acts 15:36–37). Paul looked at the *work* of God and said, "This *work* is too important to God for us to give him a second chance" (Acts 15:38). Barnabas looked at the *child* of God and said, "This *servant* is too important to God for us not to give him a second chance." Who was right? Your answer will probably be determined by your personality and the gifts of the Spirit you possess. Regardless, the contention between Paul and Barnabas concerning John Mark was so sharp, they decided to part ways (Acts 15:39–40).

But in time, something significant took place in this sensitive young man's life. In Colossians 4:10–11, John Mark (Marcus) was with Paul, and Paul calls him a "fellow-worker." He's with him again in Philemon 24, where Paul calls him his "fellow-laborer." At the end of Paul's life, he specifically requests Mark's presence, stating, "for he is profitable to me for the ministry" (2 Tim. 4:11).

Perhaps God used Paul's rejection to arrest John Mark's attention so that he could see how serious God's work actually is and to change him into a faithful servant. Or, it may have been Barnabas's ministry of consolation (Acts 4:36) that carefully restored him and gently groomed him into a place of usefulness and profitability in Christ's service. Or maybe, it was solely the ministry of the Holy Spirit of God working through John Mark as he wrote this Gospel, revealing to him what true servanthood is through the life and death of his Savior. Or it could have been a combination of all three influences! However it happened—praise the Lord!—John Mark became a faithful, useable, profitable servant of the Lord Jesus Christ.

Mark's life can be an encouragement to us in this regard. Many of us have blown a major opportunity (or many opportunities) to serve the Lord in the past. We are often prone to discouragement and defeat in our service for Christ. Maybe you are in need of a second chance … a third … or even a fourth. Allow the restored, renewed, and revived ministry of John Mark, through this Gospel God used him to pen, to point you to the one true model of servanthood, our Lord Jesus Christ!

52 WEEKS OF PURSUIT

WEEK 43, DAY 1: TODAY'S READING: MARK 7-9

OVERVIEW:
The Servant teaches (7:1–8:26); the Servant reveals that suffering leads to glory (8:27–9:13); the Servant reveals that power comes from faith (9:14–29); the Servant reveals that service leads to honor (9:30–50).

HIGHLIGHTS & INSIGHTS:
We now have all the pieces that will give us the big picture of Mark's Gospel. Today, let's begin by pulling all the pieces together into a concise, easy-to-open package.

1. **Information About The Author.**
   - His name: Mark
   - His name means: "A Defense"
   - His mother's name is Mary (Acts 12:12)
   - He is also called John (Acts 12:12, 25; 15:37)
   - He is also referred to in Scripture as Marcus (Col. 4:10; Philem. 24; 1 Pet. 5:13)
   - His uncle is Barnabas (Col. 4:10)
   - He was a minister or servant on Paul's first missionary journey (Acts 13:5)
   - He quit the team (45 AD) (Acts 13:13)
   - He was rejected by Paul as a participant on the second missionary journey (Acts 15:38)
   - He became profitable for the ministry again (66 AD) (2 Tim. 4:11)
   - He was a convert of the Apostle Peter (1 Pet. 5:13)

2. **Facts About The Gospel**
   - Approximate date of writing: 57–63 AD
   - Written from: Jerusalem
   - Dates of the recorded events: 26–33 AD
   - Theme: Christ as the Willing Servant
   - Christ is seen as: The Servant of the Lord
   - Key Verse: Mark 10:45
   - Key Words: *straightway* (19 times); *immediately* (17 times)
   - Chapters: 16
   - Verses: 678
   - Words: 15,844

3. **Features of This Gospel**
   - This Gospel refers to Christ as Lord only twice. The other three refer to Christ as Lord a total of 73 times.
   - This Gospel lets us know not only *what* Christ did in His earthly ministry, but *how* He did it.
   - This Gospel contains 11 fulfilled prophecies.

4. **A Simple Outline of This Gospel**
   - The Servant's WORK (chapters 1–10)

52 WEEKS OF PURSUIT

- The Servant's SACRIFICE (chapters 11–16)

A few "pithy" comments from verses in today's reading:

- 7:1 – As soon as you see the Scribes and Pharisees approaching, you can bet it ain't gonna be good!

- 7:7 – This little definition will let you know that the Scribes and Pharisees live on in many Bible-believing churches. The tell-tale sign is that they "teach for doctrines the commandments of men." They pride themselves in their so-called holy standards and see themselves as those who champion God's Word, while Jesus says they actually make "the Word of God of none effect through [their] tradition" (7:13).

- 7:15 – God isn't concerned about what we put in our mouths, but the things that come out of our mouths!

- 7:20–23 – As in every sin situation, "The heart of the problem is the problem of the heart!"

- 7:34 – This is an unbelievably powerful glimpse into God's heart. Before Jesus heals this guy, "He sighed." What's that sigh about? Jesus recognizes that it wasn't supposed to be this way! Sickness, disease, handicaps are all part of the curse of sin that we invited upon ourselves.

- 8:12 – This is a different sigh here. This is the "how-proud-can-these-Pharisees-get" sigh!

- 8:14 – The disciples get themselves a little worked up because there's only one loaf of bread in the boat between them all and fail to realize that the very Bread of life is in the boat! (We can't be too hard on them, however—we do the same just about every day.)

- 8:29–33 – It is amazing that people can be used of God in one breath (Matt. 16:17) and used of Satan in the next! And it's just as true about me and you as it is for the person you just thought of!

- 9:5–7 – With a bad case of diarrhea of the mouth, Peter is spouting off, talking for the sake of talking (v. 6)! And you gotta love how the Father interrupts him: "This is my beloved Son: hear him" (v. 7). If I may paraphrase, "Yeah, Peter, thank you for your wonderful ideas, but it's not time to talk right now—it's time to listen!" I wonder how many times on a daily basis God would like to speak a similar rebuke to us!

- 9:29 – Maybe this prescription is what it will take for God to answer that unanswered prayer request that you believe to be His will!

- 9:31–32 – This is a great example of selective hearing. (Ladies, you know we men have a bad case of it!) We hear what we want to hear and don't hear what we don't want to hear.

- 9:33–35 – Remember, as Laodiceans (Rev. 3:14–22; 2 Tim. 3:1–2), we are characterized biblically by the love of *self*! Sometimes rather than denying *ourselves* (8:34), we have simply traded arenas where self vaunts itself. Before coming to Christ, we vaunted ourselves in the *world*. After coming to Christ, we often vaunt ourselves in the *church*! (See 3 John 9.)

- 9:43–48 – The Jehovah's [False] Witnesses claim that hell is nothing but the grave. Dig up any grave anywhere on this entire planet, however, and you'll not find it burning with unquenchable fire!

- 9:50 – Is there anyone with whom you need to seek peace today?

52 WEEKS OF PURSUIT

WEEK 43, DAY 2: **TODAY'S READING: MARK 10-13**

OVERVIEW:
The Servant's paradoxes (chapter 10); the Servant in Jerusalem (chapters 11–12); the Servant unveils the last days (chapter 13).

HIGHLIGHTS & INSIGHTS:
In chapter 10, Jesus continues His teaching ministry. The Gospel of Mark focuses on what Jesus *did*, but not to the exclusion of what He *taught*. In this chapter, Jesus reveals that His wisdom is different than the world's and from our own natural inclinations. His teaching centers on five key paradoxes:

- Paradox #1 – Two shall be one. (10:1–12)

  God's intention in marriage has always been *one* man and woman, for *one* lifetime, because they have become *one* flesh. Jesus reveals that God has not changed His position about the sanctity of marriage. God hates divorce (Mal. 2:16), divorce was only ever a concession because of the hardness of men's hearts (Mark 10:5), and the ensuing remarriage that typically follows a divorce leads to adultery (Mark 10:11–12). Choose wisely.

- Paradox #2 – Adults must become as children. (10:13–16)

  We are constantly striving to get children to act like adults. Jesus said entrance into the kingdom of God requires adults becoming as children. Obviously, Jesus is referring to adults becoming child-*like*, not child*ish*.

- Paradox #3 – The first shall be last and the last, first. (10:17–31)

  This passage reveals at least four things that keep people from genuine salvation:

    1. A distrust in the fact of Christ's deity (that He is God!) (10:18; 1 John 2:22–23)

    2. A misunderstanding of the purpose of the Ten Commandments (10:19; Gal. 3:24)

    3. A misguided trust in our own self-righteousness (10:20)

    4. A mis-prioritized trust in riches (10:21–27; 1 Tim. 6:17–19)

  The "rich young ruler" is the only man in Scripture who came to Jesus and went away worse than he came. Sadly, many people through the years have been just as close to the King and to entering His kingdom, but followed this young man down the same "sorrowful" and "grievous" (10:22) path instead.

- Paradox #4 – The greatest of all is the servant of all (10:32–45)

  This certainly isn't true in the world's economy, but it is in God's! Jesus Himself is the greatest example of this truth: "For even the Son of man came not to be ministered unto, but to minister, and to give his life a ransom for many" (10:45). Philippians 2:5–11 provides an incredible explanation of this paradox. Though our Lord Jesus Christ has always eternally existed in perfect equality with the Father in the Godhead, He humbled Himself and took on the form of a servant. He not only humbled Himself by becoming a man, but by dying as a man. His humility wasn't just that He died, but that He died the most humiliating death of all, "even the death of the cross" (2:8). It was that very servanthood that caused the Father to exalt Him as the absolute greatest of all and that has caused us to exalt Him to the place of Lordship in our lives!

- Paradox #5 – It is the blind who see, and the seeing who are blind (10:46–52)

  The scribes and Pharisees thought that they could see perfectly, spiritually speaking, when in reality, they were completely blind. This physically blind man, however, had perfect vision spiritually. Like the scribes and Pharisees, one of the chief characteristics of Christians in our day is that we think we see perfectly in the spiritual realm, when in reality we are completely blind (Rev. 3:17–18).

Chapter 11 moves into the last eight days of Jesus's life. Because this Gospel is written to Gentiles, unlike Matthew, Mark makes a beeline toward that glorious truth that allows Gentiles to become citizens of the kingdom of God: the death, burial, and resurrection of Jesus Christ.

From a big-picture standpoint, chapters 11–13 record events that present Christ, the "Servant of all," in three of His primary offices:

- The Servant is presented as *King* (11:1–11)
- The Servant is presented as *Judge* (11:12–26)
- The Servant is presented as *Prophet* (11:27–13:37)

In chapter 13, Jesus prophesies concerning the final week of years from Daniel's prophecy (Dan. 9:24–27) that we call the Tribulation. In this passage, He unveils:

- The first half of the Tribulation in 13:5–13.
- The middle of the Tribulation in 13:14–18.
- The last half of the Tribulation in 13:19–27.

Note also the "four watches of the night" in 13:35.

- 1st watch – "Even" (or "Evening") – From 6 p.m. to 9 p.m.
- 2nd watch – "Midnight" – From 9 p.m. to 12 a.m.
- 3rd watch – "Cockcrowing" – From 12 a.m. to 3 a.m.
- 4th watch – "Morning" – From 3 a.m. to 6 a.m.

In terms of church history, the approximate dates that coincide with these "four watches of the night" are as follows:

- 1st watch – "Evening" – From c. 33 AD to c. 533 AD
- 2nd watch – "Midnight" – From c. 533 AD to c. 1033 AD
- 3rd watch – "Cockcrowing" – From c. 1033 AD to c. 1533 AD
- 4th watch – "Morning" – From c.1533 AD to c. 2033 AD

We are living in the very final minutes (and maybe even seconds!) of the final watch of the night. Take special note of Jesus's final words in chapter 13: "And what I say unto you I say unto all, watch"!

52 WEEKS OF PURSUIT

WEEK 43, DAY 3: TODAY'S READING: MARK 14-16

OVERVIEW:
The Servant's suffering (14:1–15:20); the Servant's death (15:21–41); the Servant's burial (15:42–47); the Servant's resurrection (16:1–18); the Servant's ascension (16:19–20).

HIGHLIGHTS & INSIGHTS:
These chapters break down into two clear sections: The last six places in the Servant's *walk* and the last four events in the Servant's *work*.

THE LAST SIX PLACES IN THE SERVANT'S *WALK*.

1. The town of Bethany – where Jesus was *worshipped* (14:1–11)

Jesus appreciates worship that's out of the box (14:3). When he had revealed His suffering and death (10:32–34), nobody seemed to care. Instead of asking what He meant, the disciples asked where they would be sitting in the kingdom (10:35–41). Then there was Mary. Rather than anointing Christ's body after His death (14:8), Mary lavishes her love, adoration, and worship on Him while He was still among them. But when, like Mary, our worship is outside the box, the mainstream will respond to us as they did to her: "They murmured against her" (14:5).

2. The upper room – where Jesus was *betrayed* (14:12–26)

Immediately following Mary's glorious act of worship, Mark records the most hideous act of treason: One of our Lord's own disciples would betray Him. What must have been in our Lord's mind and heart as He spent these final hours with His disciples, knowing that the same Judas who received from Him the bread that represented His body would, only minutes later, receive money for offering His actual body to be crucified.

3. The Garden of Gethsemane – where Jesus was *forsaken* (14:27–52)

Peter is a classic example of the adage, "Talk is cheap." Again, knowing full well what Peter would do in the next few hours, Jesus invites him, James, and John to go further than the rest of the disciples (14:33), allowing them to enter another level of information, as well as intimacy, with their Lord. Sadly, at the time that our Lord, in His humanness, most needed the love and support of His friends (14:34), He was forsaken. First, Peter, James and John slept through His deepest sorrow (14:37), and then "they all forsook him, and fled" (v. 50).

And it was here, before he ever got to the cross, that Jesus won the real battle—the battle between "My will" and "Thy will." Likewise, it is in the Gethsemanes of our life that battles are won or lost.

4. The High Priest's Palace – where Jesus was *denied* (14:53–72)

Here, Jesus was plotted against by the chief priests and the council, lied about by the very ones He had come to redeem, and vehemently denied by the very one who had vehemently vowed he would die before denying Christ!

Peter's track record through the Gospel of Mark is not a good one. He argued when he should have submitted (8:32–33). He talked when he should have listened (9:5–7). He slept when he should have prayed (14:37–38). He fought when he should have surrendered (14:47) and denied when he should have witnessed (14:66–71). But before we are tempted to criticize Peter, we need to realize that he sounds a whole lot like us! And more importantly, Peter was remorseful and repentant (14:72), as well as forgiven (John 21).

5. Pilate's Hall – where Jesus was *condemned* (15:1–20)

In order to condemn Jesus to death, the Jewish council had to convince Pilate that Jesus was guilty of a capital offense (John 18:31–32). Since He was obviously not guilty of a capital crime, there was only one possibility: twist His claim to be King into a statement against Rome's authority, making Him out to be a political revolutionary. Pilate realized the council's accusations were bogus and born out of envy (15:10). Hoping to avoid a controversial decision concerning Jesus, Pilate offers to release a prisoner, Barabbas or Jesus, thinking that the people would never choose to release a murderer. The chief priests, however, had worked the people ahead of time (15:11), and they demand the release of Barabbas and the crucifixion of Jesus (15:12–14). Pilate agrees "to content the people" (v.15). In our lives, too, being a people-pleaser will always lead to unbelievable and unthinkable compromise!

6. On Golgotha – where Jesus was *crucified* (15:21–41)

Mark provides us a time sequence of the crucifixion:

- "The third hour," or 9 a.m. (15:25) – Jesus was nailed to the cross
- "The sixth hour," or 12 noon (15:33) – Darkness for the next three hours
- "The ninth hour," or 3 p.m. (15:34–37) – Jesus's final words before He "gave up the ghost"

THE LAST FOUR EVENTS IN THE SERVANT'S *WORK*.
- Event #1 – The Servant's *death* (15:21–41)
- Event #2 – The Servant's *burial* (15:42–47)
- Event #3 – The Servant's *resurrection* (16:1–18)
- Event #4 – The Servant's *ascension* (16:19–20)

52 WEEKS OF PURSUIT

WEEK 43, DAY 4: TODAY'S READING: LUKE 1-3

OVERVIEW:
The introduction of Theophilus (1:1–4); the conception of John the Baptist (1:5–25); the conception of Jesus in Mary (1:26–38); Mary and Elisabeth's meeting (1:39–56); the birth of John the Baptist (1:57–66); the prophecy of Zacharias (1:67–80); Christ, the baby (2:1–20); Christ, the child (2:21–28); Christ, the youth (2:39–52); the testimony of John the Baptist concerning Christ (3:1–20); the testimony of God the Father and God the Spirit concerning Christ (3:21–38).

HIGHLIGHTS & INSIGHTS:
Whereas Matthew was written to Jews to present Christ as *King*, and Mark was written to Gentiles (specifically Romans) to present Christ as a *Servant*, the Gospel of Luke was written to Greeks to present Christ as a *Man*.

Unlike the Jews, who looked for signs, the Greeks "seek after wisdom" (1 Cor. 1:22). Historically, the Greeks were synonymous with *philosophy*, or "love of wisdom" (philos = love; sophia = wisdom). The Greeks loved wisdom and were consumed with discovering the meaning of life and morality. This Gospel, then, reveals that Jesus Christ, God in human flesh, is the true meaning of life and the ultimate standard of morality. The name Luke means "light-giver," much like the Hebrew name Lucifer ("light-bearer"), and his Gospel shines as a "light to lighten the Gentiles" (2:32). Since every generation has been influenced by the philosophical mindset of the Greeks, this Gospel gives light to every generation.

Three things make Luke's Gospel unique. First, it was written to a man named Theophilus (meaning "lover of God"). "It seemed good to me also, having had perfect understanding of all things from the very first, to write unto thee in order, most excellent Theophilus" (1:3). While we don't know who he actually was, Theophilus was obviously a believer. In the very first verse, Luke talks about "those things which are most surely believed among *us*."

Second, Luke's purpose in writing was to lay to rest any questions or doubts Theophilus had. "That thou [Theophilus] mightest know the certainty of those things, wherein thou hast been instructed" (1:4). To accomplish this, Luke focused on facts, giving a much more detailed account of the life of our Lord. (See 1:5; 2:1–4; 3:1–2 for examples of Luke's love of detail.) This is, no doubt, why Luke is the longest Gospel. (It has four fewer chapters than Matthew, but about 2,000 more words!) Finally, the Gospel of Luke is part of a two-volume set, along with the book of Acts, which begins, "The former treatise have I made, O Theophilus, of all that Jesus began to do and teach" (Acts 1:1).

The particular emphasis of Luke's Gospel is to present Jesus as a *Man*. The phrase "Son of man" is found twenty-five times, highlighting our Lord's humanity. We will see Him weeping over those who rejected Him (19:41); touching the untouchable (5:13); being touched by the unthinkable (7:39); and seeking the lost (5:31–32; 9:56; 19:10). In fact, seven times in this book Jesus invites lost people to follow Him.

The focus on Christ as a Man is also reflected in Luke's record of His genealogy. Matthew, the Jewish Gospel, uses His genealogy to identify Christ with David and traces His family line from Abraham, the father of the Nation of Israel. Luke, however, traces Christ's genealogy through His human mother, back to Adam, the first man (Luke 3:38).

Luke presents Christ as 100% man, but at the same time, He is 100% God. This is a major hang-up for Jehovah's *False* Witnesses who will throw out Luke 2:40, for example, as proof that Jesus wasn't and couldn't have been God. What they prove, however, is that they don't believe the Bible and don't have the Spirit of God in them so they can understand the Bible (1 Cor. 2:14). 1 Timothy 3:16 calls Christ's deity the "mystery of godliness" and defines it as the fact that "God was manifest in the flesh, justified in the Spirit, seen of angels, preached unto the Gentiles, believed on in the world, received up into glory."

WEEK 43, DAY 5: **TODAY'S READING: LUKE 4-6**

OVERVIEW:
The testimony of Satan concerning Christ as the Son of God (4:1–13); the testimony of the Scriptures (4:14–30); the testimony of demons (4:31–44); Jesus is the difference between failure and success (5:1–11); Jesus is the difference between guilt and forgiveness (5:17–26); Jesus is the difference between the old and the new (5:27–39); a new kind of Sabbath (6:–11); a new kind of nation (6:12–19); a new kind of blessedness (6:20–49).

HIGHLIGHTS & INSIGHTS:
Do you know who God used to provide the most content in the New Testament? The obvious answer is Paul, right? Wrong! Though Paul penned more New Testament *books* than any other writer, God used Luke to provide the most content. (This is based on the number of words and verses in Luke and Acts compared with those in the thirteen books known to be authored by Paul. A great case could be made that Paul authored the book of Hebrews during his forty days and nights in Arabia, but we cannot be dogmatic about it since the Holy Spirit did not inspire its human author to include his name.)

Yesterday we focused on background of the Gospel itself. Today we will look at its author. Who is Luke? Colossians 4:14 refers to him as "the beloved physician." Notice it is not, "Luke, the beloved *doctor*," but "Luke, the beloved *physician*." Is that a big deal? Yes! God chooses His words very carefully (Prov. 30:5). There are no indiscriminate or random words in the Bible. He calls Luke a "physician" to distinguish between his occupation and that of a doctor in that day. When God refers to doctors in the Bible (Luke 2:46; 5:17; Acts 5:34), He means theologians who were so full of head knowledge about God that they missed God when He was right in front of them. Many people know lots of information *about* God and the Bible, but they don't know *Him*. The Bible is not an end in itself; it is a means to an end. And that end is not to get to know the Bible, but to get to know God! We don't read our car's owner's manual to get to know the manual. We read it to get to know the car. Similarly, God provided us with the Bible so we could get to know Him!

Interestingly, only two physicians are mentioned in the entire Bible—Luke and our Lord Jesus Christ. Though they both possessed the ability to heal physically (Jesus through miracles and Luke through medicine), both were more concerned about the spiritual healing needed in men's souls than the physical healing needed in men's bodies! Luke pointed men to the Great Physician and His glorious cure. Jesus is both the Physician and the Cure Himself!

As we have provided for both Matthew and Mark's Gospel, the following is a basic summary of the Gospel of Luke:

1. **Information About the Author:**
    - His name: Luke
    - His name means "Light-giving"
    - He was a physician. (Col. 4:14)
    - He wrote this Gospel to Theophilus (Luke 1:3)
    - He also wrote the book of Acts (Acts 1:1)
    - He joins the second missionary team in Troas (Acts 16:1–10)
    - He stays behind in Philippi (Acts 17:1)
    - He rejoins the missionary team on their third journey (Acts 20:1–6)
    - He journeys with Paul to Rome (Acts 27:12)
    - He is also referred to in scripture as Lucas (Philem. 23–24)

2. **Facts About This Gospel:**
    - Approximate date of writing: 60 AD
    - Written from Philippi
    - Dates of the recorded events: 6 BC–33 AD
    - Theme: Christ as the perfect man
    - Christ is seen in this Gospel as the Son of man
    - Key verse: Luke 19:10
    - Key word: Man (131 times)
    - Chapters: 24
    - Verses: 1,151
    - Words: 19,482

3. **Features of This Gospel:**
    - Luke is the only Gospel that records the parable of the Good Samaritan
    - Luke is the only Gospel that records the cleansing of the Ten Lepers
    - This Gospel contains 9 fulfilled prophecies

4. **A Simple Outline Of This Gospel: The Four Periods**
    - Period #1 - A Time of *Preparation* (chapters 1–3)
    - Period #2 - A Time of *Identification* (chapters 4–8)
    - Period #3 - A Time of *Instruction* (chapters 9–18)
    - Period #4 - A Time of *Culmination* (chapters 19–24)

WEEK 44, DAY 1: **TODAY'S READING: LUKE 7-9**

OVERVIEW:

Jesus's response to the faith of the centurion (7:1–10); Jesus's response to the sorrow of the widow (7:11–17); Jesus's response to the doubt of John the Baptist (7:18–35); Jesus's response to the love of a woman with a sordid past (7:36–50); Jesus teaches His disciples about receiving God's Word (8:1–21); Jesus tests His disciples concerning applying God's Word (8:22–56); Jesus sends out His 12 disciples (9:1–11); Jesus feeds the 5000 (9:12–17); Jesus teaches His disciples about His person, His sacrifice and His kingdom (9:18–36); Jesus endures His disciples' lack of power, love, and surrender (9:37–62).

HIGHLIGHTS & INSIGHTS:

Since the Gospels record actual events, they are, for the most part, easily understood. Though each event is power-packed and full of practical application, the structure of *52 Weeks of Pursuit* does not allow commentary on every passage. While you can make much practical application from all of today's reading, we will focus on one particular story, "The Pharisee and the Prostitute" in Luke 7:36–50. It illustrates the significant contrast between the religious leaders and common, sinful people.

Lesson #1: The Pharisee was willing to interrupt his *schedule* to have Jesus in his *presence*. The prostitute was willing for the *presence* of Jesus to interrupt her *life*! (Luke 7:36)

For Personal Examination: Do I want Jesus in my presence? Or do I want Jesus's presence in me? Do I want to have Him? Or do I want Him to have me?

Lesson #2: The Pharisee wanted Jesus in his presence, but was seeking to *save* face. The prostitute wanted the presence of Jesus in her and was seeking *His* face. (Luke 7:36–38, 44–46)

For Personal Examination: What am I seeking to hold on to even while I'm telling Jesus I want His presence in me? Do I want as much of the presence of Jesus in me as I can have, or do I want as much of the presence of Jesus in me as I can have *and not lose my identity*?

Lesson #3: Jesus heard what the Pharisee was saying in his heart. Jesus also heard what the prostitute was saying in her heart. (Luke 7:39, 44–47)

For Personal Examination: What does Jesus hear when He listens to my heart? Would Jesus hear my worship if it weren't expressed with words?

Lesson #4: The prostitute was ten times the sinner the Pharisee was, but our sinfulness is not determined by the amount of sin-debt we incur, but by the amount we have to pay on the debt. We all had *absolutely nothing* to pay on our debt! (Luke 7:40–42)

For Personal Examination: Do I really understand my sinfulness before God? Do I fully comprehend the significance of the fact that, regardless of the amount of my sin, I had nothing to pay on the debt?

Lesson #5: The Pharisee's blindness to his own sinfulness *diminished* his capacity to love Jesus. The prostitute's overwhelming awareness of her own sinfulness *enlarged* her capacity to love Jesus. How you view your own sinfulness affects your ability to love Jesus! (Luke 7:40–43, 47)

For Personal Examination: Do I fully comprehend the significance of my own sin when I view the price Jesus paid for sin through His death on the cross?

Lesson #6: The Pharisee was so blind to his own sin, it opened his eyes to the prostitute's sinfulness. The prostitute's eyes were so open to her own sinfulness, she was blinded to everyone else's. How you view your own sinfulness affects your ability to see others! (Luke 7:36–39)

For Personal Examination: Has pride blinded my eyes to my own sin and opened my eyes to the sin of others?

Lesson #7: The Pharisee's so-called worship in the presence of Christ was based on *his own* worthiness. The prostitute's worship in the presence of Christ was based on *Christ's* worthiness. (Luke 7:40–50)

According to Jesus, the Pharisee's worship lacked three things: He didn't *think* enough of Jesus to provide water to wash His feet. He wasn't *excited* enough about receiving Jesus into his presence to provide an affectionate greeting. And he wasn't *considerate* enough of Jesus to provide oil to anoint His head.

But the prostitute's worship was wholly different. She broke open the box of her most prized treasure to release the fragrance of true worship. She expressed a broken and contrite heart through her tears used to wash Jesus's feet. She dismantled her glory (her hair, 1 Cor. 11:15) to give Him glory. And she let her affection and exaltation of Christ overflow by ceaselessly kissing His feet.

> For Personal Examination: Whose worthiness is the basis of my worship? Will I break open the "box" of my most prized treasure for Jesus? Is my heart calloused and cold, or is it broken open with tears to wash Jesus's feet? How willing am I to dismantle my ego and self-glory for His glory? Is my affection and exaltation of Christ apparent by my humility toward Him (kissing His feet)? In other words, will I be a box-breaking, oil-pouring, tear-washing, glory-sacrificing, foot-kissing, face-seeking worshipper of the Lord Jesus Christ today?

52 WEEKS OF PURSUIT

WEEK 44, DAY 2: **TODAY'S READING: LUKE 10-12**

OVERVIEW:

Jesus sends out the seventy (10:1–24); Jesus teaches about who our neighbor is (10:25–37); Jesus teaches us the importance of worship (10:38–42); Jesus models the importance of prayer (11:1); Jesus provides a pattern for prayer (11:2–4); Jesus teaches about persistence in prayer (11:5–8); Jesus offers promises concerning prayer (11:9–13); Jesus teaches about the devil (11:14–28); Jesus's illustrations concerning the crowds: Jonah (11:29–30, 32), Solomon (11:31), and Light (11:33–36); Jesus teaches about the hypocrisy of the Pharisees (11:37–54); Jesus warns about hypocrisy (12:1–12); Jesus warns about covetousness (12:13–21); Jesus warns about worrying (12:22–34); Jesus warns about carelessness (12:35–53); Jesus warns about lack of discernment and diligence in spiritual matters (12:54–59).

HIGHLIGHTS & INSIGHTS:

The phrase *kingdom of God* appears more times in the book of Luke than in any other book in the New Testament. Interestingly the phrase *kingdom of heaven* is found 33 times in 32 verses in Matthew, and the phrase *kingdom of God* is found 33 times in 32 verses in Luke!

As you will recall, the kingdom of heaven is the kingdom promised to the Jews all through the Old Testament and is sometimes referred to as the kingdom of Israel (Acts 1:6; Hos. 1:4). It is a literal, physical, earthly, governmental, messianic, Davidic kingdom over which Jesus rules as King from His throne in Jerusalem. The kingdom of God, on the other hand, is a spiritual kingdom that cannot be seen or touched, where Jesus rules as King on the throne of men's hearts by way of a spiritual birth (Luke 17:20–21; John 3:3; Rom. 14:17; 1 Cor. 4:20; 15:50). Luke emphasizes the kingdom of God because this Gospel is designed to present the Lord Jesus Christ as the Son of man who came "to seek and to save that which was lost" (Luke 19:10).

The Jews of Jesus's day were totally preoccupied with the kingdom of heaven and, therefore, were totally oblivious to their need to be born into the kingdom of God. It made them blind, selfish, and self-serving. Similarly, the Christians of our day are totally preoccupied with the kingdom of God and, therefore, are totally oblivious to the kingdom of heaven. It likewise makes us blind, selfish, and self-serving (Rev. 3:14–22; 2 Tim. 3:1–2). We claim the promise of eternal life, while we spend our lives seeking our own literal, physical kingdom on the earth! Now that we have been born into His spiritual kingdom, God intends that we "seek those things which are above, where Christ sitteth on the right hand of God," and that we "set [our] affection on things above, not on things on the earth" (Col. 3:1–2). God wants the literal, physical kingdom in which our Lord Jesus Christ will finally receive the "glory due unto his name" (1 Chron. 16:29; Ps. 29:2; 96:8) to so be in our hearts that it causes us to continuously pray for it to come (Matt. 6:10). Keeping these two kingdoms straight clearly has both *doctrinal* and *practical* implications.

Perhaps Luke's emphasis on the kingdom of God is why his is the only Gospel that includes the sending out of the seventy (10:1–24). Why seventy? Just as the twelve apostles are associated with the twelve sons of Jacob, the seventy must also have some significant association. Though it is difficult to determine, it seems that the seventy are associated with the seventy nations in Genesis 10. Because Luke focuses on the universality of the kingdom of God to all peoples and all nations, it makes sense that he would include the seventy being sent to spread the message to all nations.

Other tidbits to glean from today's reading:

10:1–42 – This chapter describes three places and three things we are to do in those places.

- The Harvest Field (10:1–24): We are to *represent* Him
- The Highway (10:25–37): We are to *model* Him
- The Home (10:38–42): We are to *worship* Him

10:23–24 – I hope this is the way you feel about the things the Lord has graciously allowed you to see in His Word as well as for allowing you to be a part of in His kingdom.

11:1 – The disciples heard Jesus preach the greatest sermons that have ever been preached, but they never said, "Lord, teach us to preach." They saw Him perform the most incredible miracles that have ever been performed, but they never said, "Lord, teach us to do miracles." But they heard Him pray and couldn't help but say, "Lord, teach us to pray." What a connection and intimacy with the Father Jesus must have had when He prayed! May we learn what it really is to pray!

11:24–26 – These verses reveal that we cannot simply be set apart *from* the world; we must be set apart *to* God (John 17:11–17)! It is not enough to simply *put off* the *old* man; we must *put on* the *new* man (Eph. 4:22–24; Col. 3:8–14). It is not enough that we no longer serve *sin*, but that we serve *righteousness* (Rom. 6:17–18).

52 WEEKS OF PURSUIT

WEEK 44, DAY 3: **TODAY'S READING: LUKE 13-15**

OVERVIEW:
Jesus provides pertinent answers to pertinent questions (chapter 13); Jesus addresses the guests in a Pharisee's house on the Sabbath day (chapter 14); Jesus gives three illustrations to reveal God's heart for the lost (chapter 15).

HIGHLIGHTS & INSIGHTS:
As Jesus continues His journey toward Jerusalem (9:51; 13:22; 17:11; 18:31; 19:11, 28), He is asked four questions that provide a clean breakdown of chapter 13.

1. A *Political* question about *Justice* (13:1–9)
   Jesus knows that anything He says about Pilate will certainly make it to Jerusalem before He does! Verses 3 and 4 teach us not to assume that human tragedies are divine punishments.

2. A *Legal* question about the *Sabbath* (13:10–21)
   The Pharisees, in their pride and self-righteousness, could not see that Jesus "loosing" (13:12) this woman from Satan's bond and her suffering on the Sabbath was no different from them "loosing" their ox or donkey from the stall to get water on the Sabbath (13:15). Pride and self-righteousness still cause that same blind and judgmental spirit today.

3. A *Theological* question about *Salvation* (13:22–30)
   Jesus turned the man's general question about how many would be saved into a personal question about whether or not *he* would be saved. Even today, many people ask great spiritual, theological questions they have no intention of obeying or practicing—even if they receive the answer!

4. A *Personal* question about *Death* (13:31–35)
   Instead of answering a specific question, Jesus responds to the statement in verse 31 as if the Pharisees had asked whether he was concerned about Herod's desire to kill Him. His answer is that His life was on God's timetable, not man's (John 2:4; 7:30; 8:20; 13:1; 17:1). Today (and every day) our lives are on the same schedule!

In chapter 14, Jesus is invited to one of the chief Pharisee's house for dinner after church, so to speak. Recognizing that He is intended to be the main dish, Jesus takes command of the room and, rather than be eaten alive, confronts those in attendance with their own personal issues.

- In 14:1–6, He confronts the Pharisees with their false spirituality by healing someone on the Sabbath.

- In 14:7–11, Jesus points out the other guests' self-promotion, as they chose positions in the room to make themselves appear important.

- In 14:12–14, Jesus confronts the host who had invited his guests either to fulfill an obligation or to impose a debt on them. But what about us? Where are the people who don't have an ulterior motive behind their generosity? Even when we think we're doing something for nothing, our ulterior motive is often wanting to be seen as someone who does things for nothing in return.

- In 14:15–24, Jesus reveals that the Jews were about to miss the Messiah's invitation and that He would turn to the Gentiles. In the twenty-first century, people miss Jesus for the same reasons that they did in the first century: they revel in their riches (v. 18), climb in their career (v. 19), or focus on their family (v.20).

- In 14:25–35, Jesus leaves the Pharisee's house and challenges the multitudes. He wasn't looking for people to add Him into their already cluttered lives. He was looking for those to see their relationship with Him as the most important and see Him as life itself! Jesus has never been interested in self-seeking consumers, but in self-denying disciples.

Confronting people's issues as Jesus does in chapters 13–14 doesn't fly too well today. Though we have seen that true, biblical, Spirit-anointed preaching is at least two-thirds negative (Jer. 1:10; 2 Tim. 4:2), if someone preached in most churches today the way Jesus did in these chapters, I think he'd get some pretty harsh comments.

- "Why does our message need to be so negative?"
- "People don't come to church to feel bad."
- "I'm afraid to bring visitors to church because the strong preaching may push them away."
- "I'm just not being fed."
- "I'm looking for something that has a better ministry to my kids."

But thankfully, Jesus wasn't all negative. In chapter 15, He offers three illustrations that reveal the heart of God for His lost creation. Our Heavenly Father is like:

- A Tender Shepherd (15:1–7)
- A Diligent Housewife (15:8–10)
- A Longing Dad (15:11–32)

He searches, seeks, longs for, and sacrifices to see what was lost returned to its rightful place. Praise the Lord, our rightful place is with Him!

52 WEEKS OF PURSUIT

WEEK 44, DAY 4: TODAY'S READING: LUKE 16-18

OVERVIEW:
Jesus teaches about stewardship (16:1–13); Jesus teaches about covetousness (16:14–31); Jesus teaches about forgiveness (17:1–6); Jesus teaches about faithfulness (17:7–10); Jesus teaches about thankfulness (17:11–19); Jesus teaches about preparedness (17:20–37); a lesson to be learned from a persistent widow (18:1–8); a lesson to be learned from a proud Pharisee (18:9–17); a lesson to be learned from a mis-prioritized ruler (18:18–34); a lesson to be learned from a pressing beggar (18:35–43).

HIGHLIGHTS & INSIGHTS:
There is much more action and pertinent information in these chapters than we have space to explore. So today we'll focus on key topics that have significant application for believers living in the last days.

SUBJECT #1 – STEWARDSHIP (16:1-13)
Though this steward's circumstances were somewhat different than ours, like him, we will each "give an account of our stewardship" (16:2) at the judgment seat of Christ. (See 2 Cor. 5:10; Rom. 14:10, 12.) On that day we will answer one question: "What did we do with what He entrusted to us?" We will give an account of our stewardship of:

- The *Life* of God (Gen. 2:7; Rom 5:12; Col. 1:26–27; 1 John 5:11) – He's enabled us to live righteously.

- The *Love* of God (Rom. 5:5; Mark 12:28–31; 1 John 4:14–17, 19; 1 Thess. 4:9) – He's enabled us to love divinely.

- The *Gospel* of God (1 Thess. 2:4; 1 Tim. 1:11; 6:20) – He's enabled us to impact souls eternally.

- The *Gifts* of God (1 Peter 4:10–11; 1 Cor. 3:10) – He's enabled us to serve powerfully.

- The *Resources* of God (Money: Luke 16:11; Time: Eph. 5:16; Col. 4:5; Talents: Matt. 25:14–30; People: 2 Tim. 1:5; 3:15) – He's enabled us to manage resources wisely.

I am convinced that 16:11 explains why many Laodiceans never reach people with the gospel or minister effectively. It may be that God is unwilling to entrust to them what He treasures because of they are unfaithful with their money.

But if 16:11 is a doozy, then 16:13 is a blockbuster for our generation. We convince ourselves that this verse is true for everybody but us, that we will be able to love both God and money. But what part of *cannot* do we not understand? When God looks at our lives, He will think we either love Him and hate money or hate Him and love money. He will see that we either hold to Him and despise money or hold to money and despise Him. Many modern believers are attempting to love money and love God at the same time, but Jesus said it simply *cannot* be done!

SUBJECT #2 – HELL (16:19-31)
Prior to Christ's resurrection, believers who died were held in a place of paradise called Abraham's bosom. It was close to the place of punishment called hell where unbelievers were located, but separated by a great gulf or gaping opening (16:26). Clearly, hell is a real place where real people go and experience real suffering and torment. In hell, the rich man had eyes and could see (16:23a), had a body and could feel (16:23b), had a tongue and experienced thirst (16:24), had a mouth and could talk (16:27), and had a mind and could reason (16:28).

In this passage, we learn there are no unbelievers in hell. Unbelief may have gotten them there, but as soon as they open their eyes in hell, they become believers! Sadly, it is eternally too late. We also learn that people in hell have compassion for the lost (16:28). Many believers do not have the same passion and compassion for souls that this lost rich man had! Many think that if God would just do some miraculous thing, our lost family and friends would come to Christ, but here we learn that if they refuse to believe the Bible, they wouldn't believe even if someone rose from the dead to speak to them. They already proved that by not believing in the resurrected Christ!

SUBJECT #3 – FORGIVENESS (17:1-5)

Jesus is clear: "It is impossible but that offenses will come," but forgiveness must be our response. When someone offends us, God's grace immediately kicks in to help us to bear it (2 Cor. 12:9; 1 Cor. 10:13). But we can refuse to apply God's grace or to "fail of the grace of God" (Heb. 12:15). And if we do, our unforgiving spirit will cause a "root of bitterness" to spring up in us and "trouble" us and "defile many" people around us, even leading us into sexual sin (12:16). Don't ever underestimate the importance of forgiveness!

SUBJECT #4 – THANKFULNESS (17:11-19)

In terms of these ten lepers, believers in our day are generally more like "the nine" than the "one." Jesus asked, "Where are the nine?" (v. 17). His question is a good one in our Laodicean Age, as we consider these other references to thankfulness:

- 2 Timothy 3:2 – being "unthankful" is as characteristic in our day as being "lovers of our own selves"!

- Romans 1:21 – being "unthankful" is a first step toward a "reprobate mind" (v. 28). This is serious stuff!

- 1 Thessalonians 5:18 – We cannot be in the perfect will of God and not be thankful! Again, it's serious stuff!

SUBJECT #5 – RIGHTEOUSNESS (18:9-14)

We who hold to the fundamentals of Bible-believing Christianity run the greatest risk of becoming the modern-day Pharisees. Have you become Pharisaical? Luke 18:9 identifies two tell-tale signs:

1) Trusting in your own righteousness (what you do *for* Christ, rather than who you are *in* Christ)

2) Thinking you're more spiritual than others.

The first sign is especially significant. Paul writes that those who are "ignorant of God's righteousness, and going about to establish their own righteousness, have not submitted themselves unto the righteousness of God" (Rom. 10:3). God's righteousness (on either side of salvation) could never be *achieved*! It can only be *received*! Paul desired to "be found in him, not having mine own righteousness, which is of the law [what I do for God], but that which is through the faith of Christ [what Christ does for me], the righteousness which is of God by faith" (Phil. 3:9).

But the second sign should also give us pause. What do you honestly think when you look at others? Do you secretly think that you are on a higher plane because of what you do or don't do? We must be careful!

WEEK 44, DAY 5: **TODAY'S READING: LUKE 19-21**

OVERVIEW:

Jesus as the Savior Who seeks the lost (19:1–10); Jesus as the Master Who rewards the faithful (19:11–27); Jesus as the King Who offers peace (19:28–48); a question concerning John the Baptist (20:1–19); a question concerning Caesar (20:20–26); a question concerning Moses (20:27–40); a question concerning David (20:41–44); a warning concerning the scribes (20:45–47); a teaching concerning giving (21:1–4); the revealing of the first half of the Tribulation (21:5–19); the revealing of the middle of the Tribulation (21:20–24); the revealing of the last half of the Tribulation (21:25–27); the closing admonitions (21:28–36).

HIGHLIGHTS & INSIGHTS:

Chapter 19 moves us into the last week of Jesus's earthly life. He is approaching Jerusalem, where two groups passionately await His arrival. Some are preparing to exalt a King, while others are preparing to execute a fraud.

As Jesus comes into Jericho (19:1), we meet Zacchaeus. His name means "righteous one," but he was anything but righteous! He was the top-dog tax collector ("chief among the publicans," v. 2) in Jericho, which by itself was bad enough. Jews who sold out to the Romans to extract taxes from fellow Jews was despicable in this culture. They were viewed as ruthless, heartless, conniving, lying, traitors—and those would have been their good qualities!

And evidently, Zacchaeus had made quite a reputation for himself (19:7). He was apparently sporting a major short-man complex and found he could be "taller," not by beating up bigger guys, but by making them submit to him as he gouged them on their taxes.

But, oh, the difference a day makes! When I lifted my head off my pillow on September 24, 1972, I had no idea what would take place in my life before my head hit the pillow again—but on that day, I was turned:

- From darkness to light (Col. 1:13; Acts 26:18a)
- From the power of Satan to the power of God (2 Tim. 2:26; Acts 26:18b)
- From guilt to forgiveness (Acts 26:18c)
- From serving sin to serving righteousness (Rom. 6:17–18)
- From separation from God to a relationship with Him (Eph. 2:1; Gal. 4:5–7)
- From spiritual death to spiritual life (Eph. 2:1; Rom 8:2)

Similarly, this was the day that would forever change Zacchaeus's life! He hears that Jesus is coming to town and desperately wants to lay his eyes on this One Who had been so hyped. But because of his short stature, he can't catch a glimpse. He runs ahead and climbs a tree so he can at least see Him, but he ends up getting so much more. As Jesus passes under the tree, not only does He see Zacchaeus, and not only does He speak to him, but He invites Himself over to Zacchaeus's house! Can you imagine?

Zacchaeus was stoked (19:6)! He received Jesus into His home as a guest, and in just a matter of minutes, Jesus had become its master. Zacchaeus acknowledged Christ's lordship and was saved (19:9).

In 19:8–9, Jesus wasn't saying that Zacchaeus was saved because of his pledge to give to the poor and to make right the wrong he had done by gouging people of their money. His willingness to do those things was the *visible proof* of his salvation. Big talk about salvation is one thing, but when God has a man's finances, it's a pretty good indicator that He has all of him (Matt. 6:21). In this one afternoon, Jesus caused this sinner (19:7) to live up to his name ("righteous one"), as he became a true "son of Abraham" (19:9) by faith (Rom. 4:22; Gal. 3:7).

Like Zacchaeus, we all have a short-man complex that only Jesus can help us overcome: "For all have sinned, and come short of the glory of God" (Rom. 3:23). In our lost state we tried to make ourselves appear taller through our religiosity, our good works, and our external righteousness, but it only made us shorter (Rom. 10:3; Isa. 64:6).

The good news about Zacchaeus is that, not only did everybody else know he was a sinner, he knew it and was willing to deal with it! In fact, he is the only one in the story who received salvation (v. 9). It's possible that the self-righteous, religious crowd who got so upset about Jesus hanging out with Zacchaues (v. 7) ultimately went to hell. That scenario continues to repeat itself right up to this present hour.

A couple of other comments about today's reading:

19:10 – Zacchaeus ran up the road seeking to see Jesus at the same time Jesus was walking up the road seeking to save Zacchaeus.

19:14–15 – We are living in the very last hours in that time between verses 14 and 15—between the Master's absence and His promise to return!

19:41–44 – This is only the second time that Jesus wept publicly (John 11:35). While the crowd is rejoicing (19:37), Jesus is weeping. Sounds a whole lot like Laodicea.

20:1–47 – Chapter 20 can be broken down by the four questions Jesus asks:

- A question concerning John the Baptist (20:1–19)
- A question concerning Caesar (20:20–26)
- A question concerning Moses (20:27–40)
- A question concerning David (20:41–44)

21:1–4 – Jesus isn't impressed with the size of our gift, but the size of our sacrifice.

21:5–38 – The remainder of chapter 21 lines up with the things we covered in Matthew 24 and Mark 13.

52 WEEKS OF **PURSUIT**

WEEK 45, DAY 1: **TODAY'S READING: LUKE 22-24**

OVERVIEW:
The wicked plot of the religious leaders to kill Jesus and to contract Judas (22:1–6); Jesus's last Passover (22:7–13); the converting of the Passover meal into His own supper (22:14–28); Jesus foretells Peter's denial (22:29–38); prayer in the garden (22:39–46); Jesus's arrest (22:47–54); Peter's denial (22:55–62); Jesus is mocked, blasphemed, and beaten (22:63–71); Jesus before Pilate (23:1–7); Jesus before Herod (23:8–11); Jesus returned to Pilate (23:12–24); Pilate releases Jesus to His accusers to be crucified (23:25–49); Jesus's burial (23:50–56); Jesus's resurrection (24:1–12); the ministry of the risen Christ (24:13–45); Jesus's commission (24:46–49); Jesus's ascension (24:50–53).

HIGHLIGHTS & INSIGHTS:
We have walked through these events in Jesus's life in both Matthew's and Mark's Gospels. Though we have read it twice in two weeks, may God give us a fresh sense of wonder and appreciation today. This is the manifestation of God's love for us (1 John 4:9) and the revelation of the Gospel (1 Cor. 15:1–4). As far as salvation is concerned, this is the heart of the Bible!

Because these chapters are so familiar, we will focus on Jesus establishing the observance of communion, what we refer to as the Lord's Supper (22:7–20). Because Jesus turns the bread and cup of the Passover meal (22:15) into his Supper, we will examine both meals to see how they are related.

1. The biblical and historical meaning of the Passover.
   - A general understanding of the Passover Meal

     The Passover meal was a commemorative feast to remind the Jews of what God had done in delivering them out of their bondage in Egypt.

   - The circumstances of the first Passover (Exodus 12)
     God's people were being held in bondage in the dominant world power (Egypt) by the will of its wicked king, Pharaoh. Day after day they labored as slaves under the domination of the taskmaster's whip, as they trudged out their existence in Egypt. God delivered them from Egypt by a series of plagues, ending with the curse of death upon the firstborn. The only way to escape the death of the firstborn in their house was to kill a spotless lamb and apply its blood to the top beam and the two side posts of the door. When the Lord passed through the city to execute judgment, he would "pass over" every house to which the blood of the lamb had been applied. God instituted the Passover meal on that night and commanded His people to celebrate it each year so they would remember His delivering power that was manifest in bringing them out of the bondage of Egypt by the blood of the Lamb.

   - The big picture of the Passover
     We, too, were being held in bondage in the course of this world (Egypt) by the will of its wicked king, Satan (Eph. 2:2; 2 Tim. 2:26). Day after day, we labored as slaves under the domination of the taskmaster of sin, as we trudged out our existence in of this world (Rom. 6:14; Gal. 1:4). God delivered us from the curse of death of our first birth when we applied the blood of the true Passover Lamb, the Lord Jesus Christ, to our lives (1 Cor. 5:7). God instituted a meal that He has commanded us to observe so we will remember His delivering power that was manifest in bringing us out of the bondage of this world and sin through the blood of the spotless lamb of God on the cross (Luke 22:7–20; Matthew 26:17–28).

2. The biblical and historical meaning of the Lord's Supper.
   - The transformation of the bread of the Passover: "And he took bread, and gave thanks, and brake it, and gave unto them, saying, This is my body which is given for you: this do in

remembrance of me." (Luke 22:19)

- The transformation of the cup of the Passover: "Likewise also the cup after supper, saying, This cup is the new testament in my blood, which is shed for you." (Luke 22:20)

  In other words, "From now on, don't go back to the picture; go back to the reality."

- The meaning of "eating the bread" and "drinking the cup."

  There are two basic things that a person needs to come to grips with (believe) in order to be saved:

  1. Who Christ is (that Jesus Christ is God in human flesh)
  2. What Christ did (that Jesus Christ shed His blood on the cross to atone for man's sin)

- Jesus's metaphor of "eating the bread" and "drinking the cup" in John 6.

  The religious leaders are appalled by Jesus's claim to be God. Jesus wants them to understand "If you never come to grips with who I am, and what I have come to do, you will never receive eternal life."

- The connection of "eating the bread" and "drinking the cup" in the Lord's Supper.

  We are brought back to the very two things that saved us:

  1. God opened our eyes to understand that Jesus Christ is, in fact, God in a human body
  2. We placed our faith in what Jesus Christ did through the shedding of His blood for the remission of our sin

52 WEEKS OF PURSUIT

WEEK 45, DAY 2: TODAY'S READING: JOHN 1–4

OVERVIEW:
Christ is the Word (1:1–3, 14); Christ is the Light (1:4–13); Christ is the Son of God (1:15–18, 30–34, 49); Christ is the Messiah (1:19–28, 35–42); Christ is the Lamb of God (1:29, 35–36); Christ is the King of Israel (1:43–49); Christ is the Son of Man (1:50–51); Christ and the disciples (1:19–2:12); Christ and the Jews (2:13–3:36); Christ and the Samaritans (4:1–54).

HIGHLIGHTS & INSIGHTS:
We have come to the final Gospel, the Gospel of John. An obvious questions that surfaces in every generation of believers is why there are four Gospels and not just one. Certainly, the easiest answer is that God wanted it that way! That's good enough for me, but we can easily give three basic explanations.

1. The Practical Reason.

   If a police officer was investigating an accident at an intersection and had four people who had witnessed the accident from the four corners of the scene, they would provide all the information he would need to prove conclusively what had actually taken place. The four Gospel accounts do the same.

2. The Presentational Reason.

   As we have seen, each Gospel is written to a particular audience to presenting a specific aspect of who Jesus Christ actually is. Matthew was written to the Jews to present Jesus Christ as the King of the Jews. Mark was written to the Gentiles (specifically, the Romans) to present Jesus Christ as the Servant of the Lord. Luke was written to the Greeks to present Jesus Christ as the Son of Man. And John is written to the world to present Jesus Christ as the Son of God. In fact, John uses the word *world* fifty-nine times in his Gospel (nearly a quarter of the total times it is used in the Bible). John wants every tribe, tongue, people, and nation to hear and understand that Jesus Christ is the Messiah, God in human flesh, and is the source and meaning of life. At the end of his Gospel, John declares that exact two-fold purpose: "And many other signs truly did Jesus in the presence of his disciples, which are not written in this book: But these are written, that ye might believe that Jesus is the Christ [the "anointed," the Messiah], the Son of God [God in a human body]; and that believing ye might have life through his name" (20:30–31).

   The greatest barrier to world communication is not geography or money or even politics (the world is quickly moving to a one-world government!). The greatest barrier is and has always been *language*. In his Gospel, John seeks to present Christ to the world so clearly that people in every culture can *believe* Jesus Christ is God and *receive* the life He offers (1:38, 41–42; 5:2; 9:7; 19:19–20).

3. The Peripheral Reason.

   In Revelation 4:6–7, God reveals four creatures on the four corners of His throne. John writes, "And before the throne there was a sea of glass like unto crystal: and in the midst of the throne, and round about the throne, were four beasts full of eyes before and behind. And the first beast was like a lion, and the second beast like a calf, and the third beast had a face as a man, and the fourth beast was like a flying eagle."

   By comparing the likeness of each beast to the content of each gospel, the connection between the four beasts of Revelation and the four Gospels seems clear, right down to the order in which they are listed.

   - First Beast: Like *Lion* – As Matthew's purpose was to reveal Christ as the King of the Jews,

He is presented as the "Lion of the tribe of Judah" (Rev. 5:5).

- Second Beast: Like a *Calf* – As Mark's purpose was to reveal Christ as the Servant of the Lord, He is presented as the One who *ministers* in service and sacrifice.

- Third Beast: Like a *Man* – As Luke's purpose was to reveal Christ as the Son of Man, He is presented as the perfect Man.

- Fourth Beast: Like an *Eagle* – As John's purpose was to reveal Christ as the Son of God, He is presented as the Word who descended from heaven like an eagle and was made flesh.

The Gospel of John is structured around Passover Feasts. John takes us through three Passovers in this book, which ultimately culminate with the crucifixion.

1. John 1:1–2:13 is the beginning of Christ's ministry up to the first Passover recorded in John's account.

2. John 2:14–5:1 takes us up to the second Passover Feast.

3. John 5:2–6:4 takes us up "nigh" (near) to the third Passover where Jesus eats the Passover Feast with His disciples in 13:1–2 and then moves into the night before His crucifixion.

As we saw from Luke 22, the significance of the Passover is that Jesus is the fulfillment of the Passover Lamb (1 Cor. 5:7)! In fact, John the Baptist said of Christ: "Behold the Lamb of God, which taketh away the sin of the world" (John 1:29). The Passover commemorates the most significant event in Jewish history—God's deliverance from slavery and oppression in Egypt under its wicked king. And how was Israel delivered? Through the blood of a spotless lamb. Thus, in this Gospel, John focuses on the final Passover and the shedding of the blood of *the* spotless *Lamb* of God! This one-time historical event has been delivering people from the slavery of this world (Eph 2:2) and its wicked king (2 Tim. 2:26) for nearly two thousand years!

May God use each of us to declare, along with John the Baptist, "Behold the Lamb of God, which taketh away the sin of the world"!

WEEK 45, DAY 3: **TODAY'S READING: JOHN 5-7**

OVERVIEW:
Christ and the Jewish leaders (5:1–47); Christ and the multitudes (6:1–71); the conflict over Moses (7:1–8:11).

HIGHLIGHTS & INSIGHTS:
In 20:30–31, John clearly states the purpose of his Gospel: to reveal the signs Christ performed during His earthly ministry to prove His deity, so that the gift of life—both eternal and abundant (John 10:10)—can be ours.

The Gospel of John is unique in how it fulfills that purpose. The first three Gospels are often called the Synoptic Gospels (*synoptic* means "to see together"). They cover, as we have seen, the same basic material. But over 90 percent of John's material is different from the other three. While Matthew, Mark, and Luke deal primarily with the *events* of the life of Christ, John deals primarily with the *meaning* of those events. For example, all four gospels record the feeding of the five thousand, but John follows the miracle with Christ's description of Himself as the "Bread of Life" (John 6), which provides the explanation of the miracle.

John also emphasizes the *person* of Christ. He includes Christ's "I AM" declarations, seven statements Jesus made to identify *who* He is and *what* He came to the earth to do:

1. I AM the Bread of Life (6:35, 41, 48, 51)
2. I AM the Light of the Word (8:12; 9:5)
3. I AM the Door of the Sheep (10:7–9)
4. I AM the Good Shepherd (10:11–14)
5. I AM the Resurrection and the Life (11:25)
6. I AM the Way, the Truth, the Life (14:6)
7. I AM the True Vine (15:1, 5)

"I AM" is significant because it is the name Jehovah God used to reveal Himself to Moses in Exodus 3:14. Also, biblically, seven is the number of perfection or completion, so these seven declarations reveal that Christ is perfectly and completely God (20:30–31). Lastly, while John records other times Jesus refers to Himself as "I Am" (4:26; 8:28, 58; 13:19; 18:5, 6, 8), these seven describe His deity and how He as God provides life (20:30–31).

Another distinctive of John's Gospel is that John chose (under the inspiration of the Holy Spirit) to record seven of Christ's miracles. In keeping with his purpose statement (20:31), these seven reveal that "Jesus is the Christ, the Son of God," and they are revealed in a specific order because they form a perfect and complete picture of salvation.

- The first three show the *means* of salvation:
    1. Water into wine (2:1–11) – Salvation is by the *Word of God*
    2. Healing the nobleman's son (4:46–54) – Salvation is by *faith*
    3. Healing the paralyzed man (5:1–9) – Salvation is by *grace*
- The fourth miracle stands alone to teach that dedicated disciples must give the Bread of Life to lost sinners.
    4. Feeding the five thousand (6:1–14) – Salvation is brought to the world by *human means*

- The last three show the *results* of salvation:
    5. Calming the storm (6:15–21) – Salvation brings *peace*
    6. Healing the blind man (9:1–7) – Salvation brings *light*
    7. Raising of Lazarus (11:38–45) – Salvation brings *life*

Lastly, each miracles introduces the discourse that follows. The discourse with Nicodemus follows the miracles that Nicodemus had witnessed (3:2). The healing of the paralyzed man (5:1–9) led to the discourse in 5:10–47. The healing of the blind man that resulted in him being cast out (9:34) precedes the discourse concerning Christ being the Good Shepherd Who never casts out anyone (10:1–41).

As we did for each of the other gospels, the following will provide an overall analysis of the Gospel of John:

1. **Information About The Author.**
    - His name: John
    - His name means "Jehovah (The Lord) is a gracious giver"
    - He is referred to in scripture as the disciple whom Jesus loved (21:20–24)
    - His father's name is Zebedee (Mt. 4:21)
    - He has a brother named James (Mt. 4:21)
    - He was intolerant of others (Lk. 9:49–56)
    - He is one of the two "sons of thunder" (Mk. 3:17)
    - His initial ministry was limited to Jews (Gal. 2:9)
    - He was exiled to an island called Patmos (Rev. 1:9)
    - He also wrote the books of 1, 2 & 3 John and Revelation

2. **Facts About This Gospel.**
    - Approximate date of writing: 85–90 AD
    - Written from Ephesus
    - Dates of recorded events: 26–33 AD
    - Theme: Deity of Christ
    - Christ is seen as the Son of God
    - Key verse: John 20:31
    - Key word: Believe (99 times)
    - Chapters: 21
    - Verses: 879
    - Words: 19,973

3. **Features Of This Gospel.**
    - This is the Gospel that identifies Christ as the Son of God more than any other
    - This is the Gospel that has the least number of events recorded
    - This Gospel contains 15 fulfilled prophecies

4. **Simple Outline Of This Gospel—Three Witnesses:**
    - Witness #1 – The Witness of Jesus's Words and Works (chapters 1–12)
    - Witness #2 – The Witness to His Witnesses (chapters 13–17)
    - Witness #3 – The Witness to the World (chapters 18–21)

52 WEEKS OF PURSUIT

WEEK 45, DAY 4: **TODAY'S READING: JOHN 8-10**

OVERVIEW:
The conflict over Moses (7:1–8:11); the conflict over Abraham (8:12–56); the conflict over Christ's Sonship (9:1–10:42).

HIGHLIGHTS & INSIGHTS:
In the Gospels, genealogies illustrate the unique emphasis of each Gospel. Because Matthew presents Christ as the King of the Jews, Christ's genealogy in this Gospel runs through David all the way back to Abraham (Matt. 1:1). Mark presents Christ as the Servant of the Lord, so there is no genealogy in Mark's Gospel (a servant's significance is determined by what he does (His work), not His birth). Because Luke presents Christ as the Son of Man, His genealogy is traced through His human mother back to the first man (Luke 3:23–38).

John, however, presents Christ as the Son of God, so this book's genealogy takes us back to the "beginning" (John 1:1; Gen. 1:1). It shows Christ's deity, that He is, in fact, God and very God and that He has always eternally existed in the Godhead. There has never been a time that Christ didn't exist, and there has never been a time that He wasn't God and completely co-equal with the Father. (See Heb. 1:8; Phil. 2:6.)

Today's reading is jam-packed with irrefutable biblical evidence that Jesus Christ is God. The Jehovah's *False* Witnesses often claim that Jesus never claimed to be God. All I can say is, how do you spell *blind* (2 Cor. 4:4)?

John 8:12–57 is a great example. At the end of a discussion about Abraham, "Jesus said unto them, Verily, verily, I say unto you, Before Abraham was, I am" (v. 58).

By using the same name Jehovah used when He revealed *Himself* to Moses in Exodus 3:14, Jesus was declaring to the Pharisees (and the whole world) that He is God. He is claiming to be the Great I AM! Absolutely nothing Jesus could have said would have been a stronger claim of deity than that. And Jesus didn't say, "Before Abraham was, I *was*." He is not simply claiming that He existed before His physical birth. He uses the term "I AM" to show that He was not only *a* god, but *the* God—*Jehovah God*!

And this is not my interpretation. That Christ is claiming to be Jehovah God is made abundantly clear by the Pharisee's response. They understood exactly what Jesus was claiming which is why they "took up stones to cast at him" (v. 59). Stoning, according to Leviticus 24:16, was the penalty for blasphemy. They wanted to stone Him because He claimed to be God!

The same thing happens in chapter 10. Jesus makes another claim of deity in verse 30, stating, "I and my Father are one." No matter what the Jehovah's *False* Witnesses claim, those who were listening to Jesus in this passage understood exactly what He meant by what He said. In verse 31, they "took up stones again to stone him," which, again, was the Old Testament penalty for blasphemy. And in case there was some doubt, Jesus forced them to clarify exactly why they were going to stone him: "Jesus answered them, Many good works have I showed you from my Father; for which of those works do ye stone me? The Jews answered him, saying, For a good work we stone thee not; but for blasphemy; and because that thou, being a man, makest thyself God" (10:32–33). There is no doubt about it, folks, Jesus Christ *is* God and clearly *claimed to be* God!

52 WEEKS OF PURSUIT

WEEK 45, DAY 5: TODAY'S READING: JOHN 11–14

OVERVIEW:
The raising of Lazarus (11:1–46); the Pharisees' plot to kill Jesus (11:47–57); Mary's anointing of Jesus's feet (12:1–11); the triumphal entry (12:12–19); Jesus's answer to the Greeks (12:20–50); Jesus washes the disciples' feet (13:1–17); Jesus foretells His betrayal, His death, and His second coming (13:18–14:14); Jesus promises the coming of the Holy Spirit (14:15–31).

HIGHLIGHTS & INSIGHTS:
For many reasons, the Gospel of John is the most unique of all of the Gospels. But the main reason for its uniqueness is its author. John is the greatest illustration of what a Christian should be in the entire New Testament. As far as Jesus's disciples are concerned, John is in a category all by himself.

JOHN IS A UNIQUE FOLLOWER.
In a loose sense, the Twelve represent all of Christianity. What was true about that group has been true of every group of believers who have ever gathered together.

- One made the same claims as the others. He looked like a Christian, spoke like a Christian, presented himself as a Christian. But he had never genuinely been saved. Of course, that was Judas. Perhaps that same ratio exists in the church today: one out of twelve has a *profession* of salvation, but no real *possession*.

- Then there were eight. These guys were saved and just really "good folk." They attended the meetings. They sang the songs, gave their offerings, and were part of the activities. But that's as far as it went. They were satisfied with being average, a description that fits about two-thirds (8 out of 12) of most congregations.

- But three of the disciples (Peter, James, and John) had a more intimate relationship with the Lord. They witnessed greater miracles (Matt. 17:1; Luke 9:28; Mark 5:37; Luke 8:51). The Lord revealed to them what He revealed to no one else (Mark 13:3) and shared more of His heart with them (Mark 14:32–34). It's the same in many churches today. While many are passively walking through life, these folks walk with their eyes fixed on what cannot be seen (2 Cor. 4:18). They walk up mountains with the Lord, and He reveals to them His glory (Matt. 17:1–8). They go further in their walk than everyone else (Mark 14:32–33).

- And yet, one goes even further—John. At the crucifixion, Judas had already done his thing. Peter is following from afar (Luke 22:54). All the disciples have scattered (John 16:32), except John. And where do we find John? At the cross, at the feet of Jesus (John 19:26). He's the only one who followed Jesus all the way. Are you that one out of twelve?

JOHN HAS A UNIQUE TITLE.
On six occasions, instead of referring to himself by name, the Holy Spirit inspired him to write "the disciple whom Jesus loved." No other disciple is called that. Did Jesus not love them? Certainly He did. But Jesus had a special love for John. Why did Jesus have a special love for John? Because John had a very special love for Jesus! John is a great example of what it is to love Jesus with all of your heart.

JOHN HAS A UNIQUE CONFIDENCE.
In the upper room when Jesus revealed that one of the disciples would betray Him, they "began every one of them to say unto him, Lord is it I?" (Matt. 26:22). Except John. John 13:25 says that John's question was, "Lord, who is it?" John may not have had enough spiritual discernment to figure out who would betray Him, but he knew for sure it wasn't going to be him!

JOHN HAS A UNIQUE PRIVILEGE.

But there's one last thing that makes John more unique than perhaps any other person in the Bible. John 13:25 says that in the upper room the night before Jesus was crucified, John had the unbelievable privilege of laying his head on Jesus's breast. And Whose breast is this? It is God in human flesh. John, with his head on Jesus's breast, listened to the very heartbeat of God.

In Christianity today, most Christians are so in love with themselves (2 Tim. 3:2) that they hear and know their own heartbeat. Many Christians are so preoccupied with people's opinions, they definitely hear and know the heartbeat of others (1 Cor. 4:3). Too many Christians are so enamored with the things of this world, they hear and know the heartbeat of the world. But we don't have our head on Jesus's breast so we don't hear or know the heartbeat of God! Do you know how we can hear God's heartbeat today? The Bible you hold in your hands is God's heartbeat (John 1:1, 14). Through it, you can, like John, listen today to the very heartbeat of God.

52 WEEKS OF PURSUIT

WEEK 46, DAY 1: TODAY'S READING: JOHN 15–19

OVERVIEW:
Jesus teaches about abiding in Him (15:1–11); Jesus teaches about loving one another (15:12–17); Jesus warns about persecution (15:18–16:7); Jesus's promise of the Holy Spirit (16:8–33); Jesus's prayer of intercession (17:1–26); Jesus's betrayal and arrest (18:1–14); Peter's denial (18:15–18); Jesus before the high priest (18:19–24); Peter's second and third denial (18:25–27); Jesus before Pilate (18:28–38); Barabbas is released (18:39–40); Christ's crucifixion (19:1–37); Christ's burial (19:38–42).

HIGHLIGHTS & INSIGHTS:
As we come back again to our Lord's betrayal, arrest, and crucifixion today, let's consider the centuries-old argument about who killed Jesus.

The Jewish leaders, of course, are the primary targets of the blame (rightly so) because it was their plot and their false charges that actually forced the issue. Others blame the Romans, who do deserve some of the blame because they set aside normal justice to appease an angry mob and knowingly executed an innocent man. But if you really want to get to the bottom line on who bears the responsibility for Christ's death, all you have to do is listen to Peter in Acts 2:23: "Him, [that is, Christ] being delivered by the determinate counsel and foreknowledge of God, ye [the Jews] have taken, and by wicked hands [the Romans] have crucified and slain."

Neither the Jews nor the Romans were responsible for Christ's death, though they certainly bear the guilt for the actual execution and sin that was involved. Instead, the ultimate responsibility lies with God! God destined it. God planned it. And Jesus, in an act of submissive obedience, simply carried out the eternal plan (Rev. 13:8). But don't ever lose sight of the fact that *He laid down his life*!

That's why, in John 10:17–18, Jesus said, "Therefore doth my Father love me, because I lay down my life, that I might take it again. No man taketh it from me, but I lay it down of myself. I have power to lay it down, and I have power to take it again." Though He appeared to be a victim, nothing could be further from the truth! Jesus died, not because men killed Him, but because they couldn't. Jesus could not have died had He not willed to die. John 19:30 says, "When Jesus therefore had received the vinegar, he said, It is finished: and he bowed his head and gave up the ghost." He *gave* it! He yielded His life. And just as surely as He laid down His life, He *took it again*!

Throughout today's reading, Jesus demonstrates that He is in control:

19:16 – "Then delivered he [Pilate] him [Christ] therefore unto them to be crucified. And they took Jesus, and led him away."

> It seems a minor thing to say "they led him away," but it isn't. Jesus didn't have to be driven; He went willingly. He followed them to the cross exactly as the prophet Isaiah said it would happen. "He is brought as a lamb to the slaughter" (Isa. 53:7). Unlike cattle, which are driven, sheep are led.

19:17a – "And he bearing his cross…"

> Jesus carried His own cross. Why? Because God declared it would happen that way in an Old Testament type (a prophetic picture instead of a statement) of the crucifixion. Genesis 22:6 says, "And Abraham took the wood of the burnt offering, and laid it upon Isaac his son." Isaac, a picture of Christ, carried the wood for his execution up Mount Moriah. And in John 19, as a perfect fulfillment of what Isaac pictured prophetically, Jesus, too, carries the "wood" to His own execution.

19:17b – "And he bearing his cross went forth…"

> "Went forth" indicates that Jesus was led outside the city walls. Why? Because Roman law said

that no one could be crucified inside the city. They had a place for crucifixions outside the city "called the place of a skull" (19:17c) because from a distance the mountainside resembled a skull. And that's where they took Jesus. But long before Rome built that law into its books, when God instituted the offering for sin in the book of Exodus, He said, "But the flesh of the bullock, and his skin, and his dung, shalt thou burn with fire without [outside] the camp: it is a sin offering" (Ex. 29:14). And Jesus, in perfect fulfillment of the picture of the sin offering, was sacrificed outside the city.

19:18a – "they crucified Him…"

This is another exact fulfillment—and one that the Jews couldn't have been anticipated. The Jews didn't crucify people; they stoned people. But Christ had to be crucified, a Roman way to die, because of the picture God gives in Numbers 21:6 9. When Israel was bitten by snakes, God told Moses to make a serpent and lift it up on a rod, and anyone who looked upon it would be healed. Jesus himself drew the parallel in John 3:14, "And as Moses lifted up the serpent in the wilderness, even so must the Son of man be lifted up." In His crucifixion, Jesus was lifted up on a cross, a kind of death unheard of in the Old Testament. But that's how prophecy said it would happen, so it did.

19:18b – "they crucified him, and two other with him, on either side one, and Jesus in the midst [middle]."

Is it significant that He died with criminals? Absolutely! Because Isaiah 53:12 says, "He was numbered with the transgressors."

We could continue like this through this entire passage! It is one fulfilled prophecy after another. But let's skip to the final one.

John 19:28 says, "After this, Jesus knowing that all things were now accomplished, that the scripture might be fulfilled, said, I thirst."

Why did He say this here? Was it because He was thirsty? I'm sure He was! But that's not why He said it. He said it because He knew that every other Old Testament prophecy concerning His death had been fulfilled, except that one. Psalm 69:21 says, "In my thirst they gave me vinegar to drink." So, in John 19:28, Jesus is reaching back to grab that one unfulfilled prophecy so that His death could be "according to the Scriptures." Because according to 1 Corinthians 15:3, for the gospel to actually have the power to save us, every detail prophesied in the Old Testament concerning Christ's death had to be fulfilled to the absolute letter!

John 19:30 says, "When Jesus therefore had received the vinegar, he said, It is finished." In other words, "Every prophecy has now been fulfilled. I can die now." And verse 30 continues, "And he bowed his head [no slump to the side, He bowed it!] and gave up the ghost." How did He die? Did He bleed to death? Did He die of exposure? Did He have a heart attack? Did He suffocate? No. He died because He willed Himself dead. He *gave* His life!

52 WEEKS OF PURSUIT

WEEK 46, DAY 2: TODAY'S READING: JOHN 20-21

OVERVIEW:
Christ's resurrection (20:1–10); Christ's post-resurrection appearances to Mary and to His disciples (20:11–31); Jesus's reinstatement and restoration of Peter (21:1–17); Jesus's final instructions to His disciples (21:18–25).

HIGHLIGHTS & INSIGHTS:
Today we will consider the significance of chapter 21, the conclusion to John's Gospel.

In John 21, Jesus has already risen from the dead. He has made multiple appearances, two of them to His disciples. But the disciples are in danger of drifting back into their old way of life (21:3). Even after three years with the Lord, those memories are pretty foggy right now. Things didn't go like they had planned; they've moved from disillusionment to despair. Sure, there was a tremendous rejuvenation in their hearts to realize that Jesus had risen from the dead, but the disciples still hadn't quite pieced the whole thing together.

Things were different now. For three years they had walked and talked with the Lord; they were always together. Now He appears and disappears without any notice. It's just different. And on top of that, they're all bearing the guilt of the fact that they had forsaken the Lord. All of them except John scattered when Jesus needed them most.

Still, when you come to the end of chapter 20, it feels like an ending. The main narrative builds to the great climax of Thomas's confession of faith as he calls Jesus, "My Lord and my God" (v. 28). Then John gives an explanation of his purpose in writing the book: "And many other signs truly did Jesus in the presence of his disciples, which are not written in this book: But these are written, that ye might believe that Jesus is the Christ, the Son of God; and that believing ye might have life through his name" (v. 30–31). It's a beautiful conclusion. If you couldn't see another chapter just below these verses, you'd think that the book had ended with chapter 20.

But chapter 20 is not the end! There are still some extremely important things the Holy Spirit wants us to know about the disciples' situation. And He uses chapter 21 to fill us in.

First, John, under the inspiration of the Holy Spirit, doesn't want to end his Gospel without telling his readers that Peter had been fully restored. Peter hadn't just turned his back on the Lord as had the other disciples; he had actually denied Him on three different occasions! I mean, how could someone who had done something like that still be entrusted with the responsibility of shepherding the flock of Jesus Christ? Without chapter 21, the question would remain unanswered.

Also, without this last chapter, it would be a mystery why Peter is so prominent in the first twelve chapters of the book of Acts. How does a guy go from denying the Lord when he's fifty feet away from Him to preaching boldly on the Day of Pentecost? Just seven weeks later, when he looks out on the religious leaders of Israel and all the people of Judea and Jerusalem, Peter confronted them with the fact that they had taken God's own Son, the Lord of glory, and by their wicked hands had slain Him! Those are some pretty strong words! How do you go from being a coward to having that kind of courage? Chapter 21 is the missing link.

And finally, at the end of chapter 20, the last of the disciples comes to genuine faith. That, of course, was "Doubting Thomas." One by one, they had all been convinced of the resurrection, and that was wonderful. But now what? What were they going to do about it? Chapter 21 is Jesus's call to action.

A few other things to notice in chapter 21:

21:3 – Perhaps we could paraphrase this verse, "I'll tell you what, fellas, I may not be a great preacher or evangelist, but there is one thing I do know how to do, so I'm goin' fishin'! Come on, boys, let me show ya how it's done!" And they didn't get a bite. The one thing Peter thought he could do, he couldn't do anymore (John 15:5) because God had put His hand on his life, and He was in control. Learn the lesson from Peter.

21:15–17 – No matter how our love has failed, there is restoration. Perhaps that's God's message God to you today—there *is* restoration! And the restoration was initiated by the Lord. He could have said, "You know what Peter, you're a chump! You talk a big talk, but you can't be counted on to do anything! I gave you three years of my life, and I can't even get you to follow one simple command. Just forget it, man!" But that's not what happened. Jesus initiated the restoration, providing the one who had denied Him three times the chance to affirm his love for Him three times!

21:17 – After the third time Jesus asked Peter if he loved Him, Peter appeals to the doctrine of omniscience. He says, "Lord, thou knowest all things." In other words, "Lord, you're going to have to read my heart, because I know my love for you isn't obvious by my life." The doctrine of omniscience is a tremendous thing. The fact is, if God weren't omniscient, He wouldn't know that we love Him a lot of times because, like Peter, it isn't always obvious from our lives. Sometimes, we too have to ask Jesus to look on the inside, at what is in our hearts.

21:15–17 – Saying, "Feed my lambs. Feed my sheep. Feed my sheep," was Jesus's way of saying, "I forgive you, Peter. I still believe in you, Peter. I still think you're the right man for the job."

Chapter 21 marked a turning point in Peter's life. The things that took place seven weeks later on the Day of Pentecost in Acts 2 are the proof of that. May God use this chapter to be a turning point in our lives today as well!

52 WEEKS OF PURSUIT

WEEK 46, DAY 3: TODAY'S READING: ACTS 1-4

OVERVIEW:
The messengers of the kingdom prepared (chapter 1); the offer of the kingdom of heaven to the Nation of Israel (chapter 2); a second offer of the kingdom of heaven to the Nation of Israel (chapters 3–4).

HIGHLIGHTS & INSIGHTS:
To begin, we will consider some of the basic facts about the book of Acts.

- Author: Luke, the physician (Col. 4:14); also the author of the Gospel of Luke (Acts 1:1; Luke 1:1–4)
- Approximate date of writing: 59–65 AD
- Dates of the recorded events: 33–62 AD
- Theme: God's plan for Israel postponed and the revelation of the church
- Christ is seen as our Great High Priest ministering in the heavens (Heb. 4:14–16)
- Key verses: Acts 1:6–7
- Key chapters: 7–13
- Chapters: 28
- Verses: 1,007
- Words: 24,250

As we will recall, Acts is one of the four books of the Bible (along with Matthew, Hebrews and James) where you can lose your way if you don't keep your compass pointed toward the "ancient landmark" of the Nation of Israel (Prov. 22:28; 23:10). To navigate the book of Acts effectively, we will need to keep certain "trail markers" in mind.

TRAIL MARKER #1: THE TITLE
It is significant that the book's title is "The Acts of the Apostles," not "The Doctrine (or Teaching) of the Apostles." The book of *Acts* is the historical record of the *actions* of the apostles. It's the story of what happened through the continued ministry of Jesus through the apostles (Acts 1:1).

TRAIL MARKER #2: THE KEY VERSE
Acts 1:6–7 says, "[The apostles] asked of him, saying, Lord, wilt thou at this time restore again the kingdom to Israel? And [Jesus] said unto them, It is not for you to know the times or the seasons, which the Father hath put in his own power."

At this point, the apostles are focused on the return of Jesus Christ and the establishment of His kingdom on earth. Jesus had told them they sit on twelve thrones with Him in the kingdom (Matt. 19:28), so this was a big deal to them! Jesus's answer concerning the timing of all this, however, is rather vague (v. 7). Basically, He tells them, "It depends."

At this point in the book of Acts and in the plan of God, the literal, earthly kingdom (the kingdom of heaven) and its King are still being offered to the Nation of Israel. When Jesus answered their question, it remained to be seen what Israel would do with the offer. However, if we compare Acts 1:7 where Jesus says "It is not for you to know the times or the seasons," with 1 Thessalonians 5:1–2 where Paul says, "But of the times and the seasons, brethren, ye … know perfectly," a transition has been made! By the time Paul writes to the Thessalonians in 54 AD, it's gone from, "It's not for you to know," to "You know perfectly." As we will see, the apostles' question was actually answered in Acts

7 after the Nation of Israel rejected the offer of the kingdom for the third time. This brings us to our third trail marker.

TRAIL MARKER #3: A TRANSITIONAL BOOK

The most consistent thing about the book of Acts is its *inconsistency*! God does one thing in one place and something completely different in another. He is making key transitions for key purposes throughout the book. Acts is a bridge from one dispensation to a new dispensation (the church age), and it records the transition from God accomplishing His plan through the Nation of Israel to accomplishing His plan through the church.

God's changes are demonstrated through seven transitions and three key events in the book of Acts.

- **Transition #1**: From the ministry of Jesus Christ to the ministry of the Holy Spirit (1:2)
- **Transition #2**: From the Twelve being called "disciples" to being called "apostles" (1:2)
    - Key Event #1: The Nation of Israel's final rejection of the Kingdom of heaven (Acts 7)
- **Transition #3**: From the Nation of Israel to the Samaritans, a race of half-Jew and half-Gentile (8:1–5)
- **Transition #4**: From the Nation of Israel to the church, a group composed of Jews and Gentiles (8:26–11:18)
- **Transition #5**: From the preaching of the kingdom of heaven (the literal earthly kingdom offered to the nation of Israel) to the preaching of the kingdom of God (the unseen, spiritual kingdom inside individual believers) (8:12)
    - Key Event #2: The salvation of the Gentile Cornelius and the apostles' determination that God is no longer dealing exclusively with the Jews, but has now taken salvation to the Gentiles (11:18)
    - Key Event #3: The execution of the Apostle James and the decision not to replace him and Peter's departure to Caesarea (12:1–2, 19)
- **Transition #6**: From Peter, the Apostle to the Jews, to Paul, the Apostle to the Gentiles (9:1–13:1)
- **Transition #7**: From God's base of operations being in Jerusalem to it being in Antioch (11:26–13:1)

The transition from Israel to the church and to the church age were *mysteries*, truths that were hidden from the twelve apostles. (See Rom. 11:25; Eph. 3:1–12; 2:11–22.) The Twelve believed that God dealt exclusively with the Nation of Israel (Matt. 10:5–7), and in their ethnocentric opinions, the Gentiles were pagan heathens unworthy to receive anything from God (Acts 11:1–3). Thinking they were going to find themselves in the millennial reign of Christ, the apostles actually found themselves in the church age. Needless to say, their journey was full of surprises!

TRAIL MARKER #4: SIGNS AND WONDERS

The Jews required a sign. That's what God declared in 1 Corinthians 1:22: "For the Jews require a sign, and the Greeks seek after wisdom." The signs and wonders done by Jesus and the apostles were to prove to Israel that the message and the messengers were sent by God (Heb. 2:3–4). Miraculous healings and speaking in tongues were signs for the Nation of Israel. 1 Corinthians 14:22 says, "Wherefore tongues are for a sign, not to them that believe, but to them that believe not." Tongues were a sign given to unbelieving Jews, and every time tongues occur in the Bible (only in Acts 2, 10, and 19), an unbelieving Jew is present to witness the sign. Thus, since God has postponed his dealings with Israel, apostolic healings and speaking in tongues do not occur today. Romans 11:25 makes this very clear: "For I would not, brethren, that ye should be ignorant of this mystery, lest ye should be wise in your own conceits; that blindness in part is happened to Israel, until the fulness of the Gentiles be come in." God has temporarily blinded Israel and is currently working exclusively through the church.

With these four trail markers in mind, then, let's look at some highlights in today's reading.

ACTS 2

This chapter is a vortex of doctrinal error for contemporary Christians. It is here that the modern-day Pentecostal and Charismatic churches (speaking in tongues, baptism of the Holy Spirit) and the Church of Christ and the Christian Church (water baptism is essential for salvation) lose the "ancient landmark," Israel. But if you pay close attention to the context, this chapter is easily understood.

Here's the whole chapter in one sentence:

Jews from all over the world (2:5–11) came to Jerusalem (the Jew's holiest city) to celebrate Pentecost (a Jewish holiday, 2:1) where they saw the sign of tongues (Jews require a sign) and heard a Jewish apostle (Peter) tell them that, just fifty days prior, they had killed their Jewish Messiah (2:22–24, 36) and that they needed to do exactly what John the Baptist (the last Jewish prophet) and Jesus (their Jewish Messiah) told them to do in the Gospels (repent and be baptized in water for the remission of sins: Matt. 3:1–2; 4:17; Luke 3:3; John 3:22–23; 4:1–2) to prepare themselves for the soon-coming kingdom of heaven!

Obviously, this passage deals exclusively with the Nation of Israel! Simply stated, unless you're a Jew living in 33 AD, there's no need for you to speak with tongues, and water baptism does not save you from your sins!

ACTS 3

Again, in context it is clear that God is dealing exclusively with the Nation of Israel. Peter and John (Jewish apostles) are on their way to the temple (the Jewish place of worship) at the hour of prayer (Jews prayed three times a day) and that Peter performs a miracle (Jews require a sign). Upon seeing the crowd gathering (other Jews at the temple to pray), Peter tells them that they killed the Jewish Messiah (3:13–16), but that, if they repent, Jesus will return to establish His literal, earthly, Jewish kingdom (3:19–21)! In this passage, Peter is offering Israel a second chance to accept Jesus of Nazareth as their Messiah and to prepare themselves for the coming of His literal, earthly kingdom.

52 WEEKS OF PURSUIT

WEEK 46, DAY 4: TODAY'S READING: ACTS 5-7

OVERVIEW:

Internal and external opposition (chapters 5–6); the final offer of the kingdom of heaven rejected by the Nation of Israel (chapter 7).

HIGHLIGHTS & INSIGHTS:

In chapters 3–6 of Acts, the Holy Spirit reveals two forms of Satanic opposition: external and internal. External opposition occurs as persecution. The Jewish leaders mete out two cycles of persecution on Peter and John (4:1–22; 5:17–40). But though Peter and John appear to be the objects of wrath, and though the Jewish religious leaders seem to be the persecutors, "we wrestle not against flesh and blood, but against principalities, against powers, against the rulers of the darkness of this world, against spiritual wickedness in high places" (Eph. 6:12). Jesus is the real object of wrath (4:17–18; 5:28,40), and the real persecutor is Satan. In our world, you can talk about Buddhism, Islam, Hinduism, or the occult with any group of people in any public place, but as soon as you mention the name of Jesus, an uproar is sure to follow. The devil hates the name of Jesus.

What angered the Jewish religious leaders (and the devil) the most, however, was the preaching and teaching of the gospel (4:2, 18; 5:28). Here's a good spiritual rule of thumb: if the devil doesn't like it, it must be effective, so we should do it all the more! Teaching and preaching is the primary action of the Great Commission: "Go ye therefore, and teach all nations … to observe all things whatsoever I have commanded you" (Matt. 28:19–20). Teaching and preaching is the primary function of a pastor. (See Acts 2:14, 42; 3:12; 4:31; 5:20, 42; 6:1–4; 1 Cor. 1:21; Gal. 6:6; Col. 1:28; 1 Tim. 4:11–16; 5:17; 2 Tim. 4:1–2, 17; Tit. 1:3.) Satan will do anything he can to stop the preaching and teaching of the gospel of Jesus Christ!

But if Satan can't stop the gospel with external opposition, he'll walk in the front doors of the church and try internal opposition. In Acts 5, Ananias and Sapphira sold some property. To appear spiritual, they told Peter they were offering *all* of the money for the land they had sold, but they had kept back a portion for themselves. They must have thought, "What a great plan! The church will think we're really spiritual for sacrificing so much, and we'll still be rich! No one will ever know." But though we can fool men, we can't fool an omniscient God! Peter says, "Thou hast not lied unto men, but unto God" (Acts 5:4). And they each dropped dead on the spot (vs. 5, 10). The issue, of course, was not that they didn't give all of the proceeds from the sale of their property. Neither God nor the apostles had required that. The issue was that they lied to the apostles about the money and, in doing so, lied to God Himself!

And if you're wondering whether the Sunday attendance dropped after that—it certainly did! But it was all part of God's plan. God always purges His church and purifies His people in preparation for new fruit (5:11–14).

Another form of internal opposition came from the envy, strife and complaining among the believers. The Grecians' complaint in Acts 6 was legitimate and needed to be addressed, but the devil is always happy to keep us busy with legitimate needs and good things that keep us from the best things: prayer and the Word of God. When Martha was so busy working to serve Him, Jesus said to her, "Martha, Martha, thou art careful and troubled about many things: But one thing is needful: and Mary hath chosen that good part, which shall not be taken away from her" (Luke 10:41–42). The apostles, too, chose "that good part" in Acts 6 by continuing in prayer and the ministry of the Word (6:2–4). They delegated the legitimate need to carefully selected "deacons" (6:3, 5–7) so they could carry out their primary function as leaders in the church. With regard to deacons, God even holds those with the simplest forms of service to a standard of "honest report, full of the Holy Ghost and wisdom" (6:3).

In chapter 7, we come to the first key event in the book of Acts. This is the answer to the apostles' question in Acts 1:6 concerning the time Jesus would set up His kingdom. It also marks the beginning of five of the seven transitions in the book. Acts 7 is the third and final offer of the King and His kingdom to the Nation of Israel.

Stephen preaches an incredible sermon with three significant points: that God promised us (Israel) a land (7:2–7), that God promised us a Prophet like Moses (7:20, 37), but that you leaders always kill God's prophets and fail to respond properly to God's message (7:51–53). Needless to say, the council was enraged by Stephen's message and immediately picked up stones to stone him.

Then, in verse 56 Stephen said: "Behold, I see the heavens opened, and the Son of man standing on the right hand of God." To understand the significance of this statement, we have to look at exactly what Stephen saw: "the heavens opened" and "the Son of man standing." Hebrews 10:12 tells us that, immediately following His ascension (Acts 1:9–11), Jesus *sat down* at the right hand of the Father: "But this man, after he had offered one sacrifice for sins for ever, sat down on the right hand of God." Colossians 3:1 tells us that even today in the church age, Jesus is *seated* at the Father's right hand: "If ye then be risen with Christ, seek those things which are above, where Christ sitteth on the right hand of God."

But Stephen saw the heavens opened and Jesus *standing* at the Father's right hand as he was being stoned. The next time we find Jesus standing and the heavens opened is in the book of Revelation (4:1–3; 5:1, 5–6) where Jesus rises to take the book with seven seals from the Father's hand—which marks the beginning of the Tribulation. So, why is Jesus is standing in Acts 7? It's because He is awaiting the Nation of Israel's response!

If they respond with national repentance (had the Jewish ruling council repented upon hearing Stephen's message, the entire nation would have followed their lead), then Jesus will open the first seal of the Tribulation (Rev. 6) and Daniel's seventieth week will begin. If they reject the message, then Jesus will sit back down, Israel will be "blinded in part" (Romans 11:25), and the church age will begin. Clearly, the stoning of Stephen is a rejection of God's offer, and as expected, we find Jesus seated for the duration of the church age (Eph. 1:20; Col. 3:1). Consequently, God turns His attention to the gospel of the kingdom of God (the spiritual, internal kingdom) and to all of the Gentile nations under heaven, as we will see in Acts 8.

WEEK 46, DAY 5: **TODAY'S READING: ACTS 8-10**

OVERVIEW:
The transition from Israel to the Gentiles (chapter 8); the salvation of the missionary to the Gentiles (chapter 9); the transition to the Gentiles confirmed by apostolic authority (chapter 10).

HIGHLIGHTS & INSIGHTS:
At the end of chapter 7, the Nation of Israel has clearly rejected the offer of both their Messiah and His kingdom—the literal, physical kingdom of heaven. God's plan for Israel is postponed, and the parenthesis of the church age is beginning.

The stoning of Stephen led to a "great persecution" (Acts 8:1) against the believers, causing many of them to flee Jerusalem. As they did, they preached the gospel "abroad throughout the regions of Judaea and Samaria." God used persecution to accomplish His own mission of sending witnesses to "all Judaea, and in Samaria, and unto the uttermost part of the earth" (Acts 1:8)!

Acts 8 marks the beginning of the transition from God accomplishing His plan through the Nation of Israel to God accomplishing His plan through the church, composed of both Jews and Gentiles (Eph. 2:11–22). And God makes this transition incredibly smooth. First, believers witness in Judaea (8:1c). Second, Philip, the deacon mentioned in Acts 6:5 and called "the evangelist" in Acts 21:8, preaches the kingdom of God (the spiritual, internal kingdom) to the Samaritans, who are half-Jew, half-Gentile (8:5). And third, the witness extends to "the uttermost," as Philip preaches to a full-blooded Gentile on his way home from a pilgrimage to Jerusalem (8:27–28).

Interestingly, God withheld the gift of the Holy Ghost from the Samaritans until Peter and John arrived (8:14–17). This was done for two reasons: 1) To prove to the apostles in Jerusalem that the Samaritans had truly received the Word of God and 2) To prove to the Samaritans that the apostles in Jerusalem were God's ordained authorities.

In chapters 1–7, while the kingdom of heaven was being offered to the Nation of Israel, the Apostle Peter, the apostle to the Jews, has been the dominant voice (Gal. 2:7–8). In chapter 9, a new character enters the scene—Paul.

We were introduced to Paul in Acts 7:58 where he is called by his birth name, Saul (Acts 13:9). Acts 9:1 says he "[breathed] out threatenings and slaughter against the disciples of the Lord," and Paul himself said, "I imprisoned and beat in every synagogue them that believed on thee" (Acts 22:19). You know what we call a guy like this in today's world? A terrorist! Yet Paul was one of the most religious men on earth. Paul says of his religiousness, "If any other man thinketh that he hath whereof he might trust in the flesh, I more: Circumcised the eighth day, of the stock of Israel, of the tribe of Benjamin, an Hebrew of the Hebrews; as touching the law, a Pharisee; Concerning zeal, persecuting the church; touching the righteousness which is in the law, blameless" (Phil. 3:4–6).

Religion is and has always been the most destructive force on this planet to the work of God. The religious Jewish council crucified our Lord. The religious Jewish council stoned Stephen. And a religious leader (Paul) was the most destructive force against the early church. But Paul's story doesn't end there. In 1 Timothy 1:13–16, Paul says,

> [I] was before a blasphemer, and a persecutor, and injurious: but I obtained mercy, because I did it ignorantly in unbelief. And the grace of our Lord was exceeding abundant with faith and love which is in Christ Jesus. This is a faithful saying, and worthy of all acceptation, that Christ Jesus came into the world to save sinners; of whom I am chief. Howbeit for this cause I obtained mercy, that in me first Jesus Christ might shew forth all longsuffering, for a pattern to them which should hereafter believe on him to life everlasting.

What a radical transformation! Paul goes from being the chief misery of the church to the chief missionary of the church. If God could save a terrorist like Paul, He can save and transform anyone.

In fact, Paul was saved specifically to be a missionary to the Gentiles. In Acts 9:15, God calls him "a chosen vessel unto me, to bear my name before the Gentiles, and kings, and the children of Israel." Starting in chapter 9, Peter's role as the apostle to the Jews (Gal. 2:7–8) diminishes, while Paul's role as the apostle to the Gentiles increases. After Acts 13, Peter's name is only mentioned one more time, while Paul's is mentioned 129 times! Obviously, there has been a major transition.

In Acts 10, Peter, the apostle to the Jews, reluctantly preaches to a family of Gentiles. The heavens open again (10:11), but rather than seeing Jesus standing at the right hand of the Father (Acts 7:56), Peter sees a vessel of unclean animals descending and hears a voice instructing him to kill and eat them. According to Old Testament law (Lev. 20:25; Deut. 14), Jews were to avoid eating certain kinds of animals that God called "unclean." So Peter, being a devout Jewish believer in Christ, refuses to eat the unclean animals. But God says to Peter, "What God hath cleansed, that call not thou common" (10:15). God lets Peter know that He is transitioning from Israel to the church by using unclean animals as a metaphor for the Gentiles. In effect, God is saying, "Peter, I'm doing something new now—so I no longer want you to consider the Gentiles as unclean or unworthy of salvation." But Peter has a very difficult time accepting that God will save Gentiles. At this point, we might consider him an "unbelieving" Jew!

Soon, however, Peter finds himself preaching to a family of Gentiles when they suddenly begin speaking in tongues. Since Jews require a sign (1 Cor. 1:22), and tongues are a sign for unbelieving Jews (1 Cor. 14:22), this was a sign to Peter who, in this context, is a Jew who doesn't believe that God will save Gentiles! Once the apostles in Jerusalem hear of this "casting of pearls before swine," Peter is called to answer for this blatantly disobedient act of preaching to the Gentiles (Acts 11:1–3). As Peter defends himself, the most convincing evidence he offers to the Jewish apostles is the sign of tongues (Acts 11:15–18). By the end of the meeting, the Jewish church in Jerusalem declares: "Then hath God also to the Gentiles granted repentance unto life" (11:18) The transition from Israel to the church is almost complete.

Let's briefly summarize the transitions that we've discovered:

- Acts 1–6 – God is offering the King and the kingdom of heaven to the Nation of Israel
- Acts 7 – Israel rejects the King and the kingdom of heaven for the third and final time
- Acts 8 – God makes an orderly transition from Jews to Samaritans and from Samaritans to Gentiles
- Acts 9 – The transition from Peter, the apostle to the Jews, to Paul, the apostle to the Gentiles
- Acts 10 – God's transition to the Gentiles is confirmed by the apostolic authority of Peter

52 WEEKS OF PURSUIT

WEEK 47, **DAY 1: TODAY'S READING: ACTS 11-14**

OVERVIEW:
The transition from Jerusalem to Antioch (chapters 11–12); Paul's first missionary journey (chapters 13–14).

HIGHLIGHTS & INSIGHTS:
Chapters 11–14 cover the final phases of the transition from the Nation of Israel to the church. The base of operations for the early church had been in Jerusalem. When persecution arose in chapter 8, the apostles remained in Jerusalem, but the majority of believers fled (8:1). Each time a new people group received the Word of God, envoys from Jerusalem were sent to confirm God's working among them. (See Acts 8:14–17, 25; 11:1–3, 19–22.) Even Paul himself needed the apostles in Jerusalem to validate his ministry (Gal. 2:1, 9). And it makes perfect sense that Jerusalem was the place of authority for the early church.

1. If you were a believing Jew waiting for Jesus your Messiah to return to the Mount of Olives (Acts 1:9–12; Zech. 14:1–9) to establish His kingdom at His second coming, why be any place other than Jerusalem and miss all of the action?

2. If you were seeking to reach only the Jews with the message of the kingdom of heaven, Jerusalem had the greatest concentration of Jews in the entire region, not to mention the world!

3. If the apostle to the Jews (Peter) resided in Jerusalem, where else would God's base of operations be?

But starting in chapter 11, we see God begin to move His base of operations from Jerusalem to Antioch.

Once the apostles in Jerusalem had confirmed the salvation of the Gentiles (11:18), Barnabas seeks out Paul, the apostle to the Gentiles and brings him to Antioch (11:25–26) where a multi-ethnic church of Jews and Gentiles had been planted (Acts 13:1). It was also in Antioch that "the disciples were called Christians first" (11:26). For the first ten years of the church, not one believer had been called a Christian! Only when God transitions from Israel to the church, and from Jerusalem to Antioch, are His followers called Christians—another confirmation that Antioch is the new base of operations.

In chapter 12, the apostles demonstrate that God has postponed His plan for Israel by not replacing the Apostle James after his execution. Jesus promised the Twelve, "Verily I say unto you, That ye which have followed me, in the regeneration when the Son of man shall sit in the throne of his glory, ye also shall sit upon twelve thrones, judging the twelve tribes of Israel" (Matt. 19:28). When the King and His physical kingdom was still being offered to Israel (Acts 1–7), the apostles wanted to be sure there were twelve apostles in place. That's why when Judas Iscariot committed suicide, they believed a replacement was necessary—to fill the twelfth throne (Acts 1:15–26). The fact that the Apostle James was not replaced clearly indicates that the apostles recognized that Christ's return had been postponed and the church would now be God's primary vehicle for carrying out His purpose and plan on the earth.

Another proof that Jerusalem was no longer God's base of operations is that when Peter leaves Jerusalem, he doesn't return (12:19). The leadership team of Peter, James and John is obviously being dismantled and Jerusalem's central authority is waning.

In Acts 13, God introduces His church—the new institution for fulfilling His plan. It is multi-racial, multi-cultural, and missional (13:1–4). As the Word of God was being proclaimed in this local church, the Spirit of God calls Paul and Barnabas (13:2) to perform a particular work. They were to preach the gospel and reproduce local churches—specifically, churches which would plant more local churches which would reproduce other local churches and so on (chapters 13–14). Clearly, the work of both the local church and of missionaries is to preach the gospel and to plant reproducing local churches. Though many faithful Christians serve in various capacities in missions, preaching the gospel and church planting are the preeminent components of missions.

Comparing the sermons of Peter and Paul gives further proof that God was no longer offering the kingdom of heaven to Israel, but was instead intending to bring all men into the spiritual, internal kingdom of God. Peter's sermon was, "You Jews killed our Messiah and rejected the kingdom. Repent and be baptized in water!" (See Acts 2:36–38; 3:15, 19–20.) Paul's message was, "Be it known unto you therefore, men and brethren, that through [Jesus] is preached unto you the forgiveness of sins: And by him all that believe are justified from all things, from which ye could not be justified by the law of Moses" (13:38–39). Peter's message is the gospel of the kingdom, while Paul's is the gospel of grace. (See Acts 13:42–43.)

Acts 13:4–14:26 is the record of Paul's first missionary journey around 46 AD. On this first journey, the gospel was preached and churches were planted on the Island of Cyprus, Antioch of Pisidia, Iconium, Lystra, Derbe, and Perga. All of these cities, except Cyprus, are in the region known as Galatia, in modern-day Turkey. The journey took about two years and covered nearly 1,250 miles!

WEEK 47, DAY 2: **TODAY'S READING: ACTS 15-17**

OVERVIEW:
The Jerusalem church addresses false teaching (chapter 15); Paul's second missionary journey (chapters 16–17).

HIGHLIGHTS & INSIGHTS:
In Acts 15, we discover more controversy surrounding the salvation of the Gentiles. When Paul and Barnabas return to Antioch of Syria, they find false teachers are teaching the newly saved Gentiles that they must be circumcised to be saved. Circumcision was a significant symbolic act under Old Testament law, but through the blood of Jesus Christ, the law had been satisfied, and circumcision was no longer necessary (Gal. 5:6). Paul, seeing the gospel in jeopardy, begins "no small dissension and disputation" (15:2) with these false teachers. Finally, they determine that this question must be addressed by the apostles in Jerusalem.

Peter argues that all people, whether Jew or Gentile, are saved by grace so, "why tempt ye God, to put a yoke upon the neck of the disciples, which neither our fathers nor we were able to bear?" (15:10). James settles the dispute, saying, "My sentence is, that we trouble not them, which from among the Gentiles are turned to God: But that we write unto them, that they abstain from pollutions of idols, and from fornication, and from things strangled, and from blood" (15:19–20).

But, we might ask, if the Gentiles are saved by grace, why does James make a list of things they should abstain from? Meats offered to idols, fornication, things strangled, and blood (v. 20) have nothing to do with salvation or sanctification. James answers the question in verse 21: "For Moses of old time hath in every city them that preach him, being read in the synagogues every sabbath day." These stipulations were to be followed by the Gentiles to keep the door of faith open to the Jews. This is the same principle Paul described in 1 Corinthians 9:19–23: "Unto the Jews I became as a Jew, that I might gain the Jews; to them that are under the law, as under the law, that I might gain them that are under the law … I am made all things to all men, that I might by all means save some. And this I do for the gospel's sake." To settle the issue, the apostles set a letter regarding their decision with Paul, Barnabas, Judas and Silas to the church at Antioch which, when read to the church, was cause for great rejoicing!

In about 50 AD, Paul and Barnabas determine to revisit the cities where they had preached the gospel and planted churches. But they couldn't agree on who should be their companions. Even the heroes of the faith are sometimes carnal, stubborn and self-willed! Barnabas takes his nephew, John Mark, who abandoned them on their first journey, and heads for Cyprus following the original route (15:39). Paul selects Silas (also called Silvanus) and takes a new route through Syria and Cilicia (15:40–41).

In chapter 16, Paul and Silas arrive in Derbe and Lystra. Paul is impressed by Timotheus (Timothy), a young disciple who was "well reported of" in his hometown of Lystra and into a neighboring city, Iconium (16:2). Paul invites Timothy to join them, but determines that Timothy must first be circumcised since he is half Jewish (16:1, 3). Timothy was *not* circumcised as part of his salvation or sanctification, but simply so he would not be a hindrance in preaching the gospel to the Jews (1 Cor. 9:19–23).

After passing through Phrygia and Galatia, Paul's team is "forbidden of the Holy Ghost" (16:6) to go anywhere but Macedonia. Once the team lands at Philippi, a chief city of Macedonia, we discover exactly why God wanted them there. God had arranged divine appointments with lost souls like Lydia and her family (16:14), a young girl possessed by a demon (16:16–18), the Philippian jailer and his family (16:30–34), Jews and Gentiles in Thessalonica and Berea (17:1–4,10–12), as well as Dionysius, Damaris and others in Athens (17:34). This is the biblical principle of Proverbs 16:9 in action: "A man's heart deviseth his way: but the LORD directeth his steps." Paul's heart was leading him to Asia and Bithynia, but God directed his steps to Macedonia. Imagine the consequences if Paul had been stiff-necked, insisting upon his own plans and strategy and forcing his way into Asia and Bithynia, and had neglected Macedonia. He would have missed God's supernatural orchestration of events and the precious people listed above may have entered eternity in the flames of hell!

Has God put obstacles, hindrances or roadblocks in the path of your plans? Don't be stiff-necked. Trust the Lord; He will direct our steps.

52 WEEKS OF PURSUIT

WEEK 47, DAY 3: **TODAY'S READING: ACTS 18-21**

OVERVIEW:
Paul's ministry at Corinth (chapter 18); Paul's ministry at Ephesus (chapter 19); Paul begins his journey to Jerusalem (chapter 20); Paul's arrival in Jerusalem (chapter 21).

HIGHLIGHTS & INSIGHTS:
At this point, Paul and his missionary team have preached throughout Syria and Cilicia (15:41), the cities of Lystra and Derbe (16:1), throughout Phrygia and Galatia (16:6), the cities of Philippi, Thessalonica and Berea in Macedonia (16:11–12; 17:1, 10), and Athens, Greece (17:15).

In virtually every place, the preaching of the gospel and the teaching of the Word of God have been met with great opposition and persecution. In 2 Corinthians 11:23–28, Paul described his persistent sufferings in these terms:

> In labours more abundant, in stripes above measure, in prisons more frequent, in deaths oft. Of the Jews five times received I forty stripes save one. Thrice was I beaten with rods, once was I stoned, thrice I suffered shipwreck, a night and a day I have been in the deep; In journeyings often, in perils of waters, in perils of robbers, in perils by mine own countrymen, in perils by the heathen, in perils in the city, in perils in the wilderness, in perils in the sea, in perils among false brethren; In weariness and painfulness, in watchings often, in hunger and thirst, in fastings often, in cold and nakedness. Beside those things that are without, that which cometh upon me daily, the care of all the churches.

If God's "whatever, wherever, whenever" for you and me included such persecutions, would we still obey Him? As Jesus said, "If any man will come after me, let him deny himself, and take up his cross, and follow me" (Matt. 16:24).

Acts 18 begins with Paul traveling to Corinth in the Roman province of Achaia (18:12). Corinth was a wealthy city, a center of intellectualism, and famous for its excess, carnality and perversion. Every day was Mardi Gras in Corinth. It was the New Orleans, Amsterdam, or Bangkok of biblical times! To be a Corinthian was to be associated with sexual promiscuity. In fact, "Corinthian woman" was a proverbial phrase for a prostitute and "to play the Corinthian" was to play the whore or indulge in whorish behavior. Paul was sent there to shine the light of the glorious gospel of Christ into their great darkness.

Prior to Paul's arrival, God had arranged a meeting between Paul and a Jewish couple (Aquila and Priscilla) who had been exiled there from Rome. They became faithful followers of Christ, using all of their resources to further the gospel. Paul called this couple his "helpers in Christ Jesus" in Romans 16:3, even noting that they had "laid down their own necks" for his sake (Rom. 16:4). All the Gentile churches gave thanks for Aquila and Priscilla (Rom. 16:4), and when they returned to Rome, their home became the meeting place of the church (Rom. 16:5). Aquila and Priscilla knew what marriage was all about: a joint venture in advancing the gospel of Jesus Christ!

Paul carried out a fruitful ministry in Corinth for "a year and six months" (18:11). In that time, some prestigious men came to Christ: Justus, whose house was structurally connected to the Jewish synagogue; Crispus, the chief ruler of the synagogue; and another chief ruler of the synagogue and the man who had initially caused a riot over Paul's preaching: Sosthenes. (18:17; 1 Cor. 1:1–2)

Eventually, Paul, along with Aquila and Priscilla, departed for Ephesus where Aquila and Priscilla were left. Paul went on to Caesarea before returning home to Antioch of Syria (18:22–23). While at Ephesus, Aquila and Priscilla met a Jew from Alexandria named Apollos, a powerful preacher who was not up-to-date doctrinally. He was still preaching the gospel of the kingdom of heaven and performing the "baptism of John." Apollos had no idea that Jesus the Messiah had already come and gone, that God's plan for Israel had been postponed, and that the church age was already in effect. Aquila and Priscilla corrected his doctrine, explaining "the way of God more perfectly" (18:24–26). Apollos humbly and joyfully receives the new revelation, begins preaching that Jesus is the Christ, and moves on to Corinth (19:1).

While Apollos is at Corinth, Paul begins his third missionary journey, passing through Phrygia and Galatia (18:23) and landing at Ephesus (19:1), where he finds some of Apollos's converts who, like Apollos, were only aware of John's baptism. They have never even heard of Jesus Christ or the Holy Ghost (19:1–4). Obviously, they had not been born again since salvation comes only through Jesus Christ (John 14:6) and the indwelling of the Holy Ghost is the evidence of that salvation! Romans 8:9 says it very plainly, "Now if any man have not the Spirit of Christ, he is none of his." Paul preaches the gospel of grace to them; they call on the name of Jesus, are baptized in water in Jesus's name, and immediately receive the Holy Ghost, speaking with tongues and prophesying (19:4–6). Remember that tongues are a sign to skeptical Jews (1 Cor. 1:22; 14:22). These events are exactly like the events in Samaria (Acts 8:14–16), in that Paul's apostolic authority and his message is validated by the sign of tongues. These Jewish disciples of Apollos could know with certainty that Paul's gospel is the true gospel.

Paul had a fruitful few years at Ephesus (19:9–10, 18–20), and the Word of God had free course throughout Asia (modern-day Asia Minor). However, his success was stifled by a massive riot which forced him to begin his journey to Jerusalem (19:21; 20:1). On his way, Paul revisits many of the places where he had initially preached the gospel and planted churches, ministering to and edifying the disciples.

Knowing that Jerusalem would mark the beginning of his end, Paul is not afraid to die for the name of the Lord Jesus (21:13) because long ago, at his salvation, Paul had surrendered his life into the hands of His Savior and Lord. Paul said in 2 Timothy 1:12, "For I know whom I have believed, and am persuaded that he is able to keep that which I have committed unto him against that day." Paul fearlessly and confidently declares in 2 Tim. 4:6–8, "For I am now ready to be offered, and the time of my departure is at hand. I have fought a good fight, I have finished my course, I have kept the faith: Henceforth there is laid up for me a crown of righteousness, which the Lord, the righteous judge, shall give me at that day: and not to me only, but unto all them also that love his appearing."

O God, like Paul, may we live our lives with great confidence and assurance—fearlessly abandoned to You and to Your will for our lives.

52 WEEKS OF PURSUIT

WEEK 47, DAY 4: TODAY'S READING: ACTS 22-25

OVERVIEW:
Paul's testimony before riotous Jews (chapter 22); Paul's testimony before the Jewish council (chapter 23); Paul's testimony before Felix, the governor of Judea (chapter 24); Paul's testimony before Festus (chapter 25).

HIGHLIGHTS & INSIGHTS:
Paul's arrival in Jerusalem marked the beginning of his end. In Acts 21, the Jews of Jerusalem had stirred up a riot crying out, "Men of Israel, help: This is the man, that teacheth all men every where against the people, and the law, and this place: and further brought Greeks also into the temple, and hath polluted this holy place" (21:28). The Roman chief captain of Jerusalem, not wanting this riot to reach Caesar's ears for his job's sake, immediately stepped in, rescuing Paul from certain death (21:31–32).

Chapter 22 is Paul's testimony before the Jewish crowd. As soon as he mentions preaching to Gentiles (vs. 21–22), the crowd returns to a nearly unmanageable uproar. The chief captain was about to scourge Paul until he discovered that Paul was a Roman citizen. With that revelation, Paul inserted himself into the flow of the Roman legal system, thereby guaranteeing him an audience with leading political figures in the Roman government, even Caesar himself.

The chapters that follow record Paul's testimony before a few of these figures. In chapter 23, Paul stands before the Jewish council in Jerusalem again. Having been transferred to Caesarea (23:33), the Roman provincial seat of Judea, Paul stands before governor Felix. Felix is replaced by Festus (24:27), and in chapter 25, Paul gives testimony before Festus and the Jewish council.

Though there are many details worth discussing in today's reading, let's focus on a few truths about Paul's suffering and how his suffering relates to ours.

1. Suffering was a natural part of Paul's commission, as it is a natural part of ours.

God commissioned Paul as the apostle to the Gentiles, saying: "He [Paul] is a chosen vessel unto me, to bear my name before the Gentiles, and kings, and the children of Israel: For I will shew him how great things he must suffer for my name's sake" (Acts 9:15–16). God said that Paul would have the privilege of preaching the gospel to Gentiles, to kings, and to the children of Israel, so the events of chapters 21–25 display God's faithfulness in keeping His promises. But God's commission also included the promise of suffering. And God would be faithful in keeping that promise as well. Paul displayed a unique attitude as a follower of Christ in that he joyfully accepted suffering as the normal and natural result of following Christ, declaring "the sufferings of this present time are not worthy to be compared with the glory which shall be revealed in us" (Rom. 8:18).

Paul was able to keep that perspective because he was constantly looking into the eternal realm, passionately investing his life in Christ's everlasting kingdom (2 Cor. 4:18; 2 Pet. 1:11). To those of us who desire to live like Paul, God promised: "Yea, and all that will live godly in Christ Jesus shall suffer persecution" (2 Tim. 3:12). If we, like Paul, look to the right kingdom, constantly seeking to give the gospel to the lost and to live a holy life for His glory, then we will suffer! But by investing in eternity in this way, a greater hope and reward is yet before us!

2. Suffering brings us into a deeper intimacy with Christ.

Through suffering, we are able to fellowship with Christ in a much deeper and personal way (Phil. 3:10). Paul was one of the few human beings who understood that principle. If Paul had viewed his suffering as a natural man, he would have likely responded, "God, here I am witnessing for you, seeking to live a holy life for Your glory, and this is what I get?" It's the complaint we often hear from lost people: "Why do bad things happen to good people?" Though it sounds like a legitimate question, in reality, it's a self-righteous and self-centered question! It's self-righteous because we're calling ourselves good when Romans 3:12 clearly states, "there is none that doeth good, no, not one." It's self-centered because it assumes that life is all about us when Revelation 4:11 plainly declares, "Thou art worthy, O Lord, to receive glory and honour and power: for thou hast created all things, and for thy pleasure they are and were created." The real question should be, "Why do good things happen to such bad people?"

And that was Paul's perspective. Paul was so thankful for the price that Jesus Christ paid for him that he actually considered the sufferings he endured in this life a blessing! Suffering like Christ was one of his goals in life. He says in Philippians 3:8–10,

> Yea doubtless, and I count all things but loss for the excellency of the knowledge of Christ Jesus my Lord: for whom I have suffered the loss of all things, and do count them but dung, that I may win Christ, And be found in him, not having mine own righteousness, which is of the law, but that which is through the faith of Christ, the righteousness which is of God by faith: That I may know him, and the power of his resurrection, and the fellowship of his sufferings, being made conformable unto his death.

Paul understood the biblical principle that we so desperately need to learn in the 21st century: Suffering is a natural and normal part of our calling (1 Pet. 2:21). Through suffering, we not only become more like Christ, but we become more intimately acquainted with Him. May God grant us that perspective.

52 WEEKS OF PURSUIT

WEEK 47, DAY 5: TODAY'S READING: ACTS 26-28

OVERVIEW:
Paul's testimony before King Agrippa (chapter 26); Paul's journey to and arrival in Rome (chapters 27–28).

HIGHLIGHTS & INSIGHTS:
In chapter 26, Paul gives his testimony before King Agrippa, the great-grandson of Herod the Great who sought to kill Jesus at his birth (Matt. 2:1–16). Let's focus on two key features of Paul's message before King Agrippa.

1. The *Sincere Concern* of Paul's Message

    Paul could have easily despised the corrupt and wicked rulers before whom he had been on trial. None of them were willing to take a stand for the truth and declare Paul's innocence (23:27–29; 24:12–13; 26:31). The Jews falsely accused Paul and wanted to kill him (21:28–29; 23:12–15). Felix kept Paul in prison in hopes of a bribe and to please the Jews (24:26–27). Festus also kept Paul bound in an attempt to keep the Jews happy (25:9). But instead of letting the injustice and corruption make him bitter or angry, Paul did what he always did: he passionately declared the gospel of Jesus Christ, sincerely longing for the salvation of these wicked men!

    Even when King Agrippa, one of the most perverted and corrupt men imaginable, sarcastically commented, "Almost thou persuadest me to be a Christian" (26:28), Paul sincerely responded, "I would to God, that not only thou, but also all that hear me this day, were both almost, and altogether such as I am, except these bonds" (26:29). Paul's compassion for the souls of these corrupt men let him see past their wickedness to the cross where Christ died for their sins. Paul longed to see the salvation of every man—even his persecutors—just as Jesus said in Matthew 5:44: "Love your enemies, bless them that curse you, do good to them that hate you, and pray for them which despitefully use you, and persecute you." May God fill us with the sincere passion and compassion of Paul!

2. The *Simple Content* of Paul's Message

    The content of Paul's messages in these chapters is significant. Whereas I would have tried to craft the most moving, thought-provoking, powerful sermon imaginable, Paul did not. He didn't get stressed or concern himself with brilliance or eloquence. Every single time, he simply gives his testimony and a presentation of the gospel. His message was, essentially, "I once was lost, but now I'm found!" Paul had taken to heart that he was to "witness unto all men of what thou hast seen and heard" (Acts 22:15). So that's what he did. God doesn't need us to be intellectual elites, eloquent preachers, or Bible experts. We simply need to declare boldly what we have seen and heard!

    An atheist once interrupted the great evangelist H.A. Ironside's preaching, shouting, "There is no God! Jesus is a myth!" After continuous interruptions, the man finally said, "I challenge you to a debate!" Ironside said, "I accept your challenge, sir—but on one condition. When you come, bring with you ten men and women whose lives have been changed for the better by the message of atheism. Bring former prostitutes and criminals whose lives have been changed, who are now moral and responsible individuals. Bring outcasts who had no hope and have them tell us how becoming atheists has lifted them out of the pit! And sir," he concluded, "if you can find ten such men and women, I will be happy to debate you. And when I come, I will gladly bring with me 200 men and women from this very city whose lives have been transformed in just those ways by the power of the gospel of Jesus Christ." We cannot forget that the simple testimony of a changed life is a powerful witness to the transforming power of

Christ! Ask God to open a door for you today to simply tell someone what you've seen and heard.

After a difficult journey, Paul finally landed at Rome (28:16) around 60 AD, where he rented a house and received guests, preaching the gospel to both Jews and Gentiles under Roman house arrest. For the next two years, he continued "preaching the kingdom of God, and teaching those things which concern the Lord Jesus Christ, with all confidence, no man forbidding him" (28:31). Scholars believe Paul wrote his epistles to Philemon, Timothy, Titus, the Ephesians, the Colossians, and the Philippians during this Roman imprisonment. According to the record of history, Paul was beheaded sometime after 64 AD during Nero's persecution of Christians. During this same persecution, Peter was also crucified. (History records that Peter requested that he be crucified upside-down because he didn't consider himself worthy to be crucified in the same manner as our Lord.)

But before we complete our discussion of the book of Acts today, let's consider what may be the most important lesson of this incredible book: God takes full responsibility for accomplishing His own mission!

The book of Acts is rather comical when you consider how confused these great men and women of God in the early church were for the first twenty-seven years of their ministry. In chapters 1–7, uncertain about whether Christ would immediately return to restore the kingdom to Israel, they sold their houses and all of their possessions and camped out in Jerusalem so they didn't miss His second coming. (See Acts 1:6–7; 2:44–47; 4:34–35; Zechariah 14:1–9.) The apostles were startled and confused when the Samaritans and Gentiles started getting saved (Acts 11:1–3,18). The Jewish believers had a difficult time letting go of circumcision and other components of the Mosaic law so they could be free to simply trust the death, burial and resurrection of Jesus Christ for their salvation and sanctification (Acts 15:1–2). The apostles were most certainly shocked when God postponed His dealings with Israel in order to begin working with a new institution, the church, composed of both Jews and Gentiles (Rom. 11:25; Eph. 3:1–13).

From a human standpoint, living in the time of the early church could have been frustrating and confusing *if* you were attempting to analyze and formulate God. If, however, you "walked by faith and not by sight," then every day would have been a tremendous adventure! Consider some of the incredible *acts* the Lord Jesus Christ carried out through the apostles in this book.

First, God's ancient arrangement of the Jewish holy feasts brought the Jews at "just the right time" and to "just the right place" to witness the crucifixion of their Messiah at Passover. Fifty days later at Pentecost, it brought them together again, providing the opportunity to repent of crucifying their own Messiah (Acts 2). God intervened on behalf of Peter and John, freeing them from prison to continue preaching to the people in Acts 5:17–20. He used the persecution that arose after the stoning of Stephen to motivate the obstinate Jewish believers to get out of Jerusalem and carry out His mission to Judea, Samaria, and the uttermost part of the earth (Acts 1:8; 8:1). God supernaturally arranged Philip's meeting with the Ethiopian eunuch (Acts 8:26–30). He timed perfectly the salvation of Saul (Paul) in Acts 9 and Peter's visit to Cornelius's house in Acts 10. We could go on and on with all of the supernatural acts God orchestrated on behalf of the apostles!

That's the key take-away from this amazing book of the Bible. God will accomplish His own mission despite our cluelessness and despite our human inabilities and frailties. If we surrender ourselves to Him daily, we will have the amazing honor of joining God where He is already working. Have a great adventure with God today!

WEEK 48, DAY 1: **TODAY'S READING: ROMANS 1-3**

OVERVIEW:
The righteousness of God required by the heathen (chapter 1); the righteousness of God required by the hypocrite and Hebrew (chapter 2); the righteousness of God required by all of humanity (chapter 3).

HIGHLIGHTS & INSIGHTS:
Three New Testament books act like a bridge, helping us cross from one section to another. Matthew is the bridge from the Old Testament into the New Testament. The four Gospels, then, provide four historical perspectives of Jesus Christ's person and ministry. The book of Acts reveals the transition from God's dealings with the Nation of Israel to God's dealings with the church. And the book of Hebrews makes a bridge from the church back to the Nation of Israel. Having finished the book of Acts, then, we have crossed the *historical* bridge and now enter the *doctrinal* teachings of the church age.

The book of Romans is the greatest book in the Bible on Christian doctrine. Unlike other New Testament books, Paul is not writing to address doctrinal or practical problems. Instead, this book provides a handbook for understanding God's viewpoint of what He is doing in and through His church. That's why God placed this book immediately following the book of Acts. Immediately after the historical section of the New Testament, and before the other church epistles, God gives us His handbook for understanding the doctrine of the church.

Interestingly, the order of the the New Testament epistles follow the prescription in 2 Timothy 3:16, that "all scripture is given by inspiration of God and is profitable for":

- *Doctrine* – Romans (the New Testament book on Christian doctrine)
- *Reproof* – 1 and 2 Corinthians (books that reprove sin)
- *Correction* – Galatians (a book specifically written to correct false doctrine)
- *Instruction in Righteousness* – Ephesians, Philippians, Colossians, 1 and 2 Thessalonians (books teaching righteous living based on sound doctrine)

God identifies the author of this epistle (letter) in the very first verse. It was written by Paul, the apostle to the Gentiles (Acts 9:15), as were all of the letters to the churches. Paul was uniquely qualified to write the book of Romans in that he was born a Jew (Acts 21:39; 22:3), was completely familiar with Greek culture (Acts 21:37), and possessed Roman citizenship (Acts 16:37; 22:25; 23:27).

Though God chose to use Paul to write this epistle to the Romans, Paul had never actually been to Rome. He had a passion to minister to the believers there, but when Paul wrote this letter, God, in His sovereignty, had not allowed it. In 1:9–13, Paul feels compelled to let the Romans (and us!) know that. He writes,

> For God is my witness, whom I serve with my spirit in the gospel of his Son, that without ceasing I make mention of you always in my prayers; Making request, if by any means now at length I might have a prosperous journey by the will of God to come unto you. For I long to see you, that I may impart unto you some spiritual gift, to the end ye may be established; That is, that I may be comforted together with you by the mutual faith both of you and me. Now I would not have you ignorant, brethren, that oftentimes I purposed to come unto you, (but was let hitherto,) that I might have some fruit among you also, even as among other Gentiles.

Don't you wonder why God didn't let Paul get to Rome sooner? If he's the apostle to the Gentiles, why wouldn't God allow him to minister to his heart's content? But then again, it does make sense. Most of the believers whom God would establish in Christian doctrine (1:11) through Paul would be people, like the Romans, who never had or would see Paul face to face. Through the book of Romans, then, God uses His ministry through Paul to accomplish the same purposes in us that He did in the believers in Rome in the first century! It's a subtle reminder that, when we have a passion for a good thing that God doesn't bring to pass, it's most likely because He has a much more grand and glorious purpose! If Paul had gone to Rome on his time schedule, we wouldn't have the book of Romans today!

After the introduction in 1:1–15, Paul identifies two ways God exhibits His power: He demonstrates His *righteousness* to those who receive the gospel by faith (1:16–17) and His *wrath* to those who reject His truth by ungodliness (1:18, 21). Paul then catalogs the sins of the Gentiles, beginning with their rejection of His glory (1:21–23) which resulted in their perversion physically (1:24–25), emotionally (1:26–27), and mentally (1:28–32).

Having proven the ungodliness of the Gentiles (*heathen*), he turns in chapter 2 to the sins of the *hypocrites* (2:1–16) and the *Hebrews* (2:17–29). He shows the hypocrites the inexcusableness of their behavior in verses 1–4. Anticipating their objections, Paul informs them of an inescapable appointment they have with God's judgment (vs. 5–16) and concludes by exposing the unreliable confidence the Jews place in the law (vs. 17, 23) and in the unprofitable ritual of circumcision (vs. 25–29).

In 3:9, Paul reaches the conclusion to which he has been moving since 1:18—"For we have before proved both Jews and Gentiles, that they are all under sin." In other words, whether you're a heathen (1:21–32), a hypocrite (2:1–16), or a Hebrew (2:17–29), the Scriptures conclude that "there is none righteous, no, not one" (3:10)! Paul realizes that before someone receives the good news of the gospel, they must acknowledge the bad news of their sinfulness. So chapter 3 proves humanity's condemnation before God (3:1–20) and concludes by declaring the availability of righteousness to all who choose to receive it (3:21–31). But God's righteousness is offered with three conditions:

- It must be received apart from the law (3:21)
- It is only available through Christ (3:22–26)
- It can only be accepted by faith (3:21–31)

Note some key facts and figures about the book of Romans:

- Approximate date of writing: 60 AD
- Key Verse: Romans 1:16–17
- Key Word: "Righteousness" (appears 39 times)
- Christ is seen as our righteousness (Romans 3:23–24)
- Chapters: 16
- Verses: 433
- Words: 9,477

Here is a simple outline to guide us through the book:

- The Revelation of Righteousness In The Gospel
    - The Righteousness Received In Salvation (chapters 1–8)
    - The Righteousness Rejected By The Jews (chapters 9–11)
    - The Righteousness Reproduced In Sanctification (chapters 12–16)

52 WEEKS OF **PURSUIT**

WEEK 48, DAY 2: **TODAY'S READING: ROMANS 4-8**

OVERVIEW:
The righteousness of God received by faith (chapter 4); the revelation of the righteousness of God realized in the soul (chapter 5); the righteousness of God revealed in trials (chapters 6–7); the righteousness of God represented as eternal (chapter 8).

HIGHLIGHTS & INSIGHTS:
Though many Christian circles call us to let go of doctrine for the sake of so-called unity, God is adamant about its importance! God admonishes His church to "hold fast" (2 Tim. 1:13) to sound doctrine, so that we can be genuinely unified with those who are also firmly committed to the truth of His Word! It is not simply our love that unites us, folks, but our love of the truth! (2 John vs. 1–4 uses the word *truth* five times in four verses!) In the epistles to Timothy and Titus (the pastoral epistles) Paul mentions doctrine no less than thirteen times! (See 1 Tim. 1:3, 10; 4:1, 6, 16; 5:17; 6:1, 3; 2 Tim. 3:10; 4:2; Titus 1:9; 2:1, 10.) In the book of Romans, doctrine is the entire focus—especially the doctrine of salvation! No other book of the Bible provides a more complete teaching on this important subject.

In the book of Romans, Paul uses questions to present his case. In chapters 1–3, Paul asked over twenty-five questions. It's as if he's anticipating the reader's objections to the truth he's presenting and answering their argument before they can even get there. It is a masterful teaching technique that the Spirit of God uniquely gifted Paul to employ. He will use this technique throughout the book.

Chapter 4 presents a very significant transition. Whereas chapters 1–3 focused on the fact that God's righteousness is *required by sinners*, chapter 4 focuses on the fact that God's righteousness is *received by faith*. Chapters 1–3 focused on the *what*, while chapter 4 focuses on the *how*.

In 4:1–8, Paul introduces us to the *reward* of righteousness by faith—that we are *justified*. To be justified means to be rendered righteous. It may be trite, but a great way to remember the truth encompassed in the word *justified* is that it means "just-as-if-I'd never sinned." Paul reaches back into the Old Testament, to the life of Abraham, using him as an illustration of someone who was justified by faith (4:1–8). Then, Paul reveals three truths concerning how it is that justification is actually reckoned to us:

- It is not by circumcision (4:9–12)
- It is not by the law (4:13–15)
- It is only by grace through faith (4:16–22)

The chapter closes with the promise that just as God imputed righteousness to Abraham because of his faith, He likewise imputes righteousness to each of us who receive the gospel by faith.

Having laid down the reality that the righteousness God demands is not an *achieved* righteousness, but a *received* righteousness (that is, a righteousness that is not of works, but by faith), Paul then moves in chapter 5 to lay out the fact that because we didn't do anything to *earn* our salvation (our righteousness), there is also nothing we can do to *lose* it! The doctrine of the eternal security of the believer (one of the most controversial doctrines in Christianity!) is firmly established in the book of Romans, particularly in chapter 5.

Chapter 5 can be divided into two sections. Verses 1–10 identify the *benefit* of justification by faith: security. And verses 11–21 identify the *basis* for justification by faith: atonement.

In chapters 6–8, other transitions are also being made:

- Chapters 1–5 teach about *justification* by faith. Chapters 6–8 teach about *sanctification* by the Spirit.

- Chapters 1–5 identify how God saved us from the *penalty* of sin. Chapters 6–8 identify how Christ saved us from the *power* of sin.
- Chapters 1–5 show the *gateway* to the Christian life. Chapters 6–8 show the *pathway* of the Christian life.

While there is a significant contrast between Romans 1–5 and 6–8, there is an equally significant connection between Romans 6, 7 and 8. The connection comes from a little phrase found in Romans 5:17: "reign in life." Paul does not fully explain in this verse how those who have been justified by faith in Christ shall "reign in life." Instead, the full explanation comes in Romans 6, 7 and 8.

- In Romans 6, the believer can reign in life because *sin* no longer *reigns* over us (6:12)
- In Romans 7, the believer can reign in life because the *law* no longer has *dominion* over us (7:1, 4)
- In Romans 8, the believer can reign in life because the *Spirit* now gives *life* and *liberty* to us (8:2, 4)

WEEK 48, DAY 3: **TODAY'S READING: ROMANS 9-11**

OVERVIEW:
The revelation of the righteousness of God rejected in Judaism (chapters 9–11).

HIGHLIGHTS & INSIGHTS:
Today we move into the second half of Paul's great doctrinal epistle. The purpose of the writing of Romans is to reveal the righteousness of God in the gospel of Jesus Christ (1:16–17). In chapters 1–8, Paul identified a number of *principles* related to the righteousness we receive through the gospel:

- Sin is a universal reality (chapters 1–3)
- Salvation is a free gift (chapter 3)
- Salvation is received by faith (chapter 4)
- Salvation is secure and forever (chapter 5)
- Sanctification is from sin and the law (chapters 6–7)
- Sanctification is by the Spirit (chapter 8)

Beginning in chapter 9, Paul turns his attention to some of the *problems* related to the righteousness we receive through the gospel—particularly, problems that relate to the Jews.

The first problem had to do with the fact that at the time Paul wrote the book of Romans, the Old Testament sacrifices were still being offered in the Temple at Jerusalem. The principles Paul laid out in Romans 1–8 have rendered those sacrifices completely meaningless.

The second problem was related to the reality that each time Paul preached in a Jewish synagogue, he knew that Judaism and Christianity could not co-exist. If Christianity continued to spread across the world, Judaism's fate was sealed. It was just that reality that caused Paul to so bitterly oppose Christianity prior to his conversion.

The last and greatest problem Paul faced was reconciling in people's minds the doctrines of the church with the covenants God had made to the Nation of Israel. The two questions that surfaced each time Paul preached in the presence of Jews were: "Are the promises of God to the Nation of Israel now null and void?" and "Where does the Jew stand in relationship to God in this dispensation?" The purpose of Romans 9–11 is to provide answers to those questions. The Spirit of God obviously knew that these answers would blast Satan's attempts to pervert the gospel with the false teachings of the Judaizers (those who were zealous for Judaism and sought to convert others).

Some have called chapters 9–11 a parenthesis in the book of Romans, and they are. A parenthesis is a sentence or paragraph that provides the reader with an explanation, and these chapters provide us with an explanation of how God set aside His chosen people for a period of time and how God will restore Israel at a future date and fulfill all the promises He made to them in the Old Testament. The three chapters of this parenthesis can be broken down as follows:

- In Romans 9, the emphasis is on Israel's *past election*
- In Romans 10, the emphasis is on Israel's *present rejection*
- In Romans 11, the emphasis is on Israel's *future restoration*

A couple of other side notes:

Don't freak out about Paul's statement in Romans 9:13: "Jacob have I loved, but Esau have I hated."

The "as it is written" lets us know that Paul is quoting an Old Testament reference (Mal. 1:2–3) where this statement is made in reference to *nations*, not individuals! Esau represents the Edomite nation. Jacob represents the Nation of Israel. Because of John 3:16 and countless other Scriptures, there is no way that the Bible teaches that God loves some sinners and hates others.

Concerning the hardening of Pharaoh in 9:17–18, understand that God always gives people exactly what they want. If we want truth, God will give us truth. If we want a lie, God will give us a lie. Exodus 8:15 says that Pharaoh hardened his heart. Then in Exodus 9:12, it says that God hardened Pharaoh's heart. God simply gave Pharaoh what he wanted. The same principle is repeated in 2 Thessalonians 2:8–12. This passage identifies people who have understood the truth and have had the opportunity to receive the Lord Jesus Christ and be saved (2:10), but rather than receive the truth, they "had pleasure in unrighteousness" (2:12) and, therefore, lied to themselves and rejected the truth. The passage teaches that in the Tribulation, when the Antichrist comes on the scene, God will say in effect, "You wanted a lie—so that's exactly what you'll get!" Verses 11–12 say that God Himself will "send them strong delusion" so that they will believe the lie of the Antichrist and be forever damned.

In Pharaoh's case, God hardened Pharaoh's heart because *Pharaoh* hardened Pharaoh's heart! With those who miss the rapture because they lied to themselves when God presented them the truth, God will simply give them what they proved they wanted. We might do well to ask ourselves today, "Am I telling God by how I'm living my life that I want something that, in reality, I *don't want* Him to give me?

WEEK 48, DAY 4: **TODAY'S READING: ROMANS 12-16**

OVERVIEW:
The revelation of the righteousness of God reproduced in the church (chapters 12–16).

HIGHLIGHTS & INSIGHTS:
After introducing the theme of the book of Romans, the revelation of the righteousness of God in the gospel of Christ (1:16–17), Paul walked us through eight chapters of *principles* related to that gospel. Then, in chapters 9–11, Paul identified and addressed the *problems* of the gospel as they related to the Nation of Israel. We called this section a parenthesis because if you were to read from Romans 8:39 right into 12:1, it would make perfect sense! Check it out…

> Romans 8:38–39, "For I am persuaded, that neither death, nor life, nor angels, nor principalities, nor powers, nor things present, nor things to come, Nor height, nor depth, nor any other creature, shall be able to separate us from the love of God, which is in Christ Jesus our Lord. (12:1) I beseech you therefore, brethren, by the mercies of God, that ye present your bodies a living sacrifice, holy, acceptable unto God, which is your reasonable service."

Now, beginning with Romans 12:1, we move into the third and final section of this great epistle. Having considered the *principles* and *problems* of the gospel in the first 11 chapters, in these final five chapters (12–16), Paul examines the *practice* of the gospel. These chapters provide a classic Pauline pattern that we will be able to observe in all of his writings.

In each of the letters God inspired Paul to write, he presents specific doctrines in the beginning of the book and then provides a series of practical duties which are based upon the doctrines he's presented. Paul realized the danger in laying down principles without identifying how those principles should affect the practice of our lives (receiving information with no regard for transformation!). Doctrine and duties always go hand-in-hand. Each time we approach the Word of God, we must ask ourselves two very simple questions: "What is it that God wants me to believe?" and "How is it that God wants me to behave?" You see this pattern established very clearly in the book of Romans. For the first eight chapters Paul identifies the doctrinal principles related to the gospel, and in the final five chapters, he explains the practical duties based upon those principles.

In chapters 12–14, Paul identifies the following relationships that have been dramatically affected by receiving the gospel. With each relationship he provides a corresponding responsibility:

- Our relationship to God – Offer reasonable service (12:1–2)
- Our relationship to other believers – Minister our gifts (12:3–16)
- Our relationship to our enemies – Overcome evil with good (12:17–21)
- Our relationship to rulers – Be subject (submissive) (13:1–7)
- Our relationship to our neighbors – Owe nothing but love (13:8–14)
- Our relationship to weaker believers – Receive and edify (14:1–23)

Recognizing the benefit of an example, in chapter 15, Paul provides three examples of people who ministered to others. He begins with the ministry of Christ and how He pleased and received others (vs. 1–13). Next, he provides himself as an example of one that forwarded God's message (v. 14). Finally, he holds up the Gentile churches and their sacrificial giving to the impoverished believers at Jerusalem as an example (vs. 25–33).

In chapter 16, God finds an incredible way to teach us about the important keys to Paul's ministry. Paul sends his greetings to twenty-six individuals, two households, and several churches that are meeting in people's homes. That's a lot of relationships, considering these people reside in a city that Paul's not yet been permitted to visit! As we read this list, we can't help but be impressed with the fact that Paul loved people. No doubt, many of these names represented people he had personally won to Christ in other cities who now resided in Rome. It is more than apparent that Paul's ministry centered around two key things: the *Great Commandment*—loving God and loving people—and the *Great Commission*—reproducing reproducers, or making disciples. May each of our ministries reflect the same.

WEEK 48, DAY 5: **TODAY'S READING: 1 CORINTHIANS 1-6**

OVERVIEW:
An appeal for unity (chapter 1); the wisdom of God vs. the wisdom of this world (chapter 2); eternal building vs. temporary building (chapter 3); understanding our stewardship (chapter 4); dealing with unrepentant sin (chapter 5); dealing with conflict in the body (chapter 6).

HIGHLIGHTS & INSIGHTS:
The city of Corinth was the fourth-largest city in the Roman Empire, located on one of the most important east-west trade and travel routes. It was a financial center especially noted for commerce, culture, and absolute corruption. Corinth was also the headquarters for the worship of Venus and some of the mystery cults from Egypt and Asia.

The founding of the church at Corinth is detailed in Acts 18:1–17. Paul and his missionary team established this church, and Paul spent a year and half teaching and preaching there. But by the time Paul writes this letter, the church was totally operating in the flesh. Paul finds absolutely nothing to commend them for in this entire letter! *Nothing* this church was doing should be a model in our church—or any church! They were completely messed up in their relationships with each other, their attitude toward sin, their approach to marriage, their liberty in Christ, the Lord's Supper, exercising their spiritual gifts, and, of all things, their belief in the resurrection! Even though there are no positive characteristics in this church, there is an entire movement (the Charismatic Movement) that bases many of their beliefs and practices on things the Corinthian church espoused!

However, there were bigger problems in this church than just their abuse of spiritual gifts. In fact, God does not even address their abuse of these gifts until chapters 12–14. He also did not immediately answer the questions the Corinthians had written Paul to ask. He answers those questions beginning in chapter 7, but the Spirit of God knew there were other, much more serious issues that needed to be covered first.

The biggest problem this church was facing was *division*! Paul takes the first four chapters to address this cancer that often attacks the Body of Christ. He covers many topics in these chapters, but they all ultimately come back to the issue of a *unified* body versus a *divided* body.

That Paul addresses division first and more thoroughly than any other issue facing this church should speak volumes about how God feels about unity in His church. 1 Corinthians 1:10 says, "Be perfectly joined together in the same mind and in the same judgment." This is clearly the issue we need to be most concerned about in our own local church. I'd rather partner for the cause of Christ with a genuine brother who mistakenly believes tongues are still for today, than to partner with a brother who uses his tongue to cause division in the local church! (See Prov. 6:16–19.)

In chapter 5, Paul confronts the Corinthians about the man in their church who was involved in sexual sin with his father's wife! (Paul's language makes it obvious she was his stepmother.) Rather than being appalled at such a grotesque sin—and mourning over how such an atrocity detracted from the glory of Christ in His church—the Corinthians were actually bragging about it! It's difficult to fathom the depth and perversion of this man's sin, but how much more difficult to fathom the church's perverted reaction to it. Paul is so incensed by it, he tells them that he has already passed judgment upon the man and instructs the Corinthians on how they were to pass judgment upon him in a biblical manner as well. In chapter 4, the Corinthians were casting judgment on people they *shouldn't*. In chapter 5, they were failing to cast biblical judgment on those they *should*!

In chapter 6, Paul confronts the Corinthians about suing other church members in court and addresses other instances of sexual sin that were taking place by those in the church who professed to know Christ!

This was one messed-up church! And today's reading only scratches the surface of their carnality. But it also provides a beautiful and important contrast. Because, before Paul addresses the sins in this church (1:10), he takes the first nine verses to greet them. And look at how Paul describes the people in this incredibly carnal and sinful church.

Paul refers to the Corinthians as "them that are *sanctified* [holy] in Christ Jesus" (1:2). In verse 8, he says that the Lord Jesus Christ will "*confirm* you unto the end that you may be *blameless* in the day of our Lord Jesus Christ." In verse 9, he refers to them as those who "were *called* unto the fellowship of [God's] Son Jesus Christ our Lord."

How could Paul use such commendable terms? With the horrific things they had allowed into their lives, personally and corporately, how could Paul call them sanctified, blameless, confirmed and called? There is only one reason—the Corinthians were "in Christ" (1:2)! It's one of the most incredible spiritual realities in the New Testament. The moment we called on the Lord Jesus Christ to save us, we were placed *in Christ*! God the Father chose us *in Him* before the foundation of the world because He desired us to be "holy and without blame before Him in love" (Eph. 1:4). And the only way that could *ever* happen is for God to see us the way He sees His *Son*! So when God saved us, the Spirit of God "baptized" us (12:13) into Christ (placed us into Christ), and He sealed us with His Holy Spirit to guarantee that we will remain *in Christ* until "the day of redemption" (Eph. 4:30). We will be sealed until the rapture which is the day our body will be "redeemed," making it a glorified body, one that is incapable of sinning!

Just as this was true for the Corinthians, it is true for us, too. We may wonder, "How can God see me as 'holy and without blame before him in love,' when there are times when I am anything but 'holy,' and I have plenty for which I can be 'blamed,' and I'm certainly not worthy of His 'love'?" But the spiritual reality of being in Christ is a *positional* truth. It is a spiritual placement we have received from God that remains constant regardless of our spiritual *practice* because it's based on Christ's merits, not ours. This is why Paul refers to these carnal and sinful believers in Corinth as "holy" and "blameless." It was their *position* in Christ, though not the *practice* of their lives!

And throughout his writings, Paul teaches us who we are in Christ and sets before us the spiritual goal of seeing our *practice* (the actual living of our lives) match our *position* (who God made us in Christ). That is the essence of the Christian life—becoming in *practice* who God made us in *position* the day He saved us. May that become our goal today, and every day, until we receive a glorified body "like unto His [Christ's] glorious body" (Phil. 3:21).

Finally, we would think that a letter that addresses so many sinful issues in the church would also address to that church's leadership. We certainly know, as the saying goes, that "everything rises or falls on leadership," so it would seem that the quick fix would be for Paul to get the pastors or elders to exercise their spiritual authority and leadership, right? But do you know how many times Paul actually addresses the pastors of the church at Corinth? Zero!

Does that mean that pastors don't have a key responsibility, as leaders of the church, over the overall spiritual climate of the church? Absolutely not! But in the body of Christ, we're all in this together! A pastor will most certainly give an account to God for how he led God's people and how he provided oversight of the church (Heb. 13:17). But every believer will also give an account for himself at the judgment seat of Christ (Rom. 14:12). In that day, none of us will be able to say, "Well, if my pastor would have just led/taught/preached/visited/prayed or "whatever-ed" better or more than he did, I would have been different." The lesson from 1 Corinthians is that every church operates the way it does, whether in the flesh or in the Spirit, because of all the members of the body, not just a select few. All of us need to shoulder the responsibility for our local church functioning according to the Word of God! Each of us need to constantly be examining and judging our own lives and what we're actually contributing (or not contributing) to our own local church.

52 WEEKS OF PURSUIT

WEEK 49, DAY 1: TODAY'S READING: 1 CORINTHIANS 7-11

OVERVIEW:
Marriage and divorce (chapter 7); Christian liberty (chapter 8); the purpose of our liberty (chapter 9); lessons from Israel (chapter 10); issues regarding communion (chapter 11).

HIGHLIGHTS & INSIGHTS:
In chapter 7, Paul finally begins to answer the questions the Corinthians had sent to him. The first issue he addresses is the extremely controversial subject of marriage and divorce. One of the biggest issues perplexing the Corinthian church was in marriages where one partner had come to Christ and the other hadn't. Evidently, they had concluded that divorce was a possible solution, if not *the* solution.

Instead, Paul instructs them: "No! Stay in the marriage! If your partner is pleased to stay with you after your conversion to Christ, hang in there, and seek to see them come to Christ! If, because of your connection to Christ and the transformation He is making in your life, they choose to abandon the marriage, let them depart. The Lord will release you from the marriage bond, and you are free to remarry."

Clearly, we don't have room for an exhaustive look at all of chapter 7, but there are a few key principles God establishes in this chapter that are worth noting.

- 7:2–5 – Intimacy in marriage is not optional. Paul says that the husband and wife are to give themselves to each other. A marriage that lacks intimacy distorts the picture of Christ and the church revealed in Ephesians 5:25–33 and leaves the couple vulnerable to unnecessary temptation.

- 7:10–15 – Do not seek divorce. If you're married, stay married. If for some reason there is a divorce not based on biblical allowances, Paul is clear that remarriage is not an option—only reconciliation to the former spouse. However, if an unbelieving spouse departs, Paul is also clear that the believer is free, meaning free from the marriage and free to remarry.

In chapter 8, Paul addresses the question of eating meat that had been offered to idols. Though this particular issue is not relevant to most cultures today, the principles Paul lays out are helpful in matters of Christian liberty. We can easily apply these principles to any gray area, an issue where the Bible doesn't come right out and condemn the activity, but neither does it come right out and condone it. Through the discussion of eating meat offered to idols, God provides for us His mind (1 Cor. 2:16) on these difficult topics. And God doesn't want us to simply focus on our *liberty* when dealing with a gray area. The bigger issue is *love*! Specifically, love for our brother or sister.

In the extremely pagan city of Corinth, virtually any meat in the market had at some time been offered to idols. Based on Paul's response in chapter 8, their question seems to have been posed in such a way that they would get the answer they wanted. Something like, "Hey Paul, since we know there's really only one God anyway, eating meat that has been offered to idols isn't a big deal, right? It would be okay if we ate it, right? What could be the harm?"

And Paul's answer is, "Your knowledge is exactly right! But the real issue isn't *knowledge*—it's *love*! You aren't the real issue; others are! And knowledge, as wonderful as it is, puffs *us* up, while love builds *others* up!" Paul is basically saying, "Yes, we have liberty to eat meat offered to idols, but we also have to ask ourselves: 'Is it right for me to satisfy my flesh with this meat, if by doing so, I become a stumbling block to a brother or sister who doesn't possess the knowledge I have?'" Having no regard for a weaker brother in this matter tells us that our real concern is satisfying our own sinful flesh—and by eating, we not only sin against our *brother*, we sin against our *Savior* (8:12).

In chapter 9, Paul illustrates this principle from his own life. He establishes the right he and Barnabas had to be compensated for their work in the Lord (vs. 1–14). But, Paul reminds the Corinthians, for the sake of the gospel, they willingly chose to set aside this right, because the most important thing in their lives was the cause of Christ. It was more important than their own rights, their own satisfaction, or their own personal benefit. Obviously, Paul is admonishing the Corinthians (and us) to do the same! When it comes to our liberty in Christ, we should ask ourselves two very basic questions:

- Am I more concerned about my rights and my liberty than I am the spiritual well-being of my weaker brothers and sisters for whom Christ died?
- Am I more concerned about my rights and my liberty than I am the souls of people who desperately need to be reached with the gospel of Jesus Christ?

In 10:14–22, Paul takes the discussion about eating meat offered to idols to another level. Some of the Corinthians probably thought that since an idol is nothing, there was no problem going to their neighbor's religious services with him. Paul is clear that, though there is only one true God and idols are "nothing," demon spirits actually masquerade behind those gods, so idol worship actually becomes the worship of demons!

Paul then addresses whether it was permissible for the Corinthians to eat meat that had been offered to these idols. He concludes that they did have liberty to eat it, as long as doing so did not defile their conscience—or the conscience of a brother or sister. (When our conscience seems to limit us from an activity that is not condemned in Scripture, and that other Christians seem to have no problem participating in, God may be using our conscience to keep us from that activity to spare us from what that activity might lead to which God does forbid! The activity itself may not be wrong, and it may not be wrong for others—but it may be wrong for us. Don't judge others who exercise their liberty in that area, and never violate your own conscience!)

In 10:23–24, Paul reiterates that we have liberty in gray areas, but being free to do something doesn't necessarily mean we should! We must always prioritize our brothers and sisters. This is also the context for 10:31–33. The glory of God is what should be the motivation for all we do—not our own selfish interests and desires.

Paul then tells these immature and carnal believers: "Be ye followers of me, even as I also am [a follower] of Christ" (11:1). God knows we sometimes need a model to follow, a mature Christian to model what following Jesus looks like in real life. However, God doesn't desire that scenario to continue indefinitely. As believers mature, they need to learn to "stand" (Gal. 5:1) and "walk" (Gal. 5:16) on their own two spiritual feet.

In 11:2–16, Paul discusses women wearing a covering on their head in private and corporate worship. The passage is too extensive to adequately expound here, but allow me to make just two simple, yet important, observations. First, Paul clearly states that he is not instituting a biblical requirement concerning head coverings on the Corinthians or us (v. 16). And second, Paul is discussing a woman's *hair*! Those two simple realities will guide you in this passage.

Finally, Paul rebukes them for abusing the Lord's Supper. They using the Lord's Table to exercise their carnality in eating and drinking—instead of remembering our Lord's sacrifice. God uses this passage as a reminder of the purpose of communion and shows us:

- This is a very important and meaningful time to God (11:27)
- We should examine ourselves before participating (11:28)
- There are extreme consequences to partaking in the Lord's Supper without exercising judgment upon the areas of sinfulness that have been revealed to us (11:30)

WEEK 49, DAY 2: **TODAY'S READING: 1 CORINTHIANS 12-16**

OVERVIEW:
The body of Christ (chapter 12); the priority of charity (chapter 13); the boundaries for spiritual gifts (chapter 14); the resurrection of the dead (chapter 15); structure for orderly giving (chapter 16).

HIGHLIGHTS & INSIGHTS:
In chapter 12, Paul begins to address the Corinthians' ignorance regarding spiritual gifts (12:1). Remember, they think they've got it all together when it comes to this subject (4:10). They certainly didn't think they were ignorant—they thought they were enlightened! Notice however, that Paul reminds the Corinthians in 12:2 that in their worship of pagan idols when they were in their lost state ("Gentiles"), part of their worship experience included being "carried away" and "led" spiritually by demonic spirits that masqueraded behind their "dumb idols" (12:2. See 1 Cor. 10:19–20). Historically, these euphoric spiritual experiences were called "ecstasies"[1]. Verse 3 seems to indicate that the Corinthians were bringing these pagan spiritual experiences into their "worship" of Christ in the corporate gatherings of the church—in which the "worshippers" were being carried away/led in their spiritual euphoria to actually call Jesus accursed (i.e. saying, "Jesus is damned!"). Because the Corinthians had so elevated spiritual experience above truth, they couldn't even discern that such a deplorable outburst of blasphemy wasn't being generated by the Holy Spirit! It is unbelievable that Paul actually has to say to them, "Wherefore I give you to understand, that no man speaking by the Spirit of God calleth Jesus accursed" (12:3)! This whole discourse (chapters 12-14) concerning gifts is Paul's rebuke of how the Corinthian's were abusing both the Spirit of God and His gifts!

God establishes three keys to spiritual gifts:

1. There are *diversities* of gifts (12:4) – God never intended for everybody in a church to have the same gift. For the church to function as one body, there must be a *diversity* of gifts amongst the members!

2. There are different *administrations* of the gifts (12:5) – Even when God gives people the same gift, He dispenses (administrates) that gift to them in different ways.

3. There are different *operations* of the gifts (12:6) – Even though people may have the same gift, the way the Spirit of God operates through that gift in each individual is different.

In verse 7, Paul explains the overarching principle guiding spiritual gifts. The Spirit always intends to use the spiritual gifts through individual believers to "profit withal," or for the common good. In other words, our spiritual gift is not our own personal edification or benefit; it is for the spiritual benefit of others in the body of Christ. This principle is vital for understanding spiritual gifts in general. But it is particularly relevant in chapter 14 when Paul describes how Corinthian believers (and believers all over the world in the 21st century) were abusing tongues by thinking they could use that particular gift for their own edification in what is often called a "prayer language."

God uses the human body to illustrate this principle. The hand's purpose is not to benefit that hand, but to benefit the rest of our body as that hand works in conjunction with the other members of our body. This is why it's important for every believer to be placed in a local church. Believers can get the idea that they aren't as important as other members of the body, or that other members aren't as important as them, or not as important as other members of the body. But Paul's point is that every member of the spiritual body of Christ is just as vital to Him as every member of our own physical body is to us! Thus, Paul admonishes us to exercise equal care and concern for every member of Christ's body. We're to rejoice with those who rejoice and we're to weep with those who weep, regardless of their gifts and regardless of their function in the body.

Paul asks a string of questions in 12:28–31. The answer to each question is obvious. No, we don't all have the same gifts. In fact, for the body to function, we *can't* have the same function by exercising the same gift! That's why God sovereignly gives us different gifts. Our unity in the body of Christ is manifested, not by all of us fulfilling the same role, but in our diversity! It's manifested in each of us doing different things! As Paul asked in 12:7–11, did we get to choose the gift or gifts the Spirit of God imparted to us? No! The Holy Spirit imparts our gifts to us as He sees fit so each of us may carry out our God-given role in the body of Christ.

Paul concludes the chapter with a sarcastic rebuke (v. 31). Rather than humbly and joyfully exercising the gifts the Spirit had graciously given them, the Corinthians coveted the "best gifts," specifically the showy or up-front gifts. At the end of verse 31, God introduces "a more excellent way," better than the way the Corinthians were pretentiously seeking gifts they felt would give them more prominence, preeminence and recognition in the church! And this "more excellent way" is what Paul discusses in the next chapter—the way of charity, or love!

If we fail to see the connection between the the last phrase of 12:31 and chapter 13, it can easily appear that this chapter interrupts Paul's train of thought regarding spiritual gifts. It does not! The subject of love is actually critical to understanding and exercising spiritual gifts. (And it reminds us of the principle of keeping verses, passages, and even chapters in the Bible in their context.) The Corinthians were proud and self-absorbed, considering only themselves in their pursuit and use of spiritual gifts. Paul tells them (and us) that the "excellent way" God wants us to pursue is charity. And one of the key characteristics of charity is that it always focuses on others' needs—not our own! If we, as Christians, never identify our spiritual gifts, but live a life of charity, God will be completely okay with that! Because the way of charity is the "more excellent way!"

In 13:4–7, God describes what biblical charity looks like in real life. We would do well to place our life next to his description of charity to see how we measure up. Paul's point is that these are the ways true spirituality is measured—not by our flamboyant use (or misuse!) of spiritual gifts. God again reminds us that exercising charity is superior to the gifts themselves. In fact, He says there's going to come a time when the showy gifts the Corinthians were so preoccupied with and zealous for (tongues, healing, miracles) would cease to have a function in the church age.

Again, this is not the venue for presenting a doctrinal treatise of all the reasons the sign gifts have ceased—but in a nutshell, it goes like this: During the transition when God was no longer functioning according to the Old Testament, but prior to completing the written record of the New Testament, God used miraculous gifts given as signs to authenticate both the messenger and his message (Heb. 2:3–4). After the New Testament was complete, these sign gifts ceased to have a continuing role or a biblical purpose in the church because, to determine if a message was from God, believers could simply ask, "Does this message lined up with the revealed Word of God?"

As a whole or one verse at a time, chapter 14 is often taken out of context (alongside chapters 12–13) to form faulty doctrine. Here are a important points about this chapter:

- God distinguishes spiritual gifts from prophecy (v. 1). There is a spiritual gift of prophecy, but that's not what he's referring to here. Rather, this is the ability of every believer to prophesy, to proclaim the truth of God and His Word. Earlier Paul asked, "Does every believer have the gift of prophecy?" (12:29), and the implied answer was no. But now Paul is saying that every believer can and should prophesy (proclaim the truth of God)! Think of it this way: there is a specific gift of giving and a gift of faith, but every believer is commanded to give and to exercise faith, regardless of their spiritual gifts. In the same way, we have been commanded to prophesy, whether we have the gift of prophecy or not.

- In this chapter, Paul is not seeking to elevate tongues. He's seeking to elevate *prophecy*! He's not championing the idea that we should speak words about God that nobody understands to no profit, but to speak words that people do understand so they can be edified!

- The places where Paul appears to promote tongues are actually setups to show the superiority of prophecy, or proclaiming the truth of the Word of God. Though many charismatic pastors and teachers use these verses to validate the use of tongues, not one verse is a positive reference to tongues! In the first half of chapter 14, God shows the priority of speaking His truth so that people can understand over showing off some spectacular gift. The second part of the chapter deals with the proper use of gifts within the body.

- The basic principle of chapter 14 is that things are to be done "decently and in order" (14:40). A church service is to have a sense of freedom, but it is not to be a free-for-all! Any gathering of believers that breeds chaos or confusion (which is often the case in some charismatic churches) is directly disobeying God's Word. Even at the time of the writing of 1 Corinthians, when God was still using these sign gifts to authenticate the messenger and His message, they were to maintain decency and order.
    - During corporate worship, two or, at the most, three believers were permitted to speak in tongues in any one service. They were also to speak "by course," or one person at a time (14:27).
    - Someone was permitted to speak in tongues (languages) only if there was also someone present with the gift of interpretation of tongues. Without someone to interpret, tongues were forbidden (14:27–28).
    - Prophesying was also to be exercised one person at a time. There were no restrictions, however, on the number of people who could prophesy (proclaim the truth) in a gathering of the church (14:29–31).
    - Women were not permitted to speak in tongues or prophesy in the service (14:34–35). Interestingly enough, much, if not most, of the so-called "tongues speaking" that takes place in churches in the twenty-first century is done by women!

As we've already discussed, the New Testament is now complete, so the sign gifts are no longer necessary. But even if they were operative today, I know of no churches that follow the clear instructions given for their use in this chapter. I would imagine that there are churches that do, but I personally know of none. It's one thing to believe all the gifts are still operating today—but it's quite another not to follow God's clear instructions for their use!

Paul has more to correct the Corinthians about than spiritual gifts, however. In chapter 15, Paul corrects their beliefs about the resurrection, especially the priority of Christ's resurrection. He passionately and eloquently argues that everything our faith is built upon as believers in Jesus Christ is predicated on the reality of Christ physically rising from the dead. If Christ didn't rise from the dead, none of us will rise from the dead, and we become the most deceived, disillusioned, pitiful and miserable people on this planet!

However, Christ did rise from the dead! In Adam, we were all born sinners; in Christ, we are all born righteous. In Adam, all die; in Christ, we are all made alive. In Adam, we were all born in his image; in Christ, we are all born in His image. In Adam, we were all born with a body like his; in Christ, we will all receive a glorified body like His at the Rapture.

Given the importance of Christ's resurrection and its benefits and promises, then, the resurrection should be the motivation that keeps us continually abounding in the "work of the Lord" (15:58). Are you "abounding" in the work of the Lord, or have you grown complacent and weary? If so, perhaps you have misplaced the importance or the implications of the resurrection.

Finally, in chapter 16, God instructs the Corinthians concerning the best way to receive the offerings they were collecting to relieve the saints in the church at Jerusalem (vs. 1–4). This instruction has become the prescription for how offerings have been received in local churches ever since.

Verse 9 of chapter 16 reveals a fact of ministry we must never lose sight of: open doors and adversaries go hand-in-hand! Fulfilling our mission on this planet is not a walk in the park. It is a battle. Expect resistance. Expect trials. Expect difficulties. Expect adversaries, but, by all means, expect victory! By God's grace, press on! Be strong in the Lord and in the power of His might!

---

[1]The MacArthur New Testament Commentary, 1 Corinthians; Moody Press, 1984, pp. 278-280.

52 WEEKS OF PURSUIT

WEEK 49, DAY 3: TODAY'S READING: 2 CORINTHIANS 1-7

OVERVIEW:
The key to ministry (chapter 1); the spirit of ministry (chapter 2); the proof of ministry (chapter 3); the definition of ministry (chapter 4); the perspective of ministry (chapter 5); the fellowship of ministry (chapter 6); the comfort of ministry (chapter 7).

HIGHLIGHTS & INSIGHTS:
God had used Paul to plant the church in Corinth during his second missionary journey (Acts 18:1–17). The believers there had grabbed his heart. He says in 2:4, "For out of much affliction and anguish of heart I wrote unto you with many tears." In 6:11, he says, "O ye Corinthians, our mouth is open unto you, our heart is enlarged." But because of his deep love for them, there was also the potential for deep hurt. Through their many unjust accusations, snide insinuations, and contemptuous allegations, Paul felt betrayed by them, and it had impacted him immensely (2 Cor. 12:15).

We may think the great Apostle Paul was somehow above discouragement, but Paul was as human as any of us, which we see reflected in a few places in 2 Corinthians. He confesses to the Corinthians, "For we would not, brethren, have you ignorant of our trouble which came to us in Asia, that we were pressed out of measure, above strength, insomuch that we despaired even of life" (1:8). Simply put, his sorrow was so great that he was afraid it was going to kill him, and at the same time, his sorrow was so great that he was afraid it *wasn't* going to kill him! Paul was not only discouraged, he was depressed.

2 Corinthians is the most personal of all Paul's New Testament letters. He opens his heart to reveal who he really is. At times he exudes spiritual power and strength, and at others, he exhibits his human frailty and weakness. In this book, he expresses great sympathy and tenderness, as well as great sternness and even sarcasm! As a result, it is the greatest and most practical book in the Bible on how to minister to people. As Paul said, "And I will very gladly spend and be spent for you; though the more abundantly I love you, the less I be loved" (12:15). May God give us that kind of selfless heart in ministering to others!

As we read this handbook for ministry, then, we can see Paul's theme unfold in the various chapters:

- Chapter 1 – The *Key* to Ministry: *Suffering*
- Chapter 2 – The *Spirit* of Ministry: *Forgiveness*
- Chapter 3 – The *Proof* of Ministry: *Transformation*
- Chapter 4 – The *Definition* of Ministry: *Glory*
- Chapter 5 – The *Perspective* of Ministry: *Judgment Seat*
- Chapter 6 – The *Fellowship* of Ministry: *Separation*
- Chapter 7 – The *Comfort* of Ministry: *Joy*
- Chapters 8–9 – The *Heart* of Ministry: *Giving*
- Chapter 10 – The *Mind* of Ministry: *Obedience*
- Chapter 11 – The *Enemy* of Ministry: *Satan's Ministers*
- Chapter 12 – The *Humility* of Ministry: *Grace*
- Chapter 13 – The *Power* of Ministry: *Weakness*

52 WEEKS OF PURSUIT

WEEK 49, DAY 4: TODAY'S READING: 2 CORINTHIANS 8-13

OVERVIEW:
The grace of giving (chapters 8–9); Paul defends his ministry (chapter 10); the false religious system (chapter 11); Paul's final defense to the Corinthians (chapter 12); Paul's final appeal to the Corinthians (chapter 13).

HIGHLIGHTS & INSIGHTS:
Today's reading provides the clearest and most complete principles on giving in the entire New Testament (chapters 8–9). The Corinthians had committed to supplying funds to help the church in Jerusalem, but at the time Paul wrote this letter, they had not followed through on their commitment. Paul exhorts them to fulfill their promise and, in the process, God lays out the New Testament pattern for giving. Here are some of the principles in these two chapters:

- It is the grace of God that allows us to give sacrificially (8:1–3)
- Giving should result from us having already first given ourselves to the Lord (8:5)
- By God's grace, we shouldn't just give—but abound in giving! (8:7)
- Giving is the proof of the sincerity of our love (8:8)
- Jesus Christ is the ultimate picture of giving (8:9)
- We should be a generous giver (9:6)
- We should purpose in our hearts to give the amount the Lord wants us to give (9:7)
- We should give cheerfully (9:7) (In other words, not because we have to—but because we want to!)

We also find one of the simplest biblical explanations of God's grace in 8:9, that we could express this way:

G—God's

R—Riches

A—At

C—Christ's

E—Expense

The ultimate gift is the grace that God has bestowed upon us. But perhaps grace is best understood by comparing it to justice and mercy.

- Justice is God giving us *what* we deserve
- Mercy is God *not* giving us what we do deserve
- Grace is God giving us what we *did not* deserve

In chapters 10–13, Paul challenges the rebels in the Corinthian church who were questioning his *authority*, as well as the false teachers (Judaizers) that had infiltrated the church and were attacking Paul's *gospel*. In addressing these problems, Paul teaches us two significant lessons concerning the warfare we face as believers (10:3–5):

1. Our battle is not with *people*, but with the *spiritual powers* that are often at work *through* people (Eph. 6:12)
2. We cannot win in this *spiritual* warfare using *carnal* weapons (10:4)

In chapter 11, Paul talks further about the spiritual powers that were working through the human false teachers in the first century in Corinth. Those same spiritual powers are working through the human false teachers in the 21st century! Paul tells us in 11:15 that they are actually Satan's "ministers." And Paul says, though we think it would be easy to recognize them, in the same way that Satan transforms himself into an "angel of light," his ministers appear as "ministers of righteousness" (11:13–15). In other words, they live impeccable lives, present a good, godly demeanor, and even use Christian terminology as they present their message. In 11:4, Paul says that they preach Jesus, they preach the gospel, and they preach about receiving the spirit. The only problem is, it's not the Jesus of the Bible; it's "another Jesus." It isn't the gospel that Paul preached; it's "another gospel." It isn't the Holy Spirit, but "another spirit." Like the Corinthians, we must wise up and be discerning. John urged in 1 John 4:1, "Beloved, believe not every spirit, but try the spirits whether they are of God: because many false prophets are gone out into the world."

As Paul comes to the end of this epistle, he makes his final defense of his apostleship in chapter 12, through the vision God gave to him of the third heaven. The experience was so unbelievably incredible, God not only forbade him to write about it, He felt it necessary to give Paul "a thorn in the flesh" (v. 7) to keep him humble!

By the time Paul gets to his final appeal to the Corinthians in chapter 13, he has very calculatedly opened his very soul to them, and has provided a thorough explanation of his ministry, giving detailed answers to all of their accusations and objections, as well as confirming his deep affection and love for them. In this closing section, Paul pleads with the Corinthians to make sure that his third visit to them was not laden with drama (for him or for them!) like the previous visit had been.

52 WEEKS OF PURSUIT

WEEK 49, DAY 5: **TODAY'S READING: GALATIANS 1-6**

OVERVIEW:
The priority of grace in Paul's message and life (chapter 1); the priority of grace in Paul's ministry (chapter 2); the preeminence of grace over law (chapters 3–4); the priority of standing in liberty and walking in the Spirit in grace living (chapters 5–6).

HIGHLIGHTS & INSIGHTS:
The book of Galatians is one of the most practical books in the entire New Testament, and when we understand the key issues facing the churches in Galatia, it is immediately clear why that is true. As we will see, the 1st Galatian problem is still alive and well in Christianity in the 21st century!

Let's begin with some background information. While the other letters written by Paul to local churches were addressed to one specific local church in one specific city (Rome, Corinth, Ephesus, Philippi, Colossae, and Thessalonica), this letter was written to a group of local churches in a particular region. That region, in modern-day Turkey, was known as Galatia. It had been settled by the Gauls of France, and thus became known as Galatia, or "Gaulatia," if you will. The local churches in this region were established by Paul and Barnabas on their first missionary journey in the cities of Derbe, Lystra, Iconium and Antioch of Pisidia (Acts 13:14–14:23).

Obviously, these churches were comprised of Gentile believers who had responded to Paul's proclamation of the gospel which they received by grace alone, through faith alone, in Christ alone. After they received Christ, Paul and Barnabas spent time "confirming the souls of the disciples" in each of these churches, making sure that "they had ordained them elders in every church" (Acts 14:22–23). Not long after Paul and Barnabas had grounded these churches in the truth, however, false teachers began infiltrating with what Paul called "another gospel" (Gal. 1:6). Much to Paul's shock and dismay, the disciples and elders in these churches dropped Paul and his gospel like a hot potato for a false, powerless, and even damnable "gospel" (Gal. 1:6–9). Paul literally could not believe it! He writes to rebuke and to correct these churches using some of the strongest language found in any of his letters.

These false teachers are known historically as Judaizers or legalists. They were Jews who, like Paul before his conversion, were incredibly zealous for Judaism (the Jewish religion)—thus the title, Judaizers. Their basic point of attack upon the Galatian believers was that if they, as Gentiles, really wanted to *be* saved, or if they really wanted to *stay* saved, or if they really wanted to *be spiritual*, they would have to become like the Judaizers. In other words, they would first have to become Jewish proselytes and live under the requirements and ramifications of the law—thus, the title "legalists" (*legal* being connected to law). Luke summarizes their basic false teaching in Acts 15:1: "Except ye be circumcised after the manner of Moses, ye cannot be saved."

Paul's reaction to this false teaching is what prompted the writing of this scathing letter to the Galatian churches. Paul is absolutely livid with these false teachers, not to mention the Galatian believers themselves! In Galatians 1:8–9, he says that those who preach this false gospel give evidence that they are worthy of hell, and he later says that those who are swayed by them give evidence that they have not only been misinformed or deceived, but actually "bewitched" (3:1). That's a strong word! Paul says they were acting as if they were under some sort of a Satanic spell!

The content of this letter is of utmost importance because the Judaizers of the first century were not the last preachers and teachers to infiltrate and lead churches and proclaim that there is something *more* that you need to *do* in order to...

- *Be* saved ("You must be baptized," or "You must keep the sacraments.")
- *Stay* saved ("You must hold out faithful to the end.")

- Be *Spiritual* ("You must be like us. Dress like this—not that. Wear your hair like this—not that. Listen to this kind of music—not that. Go to these places—not those.")

Even today, understanding Paul's simple message through the book of Galatians is vital to keep us off of the endless treadmill of legalism.

What the Galatians didn't understand, as is the case with most believers today, is that they were already *as saved as* they would ever be and already *as spiritual as* they would ever be. That incredible standing before God isn't based on anything *we* do or don't do; it is based solely and wholly upon who *Christ* is and what He has done! Paul said in 2 Corinthians 5:21 that we were "made the righteousness of God in Him" the moment we were saved. And it's impossible to get more righteous than that. Quite simply, our righteous standing before God isn't *achieved*, it is *received*. Paul said in Ephesians 1:6 that God "made us accepted" the moment we were placed in Christ. That means that God accepts us in the very same way He accepts Christ, His beloved Son. And it's impossible to be more accepted than that! Again, this is all totally apart from anything we do or do not do. That lesson is foreign to most believers and typically comes long and hard. The difference, however, is the difference between legalism and a life of walking in the flesh—and true, genuine biblical Christianity and a life of walking in the Spirit. And quite honestly, it is the difference between a life of bondage and a life of freedom.

The message of the Holy Spirit through Paul to the Galatian believers, and to us today, is simply this: Christ, through His death, set us free from the law. In Galatians 3:2–3, Paul asks, "This only would I learn of you, Received ye the Spirit by the works of the law, or by the hearing of faith? Are ye so foolish? Having begun in the Spirit, are ye now made perfect by the flesh?" The obvious answer is that it was through faith and by His Spirit that we were saved and were placed on the road to maturity. Based on that reality, Paul admonishes us, first, to learn to *stand*: "Stand fast therefore in the liberty wherewith Christ hath made us free, and be not entangled again with the yoke of bondage" (5:1). So that, secondly, we can learn to *walk*: "Walk in the Spirit, and ye shall not fulfil the lust of the flesh" (5:16).

Understanding the practical teaching and ramifications of the book of Galatians for new believers cannot be overemphasized. It will literally save twenty years (and that's a conservative estimate) of frustration, as the flesh tenaciously seeks and strives to produce what can only be produced by the Spirit (5:22–23) through the faith of Christ. (See Gal. 2:16, 20; Phil. 3:9; Rom. 3:20–22.) Pray that God will open your eyes to the wondrous and freeing truths found in this incredible little book of Galatians.

WEEK 49, DAY 6: TODAY'S READING: EPHESIANS 1-6

OVERVIEW:
The believer's position in Christ (chapter 1); the believer's salvation by grace through faith (chapter 2); the revelation of the mystery of the church (chapter 3); the believer's walk in the world (chapters 4-6).

HIGHLIGHTS & INSIGHTS:
There are so many things that could and should be said about the book of Ephesians, but again, this is not the venue for exhaustive commentary. At best, we will be able to establish the big picture of the book. And perhaps the best way to establish the big picture is by examining one of the most controversial passages in this book, as well as the entire Bible. I'm talking about Ephesians 1:4–5, where Paul says: "According as he hath chosen us in him before the foundation of the world, that we should be holy and without blame before him in love: Having predestinated us unto the adoption of children by Jesus Christ to himself, according to the good pleasure of his will."

Based on where you land on the interpretation of these (and similar) verses, you are labeled either a Calvinist or an Arminian. Several hundred years ago, John Calvin and Jacob Arminius popularized opposing positions on these verses. Today, the basic Arminian position is that, in terms of salvation, "whosoever will may come" (Rev. 22:17). The basic Calvinist position, as it is expressed today, is that only the elect will be saved—that the only ones who will actually come to Christ are those who, in eternity past, God chose, according to His sovereign grace, to be saved.

Many people, of course, if asked whether they were an Arminian or a Calvinist, would answer "yes," meaning that they believe both. In their minds, the Bible teaches that "whosoever will may come." And yet, they would also say that the Bible also teaches that believers were "chosen in him before the foundation of the world" (Eph. 1:4). When asked how they reconcile these two seemingly contradictory statements, they may answer, as did Charles Spurgeon, "Friends don't need to be reconciled!" They believe God put both in the Bible and conclude, therefore, that both must be equally true. And though they don't come together in the human mind, they certainly must come together in the mind of God. So let's just allow God to be God because, after all, His ways are not our ways and His thoughts are far above our thoughts (Isa. 55:8–9) and the secret things belong to the Lord (Deut. 29:29), so let's just accept it, and go on! This reasoning is often illustrated with a story like this: as we approach the gates of heaven, there's a sign over the gates that says, "Whosoever will may come." As we walk through the gates into heaven and look back above them, however, the sign says, "Chosen before the foundation of the world." That middle-of-the-road approach is rather convincing and sounds pretty *spiritual*, even humble, but none of those things are the real issue! The issue is always the same: Is it *biblical*?

So we come to Ephesians 1:4, and it says, "According as he hath chosen us in him before the foundation of the world." And there are many people who will say, "C'mon! How clear can it be? My goodness, just let the Bible be the Bible!" Well, let's do that!

First of all, let's be sure that we recognize that if this verse is teaching that sometime before the foundation of the world, God had already chosen each of us who would be saved, then what the verse is teaching is that we were "in Christ" before the foundation of the world because the verse says, "According as He hath chosen us in him before the foundation of the world." If we were placed "in him before the foundation of the world," it obviously poses a huge problem! Because the Bible clearly states that prior to our salvation, we were:

- In Adam (1 Cor. 15:22)
- In trespasses and sins (Eph. 2:1)
- In the lusts of our flesh (Eph. 2:3)

- In the world (Eph. 2:12)

Are we to believe, then, that in eternity past ("before the foundation of the world"), God placed us in Christ and then, somehow we got *out of* Christ and were found in Adam, in trespasses and sins, in the lusts of our flesh, and in the world, only so that sometime later He could put us back *in Christ* again? I can't find a way for that to make any biblical sense!

We have to understand Ephesians 1:4–5 using the first principle of Bible study: context! But many people, even pastors, teachers and commentators, come to these verses without putting them into the context of the book of Ephesians, or even of the chapter in which the verses are found. And so, ignoring the context, they read, "He hath chosen us in him," and assume that the *us* means individuals whom God chose to save.

In the context of the book of Ephesians, and specifically chapter 1, however, Paul is introducing something that no believer in Christ had actually understood prior to the writing of Ephesians—the mystery of the church. That's the *us* to whom Paul is referring in Ephesians 1:4! It is the church, in a collective sense, which Paul reveals "is his body" (1:23). The church, spiritually, is as much the body of Christ as was the physical body that Christ lived in during His 33 years on this planet. That's what the whole book of Ephesians is about and why God placed it in His Bible! To teach *us* (all of us who have called upon His name!) that *we*, collectively, are the Body of Christ!

Notice that Paul says in 1:10: "That in the dispensation of the fulness of times he might gather together in one all things in Christ." And to what time period is that referring? The church age, right?

So it goes like this …

Yes, Ephesians 1:4 clearly teaches that God made a very definite *decision* "before the foundation of the world." But does the verse actually say that He was choosing *individuals* to salvation? Absolutely not! What the verse says is that before the foundation of the world, God chose that the *church*, the Body of Christ (all of *us* who exercise our will and by faith call upon Him to save *us*) would be different than any people who have ever lived. God *chose* before the foundation of the world that our salvation would place us "in him."

And *how* did God make that choice? Verse 5 says that the choice was made "according to the good pleasure of His will." In other words, He did it because He is God and that's what He sovereignly chose to do! And *why* did God the Father choose to give us that standing? Verse 4 tells us it was so we could constantly—regardless of our attitude, our disposition, our sin, or anything we do or do not do—"be holy and without blame before Him in love." The only way that could be a reality is for God to place us in Christ. That way, when He looks at us, He sees His Son who has always, even before the foundation of the world, been "holy and without blame before Him in love"!

The only people who have ever been *in Christ* are the people who are saved in the church age. As wonderful as God thought Noah, Daniel and Job were (Ezekiel 14:20), they were never in Christ a day in their lives! That exclusive standing, decreed by God before the foundation of the world, would be totally unique to believers when God was carrying out His plan on the earth through this extraordinary thing called the church. Read Ephesians 3:1–12 carefully, and you will see that "the eternal purpose which he purposed in Christ Jesus our Lord" (3:11) was that it would be the church that would know "the manifold wisdom of God," having been placed "in Christ"!

What God is trying to communicate through the book of Ephesians is that those of us who are believers in the church age are the only ones who have ever had the distinct privilege of being "holy and without blame before him in love" (1:4). And we don't have that standing before Him because we're just so much more holy and blameless and lovable than all of the Old Testament saints. It's simply because of this supremely wonderful choice that God made in eternity past, to immediately place in Christ those of us who exercise our will in the church age by calling upon the name of His Son to save us and then, to secure that position, to seal us in Him "unto the day of redemption," or until the day we receive a glorified body that is incapable of sinning! (See Eph. 1:12–14; 4:30; Phil. 3:21.)

Even more, according to Ephesians 1:5, the only ones who have been "predestinated unto the adoption of children" are those of us who are believers in the church age. And again, what the verse actually says is not that God was predestinating *who would be saved*, but rather the fact that those of us who *are saved* in the church age would have the glorious privilege as a benefit of our salvation, to be *adopted* as God's children. Let's let the Bible be the Bible! Let's hear what these verses are saying in context, without reading something into them that just isn't there.

That's why believers in the church age are eternally secure, when that was not true for Old Testament saints and will not be true for Tribulation saints (Matt. 24:13). We are the only ones who have ever been or will ever be placed in Christ! We are the only people who have ever or will ever have their righteousness and acceptance with God, not based on *who we are* or *what we do*, but based on *who Christ is* and *what He has done*! (See 2 Cor. 5:21; Eph. 1:6.)

This really isn't hard. In fact, it's very simple when we place the verses in their context and stop reading into them things that aren't there. I agree with Paul: "Blessed be the God and Father of our Lord Jesus Christ, who hath blessed us with all spiritual blessings in heavenly places in Christ" (Eph. 1:3).

52 WEEKS OF PURSUIT

WEEK 50, DAY 1: TODAY'S READING: PHILIPPIANS 1-4

OVERVIEW:
Christ our life (chapter 1); Christ our pattern (chapter 2); Christ our righteousness (chapter 3); Christ our sufficiency (chapter 4).

HIGHLIGHTS & INSIGHTS:
Let's begin with the theme of the book of Philippians. What is this book really about? What was God's purpose in putting the book of Philippians into the canon of scripture? And just how are we to determine that?

One of the best pieces of advice I've ever received relating to Bible study is this: "Learn to emphasize what God emphasizes." God doesn't have a volume control on His voice (His Word) to accentuate a particular principle or concept. Nor did He provide a highlighter to accentuate His major themes or points of emphasis to the men He inspired to write His words down. To emphasize His point, God uses *repetition*. I said, to emphasize His point, God uses *repetition*. (I thought that if it works for God, maybe it would work for me!) We can glean amazing things from the Word of God by observing the repeated words, phrases, ideas, or concepts in a passage, chapter, or book.

In the book of Philippians, for example, the word *rejoice* (or rejoice, rejoiced, rejoicing) is found twelve times, and the word *joy* is found six times. This is an incredibly positive book! Paul's positive attitude is so clear that we might think he's halfway through a six-month sabbatical, chillin' at a five-star oceanfront condo in some resort city along the Mediterranean coast with the sun beaming down upon the beautiful terrain while he's sipping Frappuccinos and eating pistachio nuts out of a hammock!

But another word keeps popping up in Philippians that lets us know that that isn't the case: *bonds*. Paul refers to his bonds four times in chapter one alone! Far from being at some resort in some Mediterranean city, he's actually in prison. He's chained to a Roman guard. What's more, he wasn't even in prison for doing something wrong. If that were true, Paul could have acknowledged there are consequences for wrong behavior and just made the best of his self-inflicted situation. But Paul was in bonds on a false charge! And not just any false charge. It wasn't that the nasty old devil had caused lost people to lie about Paul and orchestrate some devious plot to have him cast into prison. Nope, he's there because of *gossip*! Gossip that began and spread among Christians! He is in prison because of a rumor, spread by believing Jews, who were still hanging on to and were zealous for the law (Acts 21). It just doesn't make sense for Paul to have such an upbeat attitude.

But maybe Paul had this cheery attitude because he'd only been there a couple of days? Maybe he was just keeping himself psyched up—and looking forward to including this incredibly cool story in his monthly missionary letter. No, by the time he wrote this letter, Paul had been in bonds for five years!

Nor was Paul's attitude because he was past his prime. It wasn't like he was no longer effective, so where he rode out his waning years was of no real consequence. No, when he was cast into this prison, his ministry was at its absolute peak. The five years he had been in prison should have been the best and most productive years of his entire ministry. But day after day, for five years, he's in bonds, chained to a Roman guard instead.

Now, I'm not trying to make us feel bad for Paul here. I want to make sure we get that there was absolutely no human explanation for Paul to have the attitude of rejoicing that he has in this letter! He has every right, humanly speaking, to be bitter, angry, disillusioned, frustrated, depressed and worried. And chances are good that, in some way, shape, or form, every one of us feels, to some degree, that we're in a prison, too. Not necessarily one with bars, as in Paul's case, but a prison nonetheless. Perhaps there are things in your life that have left you feeling that you are locked in. They've hindered you or restricted you in some way. They've tied your hands, so to speak. The bars are invisible; the chains can't be seen with physical eyes, but they're just as real as the ones that were restricting Paul!

Perhaps you're in a job you absolutely hate, but you see no other options, and it's a ball and chain to you every weekday of your life. Or maybe you don't have a job at all and feel that you're in a prison of a dull, unfulfilled life. Or maybe yours is a prison of loneliness. You feel imprisoned because you're single, or maybe because you're married! Or maybe like Paul, you've been the victim of gossip, and the hurt you have inside of you has left you feeling that your freedom has been taken away, and you're bound by your own emotions. Or perhaps you've been the victim of some injustice, and your mind keeps you behind bars because you can't stop thinking about it.

I don't know what kind of invisible prison you may be in, but both the human writer and the divine Author of Philippians want you to know that you can be in a prison and still find freedom and joy in life and ministry—regardless of your circumstances, no matter who was responsible for them, and even if they never change!

And by seeing what God emphasizes in this book, we can see the key to living in that kind of victory is our *attitude*. The word *mind* is found ten times in this little book. The word *think* is found five times, and *remember* is found once. That's sixteen times that God is trying to get us to see that *joy* is a *choice* we make because of right thinking. Which is actually the theme of this book.

Many of us have faced circumstances like those mentioned above. They have left us discouraged, depressed, or imprisoned. But in chapter 1, God tells us that we can find joy in our *circumstances* because Christ is our *life*. The key verse in the chapter is verse 21, where Paul says, "For to me to live is Christ, and to die is gain."

Some of us have had people who have injured us in some way, and we wrestle with bitterness and anger. So in chapter 2, God says that we can find joy in our *relationships* because Christ is our *pattern*. And the key verse in this chapter is verse 5, which says, "Let this mind be in you, which was also in Christ Jesus."

Some of us wrestle with our flesh—worldliness on one hand and good deeds on the other, but both driven by the same carnal source, the flesh! And in chapter 3, Paul says, we can find joy in our *walk* because Christ is our *righteousness*. And the key verse is 3:9 where Paul says, "[That I may] be found in him, not having mine own righteousness, which is of the law, but that which is through the faith of Christ, the righteousness which is of God by faith."

And finally, some of us are gripped by worry and fear. In chapter 4, Paul says that we can find joy in our *adversities* because Christ is our *sufficiency*. And the key verse in this chapter is verse 13, where Paul says, "I can do all things through Christ which strengtheneth me."

The book of Philippians is an extremely practical book that addresses real–life issues and points us toward the joy that is found in and through Christ alone. May it be ours as God ministers to us through this powerful book today!

52 WEEKS OF PURSUIT

WEEK 50, DAY 2: TODAY'S READING: COLOSSIANS 1-4

OVERVIEW:
The preeminence of Christ (chapter 1); four warnings (chapter 2); putting off and putting on (chapter 3); real relationships (chapter 4).

HIGHLIGHTS & INSIGHTS:
In Revelation 2 and 3, our Lord dictated to the Apostle John seven letters to seven churches in Asia Minor. The seven churches existed historically at the time John wrote Revelation, and the letters addressed actual situations those churches were facing at that time. Students of the Bible have noted for centuries, however, that beyond just the Historical aspect of these letters, there is also a Prophetic application. When placed into the context of the book of Revelation as a whole, the seven letters also provide a panoramic view of the seven stages of church history that pick up where the book of Acts leaves off in the history of the early church and takes us all the way up to the rapture of the church, which is found in the book of Revelation immediately following the seventh and final letter to the churches (Rev. 4:1).

But not only did our Lord write letters to seven churches, the Apostle Paul also wrote letters to seven churches or groups of churches (the Romans, Corinthians, Galatians, Ephesians, Philippians, Colossians and the Thessalonians).

And if we take the seven letters to the churches to whom our Lord wrote and lay them next to the seven letters to the churches to whom Paul wrote, we find an amazing similarity of content. Certainly the most obvious connection would be our Lord's letter to the Laodiceans and today's reading—Paul's letter to the Colossians. In fact, the only time other that Laodicea is found in the Bible is in the book of Colossians, where it occurs five times! Though the book of Colossians was written to address specific situations taking place in that church when the Spirit of God inspired Paul to write it, and though it has certainly had application for every local church in every period of church history, there is also a very specific application of that letter to the church of Jesus Christ in the Laodicean Period (approximately 1901 to the rapture).

Interestingly, the issues that the Spirit of God inspired the Apostle Paul to address when writing to the church in Colossae in about 62 AD are amazingly similar to the issues the church of Jesus Christ has dealt with during the Laodicean Period. So you may want to make a mental note to yourself that, when dealing with doctrinal or practical issues in the church in these last days, a good place to begin looking for answers is the book of Colossians.

To give historical context to this letter, Paul wrote to the Colossians while sitting in a prison cell in Rome. This is the first of two times he would be imprisoned in Rome—the second time would end in his death.

Also interesting is that this letter is addressed to a church Paul had not personally planted in a city to which he had never personally been. In Colossians 1:4, Paul says that he and Timothy "heard of your faith in Christ Jesus." In 2:1, Paul says, "For I would that ye knew what great conflict I have for you, and for them at Laodicea, and for as many as have not seen my face in the flesh." So if Paul didn't plant this church and had never been there, I think it's fair to ask some obvious questions.

- How did the church in Colossae get planted then? And...
- Why was Paul writing to them?

Even though Paul never visited Colossae or Laodicea, he did spend a great amount of time in Ephesus, a city about one hundred miles from Colossae that served as one of his three main bases for ministry. Paul went to Ephesus on his third missionary journey and spent three years preaching and teaching there (Acts 20:31). It was there that Paul's ministry began to explode; in the first two years, "all they which dwelt in Asia heard the word of the Lord Jesus, both Jews and Greeks" (Acts 19:10).

As people from all over Asia Minor came to Ephesus, they heard the gospel, and many would have carried it with them back to their home towns. Evidently, the church in Colossae was planted by a group of men including Philemon (Philem 1:1), Apphia and Archippus (1:2), and Epaphras who served as the pastor of this young church. Paul says the Colossians had come to faith from what they "learned of Epaphras , our dear fellowservant, who is for you a faithful minister of Christ" (1:6–7). Later, Paul describes him this way: "Epaphras, who is one of you, a servant of Christ, saluteth you, always laboring fervently for you in prayers, that ye may stand perfect and complete in all the will of God" (4:12).

And despite all the blessings God had granted the Colossian church (1:4–6, 8), Epaphras also saw some things that were extremely troubling. He was so concerned that he made the thousand-mile journey to Rome to visit Paul in prison to learn how to address these threats to the spiritual well-being of the church. And, evidently, Paul felt the issues were significant enough to receive apostolic attention. He immediately wrote this letter to the church, sending it with Tychicus and Onesimus (4:7, 9), while Epaphras remained in Rome for further tutelage and discipleship.

Basically, in chapters 1 and 2, Paul writes to the church and says, "Your pastor has told me about some of the incredible things that are happening in your lives and in your church, and I'm blessed beyond measure! But let me warn you about some other things."

- 2:4 – Don't allow "any man [to] beguile you with enticing words"
- 2:8 – "Beware lest any man spoil you through philosophy and vain deceit, after the tradition of men, after the rudiments of the world, and not after Christ"
- 2:16 – "Let no man therefore judge you in meat, or in drink, or in respect of an holyday, or of the new moon, or of the sabbath days"
- 2:18 – "Let no man beguile you of your reward in a voluntary humility and worshipping of angels, intruding into those things which he hath not seen, vainly puffed up by his fleshly mind"

Then, after addressing these *doctrinal* issues in chapters 1 and 2, Paul addresses *practical* issues in chapters 3 and 4, specifically focusing on relationships.

- 3:1–17 – Our relationship with the *Lord*
- 3:18–21 – Our relationship with those in our *Family*
- 3:22–4:1 – Our relationship with those with whom we *Work*
- 4:2 – Our relationship with those in the *Church*
- 4:3–6 – Our relationship with the *Lost World*

For those of us who know the Lord, the relationships Paul addresses in these two chapters encompass every relationship we have and provide us the practical principles we need for maintaining these relationships biblically.

52 WEEKS OF PURSUIT

WEEK 50, DAY 3: TODAY'S READING: 1 & 2 THESSALONIANS

OVERVIEW:

A model church (1 Thess. 1); a model of discipleship (1 Thess. 2); a model of faith (1 Thess. 3); a model walk (1 Thess. 4–5); comfort in tribulation (2 Thess. 1); clarification in teaching (2 Thess. 2); content on various topics (2 Thess. 3).

HIGHLIGHTS & INSIGHTS:

We noted yesterday the connection between the seven letters our Lord wrote in Revelation 2–3, and the seven letters Paul wrote, specifically the link between Paul's letter to the church of Colossae and our Lord's letter to the church of Laodicea.

Immediately following the book of Colossians (which, again, applies specifically to the church in the last days), God placed the two letters to the Thessalonians. And do you know what these two letters address? The two key events of the last days: the Rapture and the Second Coming. It is the exact sequence that is found in the book of Revelation. As soon as our Lord concludes His letter to the Laodiceans in Revelation 3, heaven opens, there is a sound of a trumpet and a voice saying, "Come up hither," and John is catapulted forward in time to experience the rapture (4:1). As he is caught up into heaven (chapters 4–5), he describes the scene of the raptured church in heaven, and in chapters 6–19, he describes the events on the earth following the rapture and provides us four accounts of the Second Coming of Christ!

As we put these details together, it becomes apparent that 1 and 2 Thessalonians are the letters the Holy Spirit inspired to teach the church about *how to be prepared for the Lord's coming*. In fact, each of the five chapters of 1 Thessalonians end with a reference to the coming of the Lord (1:10; 2:19; 3:13: 4:13–17; 5:23).

But it is also clear that, though these books deal with the prophetic events, Paul doesn't want us to approach the rapture and the Second Coming of Christ as mere doctrines to contemplate or discuss in a Bible Study. They aren't just truths to tantalize our intellect or imagination—they are biblical realities that affect *the way we live*! These *prophetic* events need to be translated into *practical* spiritual living. Based on their content, we could call these books a how–to manual for living in the last days. They offer real–world advice about what we need to emphasize, as well as how we need to approach the Lord's work, so that we can be as effective as possible.

Whereas each chapter of 1 Thessalonians ends with a reference to the Lord's coming, each chapter of 2 Thessalonians ends with a reference to grace (1:12; 2:16; 3:18). Paul is making the point that, as we labor in these last days prior to our Lord's coming, we need to both apply and rely upon the grace of God that He promised would be "sufficient … in infirmities, in reproaches, in necessities, in persecutions, in distresses" (2 Cor. 12:9–10).

Two other things worth noting from the biblical context and content of these two books:

1. Our Philosophy of Leadership.

These letters written to teach the church about effective ministry in the last days as we prepare for the Lord's coming just happen to be the only letters in the New Testament that were written as a *team effort*. The books of 1 and 2 Thessalonians were actually written by three human authors: Paul, Silas and Timothy (1 Thess. 1:1; 2 Thess. 1:1). In Paul's other letters to the churches, he mentions those who are with him in his greeting, but he then immediately kicks into the first person singular, using the pronoun *I* for the remainder of the letter. But 1 and 2 Thessalonians are different. They clearly follow Paul's writing style and reflect his personality and vocabulary, but instead of merely mentioning Silas and Timothy in the greeting, he uses the pronouns *we* and *us*. There are a few places where his apostolic authority surfaces and he uses *I*, but throughout 1 and 2 Thessalonians, Paul models for us the most effective *philosophy of leadership* in the last days: leading as a part of a team. Paul, Silas and Timothy were a unit. Paul was the leader of the leaders, but they were committed to teamwork. And if we are going to be effective in carrying out the job the Lord has for us in the last days through our local churches, we also must work as a team. Leadership that emphasizes teamwork provides accountability (Prov. 11:14), as well as wisdom and safety (Prov. 15:22; 24:6).

2. The Priority of Lordship.

1 and 2 Thessalonians begin very similarly: "Paul and Silvanus, and Timotheous, unto the church of the Thessalonians which is in God the Father and in the Lord Jesus Christ" (1 Thess. 1:1; 2 Thess. 1:1). He doesn't simply say "in Jesus Christ," but "in *the Lord* Jesus Christ." Certainly the phrase "the Lord Jesus Christ" is not unusual or unique to 1 and 2 Thessalonians. In fact, it appears eighty-one times in the New Testament. What is noteworthy, however, is that twenty of those uses are in these two books. 1 and 2 Thessalonians contain nearly one quarter of the appearances of this phrase—more than any other book, or pair of books, in the New Testament.

From the Historical context, Acts 17:7 makes clear why Paul so emphasizes this phrase. Jesus being presented as the Lord (or King) was the very issue that got the city of Thessalonica so stirred up when Paul, Silas, and Timothy came there to present Christ and His gospel in the first place. It would only stand to reason that when they wrote back to them, they would continue to emphasize that theme.

But in the biblical context, in the books that the Spirit of God inspired to teach us how to be the most effective in the last days, God is clearly letting us know that, now more than ever, people must understand *who* Jesus Christ is and the position He wants to have in His church collectively and in our lives personally—as *Lord*! And Christ's Lordship in the church in the last days is so far from a reality that Revelation 3:14–22 depicts Him actually standing on the outside of the church knocking, waiting for us to open the door.

As we read these two incredible books today, let us ask ourselves two important questions.

- Am I a part of the ministry *team* of my local church?
- Does my life reflect the fact that I am submitted to Christ's *Lordship*?

52 WEEKS OF PURSUIT

WEEK 50, DAY 4: TODAY'S READING: 1 TIMOTHY 1-6

OVERVIEW:
The proper use of the Law of God (chapter 1); the power of prayer and the place of women in the local church (chapter 2); the qualifications for church leaders (chapter 3); the contrast between false and faithful teachers (chapter 4); the responsibilities of the members of a local church (chapter 5); sound advice from God to servants, false teachers, the rich, and the educated (chapter 6).

HIGHLIGHTS & INSIGHTS:
1 Timothy is the first of the Pastoral Epistles, three New Testament books (the others being 2 Timothy and Titus) addressed to pastors of local churches and dealing with how they should conduct the affairs of the church as the under-shepherds of Christ's flock—the Lord Jesus Christ, of course, being the chief Shepherd (1 Peter 5:1–4). The instruction in these letters is very specific and certainly deals with situations pastors will encounter in carrying out their biblical office. But whether we're a pastor or not, these letters have incredibly practical ramifications for all of our lives and ministries. They are certainly addressed to those who hold the office of a pastor in a local church, but God intends every member of every local church to have a pastoral mindset toward the other members of the church, as well as toward the work of Christ in and through the church.

The Pastoral Epistles also present a great model for understanding the relationship God intends to exist between a disciple and discipler. The relationship Paul and Timothy had present one of the most detailed pictures of real discipleship in the New Testament. Timothy was responsible for the office of pastor in the church at Ephesus, but he was also an individual member of the body of Christ. He was a real person with real weaknesses, real problems, and real struggles like everybody else. God placed the Pastoral Epistles in the Bible to provide every believer with practical instruction on being a follower (disciple) of Christ—from either side of a discipling relationship.

In Acts 6, we learned that Timothy's father was a Greek and his mother was a Jew (vs. 1–3). His mother's name was Eunice, and his grandmother's name was Lois (2 Tim. 1:5). He resided in Lystra (Acts 16:1–2; 20:4) where he was raised in the knowledge of the Scriptures (2 Tim. 3:15).

Upon visiting Timothy's hometown on his second missionary journey, Paul was so impressed with Timothy's testimony in his local church he invited him to be part of their missionary team. Keep in mind that this invitation was extended to Timothy following Paul's conflict with Barnabas over John Mark in Acts 15:36–41. Paul didn't want John Mark to be included on his missionary team because he was too young, too fearful, and because he still had quite a ways to go in the process of discipleship. Because God is sovereign, and because He obviously has a sense of humor, He turns right around and puts on Paul's team a fearful young man who still had quite a ways to go in the process of discipleship. When we refuse to learn His lessons from the situations God has placed in our lives, He will simply recreate similar circumstances until we learn them.

To catch the real heart of this letter, though, let's look at a few pertinent details.

- Paul most likely led Timothy to Christ when he and Barnabas came to Lystra on their first missionary journey (See Acts 14:5–7; 1 Tim. 1:2, 18; 2 Tim. 1:2, 2:1; 1 Cor. 4:17).

- Timothy became Paul's most trusted companion and friend, and Paul used him for some of the toughest assignments and situations that arose in various churches (See 1 Thess. 3:1–7; 1 Cor. 4:16–17).

- In other passages, Paul described Timothy as a selfless individual, one with whom he was completely likeminded, and viewed serving with him as a father would with his own son (Phil. 2:19–22).

- Timothy struggled with fear (1 Cor. 16:10; 2 Tim. 1:7), which probably led to the stomach problems and other physical infirmities that Paul mentions in 1 Timothy 5:23.

- Paul wrote this letter to give young Timothy some encouragement to stay in the battle as a good soldier and to "war a good warfare" (1:18) in the midst of false teachers and backsliding believers in the church at Ephesus (1:3–4, 19–20). Paul himself had invested three years in the Ephesian church (Acts 20:31) and had an intense love for them (20:37–38). Paul writes to Timothy to encourage him to stay at Ephesus and fulfill his role and responsibility as the church's pastor, in spite of the difficulties he faced. Paul had warned the elders that false teachers would both enter the church and arise out of it, and now that it had happened, Paul felt confident that Timothy was the man for the job of shutting the mouths of the false teachers and protecting the flock of God in that church (1:3; 4:7; 6:17).

This letter was written from Laodicea (see AV 1611 postscript) and sent to Timothy in Ephesus between Paul's two imprisonments in Rome. Paul wanted Timothy to stay in Ephesus, a place "fully purposed" to do God's work (*Ephesus* means "fully purposed," Rev. 2:1–2), rather than join him in Laodicea (where the Christians felt they had "rights," Rev. 3:14–18). Paul knew where God's work could most effectively be accomplished. Practically speaking, we would do well in this age if we would just "stay in Ephesus," as opposed to living in and loving Laodicea.

Additional highlights from 1 Timothy:

- In 1:1–2, Christ is four things to those of us who know Him: Our Savior, our Hope, our Father, our Lord.

- In 1:8–10, the lawful use of God's law is two–fold: to reveal what sin is (Rom. 5:20; 7:7) and to bring us to Jesus Christ (Gal. 3:21–24).

- In 1:16, Paul's life of longsuffering is the pattern for our lives (2 Cor. 11:23–28).

- 1 Timothy 1:18–20 reveals that standing for truth will sometimes require the politically incorrect practice of naming the names of those who are disobedient and that teach false doctrine.

- As believers, prayer is the first thing we should do to maintain a close relationship with God (2:1).

- 1 Timothy 2:5 reveals that no mediator (middle man) other than Christ can bring us or our prayers to the Father. Not Mary. Not the saints. Not a priest. *Only* Christ!

- In 3:16, we learn that God was manifest (shown to us; revealed) in the flesh and it is "without controversy." Today we might say there are "no ifs, ands or buts about it!" Or, "You can take that to the bank!" (See 1 Cor. 15:1–8.)

- We should refuse to be intimidated by those who insinuate that we're too young to be doing God's work (4:11–12a). Regardless of our age, we are to preach and teach God's truth with charity, purity, humility, and authority!

- In 6:20, we are to "avoid oppositions of science falsely so called." (Evolution is called science, but it's actually a religion. By faith, Christians believe, "In the beginning, *God*." By faith, evolutionists believe, "In the beginning, *dirt*."

52 WEEKS OF **PURSUIT**

WEEK 50, DAY 5: **TODAY'S READING: 2 TIMOTHY 1-4**

OVERVIEW:
Important reminders regarding faith, fear, and holding fast sound words in the last days (chapter 1); responsibilities of believers in the last days (chapter 2); the realities of living in the apostasy of the last days (chapter 3); the Apostle Paul's final charge to preach the Word in the last days (chapter 4).

HIGHLIGHTS & INSIGHTS:
This second letter to Timothy records the last words that Paul ever communicated under the inspiration of the Holy Spirit. It was written from a prison in Rome (Mamertine Prison) where Paul was being held as he awaited execution for preaching Christ during the reign of the cruel Roman Emperor, Nero, who hated Christians and Christianity!

Paul had been arrested again since he wrote the first letter to Timothy in 65 AD. The New Testament gives little detail about Paul's ministry between these two imprisonments, but what we can conclude from Scripture is that he went to Nicopolis (Titus 3:12) and then to Troas (2 Tim. 4:13) where he had left his cloak, some books, and the parchments (the Scriptures) because of an apparent need for a quick exit. At this point, Paul's execution was drawing near (4:6). His trusted companions, except Luke, had forsaken him (4:11). He is lonely, but he is not in despair (4:17; 2 Cor. 4:8–10). He longs to see his beloved son in the faith one last time, so he writes this letter to Timothy asking him to come to Rome as soon as possible (4:9, 21). In the letter, Paul encourages Timothy not to be afraid of stepping in to assume role of leadership in the ministry of the gospel and discipleship once he had been executed (1:7–8; 2:2). We should all have at least one person to whom we could write such a letter when we are on our death bed!

Additional highlights from 2 Timothy:

- 1:7 – Any time we're experiencing fear doing the work of the Lord, we can be assured that its source is not God. It's either our own foolish insecurities and lack of faith or the work of our adversary, Satan (4:18).

- 1:12 – True believers are eternally secure because they know whom they have believed (Jesus Christ), and it is He who keeps them saved until that day, not themselves!

- 2:15 – We are commanded to "study" the Word of God to make sure that we "rightly" divide it. Without diligent study, it is possible to make wrong divisions when interpreting the scripture and end up twisting it to our own destruction (2 Pet. 3:16).

- 2:24–26 – We must display genuine meekness when seeking to reach lost people with the gospel, realizing that they have been taken captive by Satan himself and are being held in his snare. Their only hope is through the message of the gospel that has been committed to our trust (See 1 Thess. 2:4).

- 3:15–17 – Paul clearly calls the Old Testament Scriptures that Timothy had as a child "holy," and even though they were not the original manuscripts, but copies of copies of copies, the Scriptures Timothy held in his hands were the very inspired Word and words of God that had the supernatural power to "perfect" and "throughly furnish" a man or woman of God "unto all good works"!

- 4:2–4 – We have many teachers of the Bible in the world today just as the Bible predicted, but few preachers of the *Word*! What's the difference between teaching and preaching? From a general standpoint, teaching is imparting *information* while preaching is initiating *transformation*. From a biblical standpoint, though, true biblical preaching includes four key things:

    1) Preaching declares *the word of God* to the listeners! It is not simply imparting information

from the Word, *using* the Word, or *about* the Word. It is imparting *the Word* itself! It has to do with the *content* of the message.

2) Preaching *reproves* the listeners! It is intended by God to be *convicting*.

3) Preaching *rebukes* the listeners! It is intended by God to be *confronting*.

4) Preaching *exhorts* the listeners! It is intended by God to be *challenging*.

In a nutshell, we could say that biblical preaching in the 21st century is politically incorrect. May God give us a few fearless men to declare the light of His glorious Word even in these dark last days. And by God's grace, may He empower us to be in that number.

52 WEEKS OF PURSUIT

WEEK 50 DAY 6: TODAY'S READING: TITUS-PHILEMON

OVERVIEW:
Order and authority in the local church (Titus 1); sound doctrine for the people of the local church (Titus 2); the biblical way to deal with heretics (Titus 3); the Apostle Paul's letter to his friend Philemon regarding his unfaithful slave Onesimus, asking him to forgive Onesimus and accept him back into his house, not just as a slave, but as a brother in the Lord (Philem. 1).

HIGHLIGHTS & INSIGHTS:

TITUS

The Apostle Paul often relied on Titus in clutch situations because he possessed two tremendous qualities: he was trustworthy and he was faithful. In fact, in 2 Corinthians 8:23, Paul referred to Titus as his "partner and fellow-helper" in the work of the Lord. Coming from Paul, those are very powerful words of affirmation. Paul wrote this letter to Titus to instruct him on how to strengthen and establish the young churches on the island of Crete. Paul wanted to make sure that Titus dealt with the Cretans who, Paul says, were known for being liars, evil, and lazy (1:11–12). How's that for political correctness?

One key topic in this letter is the qualifications for church leaders (1:6–9). The New Testament indicates that every believer *should* possess these qualities, but Paul's point is that a man who holds the office of a bishop (pastor) *must* possess them! They are biblical requirements for holding the office, and these qualifications must be upheld in the local church. A church is destined to become carnal and spiritually deficient when the leaders do not meet these biblical qualifications, when they do not walk in "true holiness" (Eph. 4:24) as an example to the flock.

Another focus of Titus is the necessity of teaching sound doctrine because, Paul says, "there are many unruly and vain talkers and deceivers" (1:10). If there were many teachers of false doctrine in the first century, consider how many *more* there must be now! Paul was clear that "evil men and seducers shall wax worse and worse" (2 Tim. 3:13). In other words, the presence of false teachers would increase, not decrease, throughout the course of history.

Paul's answer to the dilemma of false teachers is that pastors "[hold] fast the faithful word as [they have] been taught, that [they] may be able by sound doctrine both to exhort and to convince the gainsayers" (Titus 1:9). Paul even says that the mouths of these false teachers "must be stopped" (v. 11). We desperately need the men who lead our churches to be able to do that and equip the flock to do the same.

The sound doctrine that pastors are to teach is found in chapters 2–3. In chapter 2, Paul lays out sound doctrine for older men, older women, younger women, younger men, and servants. In chapter 3, Paul commands Titus to remind all in the church of their past sinful condition and the amazing kindness and love that God has shown to them. He also lays out the biblical method for dealing with heretics (those who do not hold to or teach sound doctrine): Admonish them two times, and if they continue to hold to or teach false doctrine, put them out (3:10–11). Paul concludes with a reminder to all of us to "learn to maintain good works" so that we do not become unfruitful (Titus 3:14). An unfruitful Christian is, simply, a contradiction.

Additional highlights from Paul's letter to Titus:

- Titus 1:16 – Be discerning. False teachers profess that they know God and can present a very spiritual-looking front. Upon closer examination, however, they deny God with the life that they live. In the end, it isn't their profession that will matter, only God's (Matt. 7:23).

- Titus 2:11–12 – The same grace that *saves* us also *teaches* us to live soberly, righteously, and godly in this present world. That's why Paul said in Romans 6:1–2, "Shall we continue in sin that grace may abound? God forbid. How shall we that are dead to sin live any longer therein?" If we live with the constant reminder of what Jesus did for us when He saved us from our sin, we will stand daily in awe of His grace, and sin will no longer have dominion over us. That's how grace teaches us to live a life that is pleasing to our Savior!

PHILEMON

In Philemon, God paints for us a beautiful picture of grace, mercy, and forgiveness. Philemon was Paul's personal friend whom he had apparently had led to the Lord (v. 19). One of Philemon's slaves, Onesimus, apparently stole from his master and fled to Rome, where he is somehow imprisoned and meets Paul, who leads him to the Lord as well. Paul realized that for Onesimus to be all that God intended him to be, he would need to make things right with his master. So Paul writes this short letter to his friend, Philemon, asking him to receive Onesimus back into his house, not just as a slave, but as a brother in the Lord!

In this letter God paints a number of incredible pictures for us through the three main characters.

1. Philemon is a picture of God the Father
   - He was righteous (v. 7; Jer. 23:6)
   - He was wealthy (vs. 2, 7, 11; Hag. 2:8)
   - The church was his habitation (v. 2; Eph. 2:22)
   - He was a caring householder (vs. 2, 5, 7; Eph. 2:19)
   - He had been violated (vs. 11, 18–19; Rom. 3:23)
   - He was the legal owner (v. 16; 1 Cor. 6:20)

2. Onesimus is a picture of us, as redeemed sinners
   - He was a slave (v. 16; Rom. 7:14)
   - He was an unprofitable servant. (v. 11; Matt. 25:30; Rom. 5:12)
   - He desired freedom. (v. 15; Gen. 3:1–6)
   - His quest for freedom found him imprisoned. (v. 10; Rom. 6:17)
   - In desperation, he received God's liberating grace! (v. 11; Eph. 2:8–9)

3. Paul is a picture of Jesus Christ
   - He was a prisoner on behalf of the gospel. (v. 10; Isa. 53:8; John 18:28)
   - He intercedes to the wealthy householder for the unprofitable servant (vs. 10–11; Heb. 7:25)
   - He will do nothing without the householder's permission (v. 14; John 6:38)
   - He was willing and able to pay the servant's debt (vs. 18–19; 1 Tim. 2:6)
   - He asks that the violator be received just as he would be received (vs. 12, 17; Rom. 8:17)
   - He secures for the restored a place to dwell (v. 22; John 14:1–2)
   - He soon returns to the householder (v. 22; John 14:3)

52 WEEKS OF PURSUIT

WEEK 51, DAY 1: TODAY'S READING: HEBREWS 1-6

OVERVIEW:
Comparing Christ to the angels (chapters 1–2); comparing Christ to Moses (chapter 3); comparing our rest in Christ to the rest of the Promised Land (chapter 4); comparing Christ as our high priest to the priests of the Old Testament (chapters 5–6).

HIGHLIGHTS & INSIGHTS:
The book of Hebrews begins a section of the New Testament that often causes problems when believers view it through Christian glasses. Christian glasses are fine for a book that is addressed to the local church (or a leader of a local church), but they can pose some pretty serious doctrinal issues if you leave them on when reading other books of the Bible. As with Matthew and Acts, we must read the book of Hebrews in the correct context, keeping the Jews (the Nation of Israel) in place as the "ancient landmark" lest we enter "the fields of the fatherless" (Prov. 22:28; Prov. 23:10).

Many church-age believers struggle to "rightly" divide (2 Tim. 2:15) the book of Hebrews. But we can clear up most of the difficulties by simply asking ourselves, "To whom was the book of Hebrews written?" Was it a local church? No. Was it a pastor of a local church? No. How about Gentiles? Good guess, but, no. Could it have been … the Hebrews? Yes! You must be a seminary graduate to understand something that deep! The book of Hebrews was written to Hebrews. Imagine that! And not recognizing that Paul is specifically addressing Hebrews (Jews) in the book of *Hebrews* will make our study of this book a "fatherless field."

The twofold theme of the book of Hebrews is:

- The *superiority* of Christ
- The *New* Covenant compared to the *Old* Covenant

The key word in this book is the word *better*. We have…

- A better *testament* (7:22)
- A better *covenant* (8:6)
- Better *promises* (8:6)
- A better *sacrifice* (9:23)
- Better *blood* (12:24)
- Better *substance* (10:34)
- A better *hope* (7:19)
- A better *country* (11:16)
- A better *resurrection* (11:35)

The word *better* also provides an easy breakdown of the book:

- Christ is better than the Angels (chapters 1–2)
- Christ is better than Moses (chapter 3)
- Christ is better than Joshua (chapter 4)
- Christ is a better High Priest (chapters 5–7)
- Christ established a better Covenant (chapters 8–13)

Historically, the book of Hebrews was written to reveal the establishment of the new covenant by

Jesus Christ. It is actually the written form of what the Apostle Paul did when entering cities for the first time to proclaim the gospel. Acts 17:2–3 reveals that Paul's standard operating procedure in a new city was to go first to the Jewish synagogue and reason from the scriptures how Christ was the Messiah. In those synagogues, obviously, Paul would have been speaking predominantly to Hebrews.

Doctrinally (or Prophetically), the book of Hebrews is written for the benefit of Jews during the Tribulation. God is not finished dealing with the Nation of Israel (Rom. 11). On God's timetable, we are presently living in a parenthesis called the church age. After the rapture of the church, God will once again deal directly with the Nation of Israel. If you were a Jew in the Tribulation and you realized that you and your people had missed the Messiah when Christ came the first time, as you look through the table of contents for the New Testament, what book do you think you would be most inclined to read? How about the one addressed specifically to you? The book of Hebrews!

Devotionally, however, we can still learn a tremendous amount about the new covenant and Christ's sacrifice for us even though the book of Hebrews is not written directly to us (the church). The book also clearly reveals how Christ is the reality of the pictures and types contained in the Old Testament, as well as some of the clearest teaching on the effectiveness of Christ's sacrifice—how that from God's perspective, it was the "one sacrifice for sins for ever"! Hallelujah! So, the book has a very profitable practical application for us (2 Tim. 3:16)!

Finally, there are three clear warning passages contained in the first six chapters of Hebrews (2:1–4; 3:7–4:13; 5:11–6:20). These passages are usually a place where many well-meaning people lose their way.

Historically, these passages apply in two ways. First, to those Hebrews who had already placed their faith in Christ, these passages are an exhortation to hold fast to that faith. This would be similar to the teaching we see in Galatians, where Paul actually calls believers "foolish," even though they had trusted Christ. Second, to Hebrews who had not placed their faith in Christ alone, these warnings serve as a call to salvation. These unbelieving Hebrews needed to realize that Christ is the fulfillment of what they believed was true (the Old Testament) and to embrace the new covenant Christ had established.

Doctrinally (Prophetically), these warning passages will serve in the future as an exhortation to Hebrews during the Tribulation to remain true to Christ and endure until the end. This corresponds to Christ's teaching in Matthew 24:13, that those who endure until the end shall be saved. As we saw in Matthew 24, the context of that passage is not the church age, but rather the time immediately preceding the Second Coming of Christ, the Tribulation.

52 WEEKS OF PURSUIT

WEEK 51, DAY 2: TODAY'S READING: HEBREWS 7-10

OVERVIEW:
Christ's priesthood superior to the Levitical priesthood (chapter 7); the Old Covenant was a shadow of the real (chapter 8); the Old Covenant sacrifices were temporary (chapter 9); Christ's sacrifice is permanent (chapter 10).

HIGHLIGHTS & INSIGHTS:
Today's reading provides one of the most complete explanations about the superiority of Christ when compared to pretty much everything and the superiority of the New Covenant when compared to the Old Covenant.

In chapter 7, Paul identifies Christ as a Priest after the order of Melchisedec. (The story of Melchisedec is found in Genesis 14:17–20.) This connection is tremendously significant because it reveals to us that Christ is not a priest after the Levitical priesthood which started with Aaron (Heb. 7:11). The Levitical priesthood was comprised of *men*—men who were sinners! Before those priests could offer sacrifices for the people, they first had to offer sacrifices for *themselves* (Heb. 7:27), and these sacrifices were required to be made daily and repeatedly. But Christ is a High Priest after Melchisedec (Heb. 7:24–28)! Christ was not a sinner. Christ does not have to offer sacrifices daily. Christ is a High Priest forever because He lives forever and makes intercession for us. Perfection could never come from the Levitical priesthood; it could only come from a different priesthood and a different priest. Our perfection comes from our High Priest, the Lord Jesus Christ!

And who is this mysterious Melchisedec? Allow me to lay out what Hebrews 7 reveals concerning him:

- He is the King of Righteousness (7:2a)
- He is the King of Salem, or the King of Peace (7:2b)
- He is the Priest of the Most High God (7:1)
- He has no father, mother or descent (7:3a)
- He has no beginning or end (7:3b)
- He is great (7:4a)
- He receives tithes (7:4b)
- He receives worship (7:1d)
- He is without sin (7:27)

Obviously, Melchisedec was an Old Testament appearance of the only One this simple list perfectly describes! He is, no doubt, our very Lord Jesus Christ!

God also reveals in chapter 8 that the sanctuary and tabernacle of the Old Covenant were a *shadow* of the real sanctuary and tabernacle inhabited by God in the heavens. Obviously, a shadow is a basic representation of something tangible and real. It can form a general outline of something. It can help someone identify what a particular thing is—whether a person, a tree, a bicycle, a car. But a shadow is not, and never can be, the real thing! Imagine someone wanting to have a conversation with your shadow. It's ridiculous—and that's exactly God's point! He's trying to get the Hebrews to recognize that they were still caught up worshipping in the shadows of the earthly representation of the tabernacle and sanctuary that were intended to point them to the reality of Christ!

And this isn't just a 1st century, Jewish problem! Many Jews and Gentiles in the 21st century do the same thing by not realizing that religion is merely a *shadow*—there is nothing *real* in religion. It may make people feel better to go to church, to give their money, to do good works, to sing nice songs, or to be the best person they can possibly be, but none of these *shadows* can change the *reality* of their sin! Tragically, many people today still embrace the shadow instead of embracing the reality, Jesus Christ!

The Old Covenant revealed within itself that it was not, of itself, sufficient. The holy of holies in the Old Covenant could only be entered once per year on the Day of Atonement. Thus it could not be the way into the holiest of all (God's tabernacle—not the earthly one). It was simply a figure, a shadow, imposed by the law until "time of reformation" (Heb. 9:10). None of the work carried out by the high priest of the Old Testament could perfect his own conscience, much less the conscience of the people. But then the "time of reformation" did come—and we're not talking about Martin Luther! The real High Priest showed up—an everlasting High Priest—the High Priest of the true tabernacle. And the blood offered by this High Priest was not the blood of bulls and goats, but was *His very own* blood—the blood of God! His sacrifice can purge our conscience, and His blood established a brand new covenant.

And how much greater is this New Covenant than the old one! The blood of bulls and goats (or anything else) never could, never can, and never will be able to take away sin. But this Priest, this man, the "God–man," the Lord Jesus Christ offered *one* sacrifice for sins forever! There is no other sacrifice needed. There is no other sacrifice required by God. And any other sacrifice we attempt to offer becomes an affront to God because what it actually says is that we don't believe the sacrifice of His Son was sufficient.

And let's get practical for a minute. Sometimes after we fall prey to sin, we unwittingly add to Christ's sacrifice by attempting to feel really, really bad about our sin (a form of the unbiblical practice of the Roman Catholic penance). Other times, when we've sinned against God, we think we can sacrifice for it by giving more, reading more, praying more, witnessing more, or promising to do better the next time. But do you know how much these sacrifices actually accomplish concerning our sin? *Nothing*! We can't add anything or take anything away from Christ's one sacrifice. We must trust His sacrifice, and His sacrifice alone—not our own sacrifice, or anything we may attempt to add to the gift of Christ's sacrifice. This is why the false gospel that is preached by Roman Catholicism cannot save. It is a message that says Christ is still being sacrificed for sin (the mass) and that, although you're forgiven, you must still pay for your sin (purgatory). May we simply trust the once-for-all sacrifice offered by our perfect High Priest and rest completely in Him and the forgiveness of sin found in Him. And may we proclaim the message of the New Covenant so that others may get out of the *shadows* and into the *reality* of Christ!

52 WEEKS OF PURSUIT

WEEK 51, DAY 3: TODAY'S READING: HEBREWS 11-13

OVERVIEW:
The examples of living by faith (chapter 11); the necessity of chastisement (chapter 12:1–6); the exhortation to endure (chapter 12:7–28); remembering others (chapter 13).

HIGHLIGHTS & INSIGHTS:
Hebrews 11, the "Hall of Faith," is one of the most popular chapters in the Bible. Using real-life examples, it lays out for us what it means to live by faith. Most Christians know God wants us to live and walk by faith, but what that actually means can seem vague. In chapter 11, God presents a panorama of men and women who walked by faith so that we can see what living and walking by faith looks like in real life!

But many times, we read a chapter like Hebrews 11 and think that we could never be like these great men and women of God. How easily we forget that these "great" people were not perfect.

- Noah got drunk after the flood
- Abraham lied about his wife (twice!) because he was more concerned about himself than about her
- Sarah thought she needed to help God out with His promise to Abraham
- Jacob deceived and lied to his father in order to get his father's blessing
- Moses was willing to kill a man in his "service" to God
- Rahab was a harlot
- Samson wasted most of his life and ability pleasing himself
- David committed adultery and murder

The biblical reality of these "great men and women of God" in Hebrews 11, whom we tend to hold up as superstars (or supersaints), is that they were *flawed* men and women just like me and you. These very normal people pleased God because they did something very *abnormal*! They exercised faith in God and His Word! That, my friend, pleases our God (11:6), and ultimately, that is why we exist—to bring Him pleasure (Rev. 4:11).

Obviously, we could make tremendous amounts of personal application from this chapter, but we will only touch on two important points.

1. Biblical faith results in action

Each example God lists in this chapter is an action that had its root in faith. It was something a person did "by faith." And when we are walking "by faith," it is because we are "walking in the Spirit" (Gal. 5:16). That is crucial. Galatians 5:22 says that *faith* is part of the fruit the Spirit produces when we are walking in Him. Simply put, without faith it is impossible to please God (Heb. 11:6), but it is impossible to have faith apart from the filling of the Spirit!

2. Biblical faith changes our values

As Laodiceans, we want what we think is the best of both worlds. We want to walk with God, but we also want to enjoy the pleasures of this life (11:15, 25). Biblical faith enables us to see the emptiness and vanity of this world. Verse 14 says that biblical faith seeks a different "country," what verse 15 calls a "better country"! Biblical faith looks for a city "whose builder and maker is God" (11:10). We may need to ask ourselves, "What *city* and what *country* would God say I'm presently seeking by the actions of my life?"

3. Biblical faith is what pleases God.

We easily fall into the trap of thinking that God is pleased by all of the stuff we do: we go to church, we're good stewards of the money God entrusts to us, we read the Bible, we pray. And all of those things are important and are most certainly part of our obedience. But it is possible to do all of those things (and more!) in the power of the *flesh*, totally apart from *faith*! In light of this chapter, we should ask ourselves this simple question: Is Christ living His life *through* me by the power of faith (2 Cor. 4:10) or am I trying to live *for* God in the power of the *flesh*? Biblical faith will always result in actions, but those same actions produced by the arm of the flesh in an attempt to please God will fall absolutely flat and are nothing but wood, hay and stubble (1 Cor. 3:12).

The only way we will ever live a life of faith is to follow the admonition of 12:2: we must "look unto Jesus." Our sights must be set on Him. He must be the goal we strive to attain. And not only are we commanded and admonished to "look unto Jesus," but we are to do so "diligently" (12:15)! May we get our eyes off of ourselves, off of others, off of this world and onto the Lord Jesus Christ today May He be *pleased* by our life of *faith* in Him.

52 WEEKS OF PURSUIT

WEEK 51, DAY 4: TODAY'S READING: JAMES 1-5

OVERVIEW:
Patience in tribulation (chapter 1); encouraging impartiality (chapter 2); the power of the tongue (chapter 3); true humility (chapter 4); the failure of money (5:1–6); the blessedness of patience (5:7–12); the power of prayer (5:13–20).

HIGHLIGHTS & INSIGHTS:
Just as with the book of Hebrews, we must start in the book of James with a simple question: "To whom is this book written?" Most people read the book of James without considering that fundamental question, thinking it's just like the letters written to local churches or leaders of local churches (Romans–Philemon). But James is not written to a local church or a leader of a local church. In the very first chapter and verse, James lets us know very specifically that he is writing to "the twelve tribes scattered abroad"—or Jews!

The key principle of this book is that God intends for genuine, biblical faith to result in a changed life. Historically, this book was written to Jews who had made a profession of faith in Christ to teach them that their faith should and will change their life. Prophetically, James is written to Jews living during the Tribulation to teach them how to live out their faith in difficult circumstances. In a Devotional sense, this book is a practical manual to help us understand how our faith should be lived out.

The book can easily be broken down by chapter.

- Chapter 1 – Real faith should endure temptation
- Chapter 2 – Real faith should show no partiality
- Chapter 3 – Real faith should change our speech
- Chapter 4 – Real faith should transform our relationships
- Chapter 5 – Real faith should anticipate Christ's return

We can make many practical applications from the book of James. Here are just a few to help you get started:

- Be a doer of the Word (1:22–25)

As Laodiceans, we often feel that we are sitting in a good place spiritually because we *know* quite a bit about the Bible. God clearly reveals that it is not what you know, but what you *do with what you know* that is important. We need to judge ourselves the way God does—not based on our knowledge, but based on our walk.

- See how God sees (2:1–13)

Who do we give preferential treatment to? We may not banish the poor to the back rows while escorting the rich to the front as James describes, but do we view the poor or other people groups the same way we esteem the rich and successful? Are we willing to talk to the visitors at church that we think are sharp, but show little interest in those that don't look like "our kind"? We must seek to reach out to those whom Christ is touching regardless of their socio–economic status, race, or background.

- Watch your mouth (3:1–18)

The questions James suggests in this passage are convicting! How is it that the same mouth can speak both blessing and cursing? How can we pray and sing such awesome words to God, but be so rude and cutting when talking to and about people? James is right, "My brethren, these things ought not so to be" (v. 10).

- Humble yourself before God (4:1–10)

In our culture, when we are taught from an early age to watch out for ourselves. Our natural thought process is to lift up ourselves in the sight of others. God's command is the complete opposite. We are to humble ourselves before Him, and then His grace will work in us to lift us up. I love Andrew Murray's comment concerning humility: "Humility is not thinking meanly about yourself. It is not thinking of yourself at all."

- God answers prayer (5:14–18)

None of us would *say* that God doesn't answer prayer, but our actions often reveal that we really *believe* exactly that. Do we really believe God hears us and cares about the needs we bring before Him? Do we really believe that the "effectual fervent prayer of a righteous man availeth much" (v. 16)? If the answer to these questions in our lives is yes, it will be made manifest in at least one very specific activity—we will *pray*!

May we apply the incredibly practical truths of this book today, allowing God's grace and power to be displayed in and through us.

52 WEEKS OF PURSUIT

WEEK 51, DAY 5: TODAY'S READING: 1 PETER 1-5

OVERVIEW:
The call to be holy (chapter 1); Jesus Christ is our cornerstone (2:1–10); learning to submit (2:11–25); the relationship between a husband and wife (3:1–7); admonitions toward personal and practical holiness (3:8–12); suffering for the right reasons (3:13–4:19); admonitions to elders (5:1–4); more admonitions toward personal and practical holiness (5:5–14).

HIGHLIGHTS & INSIGHTS:
In this letter to Gentile believers who were enduring intense suffering, Peter begins by pointing out the "lively hope" that was theirs because of "the resurrection of Jesus Christ" (1:3). He reminds them that, though all of their earthly possessions may be taken away (as had happened to many of them), God has promised them "an inheritance incorruptible, and undefiled, and that fadeth not away," which has been "reserved in heaven" for them (v. 4). Peter reminds them that God's promise would make life in the future glorious and joyful, but he also recognized that, for the present time, these believers were "in heaviness through manifold temptations" or trials (1:6).

THE TRUTH ABOUT TRIALS
1 Peter 1:7 is a blockbuster verse that explains several key truths about the trials, difficulties, and sufferings we endure in this life:

1. Rather than random acts of fate, they are the God-ordained "trying of our faith." In other words, trials are God's way of allowing our faith to be put on the witness stand so He can see what it's made of (Deut. 8:2).

2. Peter has an unusual perspective on trials. They are situations where it feels as if the bottom has dropped out of our lives. But while we describe them as uncomfortable or unwanted, Peter calls them precious. Not that our trials are precious in and of themselves. They are precious because of what they accomplish! God has designed the trial of our faith so that we "might be found unto praise and honor and glory" at our ultimate accounting before the Lord Jesus Christ at His appearing. Could there be anything more valuable or precious than being found "unto praise, honor and glory" in that day? Peter is saying that knowing that future result of our trials should have a major impact on our attitude as we go through them today.

3. Peter compares our experience of these trials to the process of refining gold. For men, gold is the most precious commodity on earth, but from God's perspective, the most precious commodity is our faith. And just as gold is purified and refined in fire, so also is our faith!

Through these truths, Peter gives his readers, in the 1st century and today, the hope and confidence we need to face the trials of life.

PERSONAL HOLINESS AND TRIALS
The main theme of 1 Peter is personal holiness. But personal holiness is connected to trials. Why? The lust of the flesh does not have same pull in times of suffering that it has at other times. Peter says, "For he that hath suffered in the flesh hath ceased from sin; That he no longer should live the rest of his time in the flesh to the lusts of men, but to the will of God" (4:1–2).

Personal holiness is much more than a list of things we should and should not do. While holiness has a tremendous bearing on our actions, that's not what God meant when He said, "Be ye holy: for I am holy" (1:16). Being holy is about God working in us to make us like Himself. He changes us from the inside out, not the outside in. Holiness is, first and foremost, about being—not doing. And when we are who God wants us to be, we'll do what God wants us to do (though the opposite is not necessarily true).

PERSONAL HOLINESS AND AUTHORITIES

In 2:13–25, Peter connects holiness to submission to the authorities God has placed in our lives. Even when those authorities are wrong or have a froward attitude, we are to submit. Interestingly, in the 21st century we have Christian organizations and lawyers fighting for Christians' rights. Clearly, submission doesn't mean Christians can't use the law to change things. And if the authorities in our lives are demanding that we violate the Word of God, "we ought to obey God rather than men" (Acts 5:29)! But demanding our rights is a concept foreign to the Bible. God never intended Christians to be political revolutionaries, lest the message of the gospel be lost. In 2:21–25, Jesus is our example of submitting to those in authority even when they are wrong. In fact, God says it is "thankworthy" if we suffer wrongfully for being a Christian (2:19). When we do, we remind Him of His Son, and it fills Him with thanks. (Imagine the God of the universe thanking us!) In truth, I'm convinced that fighting for our rights is really about not wanting to suffer!

PERSONAL HOLINESS AND MARRIAGE

Holiness also expresses itself in a right relationship with our spouse, with husbands honoring their wives and wives submitting to their husbands (3:1–7). And, according to this passage, carrying out our biblical responsibilities to our spouse is not dependent on whether or not they fulfill theirs. Husbands are to honor their wives, even if she isn't worthy of honor, and wives are to submit to their husbands, even if he isn't obeying the Word of God (3:1, 7). Men cannot honor the Lord—and women cannot be subject to the Lord—without doing so. And men, pay attention to the brief statement found at the end of verse 7. If we refuse to fulfill our biblical responsibilities to our wives, God will refuse to answer our prayers. This is a key reason why men in the 21st century have so few answered prayers!

PERSONAL HOLINESS AND OTHER BELIEVERS

Peter also demonstrates that holiness expresses itself in love, compassion, and unity with other believers in our local church (3:8–11). True holiness doesn't render "evil for evil, or railing for railing: but … blessing" (v. 9). Other believers will wrong us (Luke 17:1; Rom. 12:18). But when they do, we can choose our response. Will we give evil for evil and railing for railing, or will we return blessing? Will we speak evilly and with guile or speak good things (3:10–11a)? Will we passionately seek peace, or will we allow evil to prevail in the conflict (3:11b–12)?

This is a recurring theme in 1 Peter: love the brethren and endure suffering for Christ. And those two things seem to be the hardest for us to do. Our pride makes us unwilling to cover the sins of others when they wrong us (4:8) and makes us think that we deserve better in the midst of suffering. Thus, God commands us to "humble [ourselves] …under the mighty hand of God" (5:6). How do we do that? God completes the thought in verse 7: by "casting all [our] care upon Him]! This verse is usually applied in times of sorrow, and rightfully so, because God certainly cares for us and is interested in our problems. But this verse does not apply only to the cares that make us sorrowful, but also to everything we find ourselves caring about (our finances, our careers, our families, our future). 1 Peter 5:7 says to cast *all of our cares* upon Him, to genuinely surrender every aspect of our lives to Him. That's genuine humility. And when we're completely yielded to Him, He pours out His grace (the desire and power to obey God) upon us (James 4:6).

52 WEEKS OF **PURSUIT**

WEEK 51, DAY 6: **TODAY'S READING: 2 PETER 1-3**

OVERVIEW:
The divine strategy for our spiritual growth and development (1:1–15); the superiority of God's Word to experience (1:16–21); false prophets and teachers (chapter 2); the Second Coming of Christ (chapter 3).

HIGHLIGHTS & INSIGHTS:
In Peter's second epistle, he reminds these believers of truths they already knew, but needed to have "always in remembrance" (1:12). We, too, need to be reminded of what we already know because there is a major difference between knowing something in our minds and seeing it active in our lives. That's what 2 Peter is all about.

The most important decision any person will make is the decision to come to Christ or, as Peter says, to "obtain like precious faith with us" (1:1). What an incredible reality, that the faith we have in Christ today is the same faith that apostles like Peter had. The power that saved the apostles is the same power that saved us!

In chapter 1, we discover that coming to faith in Christ isn't an end—it's the beginning! Sometimes the journey of coming to faith in Christ can be long and hard. By the time many people call on the name of the Lord by faith, they feel such a sense of relief and release. They feel the journey is over. But God has much more in mind for our lives than simply coming to faith. As vital as that is, He intends for the "grace and peace" we experienced in salvation to be "multiplied" throughout our lifetime (1:2) until we make our entrance into His "everlasting kingdom" (1:11).

In 1:5–7, Peter says that, after coming to faith in Christ, we are to "give all diligence" to add seven things to that faith. Adding these seven things is so important that he doesn't command us to just "give diligence," but to "give *all* diligence" to add them. We are to make this our focus and pursuit for the remainder of our lives!

The seven things Peter tells us to "give *all* diligence" to add are *sequential*. They are not to be added to our lives randomly over the course of our lifetime. The grammar in verses 5–7 dictates that these seven things be added in order. First we are to "give *all* diligence" to add *virtue* to our faith. Once virtue has been established, then we begin the process of adding the second thing—*knowledge*. But knowledge doesn't get added to faith—it gets added to virtue. Then when we add *temperance*, it gets added to knowledge. And the remaining four things follow this same pattern. The plan laid out in these verses is what I like to call "The Divine Strategy For Spiritual Growth." This strategy will never be improved and should be not only what we build our personal lives upon, but also the strategy every church should employ for growing its people!

That God commands us to "give *all* diligence" should certainly motivate us to drop our present pursuits and pursue these seven things continuously. But in verses 8–11, Peter pushes the importance of these things into an entirely different realm! He begins by listing three *positive guarantees* for what will happen in our lives if we will "give *all* diligence" to add these seven things.

1. We will truly *know* Jesus.

    That is awesome! And remember, knowing Him is what "life eternal" is really all about (John 17:3).

2. We will never *fall*.

    What a tremendous promise that is, especially when you stop to consider that

    - Adam, the most perfect man who ever lived other than Christ Himself—fell!
    - David, "the man after God's own heart"—fell!

- Solomon, the wisest man who ever lived—fell!
- Samson, the strongest man who ever lived—fell!
- Thousands of others through the centuries who were just as sincere in their faith as any of us are in ours—fell!

But according to Peter, if we will "give *all* diligence" to adding these seven things to our lives, we will *never fall*! That is quite the guarantee!

3. Our entrance into the everlasting kingdom will be *abundant*.

    When it's all said and done, when our life is over and we walk out of the Judgment Seat of Christ and into the everlasting kingdom, if we added these seven things, our entrance into that kingdom is going to be everything God intended for it to be. It will be *abundant*!

There simply aren't three guarantees that could be more powerful and positive then these. But Peter doesn't stop there. He also gives three *negative guarantees* if we neglect to add the seven things.

1. We will become *blind*.

    Jesus said that one of the chief characteristics of believers in the last days is that they are spiritually *blind* (Rev. 3:17). Blind to the *Word* of God, blind to the *work* and *working* of God, and blind to the *will* of God.

2. We will be unable to see into the *eternal realm*.

    Peter says that we won't be able to "see afar off" (1:9b). We won't be able to see, as Paul did, "the things which are not seen" (2 Cor. 4:18), the things in the eternal realm that are seen only through the eyes of faith.

3. We will end up *living like we did before we were saved*.

    Peter says we will forget that we were "purged from [our] old sins" (v. 9). We will end up living like we did before we came to faith.

With those six guarantees (three extremely positive and three extremely negative), how could we not spend the rest of our lives "giving *all* diligence" to add these seven things? Peter was so sure that this was what we were to give the rest of our lives to that he basically says this in verses 12–15:

"Listen—these seven things are so significant to what you do with the rest of your life, that I don't care whether you're already established in them or not. I'm not going to stop talking about them. I'm going to approach them as if you've never even heard them. I'm going to take every ounce of energy I have for the remainder of my life to stir you up about being established in these seven things because the Lord has revealed to me that my days on this planet are limited. So I'm going to 'give *all* diligence' to make sure you 'give *all* diligence' to add these seven things right now, and every day of your life for the rest of your life—even long after I'm dead and gone!"

I'd say the old boy was pretty enamored by those seven things! Oh, may we be likewise!

52 WEEKS OF **PURSUIT**

WEEK 52, DAY 1: **TODAY'S READING: 1 JOHN 1-5**

OVERVIEW:
People with the assurance of their salvation confess sin (chapter 1); people with the assurance of their salvation don't love the world's system (chapter 2); people with the assurance of their salvation purify their lives (chapter 3); people with the assurance of their salvation love God and His children (chapter 4); people with the assurance of their salvation believe the Bible (chapter 5).

HIGHLIGHTS & INSIGHTS:
Every person on this planet wants peace, joy, and security. And the book of 1 John was written and included in the canon of Scripture to explain just how we can get them.

- Peace with God

    1 John begins, "That which we have seen and heard declare we unto you, that [for this purpose] ye also may have fellowship with us: and truly our fellowship is with the Father, and with his Son Jesus Christ" (1:3). *Peace* with God is the result of *fellowship*, our relationship with God through the Lord Jesus Christ.

- Fullness of Joy

    John continues, "And these things write we unto you, that [again, for this purpose] your joy may be full" (1:4). *Joy* is the result of the first *purpose* (peace with God).

- Security for the Future

    1 John 5:13 says, "These things have I written unto you that believe on the name of the Son of God; that [once again, for this purpose] ye may know that ye have eternal life." This is really the key to the first two purposes because we will never experience the peace *of* God or peace *with* God, nor the fullness of *joy*, until we know beyond a shadow of a doubt that we have been born again. From a Devotional standpoint, the book of 1 John is in the Bible to provide the *assurance* of our salvation. (And there are people who are genuinely saved that simply don't have the assurance that they are!) It is written so we can know we're saved. In fact, the word *know*, or some form of it, is found 27 times in this book.

Every person who is genuinely born again is eternally secure. The book of Ephesians teaches us that as members of the body of Christ, upon our salvation, we were actually placed in Christ and "sealed with that Holy Spirit of promise, which is the earnest [downpayment; engagement ring] of our inheritance until the redemption of the purchased possession, unto the praise of his glory" (Eph. 1:13–14). If we have genuinely been born again, there is no question that we are eternally secure. So the first important question is, "Have we genuinely been born again?" And if we have, "How can we have assurance that we are?"

In 1 John, God provides the criteria we are to use to find assurance of our salvation: "These things have I written unto you that believe on the name of the Son of God; that ye may know that ye have eternal life, and that ye may believe on the name of the Son of God" (5:13). The "these things" that John said were written to let us know that we have eternal life are, specifically, chapters 1–5 of the book God was using him to write.

The book of 1 John actually presents two simple tests that will give us the assurance of our salvation: a *doctrinal* test and a *moral* test. Basically, all John does throughout this entire book is present and expound upon these two tests. The doctrinal test has two parts or asks two questions:

1. What did you say about sin?

    In chapter 1, those who are born again are those who have confessed that they are sinners. John says, "If we say that we have not sinned, we make him a liar, and his word is not in us" (1:10).

Salvation is dependent upon the Spirit of God reproving or convicting us of sin, righteousness, and judgment (John 16:8–11) and us responding to the Spirit's conviction by confessing to God that we are helpless and hopeless sinners before Him.

2. What did you say about Christ?

To be saved, God says you must believe that "Jesus is the Christ" (2:22). The word *Christ* means "anointed." The Hebrew word for "anointed" is *Messiah*. The Jews understood that Messiah ("the Christ") would be God in a human body (Isa. 9:6, "mighty God"). To be saved, one must believe that Jesus Christ is God, not *a* god and not one-who-was-created-at-a-point-in-time by God, but *the* one true *God* who alone can take away sin (2:22–23).

The doctrinal test says that those who are saved are those who believe that, because mankind was hopelessly separated from Him by their sin, God became a man in the person of Jesus Christ and that He is the only hope for the forgiveness of sin through the confession of sin. If you (or any person, regardless of their profession) did not believe those two things, you are, very simply, not saved.

So the doctrinal test asks, "What did you believe?" And the *moral* test, asks, "How do you behave?" The moral test, likewise, has two parts:

1. The *Obedience* test

   1 John is screaming that you can *know* you are genuinely saved by your *obedience*. Your obedience doesn't *make* you saved or *keep* you saved—the blood of Jesus Christ applied to your sin secured that (1:7). From a Devotional standpoint, your obedience provides the assurance that you are saved. John says, "He that saith, I know him, and keepeth not his commandments, is a liar, and the truth is not in him. But whoso keepeth his word, in him verily is the love of God perfected: hereby know we that we are in him. He that saith he abideth in him ought himself also so to walk, even as he walked" (2:4–6). Christians do sin (2:1) and are capable of walking in disobedience (the Corinthians!), but when they do, they will find that they struggle to have the assurance of their salvation and will therefore struggle to experience peace and joy.

2. The *Love* test

   The love test has three parts, each of which is repeated throughout the book. First of all, those who are saved *love God*. This part is put very succinctly in 4:19, "We love him, because he first loved us." Secondly, John says that those who are saved will *love their brothers and sisters*. One of the clearest examples of this part is found in 2:9–11: "He that saith he is in the light, and hateth his brother, is in darkness even until now. He that loveth his brother abideth in the light, and there is none occasion of stumbling in him. But he that hateth his brother is in darkness, and walketh in darkness, and knoweth not whither he goeth, because that darkness hath blinded his eyes." Thirdly, those who are born again will *not love the world*. 1 John 2:15–17 say, "Love not the world, neither the things that are in the world. If any man love the world, the love of the Father is not in him. For all that is in the world, the lust of the flesh, and the lust of the eyes, and the pride of life, is not of the Father, but is of the world. And the world passeth away, and the lust thereof: but he that doeth the will of God abideth for ever."

Truly born-again people can—and do—at times wane in their love for God or struggle at times to love their brothers and sisters or struggle to not love the world and the things in it. But when we do, the result will be a lack of assurance which inevitably leads to a lack of peace and joy.

52 WEEKS OF PURSUIT

WEEK 52, DAY 2: TODAY'S READING: 2 JOHN, 3 JOHN, JUDE

OVERVIEW:
The basis of love (2 John 1–3); the behavior of love (2 John 4–6); the bounds of love (2 John 7–13); the excellence of Gaius (3 John 1–8); the evil of Diotrephes (3 John 9–10); the elevation of Demetrius (3 John 11–14); the command to contend for the faith (Jude 1–4); the condemnation of the counterfeits of the faith (Jude 5–16); the call to surrender in our faith (Jude 17–25).

HIGHLIGHTS & INSIGHTS:

2 JOHN

2 John is an important book of the Bible for those of us living in the last days. Many in Christian circles today say, "Let's drop our petty doctrines for the sake of love." The book of 2 John is in our Bible to tell us the exact opposite!

In the first verse, John refers to himself as "the elder." He is not referring to a position or office in the church, but to his age. John is an old man by the time he writes this book—probably between 80–90 years old. And he is writing to "the elect lady." She is not mentioned by name, but is obviously someone with whom John has a very close relationship, as he affirms his love both for her and for her children.

While she is not named, we may surmise that this lady's husband had passed away and that her children were now grown. She has a passion for ministry, compassion for people, and wanted to use her home as a tool for the Lord by housing itinerant preachers and teachers on their journeys. She is obviously a very good-hearted and loving lady.

In John's travels, however, he has come in contact with this elect lady's nieces and nephews (v. 13), who have informed him of something that alarmed and upset him, that their Aunt, out of so-called love, was welcoming false prophets and teachers into her home (v. 10). John writes to instruct this extremely loving, benevolent, and hospitable lady that the Lord wanted her to be discriminate in her demonstration and expression of love.

The urgency of John's message to this special lady stands out in verse 12: "Having many things to write unto you, I would not write with paper and ink: but I trust to come unto you, and speak face to face, that our joy may be full." We don't know what John shared with her face to face. Obviously, we don't need to know, or the Spirit of God would have inspired John to record it for us. But the Spirit of God clearly wanted us to have the first eleven verses so that God's people would understand how God wants us to respond to false prophets and teachers. This little letter actually shows us how biblical love is to operate when it encounters false doctrine, prophets, and teachers.

In verses 1–3, John says that the basis of genuine, biblical love is *truth*. (The word is repeated five times in four verses!) *Love* and *truth* are inseparably linked in Christianity, and our love cannot be permitted to be governed by anything other than truth! According to these verses, we are not to indiscriminately share love for the sake of love. Rather, we share love for the sake of truth! And when truth is violated, love is to be redirected. Talk about going against the teaching of Laodicean Christianity. But that is the crystal clear teaching of God's Word.

In verses 4–6, we find that, though the basis of love is truth, the *behavior* of love is *obedience*. The elect lady's children are an example for sharing love: they were "walking in truth" (v. 4). And John comes back to the same point he had just made: Walking in love is walking in truth, and walking in truth is walking in love! Simply put, love obeys! It obeys the truth. And when truth is violated, love is not unleashed. The love of the truth keeps love in bounds. Yes, true biblical love has boundaries!

And John defines in verses 7–11 the *boundaries of love*. The reason we must walk in love *and* walk in truth is that "many deceivers are entered into the world, who confess not that Jesus Christ is come in the flesh. This is a deceiver and an antichrist" (v. 7). Unless we understand the biblical connection between truth and love, and unless we are walking in truth and in love, we will never respond to these deceivers and antichrists as God intends. And our response to them is extremely important to God—so important that a wrong response will have a profound impact on us at the judgment seat of Christ! Verse 8 says that we put ourselves in a position of losing rewards that we have already attained ("have wrought") through our previous work! Verse 9 tells us that truth limits the expression of our love toward those who "transgress" the "doctrine of Christ." In other words, when dealing with those who do not teach that Jesus Christ is God in a sinless human body, we are to apply the teaching of verse 10: do not let them in our house and do not tell them "God bless you." To do otherwise, John says in verse 11, is to become a "partaker" in their "evil deeds." (These verses are obviously in reference to someone who comes to you on a mission to propagate false doctrine and not simply those who may have been deceived by false teachers.)

3 JOHN

In the book of 3 John, John describes three main characters: Gaius, Diotrephes and Demetrius. He tells us:

- The excellence of Gaius (vs. 1–8)
- The evil of Diotrephes (vs. 9–10)
- The elevation of Demetrius (vs. 11–14)

And each of us needs to consider an important question: "Which of these three characters am I most like?"

JUDE

The book of Jude, from a Historical standpoint, was written to Jewish believers, charging them to "earnestly contend for the faith" (v. 3) and to endure until the coming of Lord Jesus, their Messiah.

From a Prophetic standpoint, it is written to Tribulation saints to help them identify the Antichrist and his ministers and encourage them to "earnestly contend for the faith" as they await the Second Coming of their Messiah, the Lord Jesus Christ.

And from a Devotional standpoint, Jude teaches us that if we are eagerly awaiting the return of our Lord Jesus Christ, we will also be "earnestly contend[ing] for the faith."

May that be our testimony in these dark and perilous last days!

52 WEEKS OF PURSUIT

WEEK 52, DAY 3: TODAY'S READING: REVELATION 1-5

OVERVIEW:
John's description of the risen and glorified Christ and our Lord's instruction concerning the "Revelation" (chapter 1); the seven letters to the seven churches representing seven periods of church history (chapters 2–3); the scene in heaven following the Rapture and during the Tribulation (chapters 4–5).

HIGHLIGHTS & INSIGHTS:
Today we begin one of the most incredible books of the Bible, the book of Revelation. Many have thought that this book was so shrouded with mysteries that it could never be fully, or perhaps even remotely, understood. Actually, there is very little here that is a mystery, and when it is, it is clearly presented as such and is clearly explained in the passage (1:12, 16, 20). The difficulty in understanding the book of Revelation stems from two basic problems:

1. *Not believing what we read.* When we read Revelation, we ask, "What does the verse or passage mean?" instead of asking "What does it *say*?"—and simply believing it!

2. *Not "rightly dividing the word of truth"* (2 Tim 2:15). As we read Revelation, we don't recognize the key statements or events that reveal to us where a particular verse, chapter, or passage sits on God's prophetic timeline.

One of the easiest ways to understand Revelation is to pay attention to the divisions God has already put in place. In the midst of the various events John describes, something significant happens twice: heaven opens. When heaven opens the first time in 4:1–2, somebody *goes up*. When it opens the second time in 19:11, somebody *comes down*.

In 4:1, heaven opens, and John, a picture of the church, hears a voice, the sound of a trumpet, and, in a moment, in the twinkling of an eye, finds himself in heaven at the very throne of God. Clearly this is a description of the rapture (1 Thess. 4:13–17). In 19:11, heaven opens, and the Lord Jesus Christ comes out of heaven on a white horse with His armies following behind, also on "white horses, clothed in fine linen, white and clean" (19:14). These armies" are clearly the church (19:7–8), and the event is unmistakably the Second Coming. A simple way to distinguish between these two events is that at the rapture, Jesus comes in the clouds *for* His saints (1 Thess. 4:17), and at the Second Coming, Jesus comes to the earth *with* His saints. The rapture ends the church age and ushers in the Tribulation, and the Second Coming ends the Tribulation and ushers in the millennium [*milli*= thousand; *anum*= years] (Rev. 20:1–6).

These two significant events, then, divide the book into three sections: chapters 1–3, chapter 4–19, and chapters 20–22. And in 1:19, God told John that there would be three sections to the Revelation he would receive: "The things which thou *hast seen*" (past), "The things *which are*" (present), and "The things which *shall be* hereafter" (future). So we can make the obvious connection between the three divisions created by the heavens opening and the three sections which God told John to write in 1:19.

However, there is a key we cannot miss when making these connections. John says, "I was in the Spirit on the Lord's day" (1:10). Most assume that he is talking about some Sunday afternoon, that he was simply "walking in the Spirit" as we have been commanded to do (Gal. 5:16) when suddenly he received an incredible "revelation" from God. But that is not what the verse is communicating!

Remember, the phrase "the Lord's day" isn't talking about Sunday. This is the phrase God uses to refer to the theme of the Bible, that thousand-year day that God set aside for Himself way back in Genesis 2:3 (2 Pet. 3:8). In verse 10, John is saying that the Spirit of God catapulted him forward in time to the Day of the Lord, and, from the vantage point of someone in the 21st century at the time of the Lord's second coming, he was to write in the three tenses described in 1:19. So, John wrote the Revelation from the standpoint of "the Lord's Day," and the book of Revelation actually divides like this:

- Chapters 1–3 are "the things which John *hast seen*" (1:19a)—the things which from the standpoint of "the Lord's Day" were in the past. Namely, the events of the church age to the rapture.

- Chapters 4–19 are "the things which *are*" (1:19b)—the things which from the standpoint of "the Lord's Day" were in the present. Namely, the events of the Tribulation to the Second Coming.

- Chapters 20–22 are "the things which *shall be*" (1:19c)—the things which from the standpoint of "the Lord's Day" were yet in the future. Namely, the events of the millennium on into eternity.

These divisions are necessary because this book is "the Revelation of Jesus Christ" (1:1) and our Lord Jesus Christ is He "which is, and which was, and which is to come" (1:8).

With these basic guideposts in place, the book of Revelation is really not very difficult to understand if we simply take it *literally* and *believe* what it *says*. Understanding how the book is divided lets us know what each chapter is detailing and begins to open our eyes to truths that are nothing short of astounding (Ps. 119:18).

For example, when we place the seven letters written to the seven churches in chapters 2–3 in today's reading into the right divisions of the book, we discover they actually represent seven periods of history within the church age. These seven letters outline the history of the church where the book of Acts leaves off all the way up to the rapture, which again is found in Rev. 4:1, immediately after the seventh and final letter to the churches.

The seven letters were addressed to real churches that existed historically in Asia Minor in 95 AD and addressed real needs that these churches were really facing when John received the revelation, but in their context, they also provide a perfect outline to help us interpret the events that have taken place in the history of the church age.

The following is a brief overview of church history as defined by Revelation 2 and 3:

Ephesus	Revelation 2:1–7	90 AD – 200 AD	"Fully Purposed"
Smyrna	Revelation 2:8–11	200 AD – 325 AD	"Bitterness" or "Death"
Pergamos	Revelation 2:12–17	325 AD – 500 AD	"Much Marriage"
Thyatira	Revelation 2:18–29	500 AD – 1000 AD	"Odor of Affliction"
Sardis	Revelation 3:1–6	1000 AD – 1500 AD	"Red Ones"
Philadelphia	Revelation 3:7–13	1500 AD – 1900 AD	"Brotherly Love"
Laodicea	Revelation 3:14–22	1900 – Rapture of the church	"Rights of the People"

52 WEEKS OF **PURSUIT**

WEEK 52, DAY 4: **TODAY'S READING: REVELATION 6-11**

OVERVIEW:
The first account of the Tribulation and Second Coming through the opening of the seven seals (6:1–8:1); the second account of the Tribulation and Second Coming through the sounding of the seven trumpets (8:2–11:19).

HIGHLIGHTS & INSIGHTS:
In chapters 4–5, John revealed the scene *in heaven* immediately following the rapture of the redeemed church of Jesus Christ. In chapter 6, John is revealing to us the scene *on the earth* immediately following the rapture.

This chapter begins the revelation of the Tribulation which, of course, culminates with the Second Coming of Christ. Chapters 6–19 are actually four accounts of these events. This is a significant point if we're going to keep ourselves within the framework of how God has divided the book of Revelation, and it is here that I believe most commentators, theologians, and Bible experts lose their way. They approach these chapters as if they were written linearly or sequentially (first this happens, then this happens, and next that) That is how westerners think, and it usually dictates, not only our approach to life, but also our approach to the Bible.

The Bible, however, is an Eastern book and is written circularly, not linearly. In no place in the Word of God is this more clear than in Revelation 6–19. Rather than one, continuous, sequential timeline in these chapters, God takes us through the same time period (the Tribulation culminating with the Second Coming of Christ) four different times from four different perspectives. Many commentators, theologians, and Bible experts balk at this idea, reasoning, "Why would God do something like that?" And that's a legitimate question. But it's easily answered: that is exactly what God did in the Gospels! The Gospels provide four accounts of the first coming of Christ from four different perspectives, so, because He is unbelievably consistent, before He concludes His revelation to man, God gives us four accounts of the Second Coming of Christ from four different perspectives!

If we fail to see what God is doing in these chapters, the book of Revelation becomes a chaotic nightmare requiring a lot of doctrinal gymnastics to make any kind of logical and chronological sense. With this one simple key (four accounts of the same events), however, this seemingly complex book becomes unbelievably simple.

- God brings us through the first account of the Tribulation and Second Coming through the opening of the seven seals in Revelation 6:1–8:1. Chapter 6 alone provides the first complete account of the Tribulation and Second Coming. The opening of the first five seals (6:1–11) covers the seven years of the Tribulation, and the opening of the sixth seal (6:12–17) is the first account of the Second Coming of Christ.

- In chapters 8:2–11:19, God brings us through the Tribulation and Second Coming for the second complete time through the sounding of the seven trumpets.

- The third account is found in chapters 12–14, as God brings us through the same events in this time period through the revealing of seven personages (or personalities).

- The fourth and final time through the Tribulation and Second Coming is found in chapters 15–19, through the pouring of the seven vials.

Lastly, one of the keys to understanding Revelation is recognizing that John's descriptions are not symbolism that needs to be unraveled or interpreted. Just believe what you're reading, understanding that John is a 1st century man living trying to use 1st century terminology to describe events happening in the 21st century!

52 WEEKS OF PURSUIT

WEEK 52, DAY 5: **TODAY'S READING: REVELATION 12-17**

OVERVIEW:
The third account of the Tribulation and Second Coming through the revealing of the seven personages (chapters 12–14); the fourth account of the Tribulation and Second Coming through the pouring of the seven vials (chapters 15–16); the Babylonish mother (17:1–6); the Babylonish monster (17:7–18).

HIGHLIGHTS & INSIGHTS:
In chapter 12, John begins the third account of the Tribulation and Second Coming that our Lord revealed to him. In this account, these events unfold through the revealing of the seven personages that are found in chapters 12–14.

1. The *woman* (12:1–2, 4–6, 14–17) is clearly the *nation of Israel*
2. The *child* (12:2, 4–5) is the *Lord Jesus Christ*
3. The *dragon* (12:3–4, 7–9, 12–17) is *Satan*
4. The *archangel* (12:7–9) is *Michael*
5. The *Antichrist* (13:1–10) is the *first beast*
6. The *false* prophet, or *second beast* (13:10–18), is not mentioned by name, but will work in conjunction with the Antichrist during the Tribulation
7. The *144,000* (14:1–5) is the final personage. They are the *true Jehovah's Witnesses*

Once again, there are too many things unfolding in these chapters to provide adequate commentary. But because so many Laodicean cults have been spawned by a misunderstanding of and false teaching concerning the 144,000 (the Jehovah's *False* Witnesses, the World-Wide Church of God, the Seventh-Day Adventists and the Mormons, the so-called "Latter Day Saints" and the "Reorganized Church of the Latter Day Saints"), some commentary may be helpful.

The 144,000 mentioned in chapter 14 are the same 144,000 that were mentioned in chapter 7. The only difference between the 144,000 in these two chapters is their location. In chapter 7 they are on the earth. In chapter 14 they are in heaven ("the mount Sion," 14:1).

The bigger question, of course, is who are they? According to 7:4–8, they are 12,000 from each of the twelve tribes of Israel. In other words, they are 144,000 literal, physical Jews. Unfortunately for the aforementioned cults, there is not a Gentile in the bunch! The next time an antichrist (1 John 2:22) comes to your door and tells you they are a part of the 144,000, just ask them which of the 12 Tribes of Israel they're from. Some things are just pretty simple!

These 144,000 Jews will be miraculously converted sometime at the beginning of the Tribulation (7:1–3). Revelation 14:3 says they will be "redeemed from the earth," and verse 4 says they will be "redeemed from among men." It appears that their miraculous conversion will be like that of the Apostle Paul, who referred to himself as "one born out of due time" (1 Cor. 15:8). After their conversion to Christ, the 144,000 will be sealed in their foreheads (7:3) with "the seal of the living God" which is the Father's name: Jehovah (7:2–3; 14:1). They are sealed for three reasons:

1. To Mark God's Personal Possession

    God marks them with His name for the same reason we put our name on what belongs to us. He is saying, "These are mine!"

2. To Guarantee God's Personal Protection

    Placing our name on our possessions may not deter people from messing with it, but the name of

Jehovah is completely different!

3. To Fulfill God's Personal Purpose

God's purpose has always been to reach the whole world. That was His purpose God for Israel in the Old Testament, and it is His purpose for the church. It will still be His purpose through the 144,000 "servants of our God" (7:3) during the Tribulation: "This gospel of the kingdom shall be preached in all the world for a witness unto all nations; and then shall the end come" (the Second Coming, Matt. 24:14). The 144,000 will be the "firstfruits" (Rev. 14:4) of those saved during the Tribulation, and their witness will produce an incredible harvest! According to Revelation 7:9, people from every nation, kindred, people and tongue will respond. They will be like 144,000 invincible Apostle Pauls roaming the earth, evangelizing everywhere they go (Rev. 7:3; 1 Cor. 15:8).

When chapter 14 opens, the 144,000 have been raptured to heaven (14:1–5). In 14:6–13, John reveals God's last call to lost man. This will most likely take place in the final few months, weeks, or even days of the seven-year Tribulation. God gives His last call through four voices that John hears (14:6–13). When chapter 14 closes, the Lord Jesus Christ returns to earth in judgment.(14:14–20; 2 Thess. 1:7–9).

In chapters 15–16, John reveals the fourth and final tour through the Tribulation and Second Coming, this time through the pouring of the seven vials. Think of it this way: for the last six thousand years of human history, God—Who is supremely loving, gracious, merciful and kind—has been storing up His wrath. At the same time, God's name has been defied, disgraced, defamed, ridiculed, reproached, belittled, betrayed, and blasphemed. He has watched and listened from His throne as puny little humans have exalted themselves as if they were God. But while God has been "longsuffering to us–ward, not willing that any should perish, but that all should come to repentance" (2 Pet. 3:9), His wrath has been filling up day after day, stored in seven vials (15:1; 16:1) in the temple of the tabernacle in heaven (15:5–6). The Tribulation is that time when God says, "Enough!" and His wrath is poured out of the vials upon the earth (16:1).

The "woman" described in chapter 17 (also referred to as "the great whore") is a woman we've seen throughout the entire Bible! She is the *strange woman* of the book of Proverbs. She is the *religious woman* of the Tower of Babel. She is "*that woman, Jezebel*" of the book of Revelation (2:20). In this chapter, Go reveals that "the woman" is the false religious system that the Antichrist will use during the Tribulation to unite the world religiously: the Roman Catholic Church.

Beware! The stage is being set right now in these last days of the Laodicean church period for the Antichrist to use that false system to unify the world. Recognizing that fact will help us to interpret some of the events we are presently seeing and will be seeing in the world and in Christianity in the near future!

52 WEEKS OF **PURSUIT**

WEEK 52, DAY 6: **TODAY'S READING: REVELATION 18-22**

OVERVIEW:
The fall of Babylon (chapter 18); the Second Coming of Christ (chapter 19); the millennium (chapter 20); the New Heaven, New Earth and New Jerusalem (chapters 21–22).

HIGHLIGHTS & INSIGHTS:
In chapters 6–19, John brought us through four different accounts of the Tribulation which, of course, culminates with the Second Coming of Christ. The first account (6:1–8:1) was the opening of the seven *seals* (6:1–8:1). From 8:2–11:19, John describes the sounding of the seven *trumpets*. In chapter 12–14, the third account reveals the events through the seven *personages*. And the final account (chapters 15–16) is the pouring out of the seven *vials*.

Chapters 17 and 18 do not advance the events of the book of Revelation beyond chapter 16. Instead, they provide the commentary and explanation of two key verses. Chapter 17 is the explanation of Revelation 14:8 where John says, "And there followed another angel, saying, Babylon is fallen, is fallen, that great city, because she made all nations drink of the wine of the wrath of her fornication." Chapter 18 is the explanation of Revelation 16:19 where John says, "And the great city was divided into three parts, and the cities of the nations fell: and great Babylon came in remembrance before God, to give unto her the cup of the wine of the fierceness of his wrath." Think of it this way: Revelation 17 is a *mystery* form of Babylon where she is a *religious* system. Revelation 18 is a *literal* form of Babylon where she is a *commercial city* (both a political and economic system).

Chapter 19 is the revelation of the greatest event in human history: the Second Coming of Christ (the Day of the Lord). We need to be aware of several key biblical realities about this event.

1. It is the event to which all of God's *Word* has been *Pointing*

We have seen this from the very beginning of our *52 Weeks of Pursuit*. The theme of the Bible is "the Day of the Lord." We read about it in almost every single book of the Old Testament, either specifically or in picture form. It is "that day" when the Lord Jesus Christ finally receives the glory that is due His name!

2. It is the event to which all of God's *Prophets* have been *Preaching*

That's not just my guess or opinion! That is specifically what the Bible says in Acts 3:20–21: "And he shall send Jesus Christ, which before was preached unto you: Whom the heaven must receive until the times of restitution of all things, which God hath spoken by the mouth of *all his holy prophets* since the world began." It is the same event Jude 14 says Enoch was preaching about thousands of years before the first coming of Christ!

3. It is the event to which all of God's *People* have been *Praying*

In fact, Jesus said it is actually to be the first request of prayer: "Thy kingdom come. Thy will be done in earth, as it is in heaven" (Matt. 6:10; Luke 11:2). It becomes the number one prayer of our heart when we recognize that Christ's second coming will be the first time since Adam sinned in the Garden that the Lord Jesus Christ will receive the glory He deserves! In that day, every knee shall bow and every tongue confess that Jesus Christ is Lord to the glory of God the Father (Phil. 2:9–11)!

4. It is the event at which all of God's *Hosts* will be *Praising*

Revelation 19:1–7a describes this praise. We will praise Him because...

- His *salvation* has been fully *exemplified* (19:1)
- His *justice* has been fully *executed* (19:2–4)

- His *sovereignty* has been fully *exercised* (19:5–6)
5. It is the event for which all of God's *Church* has been *Preparing*

This is the day when our marriage to the Lord Jesus Christ will be consummated. According to 19:7–8, we will be wearing the wedding garment that we prepared for ourselves through the righteous life we're presently living. How we live on the earth right now does matter in eternity.

In 19:11–21, John further describes the "greatest event in human history." By the close of the chapter, everyone gets exactly what they deserve. The Lord Jesus Christ finally gets the glory He deserves as King of kings and Lord of lords. The beast (Satan in a human body, the Antichrist), his false prophet, and all of his followers will get exactly what they deserve as they are cast into the "lake of fire" (v. 20). In that day, everyone will get exactly what they deserve, with one incredible exception—us! Because God in His mercy and grace chose to place us in Christ when we called upon His name (Eph. 1:4), He accepts us and receives us as He does His very own Son. As undeserving as we are, because of Christ, we get the glorious privilege of spending eternity with God! Somebody say, "Amen!"

Chapter 20 reveals the Lord Jesus Christ spanking the devil like a two-year-old at Walmart, exercising the power and authority that has always been His, as He establishes His millennial reign. (This is the "seventh day" that the Father "blessed" and "sanctified" for Himself as a day of rest way back in Genesis 2:1–3! 2 Peter 3:8 reveals that that "day of rest" would be a thousand-year day that would come after six thousand years of toil.)

The remainder of chapter 20 describes the fierceness of the final judgment we commonly refer to as the great white throne judgment. The description is terrifying, as will be the event itself.

Politicians in these last days have been talking about a "new world order." Revelation 21 describes "God's New World Order." There will be a New Heaven that will be inhabited by the *Gentiles*, a New Earth that will be inhabited by the *Jews*, and a New Jerusalem that will be inhabited by *the church of God* (2 Cor. 10:32).

Chapter 22 concludes with seven practical responses to the book of Revelation and to the conclusion of God's revelation to man—the Bible!

1. *Trust* the Truth of God you hold in your hand (22:6,18–19)
2. *Live* with the imminent return of the God of Truth in your thinking (22:7a, 12a, 20)
3. *Do* the Truth of God you know in your mind (22:7b,14–15)
4. *Worship* the God of Truth you have in your heart (22:8–9, 13, 16)
5. *Share* the Truth of God entrusted to your stewardship (22:10–11, 17)
6. *Work* in response to the Truth of God you have received (22:12)
7. *Walk* in the grace of the God of Truth until He comes for you (22:20b–21)

May we all say with John, "Amen. Even so, come, Lord Jesus" (22:20b)! And I say with John, "The grace of our Lord Jesus Christ be with you all. Amen" (22:21).

Mark Trotter was born and raised in Miami, Florida. He pastored First Baptist Church of New Philadelphia, Ohio, for 25 years, and served as the Teaching Pastor at Northwest Bible Church in Hilliard, Ohio, for eight years. In 2016, Mark moved his base of ministry to ONE Baptist Church in Douglasville, Georgia, following his heart's desire to wholly devote his ministry to the things for which he is passionate—namely, the reproduction of disciples/churches, and the training of pastors and leaders for ministry, both of which he does nationally and internationally. Mark and his wife, Sherry, have two grown children: Justin and his wife, Morgan, and Jacie and her husband, Justin. The Lord has also blessed Mark and Sherry with four precious grandchildren.